Strangers in the Land

COUNTERPOINTS

Studies in the Postmodern Theory of Education

Joe L. Kincheloe and Shirley R. Steinberg
General Editors

Vol. 46

PETER LANG
New York • Washington, D.C./Baltimore • Boston
Bern • Frankfurt am Main • Berlin • Vienna • Paris

Strangers in the Land

Pedagogy, Modernity, and Jewish Identity

Edited by
H. Svi Shapiro

PETER LANG
New York • Washington, D.C./Baltimore • Boston
Bern • Frankfurt am Main • Berlin • Vienna • Paris

Library of Congress Cataloging-in-Publication Data

Strangers in the land: pedagogy, modernity,
and Jewish identity / edited by H. Svi Shapiro.
p. cm. — (Counterpoints; vol. 46)
Includes bibliographical references and index.
1. Jews—United States—Identity 2. Jews—Education—United States—Philosophy. 3. Jewish teachers—United States—Attitudes. 4. Critical pedagogy—United States. 5. Education—Social aspects—United States. 6. Jews—United States—Intellectual life. I. Shapiro, H. Svi. II. Series: Counterpoints (New York, N.Y.); vol. 46.
E184.36.E84S77 305.892'4073—dc21 98-44639
ISBN 0-8204-3689-5
ISSN 1058-1634

Die Deutsche Bibliothek-CIP-Einheitsaufnahme

Strangers in the land: pedagogy, modernity,
and jewish identity / ed. by H. Svi Shapiro.–New York; Washington, D.C./Baltimore; Boston; Bern; Frankfurt am Main; Berlin; Vienna; Paris: Lang.
(Counterpoints; Vol. 46)
ISBN 0-8204-3689-5

Cover art from a line drawing by Lynn Leon
Cover design by Andy Ruggirello

For those who teach
so as to repair creation

"You shall not wrong a stranger or oppress him, for you were strangers in the land of Egypt"

Exodus 22: 20–24

"In every era the attempt must be made anew to wrest tradition away from a conformism that is about to overpower it"

Walter Benjamin

"The very fact of questioning one's Jewish identity means it is already lost. But by the same token it is precisely through this kind of cross-examination that one still hangs on to it. Between *already* and *still* Western Judaism walks a tightrope."

Emanuel Levinas

"Exile comes from forgetting. Memory is the source of redemption"

Baal Shem Tov

Contents

Foreword

Shirley R. Steinberg

Teaching has always come totally natural to me. Being a Jew has always come natural to me—I am a Jewish teacher. That may be redundant as Judaism is so deeply associated with pedagogy. Many believe that the greatest student of Jewish teachers became the Messiah for Christians; speaking in parables with humility, the pedagogy of Christ reveals an enormous irony: Jesus the Jew was such a good teacher that he started his own religion.

This is a book by good Jewish teachers. (None of whom, to my knowledge, are beginning a new religion.) Ethnically and spiritually, the contributors to this book, all are located in various positions; however, we are all connected by that amazingly complex label, the one that no one seems comfortable defining, but the entire world is capable of noticing: we are all Jews. We enter the next cycle of our adult lives having spent time evaluating who and what we were, are, and will become. Along with this self-reflection, I believe as Jews we also consider how the world, the non-Jews, view us. We can never drift far from our history, and how we have been named by others has defined much of this history. Taking this into consideration, using the name "Jew" entails much more than religion, manner, genetics, or language: "Jewness" includes all that we are, how we move, act, speak and teach. We cannot separate ourselves from this; consequently, we strive to find a comfort zone in which to combine all of our parts into "self." We also continually search for others, non-Jews, to be comfortable around and with "us."

Sometimes I feel more Jewish than at other times. Walking through Buchenwald "Camp" a month ago with my non-Jewish husband and our dear Jewish friend, Phil Wexler, I felt really, really Jewish. Every tree, building and artifact was viewed by my Jewish eyes, sounds were heard by my Jewish ears, and distinctly Jewish feelings swelled beneath the anger and fear I felt. As an unusally cold wind whipped our coats and swirled around us, stray flakes of snow pelleted my Jewish head and Jewish shoulders. We declared the weather fitting for the visit and somehow we were thankful that we were so physically uncomfortable. Naturally we saw the irony in the feeling and began to question if, indeed, we have ever really felt comfortable. We hadn't.

Writing this foreword, our visit to Germany, and recently reading "Hitler's Willing Executioners, " wove into a cloth which swaddled me in my Jewness. At this point in my life, I weave my threads within the weft of the world of non-Jews and try to make sense of the pattern. I am not a victim, nor do I view Jewishness as a victim; however, I would not be honest if I did not say that I know who I am, and how I teach is as a result of my Jewishness. And I am thankful for it. I am thankful for my colleagues and their chapters, as we have entered into an eternal conversation about our pedagogy and our Jewishness. As you read this book, enjoy.

Preface

Arthur Waskow

At least since the emancipation of the Jewish community began in Western Europe almost two centuries ago, Jewish intellectuals have struggled to understand the relationship between Jewry and the wider community.

For many, the rush of what seemed fresh and exciting Western air swept them up in an ecstatic leap—out of Judaism, into universalism. As the intellectuals realized one level or another of social injustice in Western life, they often joined in criticizing oppressive Western institutions, usually from some universalist theoretical base like Marxism or Freudianism or anarchism or feminism, occasionally with references to the Hebrew prophets as Jewish precursors of radical critics. Other Jewish intellectuals smelled serious dangers in this Western air, and chose to remain focused inward, on the Jewish people and on Torah as its Divinely taught wisdom.

Still others tried to draw from Torah a critique that would address universal issues. Martin Buber and Abraham Joshua Heschel, especially, interwined Hasidic thought and Western philosophy to create critiques that spread beyond the Jewish world. The thinking of both was rooted in the crisis of German culture and politics that led to the convulsion of Nazism and its rage against Judaism and the Jews—especially, in its deepest belly, against the image of the Eastern Jew, the Hasid. Interesting that Buber and Heschel represented exactly the reverse possibility: intertwining the highest version of German philosophy and the deepest version of Jewish mysticism.

In America, from the 1960s on, Jewish intellectuals had two extraordinarily fruitful paths open to them. On the one hand, the academic walls against Jews collapsed, and they became welcome in every place of universalist thought, radical and conservative. On the other hand, an amazing Jewish renaissance began, drawing especially on Buber, Heschel, and younger thinkers who were even more influenced by Hasidism, like Shlomo Carlebach and Zalman Schachter-Shalomi. For Jewish women, the transformation was even greater: suddenly they were welcomed (made themselves welcome through struggle, I should say) as women and Jews into the West's academic life, and as Jewish thinkers into Jewishly focused circles.

But what ideas to bring? In America, the myth of the melting pot had cased to seem attractive. It had become identified with the imperial arrogance that could drop flaming napalm upon Vietnam. Blacks challenged the hegemony of Euro-American culture. Women challenged the hegemony of patriarchal culture. Multiculturalism seemed a liberating answer to this oppressive sameness. For Jews, the question took a new turn in the spiral between Jewish particularism and humanist universalism. Many Jewish intellectuals identified with multiculturalism as a new critique of Western universalism itself!

Ahh!—But what about the rediscovery that Jewish culture itself was filled with meaning and value that had been denigrated and dismissed by the same Western culture that had dismissed and denigrated the cultures rooted in Africa, Hispanic America, Asia, and the experiences of women? What about the new Jewishly focused Jewish intellectuals, the makers of Jewish renewal and feminist Judaism, neo-Hasidism and neo-Kabbalah?

And what about the sense that multiculturalism began to chase its own tale? It might be strong critique of patriarchal white corporate techno-industrial Western culture at the intellectual level, but its very strength became its weakness—fragmenting the possibility of challenging the hegemonic culture at the level of power, politics, economics, even paradoxically at the level of culture. For even in the cultural arena where the new multiculturalism might have been expected to find support from strong constituencies, it was unable to challenge the power of the dominant corporate culture to control the mass media.

The clearer it became how each autonomous culture had been bleached and leached of its life-energy by The System, the more each culture focused on trying to renew itself - and the harder it became to build an alliance of the excluded cultures to shatter the System.

It became clear—No, we became clear—the multiculturalism is necessary, but not enough. Is there a way of joining these multiple cultures into a struggle that can give them space to breath? If they are really, profoundly, different, around what values can they coalesce?

And here we come to the essays in this book.

These authors are moving toward a new vision of the role of Jewish culture:

Not just a cranny, a ghetto, in the overall landscape of human culture, sitting in a corner of the picture, detachable.

Not just a beachhead from which to launch a radical critique of the dominant culture.

But a fragment of a hologram. For in a hologram, every fragment can be used to reconstruct the whole.

Or to use a more biological image, one DNA-bearing cell in a complex planetary organism. The DNA in every separate cell is the same DNA from which the whole body is shaped. Even though each cell is differentiated in function and even in structure from the others, it still carries within itself a way of understanding and replicating the whole.

In this way of seeing, the Jewish people with its culture is one such cell, different from all the others but bearing the crucial sacred Information—the Name—that informs all the cells. Unique, yet like all the other cells in both its uniqueness and its bearing of the Name.

This is a fruitful step beyond multiculturalism, rather than a retreat from it. It is what Buber hinted at when he drew on esoteric Hasidic teachings to generate the most widely usable notion of I-Thou. It is what Heschel was reaching toward when he turned the most Hasidisch of all thoughts, that one's whole body could pray, into his saying about the multiracial march at Selma: "My legs were praying."

For Jews this poses the question: Can we learn and teach Jewish culture both for its unique self alone and for the values and teachings it bears from within that very uniqueness that speak from, and to, all the world? Can we defend multiculturalism and go beyond it?

For those of other cultures, it means—having deconstructed Western "universalism" into its patriarchal, white secularized corporatist techno-industrial particularism, and having celebrated the many cultures this false "universalism" has tried to gobble up, can we both recognize Jewish culture as one of those cultures that needs to be nourished, and begin working toward a new universalist multi-particularism that can share a vision based on the shared "DNA" within each of these different cultures?

For both Jews and others: What is that shared DNA? What is the "Name" that all these cultures bear?

From such a project, such a praxis, we might generate a transformative politics that emerges organically, not mechanically, from a coalition of many peoples, cultures, and communities.

Not "E pluribus unum," "From many, one," but "In pluribus unum," "In many, One."

That is the project, the teaching and learning, toward which this book points. And what is more, these essays and studies begin from within the Jewish culture, building from the inside out, from the individual life stories of many of these scholars, finding within each of them in all their differences the DNA, the Name, they all share. The method and the findings cohere. And this coherence rings with truth and wisdom.

Introduction

A Life on the Fringes/ My Road to Critical Pedagogy

Svi Shapiro

Introduction

In the most recent period of my life I have begun to give serious thought to the relationship between my own Jewish identity and the radical educational project that I have been committed to over many years. Whether this is because of aging (as Erica Jong says, "The older we get, the more Jewish we become"[1], the feminist invitation to be forthcoming about our biographies, or the postmodern moment that gives so much attention to marginality, I am not too sure. Yet the impulse to do this seems strong and, as is evident from this volume, it is shared by many others. Probably all of these reasons are at work and others besides. It is hard to deny the impulse that seems to grow as one gets older, to find some integrative threads to our lives so as to bind together the disparate pieces of our precarious subjectivities. And it is true that feminism has given some of us inveterate theorists permission to see our own lives as not only interesting, but a very legitimate subject of inquiry. Indeed it may be that to avoid this dimension is to perpetuate a highly abstract discourse devoid of the embodied particularity of material human lives.

It is also a curious, if little commented on, fact, that while the "postmodern moment" has meant an unparalleled acknowledgment of the salience of "difference" and the "other" in the constitution of our social world, within critical educational studies at least, this has not included much about Jews as either an oppressed or marginalized group. Whatever the reasons (and we shall return to this later), Jews who have identified themselves with a radical or critical project in education have, for the most part, been silent on their own Jewish identities and its effect on their lives and beliefs. This is no small matter. After all what is at stake here is whether we honor the legacy and experience of Jewish life, and see in them potentially rich contributions to the renewal of a progressive culture in America (to say nothing of achieving a degree of personal integrity in our own lives). Sadly, even where Jewish experience with its distinct structures of feeling and intellect has powerfully helped to shape the political and ethical outlook of academics, these have remained, at most, shadowy influences. Jewish radical academics and teachers have typically not sought to ground their moral outrage or political commitments towards social justice in their own historical or existential experience. This is doubly surprising when found among those who have persistently tried to espouse a critical view of institutional structures at a time when the walls that, hitherto, separated the validity and value of personal experience from our public understandings and commitments have begun to fall.

In issuing an invitation to this anthology I proposed that contributors might begin to explore the connections between our Jewish experience—the way some of us have been "positioned" in the world as Jews—and the beliefs and commitments we hold as educators. The "we" in this case are those of us who have sought to connect education to the goal of self and social transformation; that is those of us for whom some variant of critical pedagogy is at the center of our work. I was cognizant that some of those who would contribute to this volume will have come from religious homes, or may now practice a traditional form of Judaism. Some would see themselves as secular Jews with a 'cultural' form of identity. Some may have become Jews through choice. Others may be the children of holocaust survivors, or marked by the effects of anti-semitism. Still others might connect themselves to the struggle for a Jewishness that centers on the ethical and spiritual notions of *Tikkun Olam* (the repair and healing of the world). In issuing the invitation to write I was also aware that for some Jewishness or Judaism is deeply problematic or simply unacceptable. This might be the result of repugnance towards its sexism or patriarchal assumptions; the unacceptability of Jewish parochialism or chauvinism; or the ossification of its religious practices. There was also the recognition that for some of the writers this would be a first attempt to articulate a narrative of Jewish identity. The anthology was as much for them as it was for those who had already expressed themselves around this theme. It would seek to provide a safe and expansive context for these individuals. Notwithstanding our differences there is the assumption that for all the contributors, Jewish experience had powerfully shaped our identity in general, and our educational outlook in particular. The book would reflect those who had come to recognize and feel the powerful and rich legacy that is our Jewish inheritance and identity. In reclaiming the threads of that which is indelibly Jewish in our lives, it would represent a significant contribution to the struggle for human renewal in a world that demeans history, trivializes identity, and commodifies ritual.

My Own Road to A Critical Pedagogy: Life on the Fringes

It is perhaps of interest that for a long time my own road to critical pedagogy seemed to be related only very marginally to something Jewish in my experience. More recently, however, through a fairly intense process of study, reflection, and conversation, I have begun to encounter the dense and undoubtedly powerful effects of this experience in the shaping of my own language of critique and possibility in the field of education. There is, for example, the effect of living in what Isaac Deutcher referred to as "the interstices of a society"[2] in the making of a Jewish radical consciousness. While my parents were born and grew up in London, the children of recently arrived immigrants from Eastern Europe, for them the English were always the *goyim*—people quite different to themselves. They consciously marked themselves as living at the cultural periphery of a society. Notwithstanding the considerable common ground they shared with other working class Londoners in language, attitudes, and outlook, the latter seemed to exist on the other side of a powerful, if invisible, social and cultural divide. My parents, for example, shared the same peculiar political outlook as many of their non-Jewish neighbors—consistent in their support for Labour Party candidates *and* in their sense of reverence for Royalty (my own early and more radical socialism that argued for the end of monarchy was little tolerated at home). Despite our constant and thorough involvement in British life—in work, school, neighborhood, attention to the news, radio and television entertainment, interest in sporting events, the sharing and celebration of the calendar (one, of course, organized around Christian holidays)—nothing fully eliminated the invisible but powerful marker of difference that one crossed on entering our home. It was, as Zygmunt Bauman has described[3] as if we lived in, but not of, the society.

Here one must note some important differences between the British and American experience. Britain, for example, does not have the immigrant myth that has made American life so psychologically conducive for Jews. Far from the notion that "we are all immigrants from somewhere", when growing up in England one was made constantly aware that there was an officially celebrated and constituted core social and cultural identity. This did not include those with names like Shapiro, even if our synagogue prayers included one for the welfare of the Royal Family. For a nation that considered its true ancestry to reach back a thousand years and more to the Saxons and Normans, and whose head of state was also the head of the established church, those who had lived there for only two generations and celebrated neither Christmas or Easter were outsiders—members of a relatively open and tolerant society, but nevertheless outsiders. Daily I moved back and forth between my school with its Christian prayers and proud motto "Loyaute M'Oblige" (to School, Queen, and State), and my home—a piece of *shtetel* life in the midst of familiar but foreign territory. Of course as a child one is apt to magnify the ways our parents and families are peculiarly different from some imagined norm. In retrospect one can understand our lives as a complex interweaving of multiple strands of influences and experiences that marked us as at once quite similar to those who shared our economic and national circumstances in post-war London, and different from those who did not know the particular insecurities, ancient traditions, and haunting memories of Jews wherever they reside. For more than a few of us growing up in these circumstances, the twin refrains of social inequality and cultural marginality not surprisingly engendered a radical world view.

Of course the sense of difference was fomented by things seemingly trivial as well as the more profound and significant; the "yinglish" (the English inflected and enriched by Yiddish words and phrases) spoken by parents and relatives; the *tzitzit*, the fringed garment worn under my clothes that would cause so much embarrassment at P.E. classes; or the inverted snobbery of my parents regarding what they saw as the inferior aesthetic or culinary taste of non-Jews. Beyond these things made so much more apparent now through generations of American-Jewish comics and writers, there was at work a deeper form of consciousness-shaping. There were the anti-semitic threats and taunts of kids at school. There was participation in that other world of Hebrew and Judaic instruction that seemed to take so much of our time—a world that seemed so remote and stultifying in terms of our adolescent concerns and interests. And there was the world of Jewish holidays. At their most mundane the holidays were a break from school, a time to eat tasty food and be with family and friends and enjoy a ritualized playfulness. At another level they represented a serious separation from the overwhelming cultural hegemony of Christian culture. Here was not just a distinction of significant dates in the yearly round and a reminder of our differences from the non-Jewish majority, but the seeds, as I now see it, of a quite different view of history and celebration. From the earliest it was a calendar that reminded me again and again that (to paraphrase Walter Benjamin) a relentless barbarism has been the underside of history. History at least for some was the constant struggle against oppression and persecution. My history was nothing, I learned, if it was not a document of savage human brutality and a people's resistance to spiritual and physical annihilation. This is the repeated saga of Passover, Hannukah, Purim, and on into the modern 'holidays' of *Yom Hashoa* and Israel Independence Day. In all of this injustice and exile are the twinned and repeated refrains that echoes through the cyclical telling of our Jewish history. And vindication, redemption, dignity, security were ultimately the achievements, not of individuals, but of a collectivity. Judaism deals with the fate of a people, a community, not of a person. How different this is (as I am reminded so often in my classes) from the Protestant view. In Jewish history justice is always *social* injustice; exile is always that of a nation or people, not just a personal or existential separation.

Passover: Memory and Exile

It is the Passover celebration that stands at the center of my childhood and adolescent experiences, a time of joyful remembrance. At the center of this stood the *seder*, the ritual meal celebrating the ancient Israelites' liberation from Egyptian bondage. It was an annual event lit up with the festive pleasures of family conviviality, song, food, wine, stories, and humor. But beyond the immediacy of this celebration were, as I have come to see, messages of extraordinary power and significance. Here was conveyed not simply history but *memory*. The contemporary commentator Lawrence Kushner has delineated this distinction well. Memory, he says, is the connections. The further back in time the connections go, the greater the meaning. And remembering, he says, may be more in the ways things are stored than what is stored:[4]

> "It is not accidental that the great feast of remembering our redemption is called simply: The order. The arrangement and interconnectedness of each of the parts preserves the message, the meaning. The story ends with redemption, not with slavery; first come the questions, then the answers, because I was once a slave, I must know how it feels. . . We take a memory of four hundred years of slavery and set it into a larger context of liberation and redemption. We then celebrate that slavery with a banquet. We further find in those four hundred years of servitude a continuing admonition to be ever mindful of the affliction of others. We find purpose and mission in our slavery. If slaveries can become freedoms and miseries can become meaningful, then the game is never over. . . Through the dynamic search for meaning the past remains eternally fluid before our eyes."

Kushner notes that over the entrance to Yad Vashem, Israel's memorial to those who perished in the Holocaust, is inscribed an aphorism ascribed to the great Jewish teacher, the Baal Shem Tov: "Exile comes from forgetting. Memory is the source of redemption". This extraordinary view of history is reiterated time and again in the Jewish calendar, which becomes nothing less than a pedagogy of critique and possibility. We learn to make the past speak to our present lives for the sake of that which is possible in a transformed future. Injustice and oppression in our past are not simply our past; they are an injunction to the present: "And you shall tell your child on that day, saying 'It is because of that which the Lord did for me when I came forth from Egypt'." (Exodus 13:8)

The seder becomes much more than a retelling of long-ago historical events. The purpose is clearly to interrogate our present world to find in it the current forms of enslavement and suffering, and to do that from the vantage point of hope and possibility about a world in which exile and injustice have ended. This was the notion of history so imaginatively construed by the German-Jewish scholar Walter Benjamin. Unlike the Greek myth of a golden age whose crucial moment was the myth of Eden, the Jewish tradition was of a revelation that made relentless demands on all subsequent generations. Each was compelled to relive the Exodus and to 'Stand at Sinai' as if they themselves were present, and to absorb and construct their meaning through a process of continuous interpretation:[5]

> "Everything originates in the incandescence of revelation, which is then sustained through time in the myriad mirrorings and refractions of exegesis. The whole system is imaginatively focused on the great moment of its origination. . . Even the landscape of redemption that is a vital element of the tradition is a projection into the future of the Edenic past reported in revelation."

The injunction to 'remember' in this Jewish sense is a clearly ethical one: "You shall not wrong a stranger or oppress him, for you were strangers in the land of 'Egypt' "(Exodus22:20). The extraordinary pedagogy of the *Seder* (one especially aimed at children) manages to fuse a celebration of survival, the demand to see the oppressions of our present 'Egypts', and the imaginary re-envisioning of a world of wholeness and justice. And in all of this there is the insistence on our own personal and collective responsibility for transformation. Such a pedagogy is a far cry from the tepid and fragmented curriculum of contemporary schooling with its modernist separations of the epistemological, the imaginative, and the moral.

Purim: Humor in a Bitter World

In thinking about Passover or some of those other holidays of remembrance it is the laughter that comes to mind in spite of the weightiness of their concerns. This, I have come to believe, was not an escape from the seriousness of the issues commemorated, but an integral dimension of a culture intent on resisting the spiritual and emotional suffocation that can be the lot of a people afflicted with so much pain. If we see our acts of remembrance as pedagogies of hope and possibility, then, as Kushner also notes, laughter at sad times more than relieves tension; it initiates healing. It reminds us of another dimension of our psyche. There is much in Jewish humor that works in that Bakhtinian way to turn the (oppressive) world upside down; the victim becomes a winner, the fool the smart one, and the pathetic the one with wisdom. In all of this, laughter provides an emotional transcendence of the world; what appeared fixed and immutable suddenly seems arbitrary and changeable. Such humor deconstructs a world that moments before appeared so unalterable. We do not simply see the world in a new and fluid light, but, perhaps more importantly, we feel it in our bellies. Humor dissolves the overwhelming facticity and solidity of a threatening world. Purim, a holiday that commemorates the foiling of our people's enemies, does so through carnivalesque celebration. We joyously upend the conventions of our world and remind ourselves of the socially imposed categories and differences that order our world. This is well described by Edward Greenstein:[6]

> "A heightened sense of imagination and fantasy is what the Scroll of Esther and its festival of Purim are essentially about. The lighthearted tone of the story . . . bespeaks the carnival atmosphere in which the scroll emerged as the first Purim Torah. Unlike some Christians and even some Jews who find

> the book offensive, most Jews have always heard the Scroll of Esther in a Mardi Gras context and have therefore taken it as fun and fantasy . . . Jews, who have suffered the cruel caprice of and persecution by gentiles time after time, permit themselves the fantasy of imagining themselves in the gentile role and the gentiles in the Jewish role."

As the saintly Jew Mordechai replaces the anti-semitic tyrant Haman in the Persian administration we, in our imaginations, replace gentiles in the scheme of the world. This injunction to see the potential fluidity of our social order, the possibilities for overturning unjust social relationships, requires also a recognition of our own authoritarian tendencies. Michael Strassfeld notes that Purim's call for the state of *Adloyada*—a blissful ignorance of reality—enables us to see how easy it is to change from Mordechai into Haman:[7]

> "from a crusader for justice into simply a crusader. That is why the Talmud says that we fully accept the Torah only on Purim, for only when we can mock the tradition can we fully accept it. Only then are we safe to do so; otherwise we make the tradition into an idolatry rather than a smasher of idols, into frozen-in-stone dogma of what once was rather a living faith."

Israel: the Dualities of Liberation

It is hard to escape the significance of these words in the light of recent conditions in Israel and in the Palestinian territories. The tendency for a people, themselves the perennial victims of persecution, to become the oppressors of another people is clear and inescapable. It has presented me, and many other Jews, with a tormenting and gut-wrenching paradox. The struggle for survival and national independence of my own people has begotten the national subjection and humiliation of the Palestinian people. Our inalienable right to national freedom has been, and continues to be, at the expense of those who have become our 'Other'. Here is obviously not the place to consider the complex historical, political, and cultural dynamics that underlie the seemingly unending conflict between the two peoples in this region. Yet mirrored in it is the unfortunate evidence that speaks to the polysemous nature of our own Jewish traditions. However much I want to read Jewish texts and traditions as powerful tribunes of the necessity for social justice and human dignity I am compelled to face the reality that these same texts and traditions become legitimations for exclusivity, intolerance, and national arrogance, to say nothing of brutality or murder. I also know the place—intellectual and emotional—

from which the latter dispositions arise.They are there in every movement that seeks to liberate itself from a history of oppression and pain, and in its rage at an unjust world is indifferent to those who seem to obstruct its will to survival. Michael Lerner[8] has described this well when he says that Jews who jumped from the burning structure of their European home cared little that they landed on the backs of the Palestinian people. Universal concerns with justice and compassion seem irrelevant for those who see a world in which one shoots or is shot at.

The polysemous texts of Judaism have always had a dual narrative of redemption—the one of social justice and peace, and the one of an exiled nation that would return to its own land. Strangely in our postmodern times the clash between universal human aspirations and particularistic dreams has given these competing narratives new moment. It is easy for me to understand how powerful was the Zionist message in my own life. Feeling the marginality and internalized vulnerability of being a Jew in England, Zionism offered a wonderful counter-narrative to that of the *galut* Jew; instead of the weakness, passivity, and embarrassment of English Jews still trying to make themselves acceptable to the *goyim* in a post-holocaust world, Israel seemed the embodiment of another kind of Jew—confident, aggressive, and tough (a very masculine image). When I was a young person, especially, Israel was seductively overpowering in its apparent inversion of the internalized messages of oppression. There I could 'resolve' my neurotic Jewish complex and become a 'normalized' individual freed from what others (like Duboise, Fanon, and Sartre) have described as a schizophrenic existence in which one is defined by the gaze of the Other. I would no longer have to feel self-conscious about my non-anglo-saxon appearance, or be apologetic about my name (indeed, in my teens, in anticipation of this, I exchanged my name for a Hebrew one), or battle the hateful stereotypes of Jews common in England.

The world of the Zionist movement was a vital and erotically charged one for young adolescents, offering us the opportunity to remake ourselves into strong and flamboyant pioneers of the land, and to do this through the life of the socialist kibbutz community. Interestingly, in the socialist variant of Zionism (the dominant one until after the 1967 Arab-Israeli war), the twin narratives of exile and social justice seemed to be reconciled—one could return 'home' *and* help to build a community freed from the disfigurements and exploitation of the capitalist world. Within 'the movement' our educational emphasis shuttled between prophetic figures, from Isaiah to Borochov, who envisioned a society of human equality, and a revitalized Jewishness that rejected the arcane dimensions of Judaism for a nationalistic celebration of the heroic and embattled Jew.

Yet I had begun to recognize even then that this reconciliation was a problematic one and that it rested on some deep distortions. Mordechai could indeed become Haman. Yet the tensions were not easily dismissed as good versus evil; each persona spoke to dimensions of my experience and being. The shame of the Jew's powerlessness in history made those images of a tough and militant Israeli state able to determine its own fate in a still anti-semitic world, not surprisingly, attractive to me. Yet, as a product of the peace-oriented, internationalist, youth movements of the sixties, the nationalistic and militarist character of so much of Israeli society gave me a sense of alienation from a good deal of what I saw there. In the period that was still close to the six-day war such sentiments felt out of place and hard to articulate. The sharp change in Israeli politics following the Labour victory in 1992, with the new government's willingness to trade land for peace and attempt rapprochement with the Palestinians, brought to the surface the full ugliness and intolerance of that part of Zionism that conceived of the Jews' world only in terms of power and force. Here was the full expression of Jewish rage after centuries of humiliation and homelessness. And, for many Jews, both inside and outside Israel, the end of this exile would justify any callousness or brutality towards those with different national interests. For such Jews these others hardly existed at all as human beings with rights and histories that needed to be honored. I do not believe now that there is some single 'soul' of Judaism, or some unitary moral essence. My claim of a Jewish experience rooted in the injunction to remember that "you were once slaves in Egypt"—a Jewishness with a deep passion for a world of justice for all human beings—would have to compete with readings of a Jewish tradition that could somehow justify indifference, oppression, and a callous violence towards the other.

The Hebrew Prophets: Jews and the Radical Spirit

Paradoxically it is this 'God of History' that impels Jews on both sides of the divide. For each there is the powerful need to be the subjects, not the objects, of history; to be the active agents (or partners) in the making of our world—of course with very different consequences. For as long as I can remember I have felt an extraordinary solidarity with all those who struggle against the fate dictated by heteronomous relations; an identification with movements of resistance against those who deny the individual and collective capacity to give shape and meaning to one's own world. I have always been deeply moved by those human struggles that seek to increase democracy and freedom. At its core I have understood Zionism in this light. I also see the Palestinian struggle in the same way; another people struggling for some collective determination over their destiny. It is clear to me that Jews have always been disproportionately concerned with and committed to the process of human empowerment. From my youth I have been inspired by Jewish involvement in struggles against unjust authority—as socialists and communists (where the latter has been a liberational force), in trade unions, in movements that are against racism and apartheid, in the struggle for women's equality, and so on. I have also been struck by how often such activists were quite removed from any overt identification with Jewish tradition or religious faith. Somehow, nonetheless, those strong ethical and social injunctions asserted themselves among Jews even (as in my case) where religion itself seemed arcane and ossified. Yet even as I understood liberational struggles to be very much the antiphonal rhythm of modernity I have come to see its' roots dug in the ancient moral and spiritual ground of Judaism. In my more recent reflections on this I have been astonished by the resonance of the critical spirit with that of ancient Hebrew prophets; a phenomenon so extraordinarily described by Abraham Joshua Heschel. He notes:[9]

> The prophet is an iconoclast, challenging the apparently holy, revered, and awesome. Beliefs cherished as certainties, institutions endowed with supreme sanctity, he exposes as scandalous pretentions. . . The prophet faces a coalition of callousness and established authority, and undertakes to stop a mighty stream with mere words. Had the purpose been to express great ideas, prophecy would have had to be acclaimed as a triumph.Yet the purpose of prophecy is to conquer callousness, to change the inner man as well as to revolutionize history.

Michael Lerner, too, whose liberational theology has been a powerful influence on my thinking, sees Jews' disposition toward radically challenging the established order as rooted deeply in our people's historical and spiritual beginnings. Throughout much of recorded history, he suggests, the oppressed have beeen socialized to believe that cruelty and oppression are inevitable, an ontological necessity, part of the structure of reality. The spiritual realm was an alternative or an escape from the reality of the material world—it embodied a purity that could not be imagined on earth. What the Jews heard, he says, was a very different message:[10]

> "that this world could be fundamentally transformed. Spirituality and morality were not features of some other reality apart from this world, but were inherently ingredient in this world . . . Judaism becomes the metaphysics of social transformation: the system of belief about reality that makes possible revolutionary change.
>
> Judaism places transcendence on the agenda of the human race. Human beings need not be stuck in a world of pain or oppression . . . Transcendence then is a psychological, political, ethical, and spiritual continuum involving a transformative and healing praxis of *tikkun*, rather than a spiritual escape from a fundamentally flawed world."

As I read Lerner and Heschel's words I am confronted by a strange contradiction. On the one hand there are recollections of growing up in a religious environment that seems to have been miles away from the revolutionary traditions described by these writers—filled by rituals and prayers that, to a great extent, seemed very far from this kind of radical moral and spiritual commitment. Yet I am still left to question whether the passion for change (so evident in the pages of this book) is only to be understood as the product of difference and marginality, the legacy of anti-semitism in both its brutal and subtle forms. I confess to finding it a compelling notion that there is, deeply insinuated in our being as Jews, some continuing, if residual, impulse toward social transformation whose progenitors are indeed those ancient Hebrew prophetic voices and ethical scriptures. In ways more mysterious than understood these have provided us with a continuing legacy of resistance to the taken for granted reality, and the imperative for a world that takes as its central moral purpose the search for social justice.

One key to this ethos of resistance seems to lie in that Jewish penchant for argument and a deep-seated attitude of suspicion to what is merely given. Certainly in whatever Jewish circles I have moved the love for argument has seemed always to be present. From my early years at home I learned the pleasures of contradiction—there was parental pride in disputatious children! Somehow in this a *talmudic* approach to the truth was I believe present (even when Talmud was not at all the subject of concern). What I have come to understand by this is that while the truth might have been revealed at Sinai its meaning is multivalent and requires an on-going re-articulation. Each generation must, as it were, stand again at Sinai finding new layers of significance and understanding in the text. Whatever is the ultimate Truth, the truth for each generation has to be won through the hard work of intellectual interrogation and critical reason. The text provides no comforting certainty of established understanding—much more, it challenges human-beings to elicit meaning from situation to situation, and from generation to generation. The only certainty is the knowledge that is produced in the well-known give and take of Rabbinic argument. Jacob Neusner has described it this way:[11]

> The Talmud taught the Jews not to be terrified by the necessity to face, and to choose among, a plurality of uncertain alternatives in an insecure world. The Talmud testified that people must choose, if tentatively and for a time only, among competing interpretations, so that the law might in fact be applied, and the ordinary folk might know what to do. So the Talmud forced choices, in a tentative and austere spirit, among the many truths available to reasonable folk. It insisted one cannot be paralyzed before contrary claims and equally persuasive reasons.

While most of us now associate *Talmudic* discourse with the arcane and esoteric this is, I believe, to miss its essence. Neusner notes that, far from a sterile intellectualism, this was, in fact, a monumental attempt to apply a practical rationality to society—an effort to figure out how a community that was dependent on the force of better argument might live:[12]

> In a word, the Talmud is a document created by the intellect devoted to morality and seeking sanctity. It takes for granted that humanity's primary capacity is to think; it therefore is to be taken with utmost seriousness.

Here in the face of continuing insecurity and epistemological uncertainty was the historical commitment to a critical reason through which a community could create and recreate its own cultural and moral practices. At the core of this process of reason and challenge was, of course, the word. Even when the word ceases to be derived from the religious text, who can deny the extraordinary relationship of Jews to intellectual discourse? In the last two centuries of modernity Jews have played an extraordinary role in the construction of our understanding of the world, one that has far outstripped their numerical presence. Long before poststructural analysis, Jews had understood the connections between the word and the world. Lawrence Kushner writes:[13]

> According to the Hebrew Bible, God made the world with words. God just spoke and the world became reality . . . Not only are words the instruments of creation, in Judaism they are primary reality itself.
>
> We ordinarily think of words as signifiers—a few syllables which denote something really real. But in Hebrew the word for *word*, *davar*, also means 'thing'. The word does not need to be made real, it already is. It needs only to be read, spoken, and interpreted. To know the word therefore is to know reality itself.

In my home, like so many Jewish homes, books and book-knowledge were imbued with an aura of high prestige. Of course mixed into this sense of value was the understanding that they were also the medium of academic achievement and social success—an especially important fact given the economic anxiety that accompanied my parents' lives. Academic success for their children was the vindication of their constant struggle against economic insecurity and lack of social status. Yet beyond this was a respect for learning and those who were seen as 'learned', as well as a value attached to reading a newspaper and knowing what was happening in the world. Perhaps this kind of knowing and reading were a surrogate form of controlling one's world—a puppet theater of politics where grasping things intellectually stands in place of actually changing the world. In this sense Jews' obsession with knowing makes sense in a world where their real power over events and conditions has been limited, to say the least. Yet I think it must also be said that in our post-Foucault world, attachment to the word seems to represent a profound recognition of what Heschel refers to as the human capacity to be co-creators of the world. It indicates that in the process of signification human beings do much more than describe some pre-existing world—they are actually *producing* the world. Here is the extraordinary power of human beings to both represent and to make a world. Of course in this recognition we have returned to the peculiarly Jewish dialectic of interpretation and action, thought and deed. The responsibility of "standing again at Sinai" is an injunction to critically struggle to make sense of our lives and our circumstances, and to feel that sense of possibility and responsibility about re-envisioning and transforming our world. It is surely this that the great secular 'Rabbi' Marx had in mind when he talked of 'praxis' —the process of understanding and action to change society.

The Sabbath: Beyond the Work and Spend Culture

Nothing in my life quite so consistently conveyed to me Judaism's marriage of the transcendent and its emphasis on the 'this-worldly' more than the *Shabbas**. Little in my childhood life is more vivid than the rituals attached to the making of the Sabbath in my home. Preparation for it actually began on Thursday when my mother began to '*kosher*' and prepare the chicken for the traditional Friday night meal. There were cakes to bake and the process of cleaning the house in anticipation of the day. *Shabbas* actually commenced with my mother's lighting of the traditional candles accompanied with a prayer said in Hebrew, plus her own more personal words of appreciation and supplication to God. Our modest living room with candles and white table cloth seemed to glow with warmth (sometimes this was literally so, given that our home like most working class houses at that time had no central heating—the living room was one of the few places in the house kept warm with a kerosene heater). The meal—always the same—of chicken soup, boiled chicken, and vegetables, seemed at the time quite delicious. My father's recitation of the *Kiddush*, the sanctification and drinking of wine that accompanies the commencement of most Jewish holidays—was usually a time of family good humor and connection. Though there were minor irritants—for example, the injunction in orthodox homes, not to write or watch television, spend money, or to travel—for the most part the time is one of warm memories, of a celebration of family and friends, of special foods and much laughter. The actual day of *Shabbas*, Saturday, was more complicated. During much of my youth, while my mother maintained the atmosphere of a sabbath at home my father was compelled to spend the day working. In my adolescence I went from the morning service at the synagogue to my father's stall in the market where I spent the remainder of the day. I traveled from the sanctity of the *Shabbat* to what I experienced as the grubby buy and sell culture of the streets. The sad necessity of economic survival produced this undesired compromise. Many years later I have come to appreciate just how schizophrenic was this experience. It made me acutely aware of how much the *Shabbat* was a taste of a world fundamentally different from that of everyday existence so captured by the imperatives of

*The Ashkenazi pronunciation of the Hebrew word Shabbat (Sabbath) used in my family.

work and spend. Reading Abraham Heschel's "The Sabbath" for the first time when I turned forty, I was moved by the resonance of his words:[14]

> "The meaning of the Sabbath is to celebrate time rather than space. Six days we live under the tyranny of things of space; on the Sabbath we try to become attuned to holiness in time. . . The Sabbath is a day for the sake of life. Man is not a beast of burden, and the Sabbath is not for the purpose of enhancing the efficiency of his work. . . The seventh day is like a palace in time with a kingdom for all. It is not a date but an atmosphere."

Letty Cottin Pogrebin, a contemporary Jewish writer, has expressed the notion of the Sabbath this way:[15]

> "The Sabbath is pure time: 'The hours of the seventh-day are significant in themselves; their significance and beauty do not depend on any work, profit or progress we may achieve.' On that one day, we are supposed to enter time's realm and treasure time for its own sake. We are not only expected to desist from manual labor ('labor is a craft, but perfect rest is an art') but to contemplate creation, the product of God's labor. . . . Rather than communicate through productivity, we are to communicate through inaction. Not writing, not driving, all this proclaims that humanity is connected to a source of productivity greater than its own."

Restricted, as it often felt, by annoying rules my *Shabbat* still conveyed an essential structure of feeling—one that has allowed me to know that there really was another way of being in the world. This liberating alternative freed me if only for a short time from capitalism's obsession with work, and from the compulsion to fill up my 'free time' with buying and consuming. It gave me a sense of the alternative to a productivist culture's notion of time with its demand for a frantic way of life in which 'doing' was everything and 'being' without any value, and in which our instrumental view of the world meant that we lived always in anticipation of our future achievements. The liberating joy of the *Shabbat* is the temporal space it provides—for stillness, reflection, relationships, and the appreciation of life. This space is a window onto the possibility of a post-messianic/postmodern time in which this experience might begin to suffuse our whole way of being in the world.

Jews, Culture and the Politics of Identity

These reflections I hope, indicate some of the connections between my life as a Jew and the transformative vision of education I hold.

Along with other writers in this book, issues of justice, marginality, exile, memory, holiness, *Tikkun Olam* dialogic ways of knowing, ethical commitments, and social responsibility are recurrent themes. Yet I am returned to the question posed earlier; why is it that in a time of unparalleled acknowledgment of difference within critical pedagogy so little is said about Jews and Jewish identity? We may need to ask here about the relationship of Jewish identity to some larger questions concerning the current politics of identity that have become a defining feature of the contemporary social landscape. Michael Lerner, for example, has commented on how the Left typically excludes Jews from the configuration of oppressed or marginalized communities in the United States; that while such exclusion might make sense when oppression is measured in economic terms, or in the more obvious forms of racism, it ignores the continued, historically rooted, forms of emotional pain that are so much part of the Jewish experience. It may be that the relative prosperity of Jews in North America, or perhaps the deeply unpalatable nature of Israel's occupation of the Palestinian people has undergirded this analysis. Here, too, we have to consider the effects of the schism between Jews and Blacks where Jews have been cast in the very unfamiliar role as significant enforcers of racism. In a parallel vein Erica Jong has recently questioned the paradox of self-denial among Jewish feminists. She asks:[16]

> "What does it mean to have self-abnegation built into the very principle of your religion? Unless we address these questions and stop hiding behind the 'huddled masses', we cannot claim our birthright: free expression . . . How ironic that we have celebrated such freedom in African-American women writers while denying it to ourselves . . . Much remains to be done. We must confess our double self-hatred to ourselves first of all and then to our writing . . . We ourselves have absorbed not only the misogyny of our culture but also the anti-semitism. We ourselves equate Jewishnesss with vulgarity and loudness, and thus we are tempted to soft-pedal it. We leave our Jewishness to be expressed by our musical comedy stars and comediennes."

In asserting the need to embrace her Jewishness as part of the search for authenticity in her writing she notes the significance of African-American, Asian-American, and Native-American writers "who have already overcome the false assimilationist stance." Perhaps , she suggests, the Jewish woman terrifies because she represents strength, sexuality, and a loud voice.

There are, of course, other reasons for the excision of a specifically Jewish discourse from our intellectual and artistic work. Roger Simon has described one aspect of this:[17]

> "For the most part North American Jews have accepted their integration into the United States and Canada on terms which have regulated the separation of public performance and private commitments. The majority of Jewish academics have entered teaching and research positions in public institutions of higher learning accepting an implicit rule that, even if some aspect of the cultural and spiritual traditions inform their work, these were not to be made evident or topical in their writing or teaching. While most Jewish university teachers are free to affirm their public identities as Jews, what must be simultaneously recognized is that the social forms which have defined university teaching have significantly limited the manner in which Jewish academics have felt it appropriate to be and to act as Jews."

Postmodern social thought has certainly brought into question these social forms and the way they shape the nature of our discourses—the rationalities, aesthetic qualities, ideological and moral commitments that structure them. A book such as this is certainly indebted to this intellectual climate. Yet it does not come trouble free. Indeed it might be ambivalence in regard to the postmodern turn toward the local and the particular that makes some Jewish intellectuals hesitant in their embrace of their own Jewishness. In his recent book, "Twilight of Common Dreams", Todd Gitlin has vividly described the intolerance, parochialism, and sectarianism that has accompanied the rise of identity politics in the United States, and with this a disparagement of those hopes for a common struggle against social injustice in the world. He writes:[18]

> "To recognize diversity, more than diversity is needed. The commons is needed. To affirm the rights of minorities, majorities must be formed. Democracy is more than a license to celebrate (and exaggerate) differences. It cannot afford to live in the past—anyone's past. It is a political system of mutual reliance and common moral obligations. Mutuality needs tending. If multiculturalism is not tempered by a stake in the commons, then centrifugal energy overwhelms any commitment to a larger good . . . Affirming the virtues of the margins identity politics has left the centers of power uncontested."

Gitlin (a Jewish radical intellectual) speaks in passionate solidarity with all those diverse groups and constituencies who have had to fight for their value and opportunities in the world. Yet, he is clear, only the moral and political support of others who, together, may constitute a majority can provide any sort of guarantee for their prospects. While universalist human agendas have taken a beating in recent times by those writing from feminist and postmodern perspectives, such 'modernist' agendas may have continuing appeal to Jewish progressives and radicals. Jews, after all, are members of a numerically tiny group who, despite the aggressive bluster of chauvinistic Zionism, know just how dependent, ultimately, our fate is on the attitudes and decisions of others. Whatever the appeal of a Judeo-centric world view, it must be tempered by a recognition of our connections and dependency on other human beings. Only nationalist zeal or dogmatic religious faith can seal the particularistic consciousness that denies anyone or anything entree into our peculiar corner of the world. To those like myself such incommensurability is an arrogant and dangerous refusal of those democratic values that make our survival, as well as that of other human beings, possible—pluralism, dialogue, reciprocity and respect. The struggle, of which I believe this book to be a part, is the effort by Jewish Left intellectuals to both find and assert their voices as self-conscious Jews, while not trumpeting a discourse that seeks to be the one and only voice of Truth in the world. If some of us have been hesitant in attempting this, it is, perhaps, our sensitivity to the cacophony of intolerant, hate-filled, self-righteous voices that deny the possibility of social struggle borne out of a compassionate and respectful understanding of the needs and being of others.

It is a paradox of postmodern thinking that while it has certainly given license to the expression of a multiplicity of voices and identities the warrant seems to have been written in disappearing ink. It has been, for example, enormously effective at demolishing claims to essentialist, i.e., natural or unchanging forms of identity. All identities, it makes clear, are historically contingent phenomena. Nor should our identities be understood as something pure, we are always made from a complicated weave of threads that make us contradictory beings. Identity is now often viewed as a tyranny that seeks to 'fix' us in a particular mode of behavior or affect—the result of a specific play of power and knowledge. We are enjoined by such thinking to resist this kind of domination through a continual deconstruction of our own or another's identity. We are urged to take an ironic stance toward every attempt to fix or name who we are. Indeed freedom from this point of view becomes our ability to explode the apparent obviousness of any given identity and show how it is entirely a figment of a suppressed relational cultural grid. Black is the obverse of white; female of male; Jew of Christian and so on. The former in each case is little more than the denied or devalorized qualities of the latter projected onto a despised group. Such thinking, I need hardly add, has powerfully upset those dangerous, racist, misogynist, sexist, or homophobic categories that paint human beings into permanent and enclosed social spaces.

It has opened up the possibility of seeing our subjectivities as fluid and always in relation to those who would like to view us as separate and other. Yet as important and as liberating as such thinking is, it offers very little that affirms the *particular* qualities and traditions of those historically constituted identities. What are we to make, for example, of a theory that offers irony and endless deconstruction for the passionately-held commitment of a people who view themselves as inheritors of a history and tradition of four millennia? It seems to offer little that affirms the extraordinary and rich texture of Jewish life or celebrates the triumph of survival in the face of a relentlessly brutal history. It speaks little to the joyful, sometimes ecstatic, inspiration that comes from participation in ancient rituals and traditions. Nor does persistent irony or endless deconstruction seem capable of addressing the intense existential yearnings that lead some of us to search for God or find holiness in an evanescent world. And identity as something to be perpetually disrupted or transgressed seems to offer little to the psychological capability for an enduring personal commitment to progressive social change in a world where such commitment is frequently derided as a pointless and wasteful effort. Without a strong sense of historical rootedness there is surely only a weak emotional capacity for the struggle, one to be continued on from generation to generation, to make a better world. Postmodern theories of cultural identity are a useful, but ultimately thin, response to the kind of human experiences found in these pages. They are, in themselves, unlikely, ultimately, to provide the existential or spiritual means that enable us to avoid the onset of cynicism or ennui. In contrast, the authors in this book, in all their diversity, provide repeated reference to that sense of communal memory, moral commitment, and historically-rooted sense of hope that seems to be present in the story of so many Jews. We find in these, I believe, the intellectual, ethical and emotional resources that so nourish our visions of a pedagogy concerned with transforming our world; a goal that (to paraphrase Heschel) we are unlikely to fulfill completely, yet compels our life-long struggle and participation.

Michael Apple's essay is certainly an example of this. His autobiographical "fragments" points to what it means to grow up as an outsider—to feel, as he puts it, the gaze of others looking at him as a "Jew", with all that this implies. For Apple, being a Jew has always meant placing oneself outside of the mainstream—both culturally and politically, and being unsure where is one's real home. Apple provides a rich family history that is a continuing legacy of struggle for social justice; of grandparents and parents who were adherents of movements for radical social change, involved in struggles against racial oppression and economic exploitation. Never a religious man, the writer's Jewishness continually points him to a vision of education deeply rooted in the importance of "interventions into oppressive social relationships, of reaching out, of real action."

Haim Beliak's piece explores the nature of Jewishness within the context of a postmodern awareness of identity. For him there is now no possibility of a stable, unified, essential notion of what it means to be a Jew. All attempts to define being a Jew must grapple with the unprecedented contingencies of life in the present world and, especially, in the United States. Jewishness is a process of learning, always unfinished and incomplete. Its external referents are anti-semitism and the defining of Jew as other; its internal ones are Jews' connections to religious texts, ideas, acts, and rituals. Beliak argues that what is new and distinct is the "space and willingness to adopt hybrid identities." For Jews this means the capability of being both anti-assimilationist and committed to the Enlightenment, being supportive of Israel while favoring diaspora, proponents of ethnic particularism while sympathetic to at least some universal ideals. The consequence of this complexity is the demise of an assumed community among Jews; yet it is precisely this that opens the door to the generative diversity among Jews. We have the possibility of valuing the numerous narratives about Jewish identity formation. We can come to appreciate Jewishness not as something monolithic and given but as a force-field of numerous and unpredictable life experiences, memories, and folkways. Beliak's Jewish "education" comprises both the intentional acts of Jewish learning and commitment, and also the "accidents" of biography. The latter is shaped by that melange of historical fate, sociology and the extraordinary mystery of human encounters and influences in our lives. His piece gives vivid testimony to this process in his evocation of an Arizona childhood in the family of camp "survivors."

David Bleich, too, situates his own ideas about teaching in the sense of antagonism and difference in regard to being Jewish, though it is combined with what he calls the "affirmative" qualities of Jewish education and Jewish practice. While also wary of notions of some unitary or essential identity, he argues that there is a distinctively Jewish contribution to the literary academy and the process of pedagogy.

This, he calls, the "living text." For Bleich this means that the classroom is a place where texts are studied in relationship to issues like collective interests and social purpose; where we can recognize and disclose our own complex identities, and assert our rights to "self-inclusion." Jewish voices in the academy have urged us to view all texts, oral, as well as written, as organic to our social relations and historical contexts. In this view personal experience is also political—that is, it reveals how one's life is about the will to survive or the promotion of justice for all. Bleich suggests that in viewing texts as "living" —i.e. "integrated into people's lived experience, studied and changed by that experience", and transformed by their transmission into new communities, what is produced is a secularized version of Torah.

Linda Bliss avows the American democratic dream of justice, freedom, and equality. But her belief in it is tempered by her growing recognition of how little it has honored the cultures of difference that constitute the society in which she lives. She was, she says, "a fairly typical assimilated New York granddaughter of third wave Russian Jewish immigrants." And as such learned to accept that the invisibility of Jewishness was the accepted price to be paid for inclusion into America. While home did transmit, in a fashion, the sense of Jewish identity, this was a private affair, not a part of the national history or public narrative. Paradoxically it is through her experience teaching others who, also, have been excluded from our representations of history and culture that Bliss begins to recognize the violence that is done in our schools towards those who are relegated to the cultural margins. Their stories would, if told, split the world open, demanding a very different account of American life and experience. In her own teaching she seeks a dialogue in the classroom so that students can begin to hear and see the others among them. Not surprisingly such a process is a risky one, opening wounds and disrupting assumptions. Yet her vision of education is one that facilitates the assertion of those previously excluded, but also works toward an understanding and solidarity across these differences. It is an education rooted, ethically, in a vision of social justice and compassion, in democratic ideals and the prophetic tradition.

Alan Block also sets out to "recover"the lost or suppressed Jewish voice in the discourses of education. He speaks, painfully, of the profound silence of educators regarding the Jewish tradition of knowing and learning. Looking sometimes through the eyes of his seven year old daughter Emma he notes the excision of Jewish experience from the rituals and calendar of public schooling. But beyond this Block looks at the way that Greek philosophy forms the bedrock of our educational world-view and, in so doing, places the Rabbinic tradition into erasure. This is no accident, he says. For what is at stake is not Truth but action—in particular, ethical action. Block argues that what he finds in Rabbinic thought is the subversive notion that "there is always another use of and an interpretation of the text because what is at stake is not fixed knowledge, but practice." Rabbinic thought, he asserts, threatens the ontological foundations of order, and jeopardizes the amoral, disembodied Western foundations upon which education has grown. He is angry to learn how those histories of curriculum consistently refuse the Jewish perspective on texts and knowledge. Even the current postmodern turn towards the plurality of interpretation is in denial of its connections to Rabbinic traditions of thought with its emphasis on the dialogic fluidity of textual meaning. To speak as a Jew, says Block, we must risk our insecurities and the comforts of assimilation; it means, in education, to connect pedagogy to an engagement with the world in order to heal and perfect it.

Miriyam Glazer's piece is a disturbing series of reflections on identity and pedagogy as these unfold in the context of her life in Israel. Her writing is rooted in a passionately held sense of connection to her Jewishness while simultaneously forcing us to recognize the complex, multivalent, and fluid qualities of what this means. She moves from her youthful embrace of the kibbutz with its image of "reborn", vital, anti-bourgeois Jews, to her later confrontation with Zionism and its Eurocentric notions of culture and education. She discovers, painfully, both in the classroom and out, how this has meant the denigration of "Levantine culture and context" with all that this implies for Israelis and Palestinians. She uncovers the lionization of the "West" with its notions of power and modernity. And as she comes to recognize the place of the "other" in Israeli culture she also comes to see the suppression of "women" in both the society she lives in and in the texts she teaches. All of this leads to transformation in her notions of pedagogy, a " drive to see, name, relate to, engage, who and what was really present in the classroom"; to remake her curriculum into a living text that would release the powerful, if subterranean, energies that were damned up by the dominant discourse and the social order. Her feminism and her concern for the rights of the other makes living in Israel an increasingly difficult proposition. Jewishness, for Glazer, comes to mean the validation of a "diasporic consciousness"—one that has meant the recognition of the importance of "sharing space with others."

For Barry Kanpol, too, there is a need to go beyond the self-enclosedness of so much Jewishness. Like Glazer, he wants an identity that affirms Jewish experience but makes room for others. He looks back on his own upbringing with a good deal of frustration—one in which Judaism seemed devoid of real meaning or purpose, full of unexamined rituals and practices, where the world of *Goyim* seemed irrelevant to issues of faith and commitment. Christianity was the locus of anti-semitism. Not till many years later would he encounter the radical message of the historical Jesus. For Kanpol, Jews, with their history of exile and exclusion, should affirm the centrality of dialogue and understanding the lives of others, in all their pain and oppression. This, for him, is the importance of the metaphor of "breaking bread" in his vision of pedagogy and social transformation. It represents "the ability to challenge forms of oppression as well as dialogue over emancipatory possibilities." It is in this process of sharing our humanity and our lives with others that we encounter a sacred joy that affirms, simultaneously, our own lives as Jews as well as the lives of others. Critical Pedagogy, argues Kanpol, must emphasize this joyful encounter if it is to be more than the usual process of academic criticism and cynicism.

Stephen Lerman's paper echoes themes found in Block, Glazer and Bleich, but here the writer speaks as a mathematics educator. There is, for example, the concern to challenge the platonic epistemology that makes mathematical knowledge appear to reflect "the way God created the world." The history of mathematics was seen as the unfolding of Truths. Instead Lerman has argued for and taught a conception of mathematical understanding that roots it in culture and human consciousness—a form of social knowledge. There is, he finds, something talmudic about the nature of mathematical problems when taken out of the right/wrong answer approach typical of schooling. In fact the problems are complex and disputable, inviting multiple proposed solutions. All of this re-situates mathematics as a form of critical education that can play a "small but significant part" in the formation of students' understanding of social relations and in questions of equitabilty. Lerman's paper adds another layer to the complex nature of Jewish identity. Writing as someone who grew up and teaches in England, he notes some of the peculiar features of that experience, especially the premium placed upon adopting the manners and behavior of the English upper middle class. He frankly acknowledges the multiple contradictions of his identity—privileged yet supportive of those who are oppressed; sympathetic to Israel and Zionism yet angry at its treatment of Palestinians; intensely self-identified as a Jew yet, till recently, seeing other identities, female, Black, working class, as more "legitimate and utterable."

Like Lerman, David Purpel, in an extraordinarily revealing exploration of his own Jewish sensibility, focuses on the frequently conflicted nature of what this means. Central to Purpel's paper are his assertions about the pre-rational nature of both identity and one's moral commitments—assertions that carry significant implications for what it means to educate for a world in crisis. Like others in this book Purpel speaks to the enormous complexity of understanding the formation and dynamics of one's consciousness. It is a process that, he confesses, challenges the security and familiarity of his usual professional discourse, and it meant embarking on a journey to systematically explore his own Jewish identity for the first time. From the outset he makes clear his own intense ambivalence about what it means to be Jewish; there is, on the one hand, the ever-present sense of fear and dread that is impossible to fully escape or deny. It is this that leads him towards the necessity of struggle against so much unnecessary human suffering, and a vision of education that connects it strongly to the quest for social justice. Yet Purpel knows it is the same fears that produces the "excessive self-absorption and neurotic xenophobia" of Jews. It is his awareness that people are formed and driven by their vulnerabilities, pains, and insecurities that has led him to see the limitations of intellect and critical reflection in education. Before thinking, he asserts, comes faith and the commitment to a particular set of moral meanings. Educators have been reluctant to affirm the moral tradition and community from which they speak. For him a crucial part of that tradition is the history of suffering and injustice as well as the sense of responsibility and hope that are the Jewish experience. Only an education that is strongly rooted in moral affirmation—whether Jewish or otherwise, disposed toward " a world of peace, justice, love, community, and joy for all"—can hope to really address the global human condition. Yet his assertion that his "deepest and strongest ties are at base irrational" leaves us with a conundrum that threatens any commitments we may still have toward the enlightenment traditions of critical reason and self-understanding.

Mara Sapon-Shevin's remarkably revealing piece demonstrates the passionate Jewish roots of her own personal and professional commitments. Indeed, for her, one of the marks of her own Jewishness is the "imperative that one's personal behavior should somehow link up with one's broader politics." She notes that her Torah study has taught her that everyday acts are infused with meaning and purpose, and that you are supposed to think about who you are and what you believe in all the time. Like David Purpel, Sapon-Shevin is clear that her work expresses deeply-held moral commitments. Academic life is the stage on which she lives out much of her devotion to an ethical vision, one inextricably connected to her Jewish experience and knowledge. In summary, she says, her work is about "paying attention to how society responds to diversity issues and struggling for belonging, safety, and respect for all people." Her life-long commitment is to the establishment of caring, nurturing communities within classrooms and schools. And all of this is connected to a powerful concern for Tikkun Olam—the repair of the world. Jewish family life provided her not only with the passion for a world of justice but also the intellectual feistiness and moral courage that such commitments in the world demand. Among the issues Sapon-Shevin raises in her paper is the disturbing question of academia itself and the extent to which it harbors latent intolerance for vocal Jewish self-assertion.

Roger Simon, too, affirms the project of diversity but raises in his paper the place and value of Jewish particularity within that project. His concern is the relationship of "a new assertion of Jewish pedagogical praxis" to our continued commitments to democracy, compassion, and social justice. For Simon this relationship is a necessarily ambivalent one and there is a need, he says, to "face its tensions head on." He notes, for example, that there is for him a definite allure to the utopian vision of a world united through the erasure of difference. There is, too, the deeply problematic issue of the way Jewish particularity is founded in a "discourse of election"—that is to say, the notion of chosenness and superiority. This is made evident in the claim of God's special love for Israel, the gift to this people of Torah, and the covenant at Sinai. This claim easily can, and has, become the basis of chauvinism. Yet Simon argues that no acceptable moral authority can be based on this notion of election. Indeed, he asserts, that there can be no assertion of one's own identity through the suppression of others' identities. How , he asks, can we in the "postmodern space" practice a pedagogy in which separate identities refuse a language of exclusivity but through their particular histories become responsible to one another; "In other words, how might one accomplish a pedagogy of Jewish particularity that would participate in a public ethical project of co-habitation?" What must be resisted, he says, is the kind of emphasis on difference that supports commmunal separation or segregation, or where difference becomes little more than the currency of the marketplace of style and performance. Jewish particularity must be more than the reinforcement of tribalization or a marker for the culturally exotic.

For Alan Weider the central question is the one about Jewish authenticity. There is no question about his being a Jew, yet just what that means is unclear to him. Nor is there doubt in his mind that his lifelong professional concern with issues of racial justice in America is strongly connected to his Jewish roots. What is most evident for him is the model of the quintessentially Jewish teacher. His own mentor was a Jew, but one far removed from the synagogue and Judaic observance. Still it is clear to Weider that all of his teaching was related to his "Yiddishkeit." All of his work was rooted in the courage to speak with honesty and conviction, to, as Mikhail Bakhtin put it, answer with one's life. And this life was about the struggle for authentic human communication and the making of a more loving world. Poignantly, Weider reflects on the notion that a person's best work is done when they "reach back to their roots"—a task that awaits him after twenty years of teaching for social change.

The diversity of voices and perspectives in this volume seems to defy any easy attempt to distill some essential Jewish view of education. Nor should we want to. The complex and broad range of meanings does not undercut the claim to some valid Jewish experience so much as insist that we see this experience in all of its variety and color. Indeed, rather than disappointment at the absence of some Weberian ideal type, the diversity speaks to a sensibility that is rich and generative in its meanings, vision, and commitments. We need to say here, too, that the voices represented in this volume are not, and are not intended to be, exhaustive of Jewish life, subjectivity, or experience. To the contrary, my hope is that this work spurs more such attempts to explore these topics and their relationship to the struggle for an emancipatory vision of education and society. Yet readers of this collection will surely be struck by the resonance and overlap between so much that is written here. Even if we are shy of offering sharp or comprehensive definitions of what Jewishness is, its existence in these pages is palpable; it is, in Cornell West's felicitous phrase, real enough. It would, for example, be hard to miss the deep concern with social justice, the painful sense of memory, or the dialogic notion of truth, that emerge from the authors here time after time, and infuse their visions of education. While all of us live much of our lives at the borders, or perhaps the ragged edges, of diverse cultural influences, this is not to say that these borders do not also represent, sometimes, fault lines beneath which are seismic energies, passions, and furies. The Jewish 'dimension' explored in these pages is surely one such fault line, passionately, sometimes angrily, drawing attention to the need for a world of loving and just human relationships.

Notes

1. Erica Jong, *Fear of Fifty* (New York: Harper Collins, 1994), p. 68.
2. Isaac Deutscher, *The Non-Jewish Jew* (London: Oxford University, 1968).
3. Zygmunt Bauman, *Modernity and Ambivalence* (Ithaca, N.Y.: Cornell University Press, 1991).
4. Lawrence Kushner, *The Book of Words* (Vermont: Jewish Lights Publishing, 1993), p. 88.
5. Robert Alter, *Necessary Angels* (Cambridge Mass.: Harvard University, 1991), p. 100.
6. Edward Greenstein in Michael Strassfeld, *The Jewish Holidays* (New York: Harper and Row, 1985), p. 192.
7. Ibid., p. 198.
8. Michael Lerner, *Jewish Renewal* (New York: Putnam and Sons, 1994).
9. Abraham Heschel, *The Prophets* (New York: The Jewish Publication Society of America, 1962), pp. 10, 16.
10. Lerner, *Jewish Renewal*, pp. 28–29.
11. Jacob Neusner, *Invitation to the Talmud* (San Francisco: Harper and Row, 1973), pp. 291–292.
12. Ibid., p. 286.
13. Kushner, *The Book of Words*, p. 11.
14. Abraham Heschel, *The Sabbath* (New York: Farrar, Straus and Giroux, 1951), pp. 10, 14.
15. Letty Cottin Pogrebin, "Time is all there is" in *Meaning Matters* (The Foundation for Ethics and Meaning, Fall 1996), p. 5.
16. Jong, *Fear of Fifty*, pp. 340–341
17. Roger Simon, "Statement of Intent Regarding Proposal to hold a Planning Conference to Establish : Mifgash; An Institute for the Integration of Jewish Learning and Secular Scholarship" (Unpublished document, 1994).
18. Todd Gitlin, *The Twilight of Common Dreams* (New York: Henry Holt, 1995), p. 236.

Chapter 1

Is that Jewish? History, Politics, and Finding One's Way

Michael W. Apple

"True" Stories

I am in a classroom at P.S. 24 in Paterson, New Jersey. It's time for the "morning exercizes." The teacher asks one child each day to lead the class in the singing of the "Star Spangled Banner," reciting the "Pledge of Allegience," and saying aloud the "Lord's Prayer." I'm called upon to go to the front of the room. I manage to mangle the song, but get through it. Everybody notices that I skip the part of the Pledge that says "one nation under God." The teacher stops me and makes a public display of her disapproval of me for this. On the playground during morning recess, I'm pushed around and called a Jew, even by some of the kids I thought were my friends. I didn't omit that "under God" phrase for overt religious reasons. My entire family believed in the strong separation of church and state. They saw the recent addition of that phrase as a right-wing attempt to establish a state religion. Yet, to all too many of the other kids I was different. I didn't go to church. I was a "christ-killer." It sure as hell wasn't good to be a *Jew* (I can't figure out a way of writing this word that incorporates the venom with which this was said) in P.S. 24, and I sure as hell didn't want to be one on the playground at recess time.

*****

I've just been hired for my first job as a teacher—as a day-to-day substitute. I have no college degree yet, since I'm still attending night school at a local teachers college. So it's $15 a day with no benefits. It's calling at 6:15 every morning to find out where I'm to teach in the slums of Paterson, in the very schools I went to only a few years before. I stop off at the Board of Education offices to do all of the paperwork for my "Emergency Teachers Certificate." (The office has agreed to count the time I had been a teacher of first aid and compass reading in the army as part of my professional training and, thus, I am somehow able to qualify for a license.) They give me endless forms to fill out and sign. One is a loyalty oath, stating both that I have not been a member of what seem to be hundreds of organizations and that I would not subvert the Constitution. Among the groups listed are some that I recognize. They include a number of leftist political and union groups that some of my family belonged to, including those that were organized to fight against the dictatorship of Franco in Spain—a person whose name was uttered as if it was a curse in my family. I refuse to sign this form. I say that it seems pointless. I tell them that if my plan was to subvert the Constitution, wouldn't I sign the oath anyway? It sticks in my craw as one more rightist assault on individual freedom. The people in the office say that no one has ever refused to sign the oath before. Why do I want to make waves? "Is it a religious thing?" I'm queasy about answering this question, since not only would I have to say, "No, it's a political thing," but I would also say that "No, I'm not at all religious." But, since the school system desperately needs teachers and I can speak a little Spanish, the form never gets signed. I am now a teacher.

*****

Years later, I am sitting in a restaurant in Amsterdam. I'm exhausted by a day spent giving lectures on the relationship between education and differential cultural and economic power. I just want to get a meal and go back to my room to get some sleep. The restaurant is crowded so I'm in a spare seat at a table with a larger group of people I don't know. My food comes; I begin to eat. A person from the larger group, who were getting a bit boisterous after countless beers, looks at me. With an odd smile, he asks, "Are you Jewish?" I ask him why he asks. He says, well I see that you are eating alone, you are reading a book, you've got a beard, and, "Well, you look Jewish." I don't know what to say.

*****

I am in a meeting in Japan. The day has been spent working with union leaders and with activists in the social movement to fight the discrimination against the Burakumin (a caste group with a long history of oppression there). A Japanese friend of mine asks if I am Jewish, assuming the answer already. He knows my politics and assumes that there is a relationship between being on the left and Jewishness. He then goes on and says, "We are very positively inclined toward the Jews here in Japan. After all, we are also very good at commerce and at running businesses all over the world." I think that this is not the time to talk about stereotypes and about the very evident contradictions in his Jewish/left/commerce equation. But it's an odd feeling to be positioned as a Jew in this context.

*****

I am meeting with my doctoral students in what is called the Friday Seminar, a weekly meeting where we read together, comment on each others' work, engage in serious political/educational discussions, and plan activity supporting struggles both here and abroad. Approximately 50 percent of the folks in the room are from outside the borders of the United States—Korea, Japan, Burma, Jamaica, India, Brazil, and even a few from the sovereign nation of Madison, Wisconsin. We are intensely discussing a number of struggles over historical memory and whose knowledge is declared to be official in schools and in the larger society. One of the students states that as long as the Jews control the media, the truth about who has real power in the world won't come out. He's from a country that has no Jewish population whatsoever. It's unclear whether he has taken this position himself or whether this is a widely held belief in his nation. Other students chime in. One after another, stereotypical and coded (and not so coded) anti-Semitic statements are made. And these are coming from people all of whom are deeply involved in struggles against oppression both here and abroad. I can't believe what I'm hearing. I can't believe they are saying this politically; and I can't believe that they are saying it when there are Jews in the room. For the first time in years, I consciously include myself in that group. That part of my identity, one that rarely comes into my consciousness and one I hardly thought existed, takes center stage. I nearly explode. The seminar spends weeks deconstructing this "common sense" and trying to rebuild a sense of mutuality and trust.

*****

We are in a crowded Palestinian taxi, crossing the line between the Israeli Army checkpoint and the city of Ramallah on the occupied West Bank. My wife Rima and I are going there to meet with a group of educational activists within the Palestinian community to lend our support to their struggles to reopen schools and universities. The meeting lasts all afternoon. Everyone is nervous. There are people in

Israel who are very upset with us for going. More importantly, the word is out that Hamas is totally opposed to the meeting and if we are found, there is the threat of kidnapping or death. For political and educational reasons, and for reasons of solidarity, while we are scared it seems worth the risk. My work is known to the Palestinian educators. Whatever I am ethnically/religiously is less important at that moment. What counts is whether I can assist them and the students whose lives they care so much about. Strangely, I do and do not feel Jewish here. But I realize that there is symbolic significance both for me and for them in our coming. There may be hell to pay later, but we feel there is no choice. It's only later, when we return to the States and help mobilize support for these Palestinian educators, that we reflect on whether there is something "Jewish" about our support for people we believe are oppressed.

Whose Stories Are These?

After such autobiographical fragments, you will forgive me if I continue this chapter with what may seem to be a rather odd statement, given what I've just said and given what will follow. I am more than a little uncomfortable with and quite mistrustful of autobiographical accounts. I do not want to slight the power and importance of the testimony of oppressed groups; Patricia Williams's *The Alchemy of Race and Rights*[1] comes to mind. However, in a time when amateur psychoanalysis, postmodern personal narratives, and all too "precious" autobiographical accounts are increasingly found in educational literature, I have a number of worries about such tendencies. At their best and when done *very* reflexively, they do remind us that behind even the most eviscerated writing stands an embodied person. They do remind us as well of Dewey's recognition that all educational events end in an act of personal knowing. They do ask us to take seriously Abraham Heschel's insight that knowing is a form of "celebration" that takes one beyond oneself.[2] And when done well, they do enable voices that are silenced to be heard.

Yet, this said, I also believe that too many of such autobiographical tendencies reflect the new middle class's infinite need for self-display. In a time of increasingly oppressive economic and cultural relations, the message of their often relatively well-positioned and well-educated authors is too often, "But enough about you; let me tell you about me."

With this in mind, I have approached writing this chapter with a good deal of trepidation. First, I am consciously experimenting stylistically. Indeed, anyone familiar with my work may have difficulty believing she or he is reading the same author. Further, I do not put too much trust in what I say here. These are tentative reflections. I do not know their epistemological status. They aren't special; they aren't any truer coming from me than anyone else. They may not even be true about me, since my own understandings of this are themselves provisional and unclear and may derive from motives that are both less than conscious and less than self-critical. They are simply my attempts to figure out what is it about what I do that one might say is "Jewish." You will forgive me I hope, but in this particular piece of writing my audience is not only you, but *me*. I am trying to employ the autobiographical fragments I include above to do some historical and political work. I am trying to understand who part of me is and where this part may largely come from. Can I say that some of this comes from being "Jewish"? I know that you have noticed the quotes surrounding Jewish in the previous sentences. They are there for a reason, one I assume is shared by many other people with similar backgrounds. And I have come to assume that the oddity of putting that word in quotes is part of a longer tradition as well. Writing this piece is not about finding an answer; it is part of learning to ask the question.

I have purposely not attempted to theorize what I say here. Too often our response to difficult personal struggles is to search for academic respectability. I don't want to slight the importance of such theoretical projects, and in fact as some of the readers of this book may know I have inflicted such academic work on more than one generation of critical social and cultural scholarship in education. However, right now I simply want to get some questions down on paper. Of course, theories are undoubtedly smuggled into every sentence here. But I'll think about that later.

Let me admit that I don't know what it means for something to be called Jewish. I know what the stereotypes say it means. But what it means to *me* is unclear. Thus, this chapter is something of a voyage of self-discovery, where I am exploring a terrain about myself that has until recently not usually been a conscious issue for me, except in instances such as those signified in the above personal fragments. I do assume one thing, however. I do assume that there are others like me who were raised in totally secular and deeply political families where the "real" religious underpinnings of their lives was an abiding commitment to social justice.

I do know that I often feel as an outsider politically and sometimes culturally in this society. I do know that the hedonistic and possessive individualism that so permeates this nation and others like it makes me deeply uneasy. I do know that as a scholar, as a teacher, as a political activist, and in other aspects of my personal life, I do not usually overtly think of myself as a Jew. In fact, if someone were to ask me who I am, the word Jewish would be well down on the list of conscious attributes and positions I might enumerate. And yet I do know that at times—even when I can't articulate it clearly—I feel the gaze of others looking at me as a "Jew" with all that such a gaze implies. I also know that at times I feel as if I must contest the public definition and stereotypes of what people believe it means to be a "Jew."

I do not want to give the impression that my personal struggle over identity is due to the fact that historically I and many others have been positioned as a Jew in a negative way. Rather, I believe that a constitutive aspect of being a secular and political Jew is a concern with where one fits, where one's "home" is.[3]

Little did I know how "Jewish" this was until recently. Actually, in a way that I still can't quite grasp, my realization of the Jewishness of this came from a book. Irving Howe's rather masculinist yet still very powerful *World of Our Fathers*[4] placed my own political biography within a much longer history of secular "Jewish" struggles. I recognized a continuity with thousands of others. It seems odd to me that a book could have such an effect. Is this Jewish?

Perhaps I can clarify to myself what I mean by this question and how I currently understand it by reflecting on my own personal history. My grandfather was a Russian immigrant who as a young man in the late nineteenth century emigrated first to England and then to the United States. He left Russia for political and economic reasons. As a communist, he was always in danger. As someone who was very poor, he had other reasons for leaving. And as someone who (the story goes) killed a policeman who was taking part in a pogrom, attacking my grandfather's immediate family, he had no choice but to leave as quickly as he could.

My first political memories include going with him to the Workingmen's Circle every week where pinochle was played and politics was talked. Talked is exactly the wrong word here. Lived, passionately argued, part of one's very being—these are perhaps better metaphors. Like other immigrant working class folks in the inner city of

Paterson, New Jersey—the home of some of the most important strikes and labor struggles in the history of the United States—life wasn't life without being consumed by politics. This was of course ratified in his daily life as a textile worker and tailor. But politics wasn't politics unless it was guided by reading everything one could get ones hands on: Books on political struggles and on world history. "Great" (especially American) novels—by Mark Twain, O' Henry, James Fenimore Cooper. (After all, we were now in America not the old world. Thus, we should now read "American" books.) The Yiddish weeklies and dailies, especially the socialist and communist ones.

I thought that *he* had personally composed one of his favorite lines: "Religion is the opium of the masses." For him, religion was what kept "us" backward and was a tool of oppression. Who "us" was meant to be was a sliding signifier—the left, Jews, workers, immigrants, and so on. Yet probably unstated, as an absent presence, within this category of "us" were people exactly like him—poor Russian communists who rose up against the oppression of workers and who also "just happened to be" Jewish. I must admit that I have no memory of him actually using that word. And, yet, he ate what might be associated with Jewish (eastern European) food—kishke, borscht, potato pancakes. But his greatest culinary love was religiously transgressive. Once a year he treated himself to a lobster. He died when I was thirteen—and his gift to me was his *books*.

Is this Jewish—this love of books, this passion for politics and involvement, this understanding that one is on this planet to make it better, this demand that one act as ethically as possible—at the same time that any overt religious identification is dismissed?

Let us move a generation in time—to a mother (the daughter of this grandfather) who herself was both antireligious and a communist, who never finished high school but still loved to write short stories and poetry (and who gave me a middle name—Whitman—that spoke to her love of the poetic and of what was at the time partly transgressive culture). She was someone who did not work for pay outside the home. She had the meals ready when we came home from school or from "work." She took care of the house, but insisted that since we all lived there, house work was everyone's work. Thus, everyone did it—washing, cleaning, etc. Yet, she was one of the founding members of the Paterson chapter of the Congress of Racial Equality (CORE) and was an activist in the poor and black communities in Paterson, an activist who came home to cook and to be a "mother." And then she went out again to struggle over education and jobs, against the forms of political patronage that denied power to poor folks, and to fight the class and especially racial structuring that dominated Paterson's political, economic, and educational realities. We too, as her children, went to these meetings and worked in the campaigns for the progressive candidates, and with others did much of the "shit work" required in mobilizations—putting together signs, distributing material, and so on. It wasn't seen as odd. We were just "Mimi's kids" and like the kids of so many other working-class, and especially antiracist activists, we were expected to pitch in. Why? Because reality is unequal. It's *our* job to do something about it *now*. (Perhaps Paul Berman is partly right when he suggests that there is a peculiar Jewish custom of rebelling? As he puts it, in a slightly reductive way, "There is an old and slightly peculiar Jewish custom of rebelling against Jewishness by identifying with the most marginal of all possible groups so as to rebel and still not be assimilated into the mainstream; and this played its part in attracting Jews to the black cause."[5]) And she read long into the night to me, at me, with me. Is all this Jewish?

Or a father, Harry—a printer from a socialist family—who worked long hours trying to make enough money to allow the family to escape the poverty of the slums of Paterson. As a printer, he was a member of one of the most historically literate and radical crafts. His sons, myself and my younger brother, spent hours at the printshop each week. From the time we were old enough to carry a broom, we worked there. We learned to set type, to deposit it in the correct place in the cases, to run handpresses and later to run larger presses. (I, in fact, worked part of my way through night school at that small teachers college by working as a printer during the day.) And we learned—viscerally—that work was crucial to becoming a person and that it must always be done in a way that respects your skills and your fellow workers. And we learned to love the printed word. From him, we also learned why he too was antireligious. He had studied for and undergone a bar mitzvah and had nothing but bad memories of the years spent in joyless study of arcane texts that were not made meaningful to him. It was simply something one did, no questions asked or tolerated. *His* children would not have to endure such things if he had anything to do about it. Was this Jewish?

Both Mimi and Harry worked at politics—in CORE, in campaigns to elect labor-oriented and/or black or Latino/a candidates. Both had an undying respect for unions and for the possibilities of collective organizations of real people. Both were cynical about the machinations behind the two major political parties. Both were (aggressively) secular and had a profound mistrust of rightist religious movements such as those that added that "under God" to the Pledge of Allegiance said by students daily in schools. And both were more than a little happy when I decided early in my life that what I wanted to be was—a teacher. To them, there was something almost sacred about being a teacher. Even though neither of them had completed high school in the allotted time, to be a teacher was to honor the family both in class terms (I was "getting ahead"), in political terms (it's up to you, Michael, to tell the truth about this society), and in intellectual terms (teaching was about literacy, about giving people power to understand the world and—maybe—to change it). And when I ultimately became president of a teachers' union, well that was even better for all of the above reasons. How much of this is Jewish?

All of these people made it clear, by their very actions, that politics and ethics were to be lived, and that "literacy" and political talk counted. Among my memories are mealtimes when everyone—including the children—was expected to have opinions about what seemed to be everything. But some everythings returned again and again to nearly every meal. Local, national, and international politics were consumed with each meal.

But of course this is partly romantic. I have dropped a net down into the past whose weave is almost guaranteed to pull up memories of this sort. Growing up poor, in a poor area, being surrounded by relatives who all seemed to live in the same area and all seemed to be in danger of constantly losing the jobs that they had—given the fact that as an aging textile city Paterson was suffering massively from what we now call capital flight—all of this made life tense and filled us with unease about the present and the future. Poverty, job loss, the inability to pay for medical care or even one's rent (these words seem too damn abstract to deal with these experiences) weren't theorized. We didn't find them important because of some text published by "The Party" or by a leftist intellectual. They were focused upon because they were part of our daily lives and the lives of everyone (African-American, Puerto Rican, Russian, Polish, Italian, Jewish) in that area of Paterson at the time. Thus, those mealtime conversations were undoubtedly filled with other "everythings"—paying the rent, talk about school, family problems. (A communist mother's family and a socialist father's family had, shall we say, interesting problems in "getting along".

I am reminded of the old adage: When leftists form a firing squad, they always line up in a circle.) These intense political discussions, where family=politics=arguing about everything, and where even children were expected to participate and to be argued with because the nascent and still not totally formed arguments of children were supposed to be serious enough to be taken seriously—are these Jewish?

I don't want to romanticize this history and these commitments, although I don't know how not to do this. Indeed, on looking back, they speak to another more contradictory politics. I remember a picture that had importance in my family. It was a reproduction of a painting by Ben Shahn. It was of two hands, a white one reaching down and clasping the other one which was black. It was as if the black hand was attached to someone who was drowning or falling and the white one was saving it. Across the top of the painting were words in both Hebrew letters and English. They said "Thou Shalt Not Stand Idly By." These words speak to the realities of the oppressive conditions of the racial state in which we live. To be black is often to be the other, to be subject to repressive economic and cultural conditions that are simply that—repressive.

However, in that picture are other messages. "We"—the anointed ones, the ones with the best social conscience, the ones who too have experienced centuries of repression—will lift "you" up. Our task is to make this society better. We know the path; we will help you along it. There is a hidden text here, one that I am perhaps reading into it but in this case I don't think so. The hidden text is one that contains a crucial sense of the importance of intervention into oppressive social relationships, of reaching out, of real action. Yet it is combined with (more than?) a hint of arrogance, of certainty in the rightness of one's position, and of which group should be in leadership in joint struggles against oppression. Is this Jewish? I can only say that it makes me listen perhaps more carefully to some of the complaints against Jewish arrogance within some parts of the African-American community, although I have no patience whatsoever for the more virulent anti-Semitic variants of this.

I do know that whatever the contradictions involved in the politics of these representations and in the assumptions that underpinned them, the expectation that one had to live the committed life did lead me to become deeply involved in antiracist struggles on the local and national levels, including my own stint while still a high school student as publicity director of Paterson's chapter of CORE and my participation in the South in the struggles to reopen schools that had been closed by white supremacist groups opposed to integration. It undoubtedly led to my activity in union politics during the time I was president of a teachers' union and to my later and continuing involvement in political activity both here in the United States and in other nations. This comes across as too self-congratulatory, and maybe—given my personal struggles to find myself in these multiple traditions—unconsciously I want it to be. But I cannot explain my relationship to whatever Jewishness means without referring to these kinds of political actions and to what I think are some of the most important driving forces behind them. Nor, as I am beginning to understand, can I explain why nearly all of my writing and research is organized around a set of (too damn complicated) issues—What is the relationship between knowledge and power in schools and the larger society? Who benefits from the ways this society is organized? What can be done about it?—without trying to understand the historical roots I may have in a set of multiple traditions (I don't know whether to call these religious traditions since I, like many others, do not feel religious) that are much larger than myself.[6] Does this recognition mean that I am now "more" Jewish?

I am not even certain why these questions are important to me now. Why did I accept the challenge of writing this chapter when—like all of us—my life is so intensified I can hardly find a moment's peace? Why do I feel the need to situate myself within something to which I have always had such ambivalent reactions? Perhaps because, whether I accept it or not, I *am* being constantly positioned as a Jew, even in places where I would least expect it. Deep down, of course, I do know (in a very complicated way) that I am a Jew; but what that actually means is, and I think must be, always contested. If identity is being part of historical community/ies, where in that community does one belong? Whose definition of that community prevails personally and politically? In Heschel's apposite words, to be human is to "wrestle."[7] Perhaps because in the face of this I need to work through a tremendously complex history of multiple traditions to find out those parts of them that I can use to make sense of why this positioning occurs. Perhaps because not only does this history work through me but I want to use it for my own purposes. And finally, perhaps because there is a politics of pleasure involved in being constantly tortured by one's own identity and politics. Yeah, I know the question: Is that Jewish too?

Afterthoughts by Way of a Conclusion

Oddly, in this reflection I have not spent much time discussing that to which I devote so much of my life right now—writing and teaching about the connections between knowledge and power in education,[8] working with dissident groups, unions, and progressive governments and universities in the United States and elsewhere on democratizing educational research, policy, and practice, and understanding and mobilizing against the conservative triumphalism now littering the landscape with the results of its arrogant and mean-spirited policies. Instead, I've focused on a series of questions that, for reasons I have yet to fully understand, have become more important to me in the last decade.

Perhaps it is because of the fact that I have a son with a serious and recurrent long-term illness and answering these questions might provide a bit of stability. (Isn't it odd that when he was at his worst, for some reason my wife and I lit candles on Friday night to signify the fact that we—and he—had made it through another week? Cultural and historical resources have complicated uses, it seems.) Placing myself in a longer (but not "religious"?) tradition may serve some purpose here. Perhaps I am not immune to the search for collective meaning that is so evident within so many other groups. And, perhaps, as someone in his mid-fifties, there is something more psychologically complex going on. I prefer to think that much of it has to do with the growth of rightist attacks, the growth of anti-Semitism and racism, the growth of dangerous strands of religious fundamentalism inside and outside of Judaism, and similar things that cause me to wonder where I and people like me fit into these dynamics. All of this creates a situation where answering the question of "who I am" in these troubling times cannot be avoided.

Who am I? Is that a Jewish question?

Epilogue

I am back in the country after lecturing in Europe and have picked up this chapter to go through it one last time for final editing. I feel that I must add this final fragment.

I've just answered the last question from members of the audience who have heard me give an invited address at the British Educational Research Association annual meeting. I've tried to show how the conservative restoration has stitched together a tense and contradictory hegemonic alliance that is effectively transforming the very ways we think about democracy, what and who education is for, and how it will be carried out. The speech seems to have gone over well (much to my relief). A number of us crowd into a car to find a place to eat. At the restaurant, on hearing the mix of American and British accents coming from our table, the owner tries to guess where we are from. Of the seven people, three are from the United States. We play along with her.

When she gets to me she says, "You're from Jerusalem, right?" I'm taken aback. In the car on the way back to the university where the conference is being held, we talk about our experiences at the dinner. Someone who's spent a lot of time in the United States notes that the restaurant owner (who it seems was originally from Malta) assumed that a New York area accent was "from Jerusalem." Another person from England in the car says to me, "Excuse me for asking, but you are *partly Jewish* aren't you?" The stress is on the word "partly," almost as if one wouldn't want to be fully Jewish, as if this is both something that explains my academic and poltical work and is something that one would want to keep largely hidden. At that very moment, we arrive back at the university and the conversation is never completed. Since I'm adding this fragment, it is obvious that I can't get the question out of my mind. I wonder what I would have said if there had been time. I think that I would have said something like, "No, that part of me that is Jewish—including the political and secular part—is *fully* Jewish." That's quite a personal realization. It would have taken hours to explain it to her. I've devoted page after page to it here trying to understand it myself. I'm (perhaps) a little less confused now.

Anyone for a nice game of pinochle and some political talk?

Notes

I would like to thank Morry Re'em for his perceptive comments on this chapter.

1. Patricia Williams, *The Alchemy of Race and Rights* (Cambridge: Harvard University Press, 1991).
2. Abraham Heschel, *Who is Man?* (Stanford University Press, 1965).
3. See Hank Bromley, "Identity Politics and Critical Pedagogy" in *Educational Theory*, 39 (Summer 1989), pp. 207–223. While I have reservations about a number of the theoretical and political assumptions behind identity politics, Bromley does raise some important issues in the context of my own discussion here.
4. Irving Howe, *World of Our Fathers* (New York: Simon and Schuster, 1976).
5. See Paul Berman, ed. *Blacks and Jews* (New York: Delacorte Press, 1994), p. 12.
6 This is *not* to imply that political concerns are not religious concerns as well. Indeed, one of the reasons I have such respect for liberation theology on the one hand, and, especially, for Abraham Heschel's work and life on the other is the recognition of the constitutive nature of this connection.
7. Abraham Heschel, "Carl Stern's Interview with Abraham Heschel," in *Moral Grandeur and Spiritual Audacity*, ed. Susannah Heschel (New York: Farrar Straus and Giroux, 1996), p. 403.
8. Let me list some of these books. It not only gives my reflections here some academic respectability, but it will provide the reader with a better sense of what I mean by having a deep concern with the relation between knowledge and power in education. See, e.g., Michael Apple, *Ideology and Power* (New York: Routledge, 1979; second edition 1990), *Education and Power* (New York: Routledge, 1985; second edition 1995), *Teachers and Texts* (New York: Routledge, 1986), *Official Knowledge* (New York: Routledge,1993), and *Cultural Politics and Education* (New York: Teachers College Press, 1996).

Chapter 2

Acts of Memory for Creating a Jewish Identity: Learning to Play Countermelody While Developing the "Weapons of the Strong," An Optimistic Postmodernism of Opportunity and Hope

Haim Dov Beliak

> That is what learning is. You suddenly understand something you've understood all your life, but in a new way.
>
> Doris Lessing
>
> The independent subject is unseated by a wordless accusation.
>
> Emmanuel Levinas
>
> It is sufficient that others look at me for me to be what I am.
>
> Jean-Paul Sartre
>
> In my view, there is no more supine form of submission than when an entire people bases its very being on the attitudes that others have toward it.
>
> Micah Joseph Berdyezewski

It is now quite acceptable in social science and humanistic academic circles for researchers to discuss and even demonstrate the conjunction of biography and social theory. Just like my friends, who have written about this conjunction of the personal and the academic for this volume, my experience too, is to report that I feel naked! Freud theorizes that this fear of being naked in public relates to the almost universal sense of inadequacy. It is a most humbling experience to write about one's self and since self-disclosure is something that we–I–do reluctantly . . . I am embarrassed. The Hebrew language three-letter root structure opens a prismatic apparatus allowing me to distinguish some of my concerns in this paper. In Hebrew, the root g l h (ג ל ה) suggests what I feel: naked, and then again, many other possible meanings. When the root is inflected it means: uncover, inform, clarify, discover, disclose, revealed, unveiled, and in a cognate meaning of the same root: exile, uproot, wander, and captive.[0] All of these meanings might serve as a cipher for my attempt to summarize how I think about my life and how social theory from education, philosophy, and sociology inform that thinking. Some of this social theory is sanctified by the theory guilds but much of it remains less than clear. Biography has a way of challenging the neatness of theory constructions.

Often in writing this essay, I asked in the middle of either personally painful recollections and unclear raging moments of theorizing incoherance: Why bother? Yet the need to tell and the need to be heard drives so much of the present moment! My parents are getting older, my children are almost in college, and I, too, am getting older in a more self-conscious way. The invitation to this volume posed a series of questions and aroused impulses rooted in the desire "as one gets older to find some integrative threads to our lives, to bind together the disparate pieces of our precarious subjectivities."[1] The sewing of those threads in my life as a father, spouse, rabbi, man, education graduate student, and child of Holocaust survivors binds my life in the midst of commitments and relationships growing out of a more fluid articulateness that is trying to overcome the modernist academically induced internal stutter—to mix metaphors and return—to clothe myself in understanding. It is reaching toward a postmodernist valorizing of "difference" and the "other."

There are other reasons to be humbled by this process of thinking about social theory, which is often less successful in capturing the turns and particulars of individual lives than it claims. I often ask myself after reading a statistically laden essay in my field of education, what do I know that is new or important? Has the meaning of something been made clearer to me through the quantification exercises? The answer is usually no. For me meanings of things come in stories, often in my mother tongue, Yiddish. My own primary way of learning has been through hearing stories and decoding something of the people and events revealed in narratives. Along with my East European Holocaust survivor parents, I have acquired a yearning for a past that is nostalgic but sadly, too often a parody of its once former glory. Along with them, I have a critical and skeptical approach to the history of Eastern European Jewish culture. Aspects of that Jewish culture were profoundly distasteful before the death of millions of Jews made us nostalgic for the shtetl. We have not sorted this confusion of nostalgia and critique regarding our past too effectively.

I often ask people if they have ever met a pious person. Most of the time the question is treated as a nonsequitur. Most people in Los Angeles have met movie stars and professional athletes. In Los Angeles you can go to certain restaurants and bars to meet them. But where would you go to meet a pious person? Would it be better to phrase the question: What would you do if you met a truly pious person? Most people are at a loss to even comprehend what the witness of such a person could tell them, not only in words but in deeds. The primary pre-cynical definition of pious is "having or showing a dutiful spirit of reverence for God or earnest wish to fulfill religious obligation."[2] As a rabbi, I have met pious people who have taught me through their life witness something about the narrative of life that can only be captured in a story. My college mate and friend, University of Southern California anthropologist Dr. Gelya Frank, writes that, "disciplined reflexivity involves the work of clarifying one's empathic tendencies, and it has an important history in the tradition of American cultural anthropology."[3] I want to claim that empathic power for the tasks of clarifying issues of Jewish identity and the role of education. But first a story. . . .

In 1986 my mother, who was born in Olkusz, Poland, and I returned to her village in the southwestern section of Poland around Katowicz. The cold war was still a presence. We stayed with Christina, a faithful Catholic Polish friend of my mother's from the time they were little girls in school and later, during Nazi occupation. Having a trustworthy and self-sacrificing Christian friend during the war meant real help, hope, and in my mother's case, her first ham sandwich. My mother was a reluctant visitor, having returned to her home town the last time for a seventy-two hour visit in Christina's home the summer of 1945. A few months after her liberation from the "death march" (described in Daniel Jonah Goldhagen's Hitler's Willing Executioners) and following, an extended hospital stay, my mother was searching for surviving family.[4] It was this friend, Christina, and her mother, who took my mother in and protected her against the other Poles. Another surviving young girl had been killed in Olkusz shortly before my mother arrived and Christina and her mother would not allow my mother to even walk across the street alone.

When we arrived it was summer and a few days before Shavuot. There were many powerful incidents during the four-day visit to Olkusz. One of the most peculiar was the only request that Christina made of us. Christina insisted that my mother and I accompany her to the Church that abutted the town square opposite of Christina's home for a courtesy visit to the local priest. To my surprise, my mother was irritated and kept refusing to go. She explained that she had lived her whole early life in Olkusz and she had never gone to the Ti'mah (the unclean place), why should she go now? Christina didn't know what a Ti'mah was. Inadvertently, my mother had used the slang Yiddish-Hebrew word for a Church (in Polish, Koshku). My mother caught herself and explained to Christina her reluctance to go to this place, full of foreboding and mystery from the days of her youth. Nevertheless, Christina was insistent that we go. She finally won my mother's consent by appealing to the notion that it would be good for the priest, the object of our visit, to meet a rabbi (me), whose mother had grown up in Olkusz. The Davkaness (roughly, "we are around despite attempts to kill us"—a powerful motivating force in my mother's life) could always be aroused, as Christina well understood.

We traversed the hundred yards from her home and were inside a massive dark and ancient church. We climbed some steps into a separate building and arrived at the Priest's office. Christina went into the office and asked the secretary to tell the priest that she was there and wanted to introduce him to friends from America. We waited about five or ten minutes and the priest emerged. I looked at my mother, who burst into tears and instantly I, too understood. I did not need an explanation but my mother said to me: "Er zeyt oyes wie zwei Yiddin." (He looks like two Jews!) My American Jewish friends of a certain age would have said: "He has the map of Jerusalem on his face."

Apparently our priest, who was a several years old than I, was a foundling. I surmised his parents had been killed by the Nazis. He had grown up in Catholic orphanages. It was not possible to converse with the priest at great length, a missed opportunity that I have regretted for years. Later, I asked Christina, who had understood all of this interaction without knowing a word of Yiddish or English, what her understanding of this face was. She very matter-of-factly called him the "Jewish" priest and that indeed was the common reference of all in Olkusz.

As much as liberal social theory denies the physicality of Jews it is a part of common knowledge. Is there a physiognomy of Jews? (How crude a suggestion!) Does this constitute Jews as a race?[5] Or perhaps we are a culture or an ethnos? Figuring out who we (I) are (am) not easy but in this story is part of the answer. Part of the story begins in sorting out the questions of race, culture, nationality, and ethnicity.[6]

I

Culture and Race

In the *The Second Sex* Simone De Beauvoir claims: "One is not born, but rather becomes a woman . . . it is civilization as a whole that produces this creature." I ponder what would be the equivalent of de Beauvoir's statement for Jews? Are Jews "produced" by civilization or culture? Or, as it seems in everything but the actual use of the word, are Jews a "race."? There are numerous examples of "civilization's" efforts to tame and define the Jew. The cultural plasticity of the category "Jews" suggest a multitude of potential cultural positions. These positions seem to multiply in nineteenth and twentiethth century Europe precisely as the ancient civic disabilities begin to fall away. Throughout the nineteenthth century, at the advent of Emancipation's impact, Jews were perceived to form a distinct caste with their own language, voice, physical body, and mind, to name but a few attributes.[7] Ironically, these post-Enlightenment constructions of the Jew(s), were a novum and were the opposite of the Enlightenment's promise of acceptance! The romantic Enlightenment promises all but disappeared under the nineteenth century's "intense nationalism, imperialism, and xenophobia."[8]

European society wanted to know: is the distinctiveness of the Jews, as collective entity, a result of cultural or racial factors? The middle term "ethnic" was not in vogue in Europe.[9] The conception of Jewish collective distinctiveness continued into the twentieth century, increasingly employing a discourse of race, often with devastating impact. In many circles, Jewish distinctiveness was seen as marking the Jew as a race in physiological and physiognomical terms and coming to eventually shape and determine the cultural tropes of Jewish life.[10]

Sander Gilman claims that this shift from cultural to physiological difference impacts how Jews too came to see and comprehend themselves. Jews began to reflect on "the complexity of being understood or seen as different and creating out of this sense of imposed difference a meaningful sense of one's identity."[11] The meaning of my encounter with the "Jewish" priest has many aspects to it but clearly an element of this 'uncanny encounter' lies in the complexity and unclarity beyond the neat categories of the Emancipation.

Cultural positions on the distinctiveness of Jews compete with a growing discourse of the racialization of Jews. Even the cultural categories appear to 'real' Jews, as either philo-semitic or anti-semitic, but hardly neutral. One would want racial categories about Jews to be cast as by definition anti-semitic, but even that clear definition doesn't seem possible. Various racial attributes are charged with meaning that is culturally shaped but often appear under subterfuge in the guise of "natural and eternal" attributes. "At the end of the nineteenth century, the terms "Jewish racial question," "Jewish question," and "Jewish problem" were used interchangeably by Jews and non-Jew alike. All these terms refer to aspects of Jewish society, or of Jews themselves, that were considered to be objectionable and in need of improvement. They were broadly defined to include the religion, culture, economic status, and political inclinations of European Jewry.[12] It becomes increasing unclear if the "natural and eternal" are racial designations or cultural. The necessity to distinguish and understand these issues becomes more complex as the counterdiscourse of philo-semitic attributions also participate in the cultural and racial continuum.[13] External and interior perceptions by "real" Jews seems to be at work too, in shaping the identity at the same time that each individual Jew must recapitulate some portion of "civilization's" contribution toward reproducing certain identity formations. John M. Efron's book *Defenders of the Race* points to the numerous strategies of nineteenth and early twentieth century Jewish anthropologists, mostly physical anthropologists including many with medical backgrounds, who attempted to navigate this shifting and confusing morass of claims about race and culture.[14] For Joseph Jacobs, one of the most prominent of these Jewish scholars, the challenges of poverty, dislocation, pogroms, and anti-semitism were met by the use of Jewish racial science that developed out of sociology and anthropology for a "new mode of Jewish self-defense: the scientific apologia.[15]

In popular and elite sectors of society questions of self-presentation and the presentation of the racialized Other becomes central, even as a self-conscious attempt to ward off the impact of negative stereotyping seems futile.[16] The presence of several minorities in America has made the self-assertions of counter-ideas about race much more a part of both the public ken of the victims and purveyors of racial ideas. Each minority has chosen an unique way of responding to negative images of themselves. Each purveyor of racial ideas is fully aware of the use of racial messages. The discourse that seeks a commonalty and solidarity among "victims" of these images is still very much in its infancy. Gilman affirms that, "the Jew in the Western Diaspora does respond, must respond, to the image of the Jew. . . ."[17] Individual Jews are often faced with a struggle to acquiesce in accepting or rejecting representations of themselves.[18] These representations primary affect is on Jews but are invoked by various cultural media such as movies, television, and museums. "The Jew, caught up in such a system of representation, has but little choice: his essence, which incorporates the horrors projected onto him and which is embodied (quite literally) in his physical being must try, on one level or another, to become invisible."[19]

The racial attributions about Jews continue to carry explosive cultural meanings. While the impact and penetration of these stereotypes have varied over time and place, they remain part of the potential lexicon of society's images of minorities. Jews share a historical representational commonalty not only with women but with "ugly" races (primarily, Africans), and other threatening elements: microbes, devils, and swine. All the attributed physical characteristics carry a moral meaning. The hidden cloven hoof, being one of the secret marks of the Jew, points to a moral degeneracy associated with devils.[20] There is a distinctive cultural projection in the representation of Jews as black, defining both as the embodiment of ugly "races" who lack any aesthetic qualities.[21] Combined with blackness is an anatomy epitomized by the nose that is a sign of pathology and disease coincident with syphilis.[22] At times both "Jews" and "women" are perceived as interchangeable tropes for the weak, both psychically and physically. Paradoxically, "Jews" and "women" are consistently charged with exercising indirect power that is secretive, devious, and conniving but capable of overcoming the objectively stronger opposite party through subterfuge and wiles.[23] This is a characteristic of devils too. "Jews," "blacks," and "women" are often yoked together as a subject category lacking their own agency and subjectivity. When agency is attributed to Jews it is has a malevolent character. Jewish men displaying agency are often perceived as pushy, grasping, oversexed, and spoiled. Jewish women are also subject to similar stereotypes, often subject to a double dose including charges of frigidity and materialism.

The malevolent association with women, Blacks, and devils is only one facet of negative stereotypes about "Jews." The evoking of additional historical images that migrate from categories of race to gender and class are equally tenacious and remain quite disturbing, even when a "positive" alterity is rendered. One example, in its American version of this alterity is found in the notion of Jewish intelligence especially as it manages to incorporate both economic superiority and Jewish superior intelligence. The acceptance of "blame" for these superiorities is turned to "credit" by reducing their threat; and by a discourse claiming that it is the proper use of these qualities—now tamed and directed—that allow the "Jewish genius" the chance to give back to society. This is the opportunity provided by America.[24] Jews are, nevertheless, parvenus in this "positive alterity" of intelligence since the accusation includes a claim against being uncomfortable with the rest of life beyond the intellectual, namely the spiritual, material, or physical. The specter of the spiritual, material or physical invokes issues of class and gender representations. The balanced life is not possible for Jewish intellectuals—both men and women—since the two categories of genius—money and intelligence—sap all other energies. Jews are "smart" but this can be a double-edged sword that threatens always to return to the European trope of Jewish intelligence as "craftiness." The negative trope of "craftiness" has its parallel in terms of gender stereotypes of American Jewish women as grasping, suffocating, and parasitic, classical stereotypes for Jewish men in European anti-semitism.[25]

Additionally, the myth-making about Jewish superior intelligence is bound up with doubts over the question of "derivative genius" versus "true genius." This latter dualism of intelligence also has an American and European version. In the writing of composer Richard Wagner's *Das Judenthum in der Musik* we have a classic portrayal of Jewish talent as inauthentic. This derivativeness is a charge made about Jews not only in music but also in the field of letters in various "native" languages such as English, German, and French. Since Jews are never "native" they are never capable of writing authentically in "native" languages. This latter representation of "foreign" superior Jewish intelligence is internalized by "real" Jews in numerous ways too, the most prominent of which is either an overestimation of originality or nervous self-derogatory depreciation. The physical inferiority of Jews is represented as a consequence of superior intelligence. The romanticizing of Jews' intellect is at the center of philo-semitic fantasies of genius even if superior intelligence is only a consolation prize.[26]

Given the rather crowded identity "space" peopled by all sorts of questionable and problematic images, is there room for creation of Jewish identities based on self-affirmation and choice? Can Jews, in the face of so many negative stereotypes and even the ambiguity of positive tropes, form an identity of their own? Is there room for a historicized analysis of the construction of Jewish identity with all the "normal" conflicts about power, gender, secular versus religious, money, and loyalty, but minus racial stereotypes? German socialist Karl Kautsky's 1914 book *Rasse and Judentum* rejects deterministic theory of Jewish behavior and chauvinism, but he writes: "Characteristically enough, there is rising within Judaism, as a reaction against anti-semitism, a similar tendency to accept and utilize the theory of race. It is a natural application of the principle: If this theory permits Christian-Teutonic patriots to declare themselves demi-gods, why should Zionist patriots not use it in order to stamp the people chosen by God as a chosen race of nature, a noble race that must be carefully guarded from any deterioration and contamination by foreign elements."[27] These questions place important emphasis on Jewish self-identity formation but do not forthrightly ask about the dialectical role of the individual and communal contexts.[28] Narrative accounts about young individuals initiated into being Jewish are often burdened considerable with problematics. Legion are the traumatic stories describing, in particular, childhood initiations into being a Jew that are less than substantive or finally decisive. Being a Jew, contrary to so much Christian and Christianized secular thought, is not a stable and autonomous identity. Even among Jews in their self-description there is a tendency to reify or essentialize. Witness the passion and shame of Linda Nochlin's admission that: "The terrible thing about the voluminous literature representing the Jew as excessive is the way it sticks in the mind, seeps into the unconscious, embeds itself in the deepest levels of my being even if I detest its assertions and, on the rational level, I realize its total irrationality. But I am irrational, too or not merely rational. I am ashamed of myself for subscribing to these hateful, phantasmagoric pseudo-identities for even an instant; but something deep inside me cannot be gainsaid. Centuries of negative stereotyping cannot be erased so easily—not even in the minds of those who would discredit the anti-Semites and defend the Jews."[29] Rarely do these negative narratives receive a close and analytic scrutiny for what might be ameliorative reponses by the educational establishment. It is much easier to read each account as signifying an era of Jewish education that has passsed from the scene or was an isolated instance of bad pedagogy. Roger Simon's attempt to provide an exemplum of such a process of scrutiny that focuses on particular articulations of "regimes of truth" is demonstrated by both self-examination and pedagogic discussion.[30]

Exposed to newer ideas many Jews now form their identity from nontraditional sources. Jews report differing sources for identification with being Jewish shaped by a broad range of ideological issues. Feminism, spirituality, and Judaisms' role in Israel are three examples of where ideology play an increasing role. Clearly the many issues in feminism have not received a definitive response from most Judaisms. Yet one perceives the outline of their new found centrality even in unexpected quarters.[31] Increasingly, questions about Judaism's capacity to guide a rich spiritual life abound in certain quarters, especially among Jews influenced by Buddism and other spiritual traditions.[32] Questions regarding Judaisms' role in the state of Israel raise many additional questions. While these are not new questions nor is this an exhaustive list, nevertheless they point to not only differences of opinion among Jews but more fundamentally, to different kinds of identification with being Jewish. To be a Jew does not seem to include the complete adoption of one set of ideas or programs that remains constant over time. These issues have the potential to create numerous kinds of Judaisms.

A focus on Jewish identity formation requires a focus on the impact of hate, anti-semitism, as another kind of external factor that is formative but are not measurable by some clear calculation. This "external" motivation, anti-semitism, seems less decisive than it once did at mid-century. What exactly is the impact of one epithet: "Dirty Jew!" What is the impact of "internal" hate uttered by an embarrassed and assimilating parent upon a child? Is it a cautionary reminder of the limits of public avowal of Jewishness? ("Don't talk that way—with your hands—people will recognize you as zhide—damned Jew.")[33] But still the question remains: Are there positive ways of becoming a Jew that are internally generated?

The religious tradition claims that the study of religious texts and the performance of mitzvot creates Jews in a positive valence. Classically, mitzvot are defined as divinely commanded obligations toward other human beings and toward the divine economy itself. This notion of "command, mitzvah" is tied to a divine revelation moving beyond, but including the popular mind's sense of mitzvah as a good deed. The heteronomous quality and origin of such obligations is a major stumbling block for moderns.[34] The challenge of an outside authority that commands is counter to reason, a key part of the modernist discourse, which seeks to submit all things to reason. The growing celebration of ritual and the interest in narrative point to new sources for developing Jewish identity beyond the formerly unchallenged sources of reason of the modern.

Contemporary constructions of Jewish identity attempt to base the project on narrative and textual strategies.[35] Can this be achieved only by learning Jewish texts and ideas? What are those texts and ideas? There are a number of suggestions that date from the early moments of this century in the work of Franz Rosensweig and Martin Buber in rereading Bible as an example of a narrative approach.[36] What is the impact of universalizing and supersessionary discourses on being a Jew? Do not the latter rhetorical challenges of universalizing and supersessionarism remove the ground upon which Judaism speaks? Even admitting the viability of such texts or ideas, which are decisive? Are the religious ideas, acts, and rituals the only ones that count? What if the ideas are no longer religious but secular? In the end, can one "really" become a Jew? How does the perennial modicum of anti-semitism or more benign "othering" intervene in this creation called Jews?[37] What is the role of individual choice? "What is the moral content of [Jewish] identity?"[38] What if all these questions are not answerable in the thought tradition of: "either this but not that." What if all these issues take on a new valence in a postmodern situation? John Rajchman writes commenting on Stanley Aronowitz's work, that: ". . . minority identity is thus not only tragic and hopeful: it also becomes problematizing when it mobilizes something 'other'—something which cannot be assimilated within visible, established, public categories, and which causes them to be rethought." All these questions about the continuum between stereotypes and reality of one's being a Jew! The lexicon of uncertainty is hardly covered or acknowledged in the listing of questions above. Much of the foregoing material leaves aside the added complication of national identity especially in its North American civilizations' new claims on Diaspora Jewish identity. It is worth repeating here that the lack of a hegemonic North American ethnic tribal identity has given little staying power to nativist sentiments in the United States or Canada.[39] Michael Walzer claims, therefore, that this lack of a nativisitic hegemony is a signal of political openness.

All the above Jewish identity questions are worlds apart from the kind of questions being asked in 1997 and earlier, in the official North American Jewish community. The "official community" is mired in a struggle to articulate its relationship to the politicized identity questions raised in Israel by the orthodox establishment's religious hegemony. What remains of the primacy of Judaism's birth dogma? Does it answer the identity question? Does it decide who you are? If you have a Jewish mother then you are a Jew! From the external standpoint this latter question—Jewishness by birth—seems increasingly irrelevant. From an internal perspective "birth Judaism," despite its shock value as a political trope for competing streams of Judaism, seems to miss the mark of the complex issues of identity formation.

II

Some Thoughts on an Expanded Idea of Becoming a Jew

I am struck by the increasing number of accounts describing middle-aged academically trained adults whose initiations to Judaism and Jewish life begin with an almost ritual confession of Jewish ignorance.[40] Their ignorance of matters Jewish, expresses a certain self-bemusement at the seeming oddity, even scandal—that reared to indifference and blissful ignorance of the Jewish situation in the world, s/he now finds an affinity with being Jewish. Their proclamation of being Jewish is often tortuous and even comical. Many of these narratives reveal an ingenuity and tenacity that is hardly an embracing of "orthodox" principles but nevertheless suggestive and even affirming, of the traces, the signs, oracles, and turning points that created this person a heterodox Jew.[41]

Having spent my entire career as a rabbi working with academics, I finally went over "to the other side." A few years back, I decided to study for a Ph.D. in Education. A subsection of my academic interest in higher education is homo academicus, the teaching and research personnel of North American universities. There are approximately 140,000 homo academicus judaeus among the 700,000 full-time faculty. These figures exclude administrators and other full-time and part-time personnel in United States universities and colleges. Except as a matter of speech, it is hard to think of Jewish academics as a species. Many academics would claim that it is more accurate to describe each Jewish academic as sui generis. It is not a rarity to meet with incredulity from a Jewish member of homo academicus protesting the mere name of the association: Mifgash: An On-going Conversation Among Jewish Intellectuals. Emanating from the liberal humanists is a challenge couched in tones of alarm and dripping disdain: Can you tell me about Jewish mathematics? Is there a Jewish physics?[42] Jews rarely see themselves as constituting a group in academic life: "We are individuals!" My indirect reference to Pierre Bourdieu's Homo Academicus invokes one of the classic studies of academics, wholely ignored by the "anthropologists" of the academic tribe, the academics who study higher education faculty. Other people who study faculty in higher education, my colleagues, display an almost "studied obliviousness" or as Bourdieu calls it "misrecognition" of what it means to study a group that one is, at one and the same time, a part of, while denying the existence of the very same group. Jewish academics deny even the implications of participation in one part of the academic tribe that includes Jews in their almost exclusive numbers, Jewish studies personnel.[43]

Now it is possible to begin discussing the history of Jewish intellectuals not only in New York literary society but also in the Academy, proper. Both "Jews" as group and individual Jews only recently organized some expression of Jewish consciousness as a recognizable fraction of the academy, with interests and various social positions.[44] For the first time, discussion of social factors, including the impact of the government's post-World War II program of educational subsidies through the GI Bill, which massively aided returning Jewish personnel in important ways to enter many fields, especially academia and the learned professions.[45] The positioning of Jews as another "allied white" community in the racialization of American society, increasingly under threat from "nonwhite" society grew steadily after World War II, aiding in the acceptance of Jews in the academy.

I do not mean to fall into the category mistake of confusing the subject matter with the background of the person studying it. This confusion is not a rare one among both academics and nonacademics. Often people thought of themselves as being the same as or identical to the subject matter they studied or the occupation they pursued. (Hubris being as common in academic circles as elsewhere, on rare occasion, some people go so far as to believe that they invented their subject matter or were summoned by it![46]) Jews in academia were often seen as having prominence in certain fields such as economics; and justly so, given stereotypes about Jews and money. In contrast, the admissions saga of Jews in fields like English literature are legion, since Jews in another set of stereotypes were represented as alien from the "native" language.[47] For a very long time, Jewish academics' fear of this "category confusion" retarded or perhaps excluded serious discussion by individuals seeking to ponder the interface between a personal exploration of assumptions, values, and methods of an academic field with questions about Jews and Judaism. This question of personal values and academic interface was the academic equivalent of the "dual loyalties" question at the founding of the State of Israel.[48] Beginning in the seventies and eighties, new academic fields influenced by feminism became less reticent about queries of a decidedly biographic nature as well as appreciating the complex ways in which biography and bias shape fields and even research in those fields.[49] The question of the ethnic bias of science or philosophy or many other sanctified fields seemed to open new areas of inquiry. Nevertheless, except among Jews who are orthodox and work in science, the idea of a distinct academic Jewish group called, pointedly: "Jews in Modern History" or "Jews in Modern Languages," seems an odd and even threatening designation to many Jews. Yet I want to claim a legitimacy for some form of discussion among various academic fields for exactly that kind of claiming of background and biography.[50]

Until recently, the self-descriptive narrative of Jewish academics was an even greater rarity. Many Jews took as their cue the remarks of Lionel Trilling of 1944 that he did not see the appropriateness of finding either "faults or virtues" in his work because of being Jewish. Since then, the "booster-bigot" approach to understanding "Jewish contributions" has prevented a very serious study fearing the uncritical celebration of "Jewish contributions" and the malevolent complaint about "Jewish influence."[51] While there is a greater forthrightness and ease for many academics in being Jewish, hard questions about the interface between Judaism and life are not articulated nor legitimated, as part of the socialization of Jewish academics. While common conversation among academics is about backgrounds of Jews as well as other people, as vital to understanding their work, rarely has that conversation been an accepted topic of written academic reflection regarding Jews. The desire to be invisible among Jewish academics is great. To some it comes as a complete surprise that Jewish specificity around the questions of social positioning has found a new opportunity for discussion in the university world of today. In addition, many other academics have ventured a step further to ask about the interface between their personal identity and the academic work.[52]

At one time it was acceptable to arrange the divide between the public and private person with absolute certainty. Jews became so accustomed to this division they developed a slogan: "Be a Jew at home and a man [sic!] in the street." Whatever the background of this admonition to Jews struggling with Emancipation in the nineteenth century, it hardly speaks to most Jewish academics today. Much has happened to vitiate the line between these two worlds. Perhaps the line of demarcation was only part of the social imagination of Jews struggling for acceptance but perhaps it partook of the tendency of literalness that Jews seemed to want to enforce upon themselves to assuage Gentile opinion. Today many would claim that a crisis exists only in the "street"—the public arena. It is only in the public arena that one has a sense of being a Jew. Few Jews claim to have a rich private Jewish life, to live or transmit. A new question has arisen. It asks what could be the content of the reacquaintance of Jews with a personal Jewish life?[53]

Given that many are puzzled, today, by the carrying forward of the bifurcated question—of personal and private worlds—what would happen if some process of acknowledging the dubious validity of isolated selves were introduced? This process of reintroducing the private and public, which is quite far advanced in feminist circles, deserves attention among Jews. A general expression of postmodern stances has created a space and a willingness to adapt hybrid identities that seem to be new. The impulse to "be one thing only" has given way to a more complex stance. Can questions of identity receive a "both/and" resolution? There will be, I believe, many "both/and" resolutions but my personal formulation would want to include at least the following: I can imagine a nuanced Jewish political and personal identity stretching out from uncomfortable uncertainty and self-doubt to a Jewish world that is "anti-assimilationist but committed to the Enlightenment, supportive of Israel while it argues for the Diaspora, and a proponent of ethnic particularism rooted in history, yet that aspires to remain in critical tension with universal ideals?"[54] What more might be added to this continuum?

This kind of "both/and" is more than a rhetorical stance that commits itself to acquiring cultural knowledge of Judaisms' pasts in an "act of memory." This stance of "both/and" vis-a-vis memory first grew out of and was recognized as the absence and even hollowness of what passed for Jewish "commitment" in the Diasporas (and in many sectors of Israeli society too) since even before World War II. The value of the Jewish cultural past that is barely recognized in its unromantized and multifaceted diversity is largely unknown territory; it was and remains suppressed.[55] Coming to terms with that past is an "act of memory" equivalent to the ancestral "we will do and then we will hear (understand)."[56] In most instances, before we have an understanding of what Jewish life is, it is imposed on us. Yet so many have failed to see Jewish life as a Good that must be embraced and this must give us pause. It suggests that strengthened by a multiplicity of possible Jewish commitments, no one authority is constituted to pass on the legitimacy of other Jewish connections and identities. That the Good of Jewish life must be embraced by each individual prior to authoritative importunings from rabbis, reasons, or logic.

The categories of identity understanding based in "acts of memory" will contain an element of the unexplained and the mysterious, but more than likely will also impinge on questions of gender, regional and national specificity, economic and class issues, and various causes and ideologies. All these commitments will challenge and shape Jewish individuals and subsequently their communal connections but for most individuals, they will not be decisive. Being Jewish may become a factor in the identity equation but again not decisive in the way it once was for persecuted Jews. Beginning in the sixties in America the complexity and hybridity of all identities became legitimated. It was only a matter of time until that became true for some Jews too.

Harold Bloom writes about his Jewish students and finds common sentiment with them in their Jewishness which is expressed "confusedly, ambivalently, ambiguously, and partly." Bloom goes on to say:

> That is the way things are, the way they are going to be. What offers itself as normative Judaism does not speak to them, as it does not speak to me. Kafka, Freud, and Scholem, unlikely but inevitable triad, do speak to my students, and so speak to me. Jewish high culture, intellectually speaking, is now an amalgam of imaginative literature, psychoanalysis, and a kind of Kabbalah. How a Jewish high culture can continue without a Judaism is a most curious question, but if a Judaism yet develops to meet this question, it seems unlikely that such spirituality will have much continuity with the normative tradition. More likely, any such spirituality will receive its Jewish information from the writing of Kafka, Freud and Gershom Scholem.[57]

While the notion of an act of memory, perceived as somehow intervening to bring an order out of chaos, appeals to certain positive restorative yearnings among Jewish loyalists, it cannot be easily achieved for the reasons alluded to by Bloom. Acts of memory such as the building of a new hybrid canon of American-Jewish literature are a positive sign of intellectual engagement but the question remains, can the momentum be sustained? Orthodox spokespeople—from the literary or religious dispensations—may look on in puzzlement or dismay at the construction of Bloom-like "heresies," that seek to derive a Jewish spirituality that is a cobbling together of American Transcendentalist intellectuals with Jewish Kabbalistic sources, viewing them as at best idiosyncratic constructions.[58]

Another supporting manifestation of an act of memory is the recent work of education theorist, Philip Wexler, who in describing the move toward "re-sacrilization" in social theory circles begins by pointing to achievements of a new perspective on social theory "show[ing] that seemingly indifferent knowledge is integral to particular forms of life, to beliefs and values, and to everyday cultural practices. Knowledge is not indifferent, only extracted from its roots and separated from its implications for ethics of being."[59] Wexler's neo-kabbalistic metaphors point to a mining of Jewish sources for social science reflection that while a bit crude its present formulation is very promising.

At the same time, the danger of Jewish fundamentalism, which once seemed a remote possibility, among American Jews can seize and appropriate the Bloom or Wexler engagements discussed above to claim that they are a misguided, reductionist, and 'goyish' endeavors. The misappropriation of Jewish sources for fundamentalist purposes is a very real danger. Acts of memory can be distorted and instrumentalized for evil mischievous aims. We are forced to recongnize that the metaphysical foundationalism promised by acts of memory cannot be attained nor made unassailable. It is more and more evident that Jewish identity achieved through acts of memory in any of its many constructions, will not provide a silver bullet solution to cultural anomie. Once the assumed or established identities or even intellectual constructions of identity—for instance, Jewish-male-socialist or the normative traditional religious identities, among many others—are overthrown, the end of stability arrives. Accustoming ourselves to live without stability as a goal means that all identity constructions are left vulnerable. This new situation of endangerment or lack of "taken-for-grantedness" is also an opportunity. It is an opportunity that requires more diligence in the identity construction process. The possibility of constructed Jewish identity(ies) opens up clearer avenues for mitigating even vanquishing identities based on Jewish indifference or self-hate. In addition, multiple identity positions are opened up to the benefit of everyone. Identity construction is a necessary but complex issue that will not disappear or even allow itself to be set aside.[60]

> Seeing truth as made, not found—seeing reality as socially constructed—doesn't mean deciding there is nothing "out there." It means understanding that all our stories about what's out there—all our scientific facts, our religious teachings, our society's beliefs, even our personal perceptions—are the products of a highly creative interaction between human minds and the cosmos. The cosmos may be found; but the ideas we form about it, and the things we say about it, are made. One of the main themes of postmodern thought is that language is deeply involved in the social construction of reality. Rorty says: 'We need to make a distinction between the claim that the world is out there and the claim that truth is out there. To say that the world is out there, that it is not our creation, is to say, with common sense, that most things in space and time are the effects of causes which do not include human mental states. To say that the truth is not out there is simply to say that where there are no sentences there is no truth, that sentences are elements of human languages, and that human languages are human creations. . . .' In the world of religion—or, to be more accurate, in the many worlds of religion—people are overhauling doctrines right and left. How could it be otherwise? If you regard the various truths and practices of a religion as socially constructed—created by certain human beings according to the needs (as they perceived them) of certain times—you are likely to feel free to reconstruct them according to the needs (as you perceive them) of the present time.[61]

Through the accounts of various Jewish academics we are reminded "that there is no privileged position from which one can speak without one's own discourse being itself put into question."[62] The willingness of people to risk revealing their stories of "origin" is what humanizes and allows for connection and emulation. This personal narrative is a sharing that moves beyond words and discourse inscribed by the half-submerged canon of Great Books lists or other distancing subterfuges bringing people closer to other people.[63] Feminist educational philosopher, Madeleine Grumet, too, makes the case for the "both/and" character of the meaning seeking narrative process. "All language is social, although historical, all form predetermined, all invention shared, all intention sabotaged . . . [yet despite that autobiographical writing is] both inner and outer, personal and public, spontaneous and considered, mind and body."[64]

Where might this lead? In practical terms it will lead to the demise of the assumed community of Jews. If once people thought of being condemned to freedom, as paradoxical situation, hardly anyone will be able to escape arduous learning and being sorely tried by the inevitability of hyperreality in postmodernity. We are subject to a new inevitability called Postmodernity, it not a matter of taste or choice but a situation. Postmodernity is defined as the situation that we find ourselves in; it will not go away. Postmodernism, the various schools and philosophies responding to postmodernity, will continue to change, adjust, and reconceive itself.[65] Postmodernism does not seem to require a finalized accounting for one's identity but rather the use of narratives and language and strategies of intellectual construction to reconfigure the various social attributions of one's life. This process will be a fluid one that is constantly open to challenges. The seeming former stability of Jewish identity will take on numerous communities or contexts of reference both internally and externally.

I believe that the Jewish community would be greatly enhanced if it acknowledged the wonderful talent and powerful interest of Jewish intellectuals, who are generally arranged along a different axis of interests than other, more traditional, parts of the Jewish community. That is to say, that academics who by virtue of the nature of their work and the kinds of institutions they work in, are most exposed to questions of identity. In turn, academics who come to view the general Jewish community as part of their own struggle for community, meaning making, and identity formation should find new acceptance and support. Until now, there has generally been a wariness and fear that has marked the relationship between the Jewish town and Jewish gown nonrelationship. In the minds of many, Jews are much more a part of the town and not the gown in society. Today, Jews are perceived as important stakeholders in the academic world. This is a fantastic and unprecedented situation for many older Jews, who still analyze the situation of Jews as close to being congenitally outsiders to academe. The suggestion that the academic world might be uniquely positioned to help the general Jewish community understand, respond, and mobilize to engage a new generation of young Jews comes as a shock. Among the common agendas for Jewish communal groups and academia is a continuum of identity issues including: individualism and communalism; gender and reproductive issues; continuity and discontinuity. It might finally occur to people that the most central and powerful institution in the Jewish community is the university!

What could we learn if we explored the proposition that we [the Jewish community/academic public intellectuals or civilization] are producing Jews—academically inclined, socially inclined, ethnically inclined, religious inclined, ethically inclined, etc.—all in a diversity that we have never known before? A reflexive and inquiring attitude toward the process of Jewish identity formation among Jewish adults, primarily academics or even more inclusively intellectuals, would challenge some part of the power of civilization to produce Jews and open up a new diversity of Jewish narratives. Hopefully, the existence of numerous narratives about Jewish identity formation will help to create a host of identities that will move us beyond many either/or oppositions that tend to essentialize.[66] Jews who will claim gay and lesbian identities and 'halfies' who will claim both of their cultures will contribute to this new Judaism in the making.[67] With the definite exclusion of Christian admixtures, most combinations will enrich and create new Judaisms. If we are living in a postmodern world that evinces an "incredulity toward metanarratives" we may need to find the specific and individual stories to appreciate the numerous and different kinds of lives being led by people.[68]

This is in contrast to a time, mythical so it seems to us, when there was an apparent unanimity among people and perhaps among Jews too. That unity fostered the appearance of universalism, largely imposed by cultural isolation. Whatever that hermetic world was it is no longer available. Attempts to re-create Jewish worlds that often begin in appeals to a romantic former context of wholeness or idealized versions of tradition can carry forward possibilities for hope. It is possible to move beyond fundamentalisms, toward a vista of

> "transformation whose outcome is unforeseen—conditions for a sort of experiment. The potential for such movements and critical experimentations within [Jewish] society shows that history is not linear or progressive, any more than it is circular or cyclical. It shows that if history is a 'web,' it is one with many gaps and holes which allow it be constantly rewoven in other ways, and that it thus carries with it the sort of 'in-between' times and spaces . . . thus one can see minorities [Jews, Jewish identity, Jewishness] not as a given, monolithic, traditional identity, but rather as a multiple, unpredictable force which comes from the intervals of official memory to problematize and recompose traditions."[69]

That fabled world contained many elements of folkways, religious texts, and ways of studying them, values and attitudes—a cultural package, elements of which are open to rediscovery and reappropriation.

These postmodern Judaism(s) are in many ways the potential beneficiary of Jewish historical experience of surplus otherness. This non-negative otherness arises from inside Judaisms' texts—its Torah in the broadest sense of that idea—and also Judaisms' historical experiences newly comprehended. The diversity of understandings opening before us are Jewish ways that were once inconceivable. At the same moment, fear that the enrichment from outside culture threatens imperialistically, as an engulfing and reductionist challenge—as it once did in several remote and recent pasts—is vastly reduced. The more open forms of Judaisms offer themselves for compelling consideration without coercion. The lack of threat assumes the commitment to building a dialogue that asks questions of/about boundaries not in panic but hope.[70] There is produced a potential for "twoness [or even more multiples] of vision" as affirmed in Laurence Mordekhai Thomas's notion of a "narrative . . . [as] a set of stories which define values and purely positive goals, and fixed points of historical significance, as well as various ennobling rituals to be performed regularly. A narrative [that] yields a set of practices that cannot readily be appropriated by others . . . a narrative . . . [that] defines a fundamental . . . conception of the good . . . an isomorphic narrative [that] Jews have been able to affirm . . . in the face of social hostility."[71] Those values and positive goals are the result of a balancing of questions of loyalty that transcend Kantian universalistic ethics and at the same time appeals to a responsibility to the embodied and real other.[72] What remains problematic is the details in the "ritual, the practices, the good." The debate over "appropriation by others" remains as a reference point in need of clarification.

Judaisms that will emerge will by necessity be a part of the postmodern dispensation. Arnold Wolf's suggestion that postmodern situation is an option that can be voluntarily chosen or denied, ignores the diversity that cannot nor should be dismissed or elided. We are condemned to a hyperdiverse forms of Jewish identification.[73] Perhaps as suggested by the recent art exhibit, Too Jewish, a collective of "Jewish-bender" identities, we have arrived to the point that we must admit into discussion identity positions that are seemingly threatening to many sensibilities. Just as the various pieces in the exhibit force a confrontation with a number of issues, among them the fixation among some Jews with Jewish physicality (Jewish noses, for example) that removes the veil of "whiteness" and challenges the canons of beauty that form once legitimated participation in polite society.

The only consolation for this radical openness of the postmodern moment to the threatened is a recognition that this is a price of freedom in a society that does not persecute Jews or others as an expression of a rejection of freedom. This freedom demands a vigilance in developing and crafting a Jewish identity, that can never again be taken for granted, even in Israel. The only recourse is an embracing of further dialogue.[74]

III

On the Role of Education in Creating Jews

So if indeed Jews are created as Jews by education of all sorts and types, how do people become Jews? As a person committed to a process of learning and growth, the idea that Jews are created by accidents of birth runs counter to the whole enterprise of education. The education enterprise claims a familiarity with means of educating people. There is a primary claim for making a difference through intentional activities that carry the banner: education! Perhaps at one time Jewish homes educated in preparations for a far less complicated world but that is not true any longer. Statistics on conversion away from Judaism suggest that large numbers of people are no longer imbued by the notion of "actively staying put."[75] Added to the conversion numbers is a very large part of the Jewish community that is not in any way affiliated or connected to Jewish life.[76] Between the twin threats of conversion and indifference, the suggestion that education for Jewish continuity has become the central concern of the organized community and the 'unorganized' community has yet to take root. Even among the most chauvinist in Israel or elsewhere, no one really believes that Jewish homes, with rare exceptions, educate as they once mythically did. The role of auxiliaries to the family in the culture,—in the university, and in the synagogue have become more significant. Therefore, while intellectually I appreciate the Reform Jewish doctrine more and more—one is Jewish through intentional acts of education and commitment, I am inspired by the welter of life stories that engender and foster commitment. I often ponder the events, people, and dynamics that shaped my own creation as a Jew. Official Judaism presents a case for birth as the deciding and shaping incident but most Jews, even the ones unschooled in Judaism of one sort or another, seem to describe a very different process of becoming.

I want to examine one case, my own. How did I become a Jew? Today, I am a Reform rabbi, a Ph.D. candidate in Education, a Yiddish and a Hebrew speaker. I am an oldest child of Holocaust survivors, who contracted their marriage of wounded desperation in the displaced persons camps in Germany, where I was born. I am a perpetual student of Jewish traditions, especially Hebrew texts. The primary site of my learning of Hebrew texts has been the Academy and not the Yeshivah. Even the rabbinical school that I attended was more an academic-professional institution than a denominational institution.

My practice of Judaism might even be classified as observant even though the label Reform Jew and academic is supposed to signal and even deny serious connections, at least in the eyes of most Jews. The term "Reform" Jews has come to mean arbitrary and capricious commitment. Most Jewish academics of my generation assumed their identity as Americans with a naturalness that comes of being second and third generation. For the first generation of Jewish academics, there seemed to be an implied choice: either to be a Jew or an academic. For the second and third generation American Jews in academia the way to academic success was not barred by being Jewish nor was it viewed as important, in any way.

My Jewish-American identity was the result of a coincidence of training and biography that allowed me to have both without choosing. (I never felt speared in that hyphen, only in the Judeo-Christian one.) Every fiber of my being is bent, woven, and knotted into the fabric of Jewish (American) life. At the same time, I enjoy being an academic "theory" junkie My return to graduate school has made me more radical politically at a time when my peers seem to be moving in a most appallingly conservative cultural and political direction. Claiming the mantle of academic interest makes me want to claim that this and so many bifurcations—academic versus nonacademic, Jew versus American—are so much stuff and nonsense!

Yes, I am disquieted by the assignment for this book since it asks for a level of intellectualization and abstraction that belies my deeper sense of what really makes me a Jew, an educated Jew, a Jewish educator, and Jew in education.[77] Is this after all only a language game or do these categories mean something? All the formal definitions that one makes seem to leak. They are not airtight.

Here are some further examples of my primal identity that go against the grain. Many Eastern European Jews of my parent's age and education rely on oracles and signs! Oracles and signs are as sure of a method of knowing the unknowable as these survivors of the Holocaust are likely to find. They are contained not in some place of pilgrimage or worship. There are, after all, no gods to appease or propitiate. This Delphi does not require pilgrimage, only invocation. Rather they are the "genetically encoded" messages, attitudes, gestures, and looks that are harvested from unsuspecting children and now, grandchildren. "Geb a kick—Give a look, he said that just like his (murdered) grandfather. The way he holds his head to the side. And now (age forty-seven), you have Beryl Zilbershtein's glatze (bald pate)." Present by their absence are the dead relatives whose names I cannot remember, cannot file away correctly, or even fully identify on the family photos, even after thousands of rehearsals. This is all a paradoxical "racial memory" or "racial forgetting."

The education granted me is inexplicably transferred to my children. The most graphic example is my youngest son, who tells us in all candor and sincerity that he cannot go to the Simon Wiesenthal Center Holocaust Museum, around the corner from our house, because he will have his bad dream again, "the one where he is 'in the Holocaust' with Bobee (grandmother, my mother) in the cellar, all thirsty and parched." Lysenkoism is the best explanation I have for this phenomenon. We have never discussed with him nor he with my mother, the scene that she separately describes and he separately affirms. It is a specific event of my mother's hiding with her younger brother while they were trying to avoid the Nazis "clearing/cleaning the Sosnoweice Ghetto"—Judenrein, in the summer of 1943. Who exactly is my son? Is he his dead uncle?

No one's Jewish identity is safe! My younger brother's query of my mother, when returning from Sunday School one afternoon in the Fifties, is still the best formulation of the dilemma, "Mom, is Rabbi Greenberg Jewish?"

I have been blessed by individuals who made me a Jew. Four of those individuals had a major impact on me years removed from my formal contact with them today. Many others are not mentioned here but had an impact on me too. Of my major teachers, three are Jews and another is not. It is still one of the best jokes that we tell about our childhood. Is Rabbi Greenberg Jewish? Hard to tell these things that abound in the world of who is who. How about Mr. Wells, who looks—in a world of imprecision, "looks"—like "two Jews." Wells is a deacon in his Protestant church and Welsh descent but remains a presence in my life today. Dr. Mayer Tuchler was a psychiatrist, family friend, and towering humanist, who was a Jew but entirely secular and even antireligious. The late Rabbi Fred Krinsky who was raised in an orthodox home and became a leading figure in Reform Judaism and academic circles as professor of government at Pomona College. This latter figure while an important adult relationship is beyond the scope of this paper.

After all this work to transform myself through learning, it is the early childhood experiences of growing up an immigrant in culturally vacuous American Jewish communities—Mason City, Iowa, and Phoenix, Arizona—that ultimately informs my most fundamental sense of being a Jew. I came to this country literally on the shoulders of my father, who is depicted in a 1949 disembarkation front page New York paper picture, carrying me down the gangplank to these shores. I look pudgy and scared . . . he on the other hand, has the nervous smile of assurance that indicates one practiced in surviving inspections.

There are many stories of wonder about coming to America! Apparently, I managed to remain a Yiddish speaker with my parents until at least four or five years old. I understand myself as being a translator to them, for them, and perhaps, back to myself. I love speaking Jewish even though fewer and fewer people understand even the most superficial Yiddish words and references with which I love to pepper my speaking. I notice that it is only around my best friends or in public speaking situations that are laden with crisis that I discover my Yiddish voice. Most of my Yiddish is mama-loshen I will translate this as "my mother's voice" usually admonishing or advising me. While other Yiddish speakers informed my being, her small town Polish sensibilities inform who I am. In crisis, A Yid get sich I-ste, "a Jew knows how to take counsel," even if it is only with him/herself and consulting with others is quite acceptable but being paralyzed with doubt is foolish!

My inner voice is in Yiddish and I want to translate for you, my readers, some of what I hear even today. My memories often carry me back to my becoming a Jew in the 'uncivilized' conditions of Arizona of the fifties and sixties. Can there be a more disappointing failure on the record of the "educational system" of this country than a Yiddish-speaking 1950s Arizonan?

IV

My Story: Learning Weapons of the Strong

My inner voice remains adulterated with that of my parents' judgments on America; it is not the naive and innocent sound of a Henry Roth character, *Ich bin nisht gekummen ka America zu shlofen* . . . "I didn't come to America to sleep." That is my dad's voice and my search for a grounding in life. He never heard about the novel or any literature, for that matter, but he had strong opinions on America and its relation to Jews and Judaism. One of them was that you had to get up at four or five in the morning to get a head start. I don't know if this was a habit from the concentration camps or before but in a way that was quite cruel, he would often yank the blankets away, early in the morning. Toughening was a way of expressing both anger and love. While always grateful for his liberation from the concentration camps by American soldiers, Dad was in no doubt about who really won World War II: the Russians. Americans were called *chocoladniks*—the candy bars boys, since they were ubiquitously eating (essentially "softies" like chocolate) and therfore, never really tested by bone numbing suffering. The proof of this decadence was America's acquiescence in the occupation of Eastern Europe. While America was sleeping the Russians had advanced on all fronts including science, technology, medicine, and politics including Poland, Hungary, Czechoslovakia, Romania and the Baltic states, the latter where he grew up. The Russians were going to win the cold war because they were strong and could suffer! The truth is that the strong have the capacity to suffer and persevere, and not to fall asleep!

Both of my parents remained skeptical of America's posturing in the cold war. Not everything that happened was automatically blamed on the Russian paranoia nor was America always right. Life had made them wary of highsounding promises. I remember three moments during my growing up that stand out as part of my political education. My parents' loyalties were decidedly Left but it was more of an ideological commitment to the common folk, *amcha*. Workers were common folk who held people with money and airs at a distance. They were outraged by the American Jewish community's abandonment of the Rosenbergs. Just as American Jewry had stood by during the destruction of European Jews so they stood by while innocents were judged guilty and executed. Gentile Americans, they thought, should not have been so ready to condemn people like the Rosenbergs without proof and this could only be explained as anti-semitism. American Jewish fear of confronting anti-semitism could not be assuaged by abandoning the Rosenbergs. This was a crime against their European sense of *amcha* (peoplehood). The betrayal of the hapless family seemed consistent to my parents with what happened to millions of others less than a decade earlier at the hands of Nazis. The 1953 execution of Ethel Rosenberg was cynical and manipulative, since clearly she was used by the courts to try to force a confession from her husband, Julius. My mother's words summarized for me the outrage. *Seh hoben zeh geharget und noch of Shabbes* [They murdered them and on top of it, they did it on Shabbes (the eve of the Sabbath)].[78]

In 1956, Israel, France, and Britain attempted to block Egypt's Nasser from nationalizing the Suez Canal. National television coverage took up the position of President Eisenhower in opposing the internationalization of the waterways by the means used by Israel and its allies. The Soviet Union and the United States found common cause at the height of the cold war against the Jews. My father's response watching the news gave me a start: *Yetz et men zeyn az mashleugt yiddin in die Goldne Medinah* (Now, We will start to see the beating up of Jews in the Golden Country,[America]). Similarly, when Kennedy was assassinated in 1963, school was dismissed early that day. The local radio programs announced that school was dismissed around 11 a.m. My brother and I took our time, arriving home around 4 p.m., as we listened to all the anti-Kennedy crosstalk and rhetoric mixed with expressions of shock and conspiracy mongering among our classmates. Conspiracy theories were a part of the Arizona landscape even then. What shocked me more than anything else was the worried and frantic look in my mother's face when we finally got home. She had assumed that the delay was a portent of things to come including the beating of Jews. *Ich beit Gott az kenn Yidd hot im nisht geharget, ich hoff az siz nisht kenn Yid* (I hope to God that it isn't a Jew that killed him!). Jack Ruby, who eventually killed Oswald, became one of American Jewry's secret and unsung heroes. He was the avenging angel for the outraged public. "Jack (Ruby–not Kennedy) we hardly knew you."

The skepticism over American purity of motives and intentions prepared me for eventually questioning Vietnam and subsequent government pronouncements. As I look back, my parents' questioning was rather brave in the face of the heated anti-Communism of America and most especially Arizona. Their appreciation of the fragile sense of all life's situations as well as their sense of Jewish patriotism were early gifts on viewing America that imparted a critical perspective and fear of herd-thinking.

For me, school was a world of books. Most important was my strange fixation on non-fiction! The world of books and reading became an important "outside" source of knowledge that seemed to challenge my parents. Even today I retain a child's crude prejudice against the world of fiction. Fiction is the world of fantasy and imagination, the "not true" explained Mrs. Mullen, my third-grade teacher in the school library tour, as opposed to the "true," on the other side of the room. I specialized in reading the "true." Favoring nonfiction over fiction seemed like the right intellectual sustenance, a breakfast of champions, showing an early propensity and need for a certitude that would serve me well in the pseudo-scientific world of the 1950s. The 1950s worshiped numbers, almost a numerology. The new math and new science were initially adopted with excitement into the Arizona schools of my youth, to help fight off the communist menace. My version of numerology meant that I read only books that were all in the Dewey decimal numbers under 200 . . . mostly religion, bible, philosophy, Greek and Roman mythology "those are true," they have numbers. I read mythology and philosophy because they had numbers and therefore were weapons of the strong. Fiction was "not true" and catalogued alphabetically by the author's name, therefore too personal, a telltale sign of weakness. Reading fiction was dangerous since it was about fantasy that you might mistake for reality. You should train yourself to block fantasy and wishful thinking. Fiction is not a weapon of survival, of the strong, but of the weak! If your imagination gets away from you, you might die or be caught napping and be killed. This piece of concentration camp rationalism was often repeated by father. It was only in my early adolescent rebellion that I began reading fiction. As I recounted in detail the novels I began reading, my mother would always tell me that she had read all of Dickens, Conrad, Tolstoy in Polish but had forgotten all of it. I would receive dispensations to stay up reading a little later and a little later. I became an apostate to the early-to-rise theologian, father!

Different degrees and shadings of "truth," these were lessons that were beyond me in grade school. I was trying to become a bearer of "the true" and gain the key to develop "the suffering fortitude" that ensures survival in times of extremes. This mobilized sense of self appeared to be ambition in the eyes of some but it was really basic training or boot camp. The world of reading became the opportunity to be created by the books that I read in preparation for a suffering that never came.[79] Reading became a world of authority and an additional voice for me. "Reading traditionally has had a mantle of morality imposed upon it: hence the dicta to read moral books, to read books for morals, and to read morally—which is to say, a reading true to the texts. . . . But the psychology of reading proposed here presents reading itself, regardless of subject material, as both an ontological and ethical act. Information is not processed; it is created. The reading creates the self and the world with which that self engages."[80]

Once, shortly before my mother's psychiatrist died, we had a conversation. Tuchler was more than a doctor in our family, he was an anchor and source of authority and love. He played trumpet with my brothers and me. His insights and friendship were important to my development as a Jew, even though he had the typical 1930s scientist distrust for religion. Even though he was a physician, as a psychiatrist he was absolutely dependent on a certain view of social science that in later years was to change radically. He introduced me to my first reflexive conversations on my parent's private hells, which he had penetrated and could indirectly help me to appreciate, while maintaining their privacy. Tuchler was part of a small number of health professionals who had taken a special interest in the families of survivors, far ahead of his profession in recognizing the special traumas and tasks of survivor families. In the 1950s, a surprising number of Jewish medical professionals had a disdain for the survivors. Some were German Jewish refugees, who had come to America in the late thirties, attended medical school, and were now serving their former homeland and the German government to certify the medical and psychological aspects of reparation claims. Fact and rumor had it that they often denied claims based on their idea of what was called *Bruckensyndrome*. Under German government protocols, psychiatric damage caused by the ordeal of the ghettos, concentration camps, and death marches was minimized. According to the protocols, after years of trauma a person should be able to pick up their life in a normal fashion if they had a normal childhood. Watching people—family members—murdered, starved, beaten, and living in terror could only impact those who had prior psychological problems. It was many years before this situation was addressed since many survivors wanted to deny the damage done them. The incidence of German Jewish doctors' lack of compassion was a source of additional agony for many survivors. Night after night the battles raged as my mother tried to convince my father to apply for reparations. My mother argued that the money could not bring back his mother, father, brothers but now, my father was a father and we had nothing! "How can we live week-to-week? What if your back injury flares up? What if you can't work? You must deal with the angry rages and nightmares!" My father's response: "No blood money! *Ich hob seh in bod.* [Fuck them!]" Tuchler tried to treat him but he was reluctant and what could a psychiatrist tell him. Tuchler persisted in trying to help for our sake. Tuchler is in many ways a model for my rabbinate.

Despite the general reverence, awe, and worshipful respect that doctors regularly received in our family, I had decided against those noble models to enter rabbinical school. This was a decision that remained inexplicable to me, my father, and mother, and to all who knew me growing up in Phoenix. In what I now understand to be a very uncharacteristic venturing forward for a therapist Tuchler said: "You are going to spend your whole life trying to make the world just, whole, and fair for your parents. Trying to make it up to them." In keeping with the "bell-bottom mentality" of the time, I thought he was wrong. This attitude was not so far from my father's. Today I look back on Tuchler's attempt to make me aware of some of my motives for choosing the rabbinate with a different sense, a second sight. The motive of repair has a name: *Tikkun*. My reaction to news and every day disparate events is informed by this idea of Tikkun. Whether it is about the near thirty-year Israeli occupation of the West Bank; the murder of Prime Minister Rabin by a messianically unhinged Jew; the unprovoked assault on an acquaintance in a foreign country by fellow Jews in a synagogue; or even the theft of Sukkot palm fronds in Los Angeles in the Fall of 1996, by unknown culprits seeking profit, the desire to stand in the breach and repair the world seems to move me. Momentarily, a cloud of unknowing lifts. But there are no acts "to make it up to them!" I attribute the impulse toward "repair" to a longing for a world that I did not know but sensed in my parents, especially my mother. My mother, aided by her surviving sister and brothers, managed to convey something of the pre-war life in their town of Olkusz. One sister was a communist during the twenties and thirties, who lived out her communism in the needle trades organizing workers in France. Her commitment to high ideals always made feel proud of her even though she was a member of the Communist Party in its Yiddish accented version. I am aware of the moral and psychological "reading" of their vanished world that still engages me.

One incident that stays with me happened after I finally convinced my mother that indeed I was going to be a rabbi. She took me aside. "I don't think that being a rabbi is a job for you. You will starve to death as a rabbi. But when poor people bring you a chicken on Friday afternoon to ask if it is kosher. [*Gedenk, Kick nisht do ober do*] Remember don't look here," pointing to the open palms of her hands at the imaginary chicken. "But look here," pointing to her eyes. This piece of advice regarding the precarious nature of poor people's financial situation or whatever else it was that tugged at their fears and their souls, is a reminder that there is always an approach to big questions that seeks the informed heart, visible through the other person's anxious eyes, and not just what is officially right or true in some abstract universal system of ideas.

The Human Face of Official Lived Judaism

Today, Rabbi William Greenberg lives in Seattle, Washington, where he is actively retired from some thirty years of teaching, supervision of kashrut manufacturing, and leading an Orthodox, Sephardic congregation. He is not Sephardic but has a love and enthusiasm for that tradition and its Jews. About once a year, I talk to him. He was in many ways an embodiment of a Jew and rabbi that I still aspire to attain.

For a period of four or five years including my Bar Mitzvah, Greenberg was the rabbi at "Betty Brew" Congregation (Beth Hebrew Congregation) in Phoenix on Portland Avenue.[81] The Eastern European flavor of the congregation in the midst of what was still a wild west town is forever stamped in my mind. Advertisements for Phoenix businesses adorned the main streets' billboards leading to 3rd and Portland, with reminders to buy cowboy boots and clothes from Riddles on 7th Street. "Betty Brew" Congregation was made up of an odd assortment of Jews who came to America before the 1924 restrictions on emigration, now retired; a few orthodox-leaning Jews who managed to come to America in the thirties; and people like my parents and myself, "recent graduates" of the concentration and, in my case, the DP (displaced persons) camps. Mostly the additional common denominator besides being Jewish was asthma. Early on, I nursed a resentment toward the few *Americaner Yidn* - The American Jews, all of whom, I believed, were rich, uncaring, and oblivious. Some members of "Betty Brew" even had the temerity to convert to Judaism and to marry Jewish doctors, the real holy men of the Jewish people! The converts were too enthusiastic about being Jewish in a "typically *goyish* way" because they were actually interested in taking Judaism seriously! I remember this particular prejudice was instilled rather early in life.

"Betty Brew" was a collection of characters, all broken and torn from another life. They make up fragments of the emotional attitudes and even passionate commitments I acquired, without ever knowing what was being taught. I can still draw the chart, kept by Mrs. Kimmel, of where everyone's High Holiday seats were and with it the traumas of each family. If I could I would write the Betty Brew response to Primo Levy's *The Periodic Table*, calling it *The Seating Chart*. each chapter would explain their story by where and how they sat in *shul*. Each family at High Holidays sat in its same place year after year. The air was thick with remembering of how things were before the cataclysm. There were Mr. and Mrs. Nudel, who sat on the aisle two rows back from us—they survived but had lost all their seven children "there." "There" (*dorten*) was shorthand for the forests, ghettos, concentration camps, death marches, wherever people died. "There" was every place but no place. We kids would take long detours to ward off the possibility of encountering Mr. Nudel. If Mr. Nudel [pronounced, noodle] got hold of you, you were in trouble. He was a big burly man with an asthmatic wheeze. He would crush your bones in a hug so warm, so fierce, and intense. All the while you tried to squirm loose only to have your cheek torn away, by one massive meaty hand in a viselike *knip* (pinch) and in another hand, a prized piece of candy from his coat pocket. I was always ambivalent because I wanted to make him happy and also get the candy but did want to crushed.

Surprisingly, it was Greenberg who didn't speak Yiddish, a *richte Americaner Roov*—real American Rabbi—that I feel the closest to, even though I now understand that by all the measures of effectiveness that I have learned to honor from educational studies and synagogue and organizational seminars he is an example of a failure, albeit a noble failure. But he was also a failure in the eyes of the Eastern European majority of his congregation. He was a failure because he was not a *Katzetnik*, a concentration camper,[82] the term used by and among the survivors, before the honorific "survivor" was sanctified in America. Greenberg also had a love for these *greene* (newcomers). Jews had their own version of the "color line." We spoke about being American in terms of color. We certainly looked down on the reform and conservative kids (white or *weise* Jews). We weren't really "*Americaner*, since we were born in Europe. That made us technically *greene* (greenies), like my parents and their friends; but I was a *gelle* (yellow), that is, someone on the road to becoming an *Americana*—that must be some one half-white. Rabbi Greenberg, a 'white', was able nevertheless to cross boundaries and barriers among his diverse congregants. Greenberg was a failure among the American Jews because he loved teaching Torah. Greenberg was an educator and not a showman, and an excellent teacher. I loved his sermons which always began with a prayerful invocations like: "Our God and God of Our Fathers." His work with teaching or living Torah (his subject matter) and crazy, wounded, and wounding people (his commonplace) transcended the categories of 1950s big congregations. He lived out his love of real Jews.

What stands out are the lived commitments and even a few remembered phrases of Greenberg's legacy to us. It was Rabbi Greenberg who taught us *Hoomish* and *Rashi*. The standard curriculum in old-time afternoon minimalist American Jewish schools had included the first five books of Moses and his eleventh century indispensable French commentator, Rashi or Rabbi Shelomoh ben Yichtzack (Rashi). (Greenberg called Rashi, the "original little old winemaker"—reminiscent of a TV wine commercial of the time. This was the first time that I ever heard that saintly rabbis had a material existence and even worked!) What a novel subject matter! Adopt the curriculum of tradition! We never learned the subject matter but that was not Greenberg's fault. Even in the mid-fifties people had transferred authority for Jewish knowledge and teaching to Hebrew-speaking Israelis and rabbis were too busy raising money for the synagogue building fund to teach. This lack was not missed since their congregants were to busy to learn. Greenberg taught us, twice during the week, and on Sunday we had Sunday School, lampooned as *Shandey* School (it was a disgrace, *shandey*, that we knew so little about our tradition!). Greenberg was teaching us directly and neither, we kids nor certainly our parents were big donors!

I did manage to learn the general outline of Genesis and remember giggling through the discussion of Abraham's circumcision and the first meaningful discussion of covenant I ever had. Since I didn't understand which physical organ was being cut, I had to go home and get the appropriate Yiddish word. Today, I would express the notion of convenant in the religio-philosophical language of Emmanuel Levinas but the essential teaching was fullblown in Greenberg's methods, including the passage I would encounter over and over again but first heard from the "rationalist" Litvak-trained Greenberg in the name of the Lithuanian Rabbi Israel Salanter: "The material needs of my neighbor are my spiritual needs."[83] Greenberg apparently didn't know that this conceptual complexity was not appropriate to our age or intellectual ability! He taught it anyway. I learned from Greenberg the meaning of the Torah's juxtaposition of Genesis 17, of Abraham's covenant with God marked by circumsicion, and Chapter 18's visit by three visitors, an annunciation of Isaac's birth to a ninety-year-old Sarah and a hundred-year-old Abraham. The very order in which in things are told in Torah is a hermeneutical hint to their meaning. Abraham is circumcised, inaugurating the covenant, and while he is healing: "He sees (has revealed to him) . . . in the heat of the day . . . three strangers whom he runs out to enthusiastically welcome . . . three strangers (disguised angels) . . . this meeting with the other . . . the obligation of hospitality, the invocation of the covenant. In pain and inconvenience, Abraham is on the lookout for strangers, who need his help and care."[84] Greenberg then recited the anthem of the Litvak spiritual ethicists: "The other person's physical needs—my neighbor, are my spiritual response." Years later I read Emmanuel Levinas, who comments about Abraham:

> . . . the one who knew how to receive and feed men: the one whose tent was wide open on all sides. Through all these openings he looked out for passersby in order to receive them. . . . Abraham must have taken the three passersby for three Bedouins, for three nomads from the Negev Dessert—three Arabs, in other words! He runs toward them. He calls them "Your Lordships." The heirs of Abraham—men to whom their ancestor bequeathed a difficult tradition of duties toward the other man, which is never done with, an order in which one is never free. In this order, above all else, duty takes the form of obligation toward the body, the obligation of feeding and sheltering. So defined, the heirs of Abraham are all the nations: any man [sic] truly [hu]man is no doubt of the line of Abraham.[85]

Levinas's philosophy begins in a stance of ethics embodied in hospitality, in the recognition of the face of another human being. Levinas argues that ethics is a precursor to philosophy, indeed to all ideas and ideology, and does not know the distinctions of nationality or social class. It is the face of the other person that creates a dissymmetry that transcends—in Levinas's connotation, meaning ruptures and opens up to the other fulfilling the idealism of Kant. "The face 'signifies' beyond, neither as an index nor as a symbol, but precisely and irreducibly as a face that summons me. It signifies to-God (`a Dieu), not as sign, but as the questioning of myself, as if I were summoned or called, that is to say, awakened or cited as myself."[86]

We live in a fourfold *Golus* (exile) but only some *Golus* leads to *Ge'ulah* (redemption)

Whatever the meaning and practice of the former Judaism might be, in some far away place and time, the invocation "before the camps" or "there" marked another time and order of Jewish practice conjured into memory by an angry sense of loss in my parents' mouth. Now, in America, a new dispensation of Judaism allowed for a defiant and even jocular recollection of the distance between what people used to do when they were children and what their children didn't know or understand about being Jewish. The gap in knowledge, experience, and sentiment formed a central topic of discussion. This too was part of the *shande* (shame)! Later in life, I would learn the appropriate way to label the myriad of discontinuities and aporias in life—*Golus*, exile.[87] As an adult I would visit my Uncle Paul, my mother's brother who would tell me his troubles. He was a very lonely man without children and with few connections to anything but the past. "*Nu, Benny, voos ken men tien, m'lieb in golus. Dus is Yoshour*? So, Benny (my preconscious American name) what can we do, we live in exile. . . This is justice?" At the recitation of a little or big injustice, present or past, he would punctuate the despair with a shrug of the shoulders and this phrase, *Dus is yoshur*? This is just? When my Uncle Paul would intone this phrase, it was not entirely resignation or even surrender as much as a quiet critique of the world in all its brokenness and dispiriting immensity. It was also a comic gesture that could tie the little problems—a flat tire, a lost sale, a broken piece of glass in his picture framing-business—to the larger issues, international and personal, including the current political crisis in the cold war, Israel's embattled political condition, and resolving the sharing of reparations money from the Germans with struggling Israeli relatives. It is hard today to gauge the desire by my uncle to address or even end *Golus*. The cosmic split in God's world between the real and ideal, even with the final note, "*Ma Darf fight'n* . . . One must struggle," was said a little too wistfully or too jocularly to judge real intention. Nevertheless, through earnestness one must recognize and preserve the issue, the problem, even though the solution was not in sight. This process of problemitization was not entirely impotent because at the very least, one should not fall victim to accepting things the way they were. A different consciousness counted for something.

I didn't know then that the concept *Golus*, exile or its ideologically sanitized expression, "diaspora," referred to the punishment of the Jews resulting in their loss of sovereignty and the expulsion from their ancestral homeland. This punishment had two contrasting meanings. First, in the mouth of Jews, it was a reference to a self-critical sense of separation from perfection, the good and God: "Because of our sins we were exiled from our land."[88] Second, in the mouth of Christian theology and its successor faiths, Islam, the Enlightenment, and Marxism, the Jewish exile was a clear sign that the Jews were the collective reprobate people of God-History and thus permanently sidelined from all endeavors. One didn't become Jewish in these Jewish and Christian narratives but was a Jew by essence or by history, for good or ill. In these narratives all things had their essence or nature and could not be changed or obliterated. A Jew is a Jew, by virtue of having a Jewish essence, and is condemned to act like a Jew. It is important to recognize that despite the significant difference in meaning, Jewish tradition, too, is here essentializing Jews. Self-attribution and self-admission of failings are here raised to a different import in the mouths of non-Jewish who repeat the very same words.

Only much later did I learn that yet a third implication of *Golus* status made me an existentialist or perhaps a mystic. Only in college, reading Sartre and Camus, did I come to know that conceptions of *Golus* were intellectually sanctified positions, at least in the university, existentialism. *Golus* was not about a people in this version but rather about the fundamental alienation of individuals in the world. My adolescent form of *Golus*—which differed from existentialism in its embracing of a crude sixties paranoia—saw plots and intrigues based on some basic animus. *Golus*'s defining moment depended on the particular social situation that served as a reminder. You Jew, you live in *Golus*! A reminder of *Golus* might arise as an angry conservative political and cultural backlash; or as a radical Left essentializing of Jews and Capitalism that collapsed the two into each other; and as out-and-out anti-semitism. In this latter invocation of *Golus*, no one was responsible or even influential for the politics of things. "Esau hated Jacob and nothing could be done about it."[89] Resignation, avoidance, and adjustment were the best and only tools of response in this situation. Consciousness about this *Golus* could lead to short-term self-protective strategies and tactics. No fundamental risk to uncover an underlying cause or ameliorative strategy to understand and deal with the condition of *Golus* was possible.[90]

A fourth version of *Golus* was introduced to me in my late teenage encounters with the Israeli disdain for *Galut*, the modern Israeli Hebrew pronunciation even sounded condemnatory! The juxtaposition of the Holocaust, with its enormous human toll, and three years later, Israeli Independence, shifted the discourse about *Galut*. The bifurcation of Jewish experience was made central to the new state. In true Manichean style all virtue applied to Israel, the fledgling state, while all vice had one reference, the Jews of the Diaspora. The place where I lived (Diaspora), was a place so dark, doomed, and unredeemable, it was Exile! In a further lesson, I was given to understand that this was not a political situation but a metaphysical one. The benighted *Golut* was infected with a kind of metaphysical corruption so thick and encompassing that it embodied a spiritual condition to causing teenage pimples, caricatures of hunchbacks, asthmatics, and cowardice among those Jews who lived outside of Israel. This last form of *Galut* was remediable but it required a change of address.[91] Yes, we Jews in

America are in exile! A Manichean doctrine that was once rejected by our monotheistic ancestors now reappeared and was adopted and naturalized under the banner of the Jewish version of "overcoming the past." In this new Manichean world there were Jews who lived in Israel and those that lived in *Galut*. The former no longer suffered from the maladies of exile! No acne, just calm, physical prowess, and noble courage! Committed Jews are those who commit themselves to physical or psychological *aliyah* (immigration to Israel).

Nevertheless and notwithstanding all the Israel inspired happy talk, triumphalism, and idle chatter about the doomed world of *Galut*-Diaspora Judaism that one could hear from Israelis and even many Diaspora denizens, what remained constant for me is a primary sense of consciousness over the brokenness of the world and the all-important sense of hope that is its antidote. I live in *Golus/t*! Today, the human condition, as *Golus*, is elided in most Jewish communal discussions including the so-called political ones. Among the liberal movements, the Reform and Conservative movements of Judaism, *Golus* was eliminated in the ecstacies over the arrival of universal culture at the end of the nineteenth century. The affirmation of Jewish nationalism did not mean the return of *Golus*. Any return to *Golus* among the orthodox is lost in the triumphalisms of West Bank fantacies and control of holy territory. *Golus* is used as a synonym for powerlessness. Powerlessness is, in turn, a term for irrelevancy.

I hasten to defend the notion of *Golus* as having a redeeming value since it retains another context for the question of the moral content of Jewish identity. The notion of *Golus* is not a version of the 'fallenness of man' that can only be redeemed in a savior à la Christian and Hassidic understandings. And even if the savior redeems, it will not avail since "the poor will always be with us." This notion of the inevitability of poverty suggests something about the lack of social imagination of religious conservatives who misquote scripture to justify human-created poverty and to justify unjust social arrangements. These contemporary responses ignore the issue of "responsibility for the other," discussed above when I invoked Levinas.

The consciousness of *Golus* or perhaps it is a "stance," questions the "can do" attitude of America and the modern world. This world has little patience for a hand-wringing discussion of plight of the poor, the abandonment of educational institutions in the public and private arena, or the violence in our society. Ah! says this impatient world, there is a solution: the application of business methods, privatization, and cutting one's losses in a lifeboat ethics! Demanding understanding of the complexity and disenfranchisement of the poor is a trap. A much easier discourse focuses on private characterological flaws of the poor and declares them lazy and corrupt completing the American denigration cosmos. The "answer" is that those people are Black or Brown. "Those people are poor because they are Black and Black because they are poor." To ponder the complexity of social problems is to give in to inefficiency and history. A hasty retreat to answers is made: one must, after all, mend the world, *tikkun olam*! Even before a healthy respect for the flaw in the world, the impulse to fix-it rushes in to ignore complexity. These "solutions" and my parody of them, seems like a loss of *Golus*-consciousness. When those "solutions" do not produce results they become a tool of "racialization" in the hands of cynical politicians whose appeal is to employ by allusion and inference the race question. The race question is the structural equivalent of old-fashion pre-nineteenth-century anti-semitism.

Even in the magisterial essay by Daniel Boyarin and Jonathan Boyarin, there is an eliding of the specific Jewish meaning of *Golus*. By using the term Diaspora, instead of *Golus*, I suspect the brothers Boyarin of attempting to get out in front of the pack of scholars writing about Diaspora Studies.[92] While the Boyarins' point seems to suggest that just as the concept of monotheism in the nineteenth and twientieth century carried *theapologia* for the unique contribution of Judaism to the world, so too, now, does Diaspora (to use their term for *Golus*). That *Galut* is defined by the Boyarins in a unidimensional fashion as a "renunciation of . . . temporal power . . . precisely the most powerful mode of preservation of difference and, therefore, the most effective kind of resistance . . . to . . . any possibility of domination over Others by being perpetually out of power."[93] The Boyarins seem to move too close to a complete condemnation of Jewish political independence. They seem to repeat the Manichean mistakes over again, this time virtue is found only the Diaspora! Disallowing a Jewish state since the Jews exercising sovereignty in the Israeli state have been found wanting in terms of its moral *bona fides*, seems to be going too far in the opposite direction. The Boyarins are seeking a synthesis for a "stubborn hanging-on to ethnic, cultural specificity but in the context of deeply felt and enacted human solidarity [universalization]. For that synthesis, Diaspora provides a model, and *only in conditions of Diaspora can such a resolution be even attempted*."[94] The valorization of Diasporism over "statism" does not convince, since it is unlikely that only one site or even several Diaspora(s) allows for both cultural specificity and universal concern. It would seem to be possible to live in Israel and retain a sense of *Golu*. The sense of being exposed and living with uncertainty—both moral and physical—is part of my construction of a postmodern sensibility.

Moreover the attitude of ignoring the deeper problem for the sake of a quick solution has an additional moral dimension. The person of the Other is now reduced to a political calculation. Morality and consideration of the Other is not as central as it once was in the Jewish community. We have discovered our interests over our values. The thirty-six repeated invocations of Egyptian bondage (versions of "Remember that you know the heart of stranger because you were strangers in the land of Egypt") in the Torah used to serve as a reminder to treat the stranger, poor, and widow with respect. Today it is hard to imagine a serious public (both Jewish and non-Jewish) conversation about social and political treatment of the immigrant, the widow, elderly infirm; or the orphan. One need but recall the injustices done to the Jews in most audiences to gain sympathy; but how quickly our ancestors' suffering is made a mandate for our lack of concern for others. This moral coarseness does seem to have explanation(s) in both Diasporism and statism.

I have come to associate the sense of *Golus* with the trope in critical pedagogy that seeks to "problematize" the world in which we live. The aspects of the world that we once took for granted can be questioned and challenged. There always were moral voices of Judaism that did not accept as "ordained" or "natural" the twins of poverty and social inequity as a representation of a divinely ordained order. The moral voices that have moved me in the educational endeavor have come in our time from Freire, Heschel, and Purpel each of whom is inspired by the prophetic voice. "The educator as prophet does more than re-mind, re-answer, and re-invigorate—the prophet-educator conducts research and joins students in continually developing skills and knowledge that enhance the possibility of justice, community, and joy."[95]

Moral Self-containment Rather than Anger; Small and Mundane Acts

Rabbi Greenberg treated the survivors of the concentration camps with respect, understanding, and love, even when they acted in a knowingly inappropriate manner. Among the survivors were those who sought to provoke—*Le-Hachees or Of-szte-loches*. . . . How many times did Greenberg meet the man sitting on the lawn on Yom Kippur afternoon with five or ten dollars worth of hamburgers (five and six hamburgers for a dollar) and not react? The holiest day of the year in which one fasts out of love to align oneself with God's love for us and this man publicly flaunts the fasting ritual! The man says to all who can hear, "*Du meinst az emetzer hert inner-wenig? Ich hob ge-fa'ast far alemen dorten.* [You think Anyone is listening inside? I fasted enough for everyone—'there.']" Then there was the year that on Rosh Hashanah, that the plumbing broke and the same man and his friends are repeating, loudly, "I always knew the Jews stink." The memory of the assault by means of excrement from the days of the camps comes flooding into Arizona desert landscape.[96] Greenberg calmly responds to their expression of self-hate and disgust: "It's just plumbing, we are not 'there' Mr. Weiss, can you call the plumber?"[97]

But Greenberg didn't build a large congregation in his tenure in Phoenix. He may have been the last effective rabbi that "Betty Brew" had. He was also a bit of a magician and was an engineer by schooling. I didn't know which was which. He rigged up the red, green, and yellow lights that told us when to boo Haman, the villain of the Purim story. This was an innovation by the lights of the Eastern European Jews. Even here in this once a year traditionally sanctioned loosening of the boundaries, Greenberg taught about appropriate limits. About Mordechai, Esther's uncle and guardian, Greenberg told us, "A Jew doesn't bow down to an idol, but stands up for the weak, for his people, and fights back! Fighting back means using your rage in a constructive manner." Greenberg taught about the sacred, the holy, and the transcendent. He also taught how to not give in to despair and anger. The qualities of *menshlischkeit* were enacted by not getting angry, by not giving in to anger. I tried to emulate Greenberg one year, a couple of months before my Bar Mitzvah. One Yom Kippur, I beatup the *Americaner* bully, Murry S., who for years had been beating all of us younger kids up. He was so big and fat that he would vanquish us all by just sitting on us. When Murry started in on us, I calmly kept punching him in the face until he fell against the exit door of the synagogue and made such a racket that Rabbi Greenberg came running out to scold us. So I didn't learn everything Greenberg taught before my Bar Mitzvah!

Arizona School Experiences

Arizona of the 1950s was not an exclusive paradise "for whites only" as it seemingly has become today. Many of the children, I went to school with were Mexicans and Indians. The terms Chicano and Native Americans were not yet invented. Our school was on land that had originally been Indian land and so it carried the obvious and unmistakable claim of being on Indian School Road. There is some kind of ironic, perhaps dialectical injustice in the fact that all the land that was supposed to belong to the Indians forever had a school called Longview on it. As if to announce that this additional appropriation of native land—minor by larger standards—was just one more farsighted improvement in the condition of humanity, despite promises, treaties, and solemn undertakings. Discourses of universalism were employed regularly to subsume any disturbing attempts to face an encounter or an engagement with questions of justice over particular cases, like the Native Americans. Arizona had a good deal of multicultural diversity but we were being cured of the "differences that cause dis-ease in the body politic."[98]

Most of the kids were lower middle-class but a significant portion lived in the Phoenix Country Club, a restricted area—no Jews, Blacks, Indians, and Mexicans could live there. The Country Club kids were always in the upper one or two classes of the four tiered divisions in each grade. My first four years in grade school, I studied with the Mexican, Indian, and other immigrant kids in what was called, without hesitation, the lowest and the next-to-the-lowest classes. It was the Mexicans, Indians, and few Blacks that were my friends and allies against the richer, more aggressive blond Americans. In the second grade, I remember Rupert Lopez leading a charge on crutches against the white kids who called me a dirty Jew. This was the wild west and things were settled by fighting. Eventually the Mexican, Indian, and Black kids were tracked out, down into the lower classes; they finally disappeared in high school. By the twentieth reunion, by virtue of being the only clergy type, I read the necrology of my high school class, over a hundred had been killed, mostly in Vietnam or drug-related incidents. A very high percentage of the dead were from non-white backgrounds.

Until about fifth or sixth grade, all of us tracked into the lower classes were close friends, but then my life began to change around the arrival and impact of a new teacher, Mr. William Wells. Wells was a music teacher, band and orchestra. He turned out to be my savior. In the fifth grade, I was moved to the highest class. I remember that summer my life began to change; I discovered a fever for reading, perhaps I had learned enough English! But more important was the dynamic and fun-loving man, who was a friend and confidant all through high school. His different and more sedate World War II experiences, fighting the battle of San Francisco as a saxophone player in the United States Navy Band, became a part of my life. The American slang I learned, I learned or copied from him. He could reprimand and cajole and win loyalty. It is amazing to me thinking back on his ability to shape me and my brothers. He was a fierce and inspiring presence. One reprimand would include the following dialogue. "Why are you being such a hamburger? Do you want to be just a hot dog on the mustard trail? Get with it." "It" covered a multitude of things from get your homework done, don't sulk, pay attention, show up to rehearsal on time, memorize your lines, learn your music. . . .

I had a prior experience with the music world. I had signed up or was drafted into the school chorus about three or four weeks before the Christmas Concert. I had gone to rehearsals, . . . loved the songs, and have no recollection of feeling an outsider or even afraid of the religious meanings behind the songs. Most of the songs were quite happy and I too was happy to be happy. I was a fifth-grader and pretty much a conformist. What all the other kids did I wanted to do too. Being a part of the chorus was my first big group experience. The concert came and I sang my heart out. I had never been in a performance before and thought it was wonderful! No fear and no anxiety, just singing. People applauded and we were warmly received by all. The next Monday, Mrs. Kramer, the chorus director, got us up in the bleachers and warmly thanked us all for our hard work, told us how much everyone enjoyed the concert, we had sung so well—all except for one person. The principal had loved the concert but he couldn't help noticing that one exception. What had that one person done? We were all waiting ready to condemn this miscreant. He had smiled, waved, fidgeted about and sung without looking at the director! You had to keep your eyes on the director at all times. "That person is Benny Beliak." She moved forward, grabbed me by the arm, and pulled me down from the middle bleacher. She told me that I could never be in the chorus again and to leave immediately. In front of all my friends, all the other classes, I was denounced and I was condemned, I had ruined the Christmas Concert! I have always wondered since if there was not some unspoken text in the act of Mrs. Kramer. Perhaps I was Judas, the betrayer? In any case, I don't sing or perform with abandon any more.

About a week later, the newly arrived Mr. Wells announced over the public address system that band tryouts were taking place and everyone was invited. Then he read a list of names of people that were specifically invited, including me. I went to the tryouts which consisted in Wells tapping out a certain rhythm that each of us was supposed to copy; followed by a round of asking each of us which note was higher or lower from various keys on the piano. I failed both tests miserably and therefore was given a big silver-colored horn that was just a bit smaller than a tuba; it was called a baritone horn. I was charged with the task of lugging this instrument home and back for the next two and a half years of grade school. Band practice was at 7:15 each morning and sometimes after school. I was part of something big! In our first concert, we played a medley of Disney tunes, a reprise of "South of Pacific," and a few marches, but the key was the two or three parts were I played alone, or the countermelody. While band music is classically constructed around the idea that various sections of the band trade off playing the melody line and the drums and tubas play a kind of percussive rhythm, the oomphas, there is the little-noticed but to my way of thinking all-encompassing importance of the soaring, contrasting, counterposed melody. The trick was to know when to come in, what the right dynamics of the section were, and, of course, keep your eye on the conductor.

I credit Wells with having given me a new task in life: sounding the counternote in a way that it could be appropriately heard. On rare occasion, when the trombones were weak I would double on their parts and play melody but that was rare. Most of the time they were enlisted to help me! To this day in synagogue, I am more likely to have developed a countermelody to the favorite tunes of *Adon Olom* and *Yigdal* and every political and cultural issue that comes along. I think it is what has shaped my teaching style. What is missing in this perfect representation? Yes, the countermelody!

Later in life, as a Chaplain and Hillel director, I always looked for the missing voice, the countermelody. When social action and Israel-related programs were all the rage on campus for the beginning years of my career, I insisted that we do pure socials, parties. When Israel fell into disfavor because of the right-wing turn to fascism in the election of Menachem Begin, I taught the proto-Zionist enlightened philosophy of the nineteenth century - Alkalai Kalischer, Hess, and others. When the "Me generation" of the eighties held sway my office opened a emergency food pantry for the homeless and needy in an abandoned building surrounded by a junkyard recycling center.

For seventeen years, as one of three equal chaplains, I was the add-minister at the Waspy Claremont Colleges. In theory we were three equal chaplains serving the students with special responsibility to our home religious community. In the early seventies, I served as the advisor to a host of campus "marginal groups," including gay and lesbian students' group and Arab students, when the Tunisian and Moroccan Arab students were the majority at the Claremont Graduate School; and as advocate of AIDS education on campus, just after the discovery of the disease. Playing countermelody was good training for being a Jew in the assimilationist sixties and even better for choosing to study education mid-career instead of graduating to an urban pulpit. A sense of my own marginality helped me to appreciate my Irish Catholic priest colleague who stated, "there is no anti-semitism or anti-Catholic sentiment at The Claremont Colleges, only Enlightened bigotry!" So what is a Jew to do? Continue playing countermelody was my response. Or go to graduate school in education and learn that there is a whole school of countermelody called critical pedagogy.

Jewish "Looks" and Race

During the summers, my grade school had a juvenile diversion program, where we played Monopoly and Ping Pong in the air-conditioned cafeteria. Wells taught fairness, fun, play, and strategic thinking. "Wells looks like two Jews"—so my mother said and she was right. Several years later when Wells showed up on time ("poor Gentiles they don't know better") to my Bar Mitzvah, old Mr. Weiss came over and put a *tallis* (prayer shawl) around his shoulders, with the superior disdain reserved for American Reform Jews (*Americaner*), who should know better but haven't learned that you are supposed to wear a *tallis* in *shul* on Shabbas morning!

Wells was a key mentor in all things American and worldly. I heard my first classical music under his tutelage. I even went to concerts because he talked and taught about that boring music. I even listened to opera on records and on the Texaco Opera Radio show. I knew that according to Wells, when I got married I should wait two years before having any children and save the money for the expenses of a down payment on a house. What twelve year-old had ever achieved such exalted initiation into the secrets of life! This was all important advice for life!

In my last year in grade school I continued to learn about America and the world from Mr. Wells. Two moments from my eighth grade experiences at Longview Elementary taught me about the use of culture, even high culture, to harm others. First, late in the seventh grade, four of us were chosen to sing, play duets, quartets, and tell stories in a minstrel show in blackface. This was 1961! The show opened with my joke. The interlocutor said: "Gentleman be seated! Mr. Bones (that's me) you appear to be sleepy." "Ya-sur, I didn't get much sleep last night. I dream'd I was pitchin' pennies and I tossed all night," I responded. The second moment of high culture learning happened around the eighth grade graduation. I played a baritone horn solo accompanied by Monica Monroe, one of my earliest crushes. The music came from Richard Wagner's Lohengrin, "The Evening Star." It is a beautiful piece of music, which I loved without any real knowledge of who Wagner was or how much his anti-semitism had been used by the Nazis.

In short order, I had been initiated into America! Becoming American had an element of betrayal so primary that I still shudder![99] By the eighth grade, I was appearing in blackface as people were being hosed down and chased by dogs in the evil South. I was playing the music of the greatest anti-semitic culture leader of his day to my parents and their friends, who were Holocaust survivors. American schools had a way of invoking culture without history or context. Who needed to come to consciousness and history when you have America and its crushing engines of inclusion and exclusion?

I don't remember any teachers or parents comments from that time questioning the social meaning of the minstrel show or the Wagner music. There were black students at Longview, or were there? My parents knew of the cultural iconic role that Wagner played in Nazi German's life. They never said a word to me. It is only in reflection that I wonder about my belated good conscience at being able to tell this story. It was a time when American education could inflict tremendous hurt without being held accountable for it.

For many years, I would recite the jokes from the minstrel show to friends and I have had a secret and guilty love of Wagner's music all my life. The tools of hate and disparagement were naturalized in my world. I wonder why I didn't connect the "Small World" of the aesthetic to the larger issues that were happening all around me?[100] By high school and certainly college, I learned not to talk about minstrel shows but I also learned to appropriate the jokes and punch lines, now in disguised form, from the minstrel show. There was just enough overlap, so that when I wrote a few skits and gags for the children's television show It's Wallace or Wallace and Ladmo I could draw all my parodies from the Bible prophets and the pseudo-black voice, for the two characters that I knew how to best assume—Captain Super and Gerald. Captain Super was a bungling superhero with an ego a full cubic mile in dimension and Gerald was a spoiled, tantruming rich kid. A brief career in television writing and production went a long way to helping me appreciate the role of cultural borrowing—expropriation—in shaping attitudes and stereotypes.

The minstrel show was not the only opportunity to learn about the privileges of white skin in the context of becoming an American and, more important, an Arizona conservative. It played an important role in my understanding of the relationship of American Jews to African-Americans, at least from the Jewish side. When I began to think critically about my participation in the minstrel show my mother's oft-repeated sardonic statement came back to me: "*A dank Gott az mir hoben Shwartzes dow, onstand et men harginen Yidn.* [Thank God that there are Blacks in this country, otherwise they would kill Jews.] Throughout my youth, I would refer to myself as the "icebreaker," often the role of the oldest child in immigrant families. Being the first in my family or among the *greenies* to do things conferred certain privileges and expectations. My children have been discussing the colleges they would like to attend since the age of six or seven. I compare that worldliness with my "discovery" of college at the end of my sophomore year in high school!

Since "discovery" was often a hit-and-miss thing, it also meant encountering the underside of American life early. But it was my father who was certainly the most exposed to America and its codes. I remember an incident from around the age of ten or eleven as being particularly telling. My father was always looking for extra work to supplement the wages he earned at Arizona Sash and Door. He would often take on extra jobs with other cabinetmakers, to be completed on weekends and nights. One time, my dad came home angry at a fellow coworker and partner in one of these projects. He was a Black man. Dad's remarks made clear that he had learned the language and the symbols of American hate quite well. When my mother recovered from her shock at hearing her husband she said, "*Whilst machen afer'geneegen far die Goyim?* [You want to provide satisfaction and comfort to Gentile sensibilities?]" This complex question suggested that my mother did not understand that we were in a country that did not hold primary the Jews and the Gentiles, but its ever changing version of race: black and white. My dad was assimilating by announcing his anger at the easy target, Blacks. There were very few Blacks in

Phoenix and they were often limited by social convention to the "Southside." By siding with the whites my dad had discovered that he could belong to America in a way that was impossible for him in his native Latvia. Latvia, before the arrival of Nazis, had been a country where he had given his genuine loyalties, only to see his family murdered by classmates. The diminution of Blacks was a way of becoming white. Becoming "white" for Jews, is another way to triangulate the ravages of assimilation and loss of identity. Whiteness is a more acceptable way of assimilating away from the Jewish community. Becoming "white" for Jews is a way of losing one's identity by folding into the larger American identity a solidarity with the process of racialization and a consequent annihilation of the last vestiges of being Jewish. It is not perceived to be a more pernicious achievement than apostasy by the guardians of Jewish boundaries, rabbis et al., because it is not marked by a crossing of religious boundaries, yet its impact is quite telling.[101]

This capacity for "white" assimilation is challenged by the recent controversies surrounding the culture wars, including the question of the role of multiculturalism on American campuses and general culture. It wasn't too long before the question of the impact of multiculturalism would be asked about Jews. To my mind a salutory reaction has been the making of the color "white" visible. In its new visibility, "whiteness" contains many things with which Jews do not wish to associate. The assimilating power of being "white" for Jews may diminish. This may make room for a more independent struggle with Jewish identity formation in Diaspora. Second, as the actual history of Jews as subjects of the Enlightenment, nationalist and colonialist enterprises in Europe become more apparent, this too proves a disincentive for being assimilated into being "white."

When the focus shifts from exclusive analysis of African, North American, and South American histories but includes Eastern Europe, Spain, and North Africa, Jews are among the first victims of these early processes of colonialization. Jewish academics, who are surprised to be accused of erecting the imperialist and colonialist cultural barriers, are suddenly reintroduced to the new dialectics of double consciousness. The signs of this reappropriation are everywhere.

Notes

0. Reuben Alcalay. The Complete Hebrew-English Dictionary (Hartford, Connecticut: Prayer Book Press, Inc., 1965) pp. 352–353.

1. Correspondence from the editor, Svi Shapiro, August 29, 1995.

2. Stuart Berg Flexner, ed. The Random House Dictionary of the English Language, (New York: Random House, 1987) p. 1474.

3. Conversation with Gelya Frank.

4. Daniel Jonah Goldhagen. Hitler's Willing Executioners: Ordinary Germans and the Holocaust (New York: Alfred A Knopf, 1996) pp. 327–271.

5. Naomi Zack. Race and Mixed Race (Philadelphia: Temple University Press, 1993), p. 5. It is important to affirm Zack's words: "Racial categories are primarily cultural categories: The facts of human biology and anthropology do not support a belief in the existence of racial characteristics as traits, which for any given race, are present in every individual member of that race. Nevertheless, ordinary concepts of race are based on assumptions that such support is present." p. 5.

6. As I read the proofs for this essay Madeline Albright, the newly appointed Secretary of State in the second Clinton administration, has been "outed" as having at least three Jewish grandparents. Albright could stand in with Betty Friedan and my mother in a "family" picture and people would lovingly ask: "How well did the sisters get along?"

7. Sander Gilman. The Jew's Body (Routledge: New York, 1991)

8. John M. Efron. Defenders of the Race: Jewish Doctors and Race Science in Fin-de-Siecle Europe (New Haven, Conn.,: Yale University Press, 1994) p. 1.

9. Richard D. Alba. Ethnic Identity: The Transformation of White America (New Haven, Conn.: Yale University Press, 1990) p. xiii–xiv and p. 1.

10. Bauman, Zygmunt. Life in Fragments: Essays in Postmodern Morality (Oxford, UK: Blackwell, 1995), p. 208. Bauman suggests that anti-semitism is not a problem of heterophobia, "the resentment of the different," but rather a question of proteophobia "the apprehension and vexation related. . .to something or someone disquieting . . . that does not fit the structure of the orderly world, does not fit easily into any of the established categories. . . ." Bauman further suggests that, "the vagueness and diffuseness of the proteophobic anxiety, and the categorial elusiveness of the Jews who for important part of European history tended to sit astride all the usual divides and elide all the criteria normally deployed to draw them."

11. Ibid., Body, p. 1.

12. Ibid., Defenders, p.3.

13. Ibid., Bauman, p. 207. Bauman makes an important distinction between thinking of hostility toward the Jews as either "hostility to the Jews and hostility to the Jews." p. 207. Bauman also suggest that we introduce another term borrowed from Artur Sandauer, 'allosemitism.' "Allosemitism refers to the practice of setting the Jews apart as people radically different from all the others, needing separate concepts to describe and comprehend them . . . —since the concepts and treatment usefully deployed when facing or dealing with other people or peoples, simply would not do. 'Allosemitism' is essentially noncommital, just like the above practice is; it does not unambiguously determine either hatred or love of the Jews, but contains the seeds of both. . . ." p. 207–208.

14. Ibid., Defenders, p. 82. "What are the qualities, if any, that we are to regard as racially characteristic of the Jews? Much vague declamation has been spoken and written on this subject. All the moral, social, and intellectual qualities of Jews have been spoken of as being theirs by right of birth in its physical sense. Jews differ from all others in these points, it is true . . . but the differences are due in my opinion, to the combined effect of their social isolation and their own traditions and customs, and if they have nowadays any hereditary predispositions towards certain habits and callings, these can only be regarded as secondarily racial, acquired hereditary tendencies which cannot be brought forward as proof of racial purity." This a quote in Defenders from Joseph Jacobs's book Jewish Statistics: Social, Vital, and Anthropolometric (London: D. Nutt, 1891), p. iii.

15. Ibid., Defenders, p. 90.

16. van Dijk, Teun A. Elite Discourse and Racism (Newbury Park, CA: Sage, 1993) pp. 46–47. "A good education and control of public knowledge, beliefs, and discourse are the major power resources of . . . symbolic elites.

17. Ibid., Body, p. 4.

18. Prell, Riv-Ellen. "Rage and Representation: Jewish Gender Stereotypes in American Culture" in Uncertain Terms: Negotiating Gender in American Culture edited by Faye Ginsburg and Anna Lowenhaupt Tsing (Beacon Press: Boston, 1990) p. 249–266. This is an excellent example of this genre tied to issues of gender stereotyping of Jewish women.

19. Ibid., Body, p. 236. Gilman here is summarizing and argument make by Lyotard in which Jews are reduced to an essence and ignored in their complexities and diversity. The issue of the drive toward invisibility by Jews is made more nuanced and complex by Gilman's work that seeks to clarify the sometimes complex and murky language used to talk about Jews.

20. Ibid., Body, p. 242.

21. Ibid., Body, p. 174.

22. Ibid., Body, p. 174.

23. The use of the word "Jews" or "jews" in scare quotes is meant to evoke a usage by Jean-Francois Lyotard in Heidegger and "the jews" (Minneapolis: University of Minnesota Press, 1990), p. xii. David Carroll's introduction to the book explains that "the jews," ". . . refers neither to a nation, nor to a political, philosophical, or religious figure or subject. It is neither a concept nor a representation of any specific people as such. "The jews,". . . should not be confused with real Jews." The same point holds for Blacks and women. While it is not convenient to maintain the scare quotes through out this is essay it allows us not to loose an important trope.

24. Sander L. Gilman. Smart Jews: The Construction of the Image of Jewish Superior Intelligence (Lincoln: University of Nebraska Press, 1996), pp. 178–179.

25. Ibid., Prell. This article's argument is more subtle than it is possible to present here.

26. Ibid., Smart, p. 28. The recent movie, Independence Day managed to hit both the weak feminized and genius notes in the Michael Goldman part of the computer nerd, who transforms himself into a space cowboy thus winning back "his girl" through his new found macho performance of "sticking it" to the aliens. The post-battle walk of the transformed cowboy, who is no longer nauseous, allows him to smoke a cigar. The cigar is emblematic of the "sissified" environmental and health concerns of the computer nerd. The African-American character, an ace pilot overcomes stereotypes of a lack of constancy, loyalty, and skill by teaming up with the Jew. More could be said about the stereotypes of this "send off (up)" of some of the most current depictions of Vietnam era veterans, women, politicians, aliens, Jews, and African Americans.

27. Ibid., Defenders, p. 124. The quote is used in Defenders and comes from Karl Kautsky's Are the Jews a Race? (New York: International Publishers, 1926), p. 17.

28. Joan W. Scott. "Multiculturalism and the Politics of Identity," in The Identity in Question edited by John Rajchman (New York: Routledge, 1995), p. 8.

29. Linda Nochlin. "Introduction: Starting with the Self: Jewish Identity and Its Representation" in The Jew in the Text: Modernity and the Construction of Identity, edited by Linda Nochlin and Tamara Garb (London: Thames and Hudson, 1995), p. 8. The latter part of the quote refers to the important essay by Susan Rubin Suleiman in the same collection about Jean-Paul Sartre's post-World War II essay the The Anti-Semite and the Jew.

30. Roger Simon. "Beyond the Racist Text: Jewish Applause for a Yiddish Shylock" in Teaching Against Grain: Texts for a Pedagogy of Possibility (New York: Bergin & Garvey, 1992), p. 118. I would include the novel Operation Shylock by Philip Roth for its power to evoke many of the demons of modern Jewish life and put perspective on them.

31. Melanie Kaye/Kantrowitz. The Issue is Power: Essays on Women, Jews, Violence, and Resistance (San Francisco: Aunt Lutte Books), pp. i–iv and pp. 103–4. So many books could be included in a growing list but I choose this one because of its ability to formulate the problems. Debra Orenstein. Lifecycles, Volume 1: Jewish Women on Life Passages & Personal Milestones and Lifecycles, Volume 2: Jewish Women on Biblical Themes in Contemporary Life (Vermont: Jewish Lights Publishing, 1995 and 1997).

32. Roger Kamenetz. The Jew in the Lotus: A Poet's Discovery of Jewish Identity in Buddist India (New York: HarperSan Francisco, 1995). This book which is just one of a growing number of what can be termed a genre.

33. Zhide is a Polish word suggesting a slang short hand for Jews that employs intonation with an emphasis on zh sound to convey the disgust.

34. Nathan Rotenstreich. Jews and German Philosophy: The Polemics of Emancipation (New York: Schocken Books, 1982), pp. 3–8 and 61-70 are helpful in appreciating the nature of the modern "refusal" embodied in Emmanuel Kant and Hermann Cohen.

35. The contemporary constructions of Jewish identity include a number of evocative narratives that have impacted me are mentioned through out this paper, such as Philip Roth's Operation Shylock but also travel stories such as Roger Kamenetz's The Jew in the Lotus.

36. The construction of Jewish identity proposed by Rosensweig and Buber is best exemplified in their attempt to read the Bible in a phenomenological fashion. For a discussion of this approach one might profitably refer to the introduction of Everett Fox's discussion in The Schocken Bible: The Five Books of Moses (New York: Schocken Books, 1995), p. xxv.

37. Alain Finkielkraut. The Imaginary Jew (Lincoln: University of Nebraska Press, 1994), p. 34. Finkielkraut is certainly celebrated as a "find" in contemporary Jewish discourse but his understandings while pertinent remain quite conservative for my taste. "The Jew may be civilization's Other, but it is an otherness none can possess. To put it bluntly: the Holocaust has no heirs. No one can cloak himself in such an experience, incommunicable, if not the survivors. Among the people that constitute our generation, it is given to no one to say: I am the child of Auschwitz. As an imaginary Jew, I have long lived my faithfulness to my Jewish background in a kind of appropriation. . . . Now I know that I am not a Jew in the same way I am dark, curly-haired, worrisome or timid. . . . To the question "Who am I?" the answer "Jew" is never a pertinent response. The past, from which I refuse to avert my gaze, reflects more than an embellishment of my looks. For if Judaism in fact has a central injunction, it should be thought of not as a matter of identity, but of memory: not to mimic persecution nor make theater of the Holocaust, but to honor its victims."

38. Cornel West. "A Matter of Life and Death" in The Identity, p. 17.

39. Michael Walzer. "What Does It Mean to Be an 'American'"? in Brettschneider, Marla, editor. The Narrow Bridge: Jewish Views on Multiculturalism (New Brunswick, New Jersey: Rutgers University Press, 1996). Originally, published in Social Research (Volume 57:3, Fall 1990).

40. Jeffrey Rubin-Dorsky and Shelley Fisher-Fishkin. People of the Book: Thirty Scholars Reflect on Their Jewish Identity (Madison, Wisconsin: University of Wisconsin, 1996). David Theo Goldberg, and Michael Krausz Jewish Identity (Philadelphia, PA: Temple University Press, 1993). My favorite in the People of the Book for its humor is by Herbert Lindenburger, "Between Texts: From Assimlationist Novel to Resistance Narrative."

41. While this kind of talk raises the specter of "essentialism," I wish to take refuge in the rhetorical device of a strategic essentialism. Ewa Ziarek's "Kristeva and Levinas: Mourning Ethics and the Feminine," edited by Kelly Oliver in Ethics, Politics, and Difference in Julia Kristeva's Writing (New York: Routledge, 1993), p. 62 and the accompanying references to Spivak and others in footnote 1 on p. 76. In his article Herbert Lindenberger carries on a dialogue with himself denying being labeled a Jewish-American as a "hybrid new concoction based on some fashionable model" (p. 357). At the conclusion of a sharp sometimes biting series of questions put to Lindenberger by the persistent interlocutor, the interlocutor finally manages to wring from Lindenberger the story of a cousin who was part of the resistance to Hitler, in the Baum group. This leads to a denouement in which against all that he has recited acknowledging the rule of universal norms, Lindenberger announces his "tribalism in a self-contradictory fit of pique" (p. 373).

42. Howard R. Bowen and Jack H. Schuster. American Professors: A National Resource Imperiled (Oxford University Press: New York, 1986). The latest research on the numbers of Protestant, Catholic, and Jewish academics, was completed in 1975 by Everett C. Ladd and Seymour M. Lipsett which claimed that Jews were 9 percent of the academy. The present estimate of 20 percent is a guess based on extrapolations.

43. Pierre Bourdieu. Homo Academicus (Stanford, CA: Stanford University Press, 1988) p. xi and xii. Bourdieu writes, ". . . that an ethnologist would domesticate the exotic, but, if I may venture the expression, exoticize the domestic, through a break with his initial relation of intimacy with modes of life and thought which remain opaque to him because they are too familiar. . . . Only a sociological self-analysis of this kind, which owes and concedes nothing to self-indulgent narcissism, can really help to place the scholar in a position where he is able to bring to bear on his familiar world the detached scrutiny which, with no special vigilance, the ethnologist brings to bear on any world to which he is not linked by the inherent complicity of being involved in its social game, its illusio, which creates the very value of the objectives of the game, as it does the value of the game itself." The illusio of Jewish academics would add one more layer of analysis complicated by the usual questions of special relationship to an educational institution, "which has been socially licensed as entitled to operate an objectification which lays claim to objectivity and universality."

44. Paul Ritterband and Harold S. Wechsler. Jewish Learning in American Universities: The First Century (Bloomington, IN: Indiana University Press, 1994). David A. Hollinger. Science, Jews and Secular Culture (Princeton, New Jersey: Princeton University Press, 1996). In addition, mention of the several articles by Evelyn Torton Beck, "The Politics of Jewish Invisibility in Women Studies" in Transforming the Curriculum : Ethnic Studies and Women's Studies (Albany: State University of New York Press, 1991) and "Jews and the Multicultural University Curriculum" in The Narrow Bridge see footnote 16. It is important to mention also Howard Adelman's "Is Jewish Studies Ethnic Studies?" in Transforming. The recent work of Rael Meyerowitz, Transferring to America: Jewish Interpretations of American Dreams (Albany: State University of New York, 1995) is important to mention since its central argument poses the question that the work of Harold Bloom, Stanley Cavell, and Sacvan Bercovitch each represent an instance of "transference" in both the psychological and physical sense of aspirations and intentions regarding the American texts from their second generation immigrant position of ambivalence that retains a Jewish sensibility. There is not sufficient time to explore this book here.

45. Karen Brodkin Sacks "How Did Jews Become White Folks" in Race (New Brunswick, New Jersey: Rutgers University Press, 1994). See also Hollinger's Science, Jews p. 163. The GI Bill like affirmative action today helped those positioned to take advantage of the opportunity. Jews and other returning enlisted men often finished high school and entered college with the help of the stipend allotted them.

46. Rael Meyerowitz. Transferring to America: Jewish Interpretations of American Dreams (Albany, New York: State University of New York Press, 1995), p. ix–xi. Many examples could be added. See footnote 53.

47. Ibid., Science, Jews p. 159, and see above discussions. "We need to remind ourselves that in those years ['30s and '40s] the notion of a "Christian" culture still carried vivid connotations of anti-Semitic barrier(s). . . especially in the humanities and social sciences. . . . In Columbia's English department, the appointment of Lionel Trilling as assistant professor in 1939 was a breakthrough so striking that its story is still told by aging English professors around the country, in tones that Civil War buffs reserve for describing the battle of Gettysburg."

48. Since the French Enlightenment, Jews answered with caustion the question of dual loyalties when there was not a Jewish state. That question continued to echo even after 1948 when the state was founded. The question among Jews and in general society is symptomatic of additional false dichotomies and xenophic public culture.

49. Harding, Sandra The Science Question in Feminism (Ithaca, New York: Cornell University Press, 1986). The subtlety of Harding's understandings are exemplary for their willingness to ask the hard questions and patiently arrive at partial and narrow answers. It is also interesting to note the increasing genre of biographical studies appearing now, about all manner of greater and lesser lights of the academic establishment. The bibliography is enormous. It is im-

possible to encapsulate Harding's contribution but perhaps one quote that gestures toward uncovering the andocentric bias in science and might serve as key to asking a similar question regarding Jews and Judaism: ". . . th[e] masculine bias is evident in both the definition of what counts as a scientific problem and in the concepts, theories, methods and interpretations of research." The exploration of bias and biographical standpoints are necessarily tied to each other. Emmanuel Chukwudi Eze introduced and edited an important series of essays Race and the Enlightenment: A Reader (Cambridge, MA: Blackwell Publishers, 1997) in he argues through the texts of prominent philosophers [Hume, Kant, and Hegel] of the age the "enlightenment philosophy was instrumental in codifying and institutionalizing both the scientific and popular European perceptions of the human race. . . . The numerous writings on race . . . reveal, "reason" and "civilization" became almost synonymous with "white" people and northern Europe, while unreason and savagery were conveniently located among the "non-whites" . . . outside Europe."

50. Gelya Frank. "Jews, Multiculturalism, and Boasian Anthropology" in the American Anthropologist 99:4 p. 731–745, December 1997. I point to the work by Dr. Gelya Frank, an anthropologist at University of Southern California, on the Jewish background of prominent Jewish anthropologists such as Boas et. al. and the strong apologia that this academic field developed so as not to acknowledge the obvious positioning of these people as Jews is an important example of the illusio genre, mentioned above.

51. Ibid., Science, Jews, p. 11. These ideas are taken from Hollinger's book.

52. Brettschneider, Marla, editor. The Narrow Bridge: Jewish Views on Multiculturalism (New Brunswick, New Jersey: Rutgers University Press, 1996). In this book especially important is the essay by Evelyn Torton Beck, "Jews and the Multicultural University Curriculum."

53. Kaye/Kantrowitz, Melanie. The Issue Is Power: Essays on Women, Jews, Violence and Resistance (San Francisco: Aunt Lute Books, 1992) especially the essay, "Jews, Class, Color and the Cost of Whiteness" p. 146.

54. Ibid., Imaginary, p. xiv–xv. While these words are summary of Finkielkraut's ideas presented by the translator of his work, they are sufficiently concise to be useful here.

55. Ibid., Imaginary, p. xvii–xviii.

56. Emmanuel Levinas. NineTalmudic Readings (Bloomington, IN: Indiana University Press, 1991) translated and edited by Annette Aronowicz. The reference to "we will do and then we will hear" (Exodus 24:7) takes up the unusual order of the verse and is the subject of Levinas's thoughts on the question of the limits of knowledge. Levinas calls this the "temptation of temptation" in that rather than suspending commitment until one had all the facts, weighed all the possibilities, and experimented with alternatives the Jewish people committed themselves to the Good. "To accept the Torah without reasoning about its value is to accept that the commitment to the Good is never freely

chosen, never the end result of knowing. The Good, the rabbis are saying . . . is of such a nature that it takes possession of a person before the person has time to evaluate it. To receive it (the Good) as such means to acknowledge that all knowing takes its direction from it, rather than the other way around."

57. Ibid., Transferring, p. 128 quotes this passage from Harold Bloom's privately published 1987 article (p. 77), The Strong Light of the Canonical: Kafka, Freud and Scholem as Revisionists of Jewish Culture and Thought. Meyerowitz has performed an important service excellently in capturing so much of the intellectual ferment in her important book.

58. Ibid., Transferring, p. 141. Meyerowitz discusses Cynthia Ozick's demurals from "Literature as Idol: Harold Bloom."

59. Wexler, Philip. Holy Sparks: Social Theory, Education and Religion (New York: St. Martin's Press, 1996), p. 4. Wexler's solution is to invoke Kabbalistic theory as part of the strategy of resacrilizing education. He builds on the theoretical insights of Basil Bernstein, Emile Durkheim, and Harold Bloom while calling for a return to the religious roots of education. Wexler points to Durkheim's state: "As we have progressed, we have established the fact that the fundamental categories of thought, and consequently of science, are of religious origin." p. 94. It is surprising that Wexler seems unaware of the pioneer work of David Purpel in this area.

60. Craig Calhoun. Social Theory and the Politic of Identity (Oxford, UK; Blackwell, 1994), p. 4. Calhoun astutely claims that identity politics has always constituted at least a part of the American reality but theories about the social realm misled people to assume that these were settled, immutable or at best, epiphenomena that had no business in the public sphere. Political theory 'misrecognized' and elided identity as a category for a vision a standard interchangeable individual—a citizen—which was the only thematized category.

61. Anderson, Walter Truett. The Truth about the Truth (New York: Putnam, 1995), p. 8–9.

62. F. Elbaz and R. Elbaz. "Curriculum and textuality" in Journal of Curriculum Theory 8:2, 127–128. Quoted in Understanding Curriculum: An Introduction to the Study of Historical and Contemporary Curriculum Discourses (New York: Peter Lang, 1995), by William F. Pinar, William M. Reynolds, Patrick Slattery, and Peter M. Taubman, p. 539.

63. L. L. Langness and Gelya Frank. Lives: An Anthropological Approach to Biography (Novato, CA: Chandler & Sharp Publishers, Inc., 1981), p. 97–100.

64. Grument, Madeline. "Retrospective: Autobiography and the analysis of educational experience" in Cambridge Journal of Education 20:3, p. 322. Quoted in Understanding Curriculum p. 540. This notion of being "put into question" is part of the growing acknowledgment of the multiple realities that postmodernity world makes prominent.

65. Ibid., The Truth about, p. 7–8.

66. Ibid., Social Theory, p. 4. An important and relevant debate on essentialism in the identity issue is taken up in Identities edited by Kwame Anthony Appiah and Henry Louis Gates, Jr. (Chicago, Ill., The University of Chicago Press, 1995) in two essays by Walter Benn Michaels and the other, by Daniel and Jonathan Boyarin.

67. Zack, Naomi. Race and Mixed Race (Temple University Press: Philadelphia, 1993). Khanga, Yelena. Soul to Soul: A Black Russian Jewish Woman's Search for Her Roots (W. W. Norton & Company, Inc.: New York, New York, 1992). Only Khanga's book attempts to come to terms with the Jewish identity but since Judaism is only a cultural position with no spiritual valence, Judaism must of necessity be presented as empty.

68. Jean-Francois Lyotard. The Postmodern: A Report on Knowledge (Minneapolis, Minnesota: University of Minnesota, 1991), p. xiv.

69. Rajchman, John, The Identity in Question (New York: Routledge, 1995), p. ix. The additions in the square brackets are not in the original and there are a few additional minor emendations.

70. This optimistic assessment is grounded in an awareness of certain basic acknowledgments of what is possible in the postmodern situation that has opened up for Jews which will be elaborated below.

71. Laurence Mordekhai Thomas. "The Soul of Identity: Jews and Blacks" in Rubin-Dorsky, Jeffrey and Fisher-Fishkin, Shelly, People of the Book: Thirty Scholars Reflect on Their Jewish Identity (University of Wisconsin Press: Madison, Wisconsin, 1996) p. 172 and 176. While Thomas's work attempts to analyze two identity group narratives—African-Americans and Jewish-Americans—who are seemingly incommensurable in their claims about themselves. Thomas also provides an important case for the power of history to inform and particularize history to achieve a 'non-competitive' clarity. Important to mention also Vessels of Evil: American Slavery and Holocaust (Philadelphia: Temple University Press, 1993) which the full statement by Thomas of his position. I should note that "twoness" is now being claimed as having "multiplied" the identity commitment.

72. George P. Fletcher. Loyalty: An Essay on the Morality of Relationships (New York: Oxford University Press, 1993).

73. Arnold Wolf. Shema Volume 26: Issue 505, January 5, 1996. Writing in the pages of Shema, Wolf reported on the impossibility of postmodernity being of any Jewish interest with the possible exception of Emmanuel Levinas.

74. In Marla Brettschneider's study of the politics of Jewish community struggles over peace in the Middle East she points to the emergence of subcommunities within the Jewish community that are often ignored. Conerstones of Peace: Jewish Identity Politics and Democratic Theory (New Brunswick, New Jersey: Rutgers University Press, 1996).

75. Quoted in the name of Eric Erikson in Loyalty p. 5.

76. See Barry A. Kosmin et al. Highlights of the CJF 1990 National Jewish Population Survey (Council of Jewish Federations, nd).

77. Jeffrey Rubin-Dorsky and Shelly Fisher-Fishkin. People of the Book: Thirty Scholars Reflect on Their Jewish Identity (Madison, Wisconsin: University of Wisconsin Press, 1996). In this regard, I am struck by the advertisement for this book. The advertisement says: . . .Thirty Jewish Educators Reflect on Their Jewish Identity. But that seems a misnomer since none of the people included—all of whom are educators teaching in universities—are in either Jewish or education academic slots. I doubt that more than five of the thirty would be recognized in any Jewish educational institution as Jewish Educators. None even teach the topic: education in major universities, and even if all of them are Jews, none are considered Jewish educators. They hardly would recognize themselves as Jewish Educators. The one exception in the book is Dr. Miriyam Glazer of the University of Judaism.

78. In the early 1950s, the Rosenbergs were accused of stealing atomic secrets and transmitting them to the Soviet Union. They were put on trial and convicted. There never was any evidence linking Ethel Rosenberg to the alleged crimes and nor was there any conclusive evidence against Julius Rosenberg. The fact of the execution taking place on Friday, the eve of the Sabbath, was for my mother further proof of the anti-semitic intent.

79. Block, Alan Occupied Reading: Critical Foundations for an Ecological Theory (New York: Garland Publishing, Inc.: New York, 1995), p. 103.

80. Ibid., Occupied, p. 116

81. I am indebted to the owner of the Milky Way Restaurant in Los Angeles for this wonderful reminder of how English was spoken in the congregation.

82. The term Katzetnik was taken by one survivor as his literary moniker after the war.

83. Israel Salanter (1810–1883) was one of the disciples of the Vilna Gaon, and together their teaching tradition is associated with the emphasis of ethical grounding called Musar. Vilna, Lithuania, where Levinas was born, was its stronghold. A Litvak, is the term for the more rationalist ethical bent of the region's most predominate school of thought andWeltanschang. For Musar the ethical was a Weltanschang and not a series of 'what-if-questions.'

84. Ibid., Nine, p. 99.

85. Ibid., Nine, p. 99. "Nothing is more foreign to me than the other; nothing is more intimate to me than myself. Israel would teach that the greatest intimacy of me to myself consists in being at every moment responsible for the others, the hostage of others. I can be responsible for that which I did not do and take upon myself a distress which is not mine." ("As Old as the World," p. 85. Other quotes from Levinas (pp. 47–48) aid in contextualizing his pre-

philosophy's ethic in "The Temptation of Temptation." "The direct relation with the true, excluding the prior examination of its terms, it . . . can only be the relation with a person, with another. The Torah is given in the Light of a face. The epiphany of the other person is ipso facto my responsibility toward him: seeing the other is already an obligation toward him. A direct optics—without mediation of an idea—can only be accomplished as ethics. Integral (integrity) knowledge or Revelation [the receiving of the Torah] is ethical behavior. . . its messenger is simultaneously the very message)."

86. The source of this quote escapes me.

87. This term, Golus, in Yiddish and Ashkenazi Hebrew is Galut, in Israeli Hebrew. See the beginning of this essay for an earlier explanation of the meaning of the root of this word. See pp. 60–61.

88. This is the exculpatory phrase explaining why actual sacrifices were not being offered from the "Additional Service" (Musaf) for Festivals.

89. This is another classical Rabbinic invocation of a phrase explaining ancient anti-semitism that was "unmerited" and "causeless" hate and jealously. Esau is essentially all anti-semitic gentiles. Jacob is the representation of the Jewish people.

90. On a personal level, this strategy of Golus survival was exemplified by my mother's insistence that she would buy my wife an expensive ring for our engagement since "you never know, you might have to use it (the ring) to buy your life from a goy."

91. The list of "maladies" has shifted in their cultural meaning. For instance, asthma was at one time read as a sign of one's Aryan racial identity. See p. 167 in Gilman's Smart Jews.

92. Daniel Boyarin and Jonathan Boyarin. "Diaspora: Generation and the Ground of Jewish Identity" in Identities (Chicago, Illinois: University of Chicago, 1995) edited by Kwame Anthony Appiah and Henry Louis Gates, Jr. I am in sympathy with them at the silence of Jewish scholars to invoke this category "Diaspora" in contemporary discussions but wish to suggest that Golus means something more.

93. Ibid., Diaspora, p. 333–5. I have scrambled the words in the quote but I believe it correctly reflects the sense of their argument. "Crucial to this construction of Jewish history and identity is the simple fact, often consciously or unconsciously suppressed, that Diaspora is not the forced product of war and destruction—taking place after the downfall of Judea—but that already in the centuries before this downfall, the majority of Jews lived voluntarily outside of the land. Moreover, given a choice between domination by a foreign power who would allow them to keep the Torah undisturbed and domination by a Jewish authority who would interfere with religious life, the Pharisees and their successors the Rabbis generally chose the former. . . . We want to propose a privileging of Diaspora, as dissociation of ethnicities and political he-

gemonies as the only social structure that even begins to make possible a maintenance of cultural identity in a world grown thoroughly and inextricably interdependent." Just as utopian notions of nation states are dangerous so would a utopian valorizing of Golus miss the point.

94. Ibid., Diaspora, p. 332. The Boyarins quote Judith Butler, who asks, "How is it that we might ground a theory of politics in a speech situation or subject position which is 'universal' when the very category of the universal has only begun to be exposed for its own highly ethnocentric biases?" Judith Butler, "Contingent Foundations: Feminism and the Question of 'Postmodernism," Praxis International 11, [July 1991]: 153. My response is that not all universals are automatically guilty and must be examined one at a time.

95. David Purpel. The Moral and Spiritual Crisis in Education: A Curriculum for Justice and Compassion in Education (New York: Bergin & Garvey, 1989), p. 105.

96. The man on the lawn was also famous for timing his Saturday (Shabbat) morning drive to work so as to drive by Greenberg walking to shul greeting him with, "What happened, Rabbi? Did your car break down? Can I give you a lift?"

97. I imagined that Jerome Weiss was the president of "Betty Brew" forever.

98. Marla Brettschneider, The Narrow Bridge: Jewish Views on Multicaulturalism (News Brunswick, New Jersey Rutgers University Press, 1996) p. 3.

99. Ibid., Narrow, p. 274. Walzer discusses the "best" American citizen as the one with amnesia.

100. The "Small World" of the aesthetic is a reference to Ingmar Bergman's film Fanny and Alexander and the world of aesthetic diversion that is portrayed as harmless and yet soulful in contrast to the dour world of the Protestant priest's mummified life across the treacherous ravine.

101. Claire Pajaczkowska and Barry Curtis. "Assimilation, Entertainment and the Hollywood Solution" in The Jew in the Text: Modernity and the Construction of Identity edited by Linda Nochlin and Tamara Garb (London: Thames and Hudson, 1995) present a very compelling case for two kinds of assimilation, active and passive.

References

Alba, Richard D. *Ethnic Identity: The Transformation of White America* (New Haven, Conn.: Yale University Press, 1990).

Alcalay, Reuben. *The Complete Hebrew-English Dictionary* (Prayer Book Press, Inc.: Hartford, Connecticut, 1965).

Anderson, Walter Truett. *The Truth about the Truth* (New York: Putnam, 1995)

Appiah, Kwame Anthony and Henry Louis Gates, Jr., editors.*Identities* (Chicago, Ill., The University of Chicago Press, 1995)

Bauman, Zygmunt. *Life in Fragments: Essays in Postmodern Morality* (Oxford, UK: Blackwell, 1995).

Bourdieu, Pierre. *Homo Academicus* (Stanford, CA: Stanford University Press, 1988)

Bowen, Howard R. and Schuster, Jack H. *American Professors: A National Resource Imperiled* (New York: Oxford University Press, 1986).

Boyarin, Daniel and Jonathan Boyarin. "Diaspora: Generation and the Ground of Jewish Identity" in *Identities* (Chicago, Illinois: University of Chicago, 1995) edited by Kwame Anthony Appiah and Henry Louis Gates, Jr.

Brettschneider, Marla. *Conerstones of Peace: Jewish Identity Politics and Democratic Theory* (New Brunswick, New Jersey: Rutgers University Press, 1996).

Brettschneider, Marla, editor. *The Narrow Bridge: Jewish Views on Multiculturalism* (New Brunswick, New Jersey: Rutgers University Press, 1996).

Efron, John M. *Defenders of the Race: Jewish Doctors and Race Science in Fin-de-Siecle Europe* (New Haven: Conn.: Yale University Press, 1994).

Elbaz, F & Elbaz, R. "Curriculum and textuality" in Journal of Curriculum Theory 8:2, 127–128. Quoted in *Understanding Curriculum: An Introduction to the Study of Historical and Contemporary Curriculum Discourses* (New York: Peter Lang, 1995) by William F. Pinar, William M. Reynolds, Patrick Slattery, and Peter M. Taubman.

Finkielkraut, Alain. *The Imaginary Jew* (Lincoln: University of Nebraska Press, 1994).

Fletcher, George P., *Loyalty: An Essay on the Morality of Relationships* (New York: Oxford University Press, 1993).

Flexner, Stuart Berg, ed. *The Random House Dictionary of the English Language*, (New York: Random House, 1987).

Fox, Everett. *The Schocken Bible: The Five Books of Moses* (New York: Schocken Books, 1995).

Frank, Gelya. "Jews, Multiculturalism, and Boasian Anthropology" in the American Anthropologist 99:4, pp. 731–745, December 1997.

Frank, Gelyá, a conversation with Professor at University of Southern California.

Khanga, Yelena. *Soul to Soul: A Black Russian Jewish Woman's Search for Her Roots* (New York, New York: W. W. Norton & Company, Inc., 1992).

Kosmin, Barry A. et al. *Highlights of the CJF 1990 National Jewish Population Survey* (Council of Jewish Federations, nd).

Gilman, Sander. *The Jew's Body* (New York: Routledge, 1991).

Gilman, Sander L. *Smart Jews: The Construction of the Image of Jewish Superior Intelligence* (Lincoln, Nebraska: University of Nebraska Press, 1996)

Goldberg, David Theo and Krausz, Michael *Jewish Identity* (Philadelphia, PA: Temple University Press, 1993).

Goldhagen, Daniel Jonah. *Hitler's Willing Executioners: Ordinary Germans and the Holocaust* (New York: Alfred A Knopf, 1996).

Grument, Madeline. "Retrospective: Autobiography and the analysis of educational experience" in Cambridge Journal of Education 20:3, p. 322. Quoted in *Understanding Curriculum: An Introduction to the Study of Historical and Contemporary Curriculum Discourses* (New York: Peter Lang, 1995) by William F. Pinar, William M. Reynolds, Patrick Slattery, and Peter M. Taubman.

Langness, L.L. and Frank, Gelya. *Lives: An Anthropological Approach to Biography* (Notvato, CA: Chandler & Sharp Publishers, Inc., 1981)

Kamenetz, Roger. *The Jew in the Lotus: A Poet's Discovery of Jewish Identity in Buddist India* (New York: HarperSan Francisco, 1995).

Kay/Kantrowitz, Melanie. *The Issue is Power: Essays on Women, Jews, Violence, and Resistance* (San Francisco: Aunt Lutte Books, 1992).

Levinas, Emmanuel, *The Talmudic Readings* (Bloomington, IN: Indiana University Press, 1991) translated and edited by Annette Aronowicz.

Lindenburger, Herbert. "Between Texts: From Assimlationist Novel to Resistance Narrative" in Jeffrey Rubin-Dorsky and Shelley Fisher-Fishkin. *People of the Book: Thirty Scholars Reflect on Their Jewish Identity* (University of Wisconsin: Madison, Wisconsin, 1996)

Lyotard, Jean-Francois. *Heidegger and "the jews"* (Minneapolis: University of Minnesota Press, 1990).

Lyotard, Jean-Francois, *The Postmodern: A Report on Knowledge* (Minneapolis, Minnesota: University of Minnesota, 1991) p. xiv.

Meyerowitz, Rael. *Transferring to America: Jewish Interpretations of American Dreams* (Albany, New York: State University of New York Press, 1995).

Nochlin, Linda. "Introduction: Starting with the Self: Jewish Identity and its Representation" in *The Jew in the Text: Modernity and the Construction of Identity,* edited by Linda Nochlin and Tamara Garb (London: Thames and Hudson, 1995).

Orenstein, Debra. *Lifecycles, Volume 1: Jewish Women on Life Passages & Personal Milestones* and *Lifecycles, Volume 2: Jewish Women on Biblical Themes in Contemporary Life* (Vermont: Jewish Lights Publishing, 1995 and 1997).

Pajaczkowska, Claire and Curtis, Barry, "Assimilation, Entertainment and the Hollywood Solution" in *The Jew in the Text: Modernity and the Construction of Identity* edited by Linda Nochlin and Tamara Garb (London: Thames and Hudson, 1995).

Prell, Riv-Ellen. "Rage and Representation: Jewish Gender Stereotypes in American Culture" in *Uncertain Terms: Negotiating Gender in American Culture* edited by Faye Ginsburg and Anna Lowenhaupt Tsing (Boston: Beacon Press, 1990).

Purpel, David. *The Moral and Spiritual Crisis in Education: A Curriculum for Justice and Compassion in Education* (New York: Bergin & Garvey, 1989).

Rajchman, John. *The Identity in Question* (New York: Routledge, 1995).

Rotenstreich, Nathan. *Jews and German Philosophy: The Polemics of Emancipation* (New York: Schocken Books, 1982).

Roth, Philip. *Operation Shylock* (New York: Vintage Books, 1993).

Rubin-Dorsky, Jeffrey and Fisher-Fishkin, Shelley *People of the Book: Thirty Scholars Reflect on Their Jewish Identity* (Madison, Wisconsin: University of Wisconsin, 1996).

Sacks, Karen Brodkin. "How Did Jews Become White Folks" in *Race* (New Brunswick, New Jersey: Rutgers University Press, 1994)

Scott, Joan W. "Multiculturalism and the Politics of Identity," in *The Identity in Question* edited by John Rajchman (New York: Routledge, 1995).

Shapiro, Svi correspondence with Shapiro August 1995.

Simon, Roger. "Beyond the Racist Text: Jewish Applause for a Yiddish Shylock" in *Teaching Against Grain: Texts for a Pedagogy of Possibility* (New York: Bergin & Garvey, 1992).

Thomas, Laurence Mordekhai*Vessels of Evil: American Slavery and Holocaust* (Philadelphia: Temple University Press, 1993).

Thomas, Laurence Mordekhai, "The Soul of Identity: Jews and Blacks" in Rubin-Dorsky, Jeffrey and Fisher-Fishkin, Shelly, *People of the Book: Thirty Scholars Reflect on Their Jewish Identity* (Madison, Wisconsin University of Wisconsin Press, 1996) van Dijk, Teun A. *Elite Discourse and Racism* (Newbury Park, CA.: Sage, 1993).

Walzer, Michael. "What Does It Mean to Be an 'American'"? in Brettschneider, Marla, editor. *The Narrow Bridge: Jewish Views on Multiculturalism* (New Brunswick, New Jersey: Rutgers University Press, 1996).

West, Cornel. "A Matter of Life and Death" in *The Identity in Question* edited by John Rajchman (New York: Routledge, 1995).

Wolf, Arnold *Shema* Volume 26: Issue 505, January 5, 1996.

Zack, Naomi. *Race and Mixed Race* (Philadelphia, PA: Temple University Press, 1993).

Ziarek, Ewa. "Kristeva and Levinas: Mourning Ethics and the Feminine," edited by Kelly Oliver in *Ethics, Politics, and Difference in Julia Kristeva's Writing* (New York: Routledge, 1993).

Chapter 3

The Living Text: Literary Pedagogy and Jewish Identity

David Bleich

I Introduction: Borders and Mixtures

Lately, in literary and other disciplines, attention is being paid to the ideas of borders, boundaries, intersections, crossings, and transgressings. For years, neither people nor genres were thought of as having mixed identities, but now, urged by those who already recognize themselves as "mixed," we are more ready to think of every person and every genre in this new sense. Another take on this situation is that yes, we were aware that people and genres were mixed, but we *studied* them only as if they were pure or homogeneous. What was previously peripheral in our perception has become the main item: The fact of mixed kinds has become a social and a textual issue in the humanities.[1]

For Jews like myself who have followed the paths of assimilation into American society, social and textual mixture has been more commonplace in our experience. Our ways of coping with it have been shaped by how society has hosted our communities and by what our professional priorities have been. As an example of problems posed by mixture and assimilation, consider what Chaya Shoshana reports

> Different. How? Because I am not born a Jew endowed with the birthright of authenticity. Different because others ask me to explain or justify my presence in the community, whereas born Jews carry with them the assumption of authenticity. (One of the most common statements I hear when longtime Jewish friends or colleagues learn of my conversion is, "I thought you were a *real* Jew.") Different because my very presence, very existence as a Jew serves as a catalyst for questions: Who is a Jew? What is a Jew? I am a living

> projective technique. My presence often causes discomfort and raises issues of trust and safety. My presence as a member of the community causes the members to stretch the limits and the definitions and the assumptions of Jewishness.
>
> Although I must tell you: I believe now that we are ALL "different" kinds of Jews. (95).[2]

Because we accept that Chaya Shoshana is a Jew, we also should acknowledge that those of us who were "born" Jews also have made choices regarding how we are to be Jews, thus making us all, each, different kinds of Jews.

In Uganda, there is a group called the Abayudaya, black Africans who practice Judaism.[3] This group of only a few hundred people has been practicing Judaism since 1925. They are not like the Falashas of Ethiopia; they are different in that their voluntary, non-rabbinic conversion to Judaism has been historically documented. Some historians of Jewish life have not "recognized" this group, because they are not "really" Jews. Their religious practice is a mixture of Jewish and Ugandan religious practices, but they call themselves Jews and identify with Jewish Biblical tradition. Which Jews may judge whether this multigenerational group of Jews is "real" or not?[4]

We are not in position to decide who is to be included or excluded from our groups. We may continue to choose our own friends and associations, but how can anyone judge that the collectivity of Jews does or does not include people like Chaya Shoshana or the Abayudaya? The idea of Jewish identity has begun to exist mainly in an affirmative sense, while those who are not Jews affirm something else. The affirmative sense of Jewish identity seems not to be affected by reflection on what the "boundaries" of one's Jewishness may be. We assert and celebrate being Jews, but parts of our identities have been taken from non-Jewish societies and practices.

However, there is a different side to the affirmative feeling of Jewish identity: the feeling of solidarity that was created through historical opposition. In 1926, Freud wrote,

> My language is German. My culture, my attainments are German. I considered myself German intellectually, until I noticed the growth of anti-Semitic prejudice in Germany and German Austria. Since that time, I prefer to call myself a Jew.[5]

Although this path may not have been followed by most Jews in America, it is also true that once we become alert to antagonism toward our own cultural group, we feel our own membership in that group more acutely. Jewish identity as derived from having been opposed has as much historical momentum as does the mixed character of Jewish identity.

II Autobiographical Contexts

Both the history of antagonism toward Jews and affirmative Jewish education and practice have contributed to my feeling certain of my own Jewish identity. This feeling is so stable as to render the question of its "boundaries" irrelevant to me. Having internalized a well-documented history of hostility from host societies, the oppositional aspect of being a Jew is familiar to me. That aspect is combined with other ones: things I acquired unconsciously from the deportment and formulations of my parents' secular Yiddishist community in New York, and from eight years of Jewish and Hebrew education. Distinctive values of Yiddish culture and Jewish history were combined with a sense of living in opposition, increasingly in America, to create for me a seamless feeling of belonging among Jews. Although I don't need to describe this feeling using the vocabulary of borders and definitions, someone else might justifiably describe me in such terms. For me describing myself, the distinctions that I might make follow from my affirmative sense that I am a Jew and that it is good to be a Jew.

The main thought of this essay is to show how the early forms of Jewish self-differentiation in the literary academy represent a distinctive contribution, one that continues in today's literary academy and that has, in an important sense, joined with a major strand of feminist thinking to represent a distinctive perspective. I will review the contributions of Lionel Trilling and his lesser known exact contemporary, Rosenblatt, and then I will present some of the contemporary evidence of the Jewish values now observable in the literary academy. I am calling this Jewish strain in academic literary culture, "the living text."

In 1939, Columbia University admitted Lionel Trilling as its first Jewish faculty member to its English department.[6] He joined a struggle by some Jews to produce changes in the academy, to transform it from a place where only the privileged gathered to a resource for every citizen. By virtue of Jews' minority status in society, they have been a constituency wishing both to get into the academy, and to make it available to other groups who want to enjoy its benefits. Over about the past three decades, this history has been significantly affected by feminism. There are some instances in which feminist and Jewish influences on the teaching and study of literature overlap.[7] In offering this autobiographical material, I participate in the recently growing practice of self-inclusion in academic treatises, a practice partly deriving from certain Jewish values, and I will return to it in Parts IV and V.

I first understood the academy into which I was to enter when I wrote (in 1960) my bachelor's thesis on T. S. Eliot's last four plays. Preparing this sixty-four page essay, I learned how to focus exclusively on the literature, the plays themselves and what criticism was written about them, and to sustain a long discussion demonstrating the existence of a single theme in the plays. My thesis director was at first skeptical of my ability to do this task, based on his reading of my first draft. But something happened, suddenly, and I grasped the genre of New Criticism, including many of its subgenres, special sentence forms, hedges, qualifications, and styles of assertion. My thesis director recognized that a significant change had taken place in my writing, and he admitted that it "belonged" to that class of writings called New Criticism.

This critical school at first included no Jews. Its practice was reasonable in terms of its privileging of "close reading," yet Jews practiced such reading for centuries, though in social contexts different from those in the American academy. When Jews finally became members of English departments, they too practiced close reading. Originally, however, Eliot was himself one of the fountainheads of New Criticism, while William Wimsatt, Monroe Beardsley, Cleanth Brooks, Austin Warren, and others articulated a set of principles that separated the study of texts from everything else that contributed to reading practices. Among the most significant of the excluded matters were the emotional lives of authors and readers, and the social circumstances of the society out of which the literature sprang. It was "fallacious,"[8] it was taught, to try to derive the meaning of a text from either the author's intentions or from the readers' responses. The most authoritative source of meaning in a work of literature was the organic unity of its image patterns and other configurations of language and metaphor found in "the work itself." In 1960, I learned how to practice this "New Criticism," and in graduate school, I did it fluently and understood its value as a means of qualification of academic work. To some extent, I still practice New Criticism.

However, some years into graduate school it began to seem clear that New Criticism was at odds with what I considered to be Jewish interests. One of the prods toward this perception was that one of my teachers, a Jew, was an expert in Eliot, Pound, and Yeats. His course in the New Criticism clearly announced through emphasis and vocabulary the superiority of "intrinsic" criticism—study of the work itself, a form of attention he derived in part from the early critical essays of Eliot. However, the sense of oddness came more from the fact that he taught that the anti-Jewish aspects in the works of Eliot and Pound were distant from the value, the greatness, of their poetry.[9] It was this thought, presented to me about two years after I finished my bachelor's thesis on Eliot, that began my private review (that is, not for print or classrooms) of the academic identities of literature, language, and writing.

Why did some Jews overlook the anti-Jewish thoughts in literature they taught? Why did they assist in the promotion of the reputation of those who libeled Jews? In part, I recognized, the demands of assimilation superseded the need to oppose what looked like small pockets of malice: If assimilation was proceeding, as it was when my teachers were educated, it may have been a small price to pay to mention only marginally the malice also taught by the works of influential writers. Because Jews finally did enter the academy forty and fifty years ago, Jews like myself today have the chance to call attention to what Eliot and Pound did.[10] That a volume such as this is being collected is a sign that the cycle of assimilation is perhaps moving in another direction—differentiation within the whole society. Yet, differentiation of Jewish thought from more established mores of literary study was also present during the more urgent press for admission in the forties and fifties, and it took place through choices of subject matter.

III Lionel Trilling's Achievement

The work of Lionel Trilling represents a way of thinking counter to the New Criticism, whose growth was contemporaneous with his. Trilling's subject, which continues from his doctoral dissertation study of Matthew Arnold, was culture and how literature carried, promoted, and taught it. Now, fifty years after Trilling used this perspective, it has become one of the mainstays of the literary curriculum, motivated by assimilationist concerns of African Americans and other underrepresented groups. Similarly, it was partially in the cause of assimilation that Trilling viewed culture as the basis of his engagement with literature. He sought a society that could include people of many cultures, thus implicitly providing his colleagues with a basis for recognizing his inclusion in their ranks. His program had the virtue of serving the whole community, not just his own needs: the idea of culture as a literary subject matter was then, as it is now, the basis for striving after a more inclusive community.

Trilling's idea of culture is connected with the needs of Jews to belong to the community of American literary scholars, with the historic orientation of Jews to "host" cultures," and with, perhaps, one element of Jewish messianism that teaches Jews that even small injustices are signs that the messianic period has not arrived. This feature of Jewish messianism is distinct in its pragmatic character: Unless people and nations are actually at peace, we have not gotten there. No individual or state of belief is enough to announce the transformation of society: it really has to happen.[11]

In response to the last issue, consider Trilling's response to Eliot's *Idea of a Christian Society* (1939). Trilling's tone is respectful and conciliatory. But his subject is Eliot's "politics," and Eliot's attempt to derive his politics from the assumption of a society governed by Christianity. He credits Eliot with "honesty" (169) in admitting his religious assumptions. But he also suggests that Eliot is "deceiving himself" if he thinks that any church, as a practical governing institution, will be anything but "maleficent":

> If I have tried to say that the assumptions of materialism have largely failed us, it was surely not to conclude that the assumptions of supernaturalism can aid us. Based as it is on supernatural assumptions, Mr. Eliot's politics is . . . thoroughly vulnerable.[12]

As a Jew opposing a literary Christian who has some history of anti-Jewish sentiment, Trilling is circumspect, saying only that Eliot's supernaturalism (rather than his Christianity) cannot become the basis for a society. The middle ground between supernaturalism and materialism is a social meliorist position—liberal, in some people's vocabulary, progressive in others', pragmatic in still others, a vision not bound by extra- or meta-human bases for culture. *People* occupy the space between materialism and supernaturalism; this is an axiom of Trilling's liberal humanism.

In an essay written in 1945, five years after his comment on Eliot's politics, Trilling responded to a conference on the humanities in which he noticed how professors wanted to assign to high school courses the "functions of a whole ideal culture," and to universities the functions of a national or "as yet unrealized world state." Trilling had sympathy with the intentions of these professors:

The Conference wanted to say that it was worried by a society that is dominated by acquisitive ideals, by possibilities of enormous scientific power, and by the tendency of government to be less immediate to its citizens.[13] But conference constituents had, instead, exaggerated their expectations. Trilling's "answer" to this exaggeration is his statement of what the study of humanities can achieve. These humanities are "great books, music, and pictures."

> They will not save society or reform it. Their only effect is the one they have been traditionally observed to have—they give a kind of pleasure which, as their name implies, makes men more human. And that, as the Conference would admit, is the one aim of society itself.

The "pleasure" of involvement in literature and the arts, Trilling reflects, fulfills "the one aim of society": the humanization of its constituents. He may also be implying that humanities education does what others have sought from other subjects in more naive senses: unattainable social ideals were expected to be fulfilled by all subjects in schools and universities. He cites statements of goals referring to broad abilities of ethical citizenship that many educators considered should be attached to subject matters. He implies that the ordinary study of literature and the arts is a clear path toward the liberal ideal, the way academic work should oppose greed, scientific excess, and governmental detachment. Participating in the slow progress toward humanizing all of society is one pragmatic way in which Jews tried to live up to the messianic ideal. Trilling brings with him a part of this ideal, liberal humanism, into the American academy.

Trilling's early essay, "The Changing Myth of the Jew" (1930) published in *The Menorah Journal*,[15] suggests that he expected that his professional identity might permanently represent a Jewish perspective. The essay is a survey of literary treatments of Jews in English literature from Chaucer to George Eliot. Most of the essay informs readers what these treatments were and where they can be found. At the beginning, however, Trilling describes his perspective in more general terms.

> The Jew in fiction was always an abstraction, a symbol, a racial stereotype created by men whose chief concern was obviously much less to tell the truth about the character of the Jew than it was to serve their own political and economic interests and their own emotional needs.
>
> In short the Jew in English fiction is a myth . . . And as with all myths, it tells more of the hopes and fears of the people that needed it and created it than of the Jews that figure in it. . .

He [the Jew] fulfilled the mystical social function of scapegoat, on which was bound the sins of the community.

In the essay, Trilling does not specify for each case that he described just how the literary mythical Jew served the needs of its non-Jewish reading communities. The lack of specificity made it easier for Trilling to be seen as belonging to both the literary and the Jewish communities. He is trying not to offend the majority community: at the end of his essay, he allows that "in the mythical, there is usually, of course, a little of what is true." But he also accurately describes the Jewish community's perspective: literature by non-Jewish host societies used myths of Jews to serve its own economic and emotional purposes. While there is a feeling of both principle and fairness in his discussion, it is still the feeling of one who is circumspect in the service of continuing to balance the conflicting needs of a Jew in a suspicious host community.

In the late fifties, Trilling published two essays showing other features of his humanist orientation—his sense of what culture is and his sense of the importance of the individual artist as a person. These essays, while not argumentative, nevertheless set out a position contrary to the New Critical ethos that was at its height during these years. This opposition is a manifestation, in the area of literary studies, of the opposition between the social orientation of Jews and the individualist scholarly orientation of the Christian literary establishment.

Consider the later essay first, "Reflections on a Lost Cause: English Literature and American Education."[16] Trilling considers why English literature is decreasing in university popularity. On the one hand, Trilling observes, there is significant interest in "literature" in general, including European and American. For Trilling, the virtue of having English literature at the core of the literary literature. But on the other hand, English literature as a subject is "in decline." curriculum was that it most clearly represented a *historical culture.* The study of English literature meant to him the learning of what a culture was to begin with. He understood literary history as *cultural history.* He argues for having culture as a whole as the foundation of the literary curriculum. The New Criticism was the opposite of this approach, aiming to isolate literary texts from everything else. Trilling, while disclaiming a specific stance with regard to criticism, is disturbed by the sudden increase in concern with critical method. This concern produces "emphasis on the single isolated work rather than upon the breadth and catholicity of reading which one was assumed to be the goal of the study of English literature." He notes that a literary work often becomes a "problem" or a "puzzle" to be solved by the student, rather than a part of a wider culture to be understood. The practice of interpretation, he fears, has been narrowed considerably, perhaps in the service of expedience in education, instead of broadened to apply to the scholarly study of society as a whole. "The lively and informed awareness of another culture is still of very great importance in education." The study of culture partly refers to studying the "Other," in senses similar to the ways "Other" is used today. There is fundamental educational value in self-consciously viewing English culture as "other." But this value too, if viewed from a Jewish perspective, is an important strategy of living as a Jew: since one is always living in another culture, it is essential to learn "the other."

For Trilling, this is a matter of survival. It is of pragmatic value to know both one's own perspective as well as that of the "other." The learning of the "other" is fundamental in the process of disillusioning oneself about oneself and one's own situation. Trilling is advocating, before others did, the survival value of cultural pluralism, a value that, in a sense, Eliot already opposed, and even more so when his religious devotion became more pronounced.

In another zone of the critical context of "the work itself" is the individual artist. Study of authors and their intentions was opposed by New Critical philosophy. The "meaning" of the work—which was considered in some sense its essence—was to be studied apart from the intention or the biography of its author. The work was assumed to be autonomous. Trilling, however, says that "it is quite wrong" to think that there is "something illicit and low, or at least un-literary, about inquiring into the personality of the man whose name is signed to the work. . . . No question is more justified, or more beautiful, than that which asks how the ordinary human being transcends himself in art."[17] (285)

Trilling's subject is James Joyce, and in the essay, he expresses his own fascination with the historical figure of Joyce, his opinions, his ways of functioning in society. One of his observations is germane to our discussion of assimilation and Jewish identity:

> I leave it to better scholars than myself to say whether Joyce's antagonism to psychoanalysis kept him from observing that his name and Freud's mean the same. And although it may at first seem an odd comparison, the two men were in many respects very like each other. They share the avowedly heroic

> intention and the ability to wait long for achievement and fame. They share a fierce, isolate pride, and the need for loyalty. They are at one in the point family feeling, especially in the disillusioned attachment to the father. And they share the paradox of being revolutionary in their work and rigorously conventional in their lives, a corollary no doubt, of their family feeling.

This is a comparison of two people, of their cultures, and of the senses in which each person, in being similar to the other, helps to form a common culture. These comparisons also bespeak Trilling's way of living, bringing some of his Jewish values into the new culture, and yet still striving, through kinships with members of the new culture—that of the literary academy and the culture of England and America—to form a more inclusive culture of "humanism." Similarly, the relation of Ireland to England and of Jews to England (or America) may also be noted. For Freud, Joyce, and Trilling, there was some sense in which "their own" was bypassed in the service of joining a larger culture. In addition, the process of joining the larger culture had an oppositional feature in which the pursuit or exercise of "one's own" became part of the ways in which the larger culture was joined. Trilling joins the host culture by advocating humanism in opposition to New Criticism. He thus promulgates a value contrary to oppose New Critical "method," which does not apply to the study of people as individuals and as members of a culture. Trilling affirms the historical personhood of literary figures, their susceptibility to historical and cultural understanding, and thus, the importance of viewing them this way in the study of literature.

Trilling tried to integrate his own historical identity with the different kinds of identity in American academic culture. A part of his achievement that Jews may wish to claim is his commitment to the priority of the study of culture and his attempts within the academy to promote this ideal, even as, in his own time, other contrary ideals of the academy and society were in the ascendency.

IV The Delayed Recognition of Louise Rosenblatt

About a year before Trilling was appointed at Columbia, Louise Rosenblatt, a teacher educator at New York University, published *Literature as Exploration*. This work, and a related one published forty years later, *The Reader, The Text, The Poem,* set out a view of reading that took the perspectives and the responses of the reader seriously. She proposed a different and highly socialized view of reading with some kinship to Trilling's view and in opposition to New Critical principles. Rosenblatt's earlier book, coming out of a 1937 conference on progressive education, was written while John Dewey's view of education still had some currency. It then went out of print and receded until the sixties as an approach to teaching literature in secondary schools. Several factors may explain the disappearance of Rosenblatt's book: the "stock" of progressive education fell; anything associated with the "left" in the fifties and sixties was regarded with suspicion; New Criticism was becoming the dominant literary approach. Rosenblatt's book was rediscovered in the late sixties, as literary response, now often referred to as "reader response," began to emerge in circles of literary theory. "Response" was related at some remove to poststructuralism and its emphasis on the "play" of language. However, some of the "reader-response" theorists of the sixties and seventies were as interested in "method" as were the New Critics of the thirties, forties, and fifties.[18] Rosenblatt's work reentered the academic literary community, but it acquired a living importance as a result of its being reread by feminist scholars. It is also important now because of its promoting of values similar to Trilling's and Jewish social attitudes.

The story of Trilling's entrance into the academy is, as Klingenstein details,[19] the story of how a Jewish man entered a fraternity of Christian men. In the sixties, Jewish assimilation into the academy, like other academic changes, was affected by the influence of feminism. In 1963, Betty Friedan's *The Feminine Mystique* was one of those statements that set the pace.[20] Jewish feminists, along with those from other American minority communities, took on a more visible identity. Many Jews, in a sense, "came out": They no longer behaved as if their being Jews made no difference. The metaphor of the melting pot was replaced by the figure of the mixed salad. However, because women were still not welcome in the academy, whatever Rosenblatt taught was heard primarily by the women who became teachers, a class itself considered as "secondary" as the schools at which they taught: secondary, that is, to the "main" teachers, critics, and thinkers at the elite universities. A review of Rosenblatt's work in the context of my discussion of Trilling highlights her kinship with him as shown in her views of reading, literature, and culture. Both may be described as committed to "the living text" as a Jewish strand in the teaching and study of literature.

Here is a statement[21] of one of Rosenblatt's main contributions—the need, in the study and teaching of literature, to find ways to note what readers bring to their reading.

> The reader's fund of relevant memories makes possible any reading at all. Without linkage with the past experiences and the present interests of the reader, the work will not "come alive" for him, or rather, he will not be prepared to bring it to life. Past literary experiences make up an important part of this equipment which the reader brings to literature, but these have usually been emphasized to the exclusion of other elements derived from general life experience. In order to share the author's insight, the reader need not have had identical experiences, but he must have experienced some needs, emotions, concepts, some circumstances and relationships, from which he can construct the new situations, emotions, and understandings set forth in the literary work.[22]

The idea of a reader bringing a text to life is no newer than the idea of a performance bringing a script to life. Rosenblatt, by alluding to the life-giving function of the reader, brings literature's social identity to the private styles of reading urged in American schools. Encouraging the public disclosure of literary response, she encourages respect for the pedagogical authority of readers' previous life experience.

American society had retained the view of teaching in which knowledge is given by teachers to students.[23] In part Trilling also assumed this narrow view, advocating the bringing of wider cultural perspectives to students *by learned faculty*. Rosenblatt, however, claims that students *already have* some basis in experience to assimilate new works of literature, a basis that pedagogy previously ignored in its assumptions of the "blank slate." Readers, she reasoned, have already been in enough life situations to call on them in the process of more self-consciously reconstructing the literary text. The act of rebuilding or recreating by readers makes texts live. The students and teachers need to have real exchanges for the response process to work.

Rosenblatt describes how the living recreation is not private or purely internal: she characterizes it as a sharing of experience with the *author*. Where Trilling reaffirmed interest in the author as having been a living person connected to the texts under study, Rosenblatt uses this assumption in taking seriously a reader's *sharing* of experience with that person whose having lived is represented in the texts left behind. Rosenblatt describes how in reading, a synthesis must be made between the perspective developed by the reader's experience and the perspective in the text, recorded by the author's experience. Previously considered private, reading, for Rosenblatt, is interactive.

Authors do not act directly on the scene of reading. The outcome of assuming the reader's interaction with a text, or of his/her bringing it to life, is a new idea in criticism: the assumption of an active reader as opposed to one who is only receiving the work through reading. This fact has consequences that render individuals' readings collective. On the one hand, as Rosenblatt observes, the reader's own reactions, like the work of art, are the organic expression not only of a particular individual but also of a particular cultural setting. The reading, like the work, has been urged by a collective situation; readers read as social figures. Because of this fact, the teaching of literature should resocialize the individual reading. "It is important to place the discussion of the text in this matrix of personal response." But classrooms as usually conducted, tend to prevent the use of response:

> If [students] have thus far been subjected to the typical school routine, the tendency is at first for them to address themselves only to the teacher; the conversational ball is constantly thrown to the teacher, who then throws it to another student, who again returns it to the teacher, and so on. In a more wholesome situation the ball is passed from student to student, with the teacher participating as one of the group. This interchange among students must be actively promoted.

In 1938, Rosenblatt described what today is identified as a student-centered class. This style of classroom activity makes it possible for students' literary responses to get a social re-creation, which is necessary to validate the individual re-creation of the literary work by active readers. Rosenblatt assumes that teachers read as actively as students do; in fact all class members should be considered "students" in the sense that each produces a somewhat different re-creation. This collective validation of readings is also the social continuing of an original social situation of the writer and his or her original audiences.[24]

The term "human" appears repeatedly in Rosenblatt's discussion: "These concentric circles of interest focused on the students' sense of a work will involve him in still deeper concern with human relations." The literary experiences reported by readers are characterized as "human." The response process depicts what Rosenblatt calls the "human basis of literary sensitivity." Sometimes, the terms "human" and "social" can be used interchangeably in her work, though the former term has the broader reference. The "human" context for reading is the broadest: it is a center for each reading as well as an ultimate but unlimited perimeter. Texts gain life in consequence of the social situations in which they appear and in which they are subsequently read. Rosenblatt presents teaching as responsible for deepening the socialization of students by soliciting their attention to their reading experiences and then asking that these experiences be reported in "public," that is, as part of the curriculum.[25] Such experiences are then meant to be added to the materials of literary history learned in more Trillingesque senses—cultural history as reflecting the human condition. A sense of connection is constructed out of individual reading experience (the sharing with the author), classroom reading experience (the sharing of the individual readings), and the collective experiences of society and culture. When a text finally lives in its new pedagogical society, for Rosenblatt, its life has all of these dimensions.

The living text as a Jewish idea is related to the main event in the Sabbath religious services: the reading of the law. The Sabbath is more than a day of rest; it is when the law of society is learned, first by means of a live reading, and subsequently in study groups on the Sabbath and other days. The reading of the law and its study are, in turn, connected with the practices of everyday life, including eating and cleaning, as well as business and earning a living. The study of Torah is a religious practice, but in contrast to religion in the Christian sense, a religious practice is one that is integrated into the ordinary social life of people. The life of Torah is its continuousness with the daily life of the readers—all members of the community—even those (women) who were forbidden until recently to read it in religious contexts.

Rosenblatt promoted this sense of the literary texts in her work as a reader, a teacher, a thinker, and as a member of the academy oriented toward contributing to social progress. Perhaps her vision is a secular version of the role of Torah among observant Jews. Perhaps people like her and Trilling secularized Torah by saying that texts that matter in society must be treated as living texts—ones integrated into people's lived experience, studied and changed by that experience, transformed by their transmission to new living communities: classrooms and the wider society.

We "reader response" critics and scholars[26] who have belatedly taken up Rosenblatt's efforts share many of her values. I, at least, feel something Jewish about beginning in the classroom with the palpable subjective experiences[27] we have had while reading and studying our texts, and then viewing these experiences in wider contexts, and then recognizing how we share them with other readers in our classrooms and in other cultures. Those of us today who no longer question the relevance, importance, and practicality of taking readers' literary responses seriously have also become involved in Rosenblatt's and Trilling's ideals of understanding ourselves in full social and historical contexts. The practice of literary response and cultural awareness advocated by Rosenblatt and Trilling have now an important new constituency: those who recognize the multicultural pluralist society and those who adopt the feminist principle that "the personal is the political." This latter principle urges us to expect living texts. From individual "readings" emerge social and political principles through the processes of sharing and interaction. School has become the key site for these processes, and the style in which much teaching is now taking place resembles styles of teaching Torah. New elements of personal experience are now more frequently understood as political, just as readings of the mixed genre of Torah have been given as simultaneously personal, social, literary, religious, legal, psychological readings. Rosenblatt, Trilling, and others like them have helped introduce, perhaps through the mediation of classic Jewish practices and values, hopeful, progressive strains in society.[28]

V Self-Inclusion and Social Purpose in Contemporary Criticism

Today, autobiographical literary criticism is part of a larger genre of academic writing, the scholarship of self-inclusion. In this genre, scholars disclose their senses of where they are in the life cycle, in society, in geography, in their discipline, in the academy.[29] This genre combines their writing about subjects of common interest with the local movements of life-writing. The resulting statements have a historically novel authority, neither transcendental nor personal, but clearly visible as social, political, and directed toward others who can act. Before taking a closer look at autobiographical statements by literary figures, a word about the wider context.

The contemporary feminist movement studies letters, diaries, and journals with new purposes, changing their status as academic documents. Previously, when such documents were studied, they were more often the marginalia of the canonical male writers, the personal background to what was considered to be the main material, the literature. Those who edited such texts did not have the same professional status as did scholars, critics, and theorists who dealt directly with the literature. When women's and minorities' accounts of their lives and experiences started gaining attention in the late sixties, they were part of moves to change and enlarge the canon, as well as interests in placing a wider range of cultural subjects on the academic literary table. The context of the new attention to women's documents was social, political, and historical, aiming to provide a fuller, more accurate picture of what American history is.[30]

Two recent literary voices, those of Diane Freedman and Adrienne Rich, announce themselves as having mixed identities, one of which is that they are children of mixed marriages of Christians and Jews. Their work suggests an identity implied by the perspectives of Trilling and Rosenblatt: belonging to a culture in which being "mixed" becomes itself a whole identity to be accepted in unified terms. At the same time this identity is one that emerges within the processes of assimilation, yet resembles what could be a "traditional" Jewish identity.

Diane Freedman describes how feminist attention to psychoanalytic "self-other" problems (sometimes referred to as "object-relations theory") helped her to "case the [academic] joint" to discover where her vocational calling may be. She cites Judith Kagan Gardiner's observation that "women's writing may blur public and private and defy completion. . . . many contemporary women writers want an intimacy with their readers and subjects as well as with themselves."[31] Freedman reports how she used the feminist critique of psychoanalysis as the path toward re-evaluating and then reconciling conflicting cultural forces in her life. On the one hand there was her mother's Catholic side—people who "worked in factories or service positions"—and on the other, her father's Jewish side—the "Jewish intellectual tradition." As a result of her involvement in feminism, Freedman reports finding value in both sides of her family—"I grew proud of both my heritages"—so that each becomes a resource in her work as a poet, a scholar, a critic, and a teacher. In my childhood and youth, such resolutions were uncommon. Friends from mixed marriages were "nothing" more than they were "both." Even in today's classrooms, there is strong conflict on questions of intermarriage. Some Jews report being urged by their parents, against their own inclinations, to "marry a Jew," while others insist that to marry a Jew enacts their responsibility to keep alive the "tree of Judaism."[32]

Most of us cannot discern how best to act with regard to assimilation and the preservation of Jewish historic identity. My father, an immigrant, concluded sadly one day in his fifties, that perhaps his style of secular Jewish commitment was inadequate and only the religiously observant can really perpetuate the Jewish people. I and others like me who bear the heritage of an immigrant generation, also do not know how Judaism might change as it increasingly recognizes the voices and contributions of women as a class, a consideration that did not occur to my father. Freedman's response to the mixed family situation is a combination of Jewish and feminist ideals—the honoring of those contributions to one's life that promote survival and justice for all people, not just Jews. Her individual accommodations are consistent with (though not identified with) classic ideals of Jewish messianism.

Adrienne Rich's essays make a similar point, perhaps more explicitly; first in "Split at the Root" (1982) and then in "If Not with Others, How?" (1985). Her earlier essay expresses frustration with her having concealed her Jewish half for so long in senses not unlike her long concealment of her lesbian identity. She reports that her "first full-fledged act [as a lesbian] was to fall in love with a Jewish woman." She recounts how it seemed to her at first that Judaism was just another form of patriarchy. Yet reflection led Rich to a temporary uncertainty: "If you really look at the one reality, the other will waver and disperse."

> And sometimes I feel inadequate to make any statement as a Jew; I feel the history of denial within me like an injury, a scar—for assimilation has affected my perceptions, those early lapses in meaning, those blanks, are with me still. My ignorance can be dangerous to me, and to others.[33]

She refers to moments of social mystification caused by the collective denials she had to adopt because she was a mixture of the Jewish lesbian, both concealed, and the heterosexual gentile, both affirmed. In reality, she was neither one nor the other, but both, or all four. In 1982, she is the "poet who knows that beautiful language can lie, that the oppressor's language sometimes sounds beautiful. The woman trying, as part of her resistance, to clean up her act."

By 1985, this uncertainty fades, and while her new perspectives are not more rigid, they are more affirmative and seem to resemble the solution reached by Freedman. One of the ways she aims to "clean up her act" is by thinking through her relation to the State of Israel. She considers that both American Jews and Israelis are "captives of denial." She takes a longer, historical measure of the histories of the two countries as having "swept aside" native peoples in order to establish their own nations. She asks her readers not to view her discussion as anti-Semitic, and she cites an Israeli critic of Israel's aggressive policies to suggest that her views are part of contemporary Jewish and Israeli opinion. Her path toward a reasonable distribution of loyalties is Torah:

> Torah itself is not a closed system; we have been a people unafraid of argument, a people of many opinions. Our forebears were instructed to commit suicide rather than idolatry; yet Israel has become a kind of idol for many American Jews. Israel is not seen and cared about as an unfinished human effort, harrowed and flawed and full of gashes between dreams and realities, but as an untouchable construct: The Place Where Jews Can Be Safe. I think that the taboo on dissent among American Jews damages all Jews who, in the wake of the Holocaust and the birth of a Jewish state, are trying to imagine a Jewish future and a Jewish consciousness that does not stop with Hillel's first question.[35]

This critique of American Jewish attitudes about Israel is also a critique of masculine political styles: the oversimplification of a complex society (Israel's), resulting in the constant need for militancy in a self-righteous cause. She implies that idol-worship and militancy go together as expedients, that Israel as an ideal is cordoned off from real "human" considerations, thus helping to censor another, perhaps more valuable Jewish ideal—the flexible law (Torah), always renegotiated in the light of historical and social change. To this latter ideal, Rich attaches herself as a feminist and a Jew.

But, for Rich, there is something important missing from Hillel's vision of ethical necessity that is the premise on which the "conclusion" of her title is based: the extension of his second formulation, "If I am only for myself, what am I?" This question, by implication, makes a point we can accept: Exclusive attention to ourselves turns us into people we would not want to be. Rich calls attention to the implied individualism of Hillel's first two formulations, to their exclusive orientation around the "I." She has identified a source of patriarchy by showing an individualist orientation in Jewish social and ethical folklore. To *think* exclusively about the "I" leads to the inability to revise patriarchal values. By introducing the term "Others" in her expansion of the Talmudic formulation, she revises it toward the egalitarian, and even messianic vision she implies in her reflection.

The citation of the "Other" is at first the basis of her critique of America and Israel. But she soon tries to include all "others" in her perspective:

> All of us here live in two different worlds. There is the world of this community and others like it in America: Jewish and gentile, men and women, Black and brown and red and yellow and white, old and young, educated in books and educated in what Tillie Olsen has named "the college of work," in poverty or in privilege. . . . In this world of vision and struggle, there is still myopia, division, anti-Semitism, racism, sexism, heterosexism. But there is

> also passion, and persistence, and memory, and the determination to build what we need, and the refusal to buy safety or comfort by shutting up.

I hear the messianic overtones of this formulation. Rich, like many, perhaps most, Jews in history, *waits* for the arrival of universal social justice. When Rich says "If not with Others, How?" the interrogative signals the continuity of waiting, the sense that social justice is not here. However, she is using the universalist senses of feminism to add to the traditional Jewish vision: the need to reach out to the others among whom we are living, and to use the paths of feminism for this initiative.

Rich's vision is also pragmatic in that she derives from the history of others who survived racism a contemporary role for assimilating American Jews.

> As American Jews, our losses are not from the Holocaust alone. We are citizens of a country deprived of the effective moral, ethical, and aesthetic vision of those whom white racism had tried to quench in both subtle and violent ways, whose capacity, nonetheless to insist on their humanity, to persevere and resist, to educate their fellow citizens in political reality, to carry their "message for the world," as W. E. B. Du Bois called it, should be supported and celebrated by Jews everywhere. . .
>
> We must continue to insist that the concepts of Jewish survival and "what is good for the Jews" have an expanding, not a constricting, potential. I long to see the widest range of progressive issues defined as Jewish issues everywhere in this country.

Returning to the principle of affirming "humanity," Rich says explicitly, in new social circumstances, what Trilling said indirectly: There is a universalist sense of the Jewish idea of culture that can be assimilated into American society with a sense of Jewish and American common purpose. In comparison to Rich's voice, Trilling's was so reserved, so circumspect, so clearly mindful that he could not provoke or antagonize the host from whom he is asking admission as an equal. Yet there is no lack of self-regard or of respect for the host on Rich's part. The "I" is so clearly present in Rich and so conspicuously absent in Trilling. This is the "I" of one who has "come out," one who has announced in public what is true about herself and her place in society. It is an I that is for herself, the I that is not only for herself, and it is the I that declares solidarity with others. And finally it is an I that speaks out now and not later.

In retrospect, it seems that self-inclusion and social purpose describe what Trilling and Rosenblatt stood for as much as they describe the approaches of Freedman and Rich. Moreover, except by studying and describing the work of other Jews involved in the processes of assimilating into the academy and in society, it is not possible to identify these ideals as peculiarly Jewish or as only Jewish. But they do describe the work of many Jews who have created distinctive voices in the literary academy. These voices—the ones discussed above at some length as well as those I mentioned in the notes—do urge us to view all texts, the oral as well as the written, as living. This means, for one thing, the study of texts in relation to collective interests and concerns; it means that viewing our classrooms like everything else in society, as places where real social relations can grow, and not preparatory stages for some more important activity; it means using these texts to discover, identify, and disclose our sense of mixture within and multiple belongings without.

The reader may note that my partial identifications with those whose work I have been discussing places me within this viscous process of assimilation. Yet the reader may also wish to consider why, nevertheless, I feel no ambiguity about being a Jew, no sense of being pulled in different directions, no conflict over being a mixed entity with several languages that hold my thoughts. I do not think about why I have no such conflicts: There are enough conflicts in daily life deriving from this stable identity to occupy me for a long time.

Notes

1. Ralph Cohen has given new impetus to the study of genre in literary theory, starting in the early 1980s His key ideas, published in several essays and public lectures, are that all genres are mixed (made up of other genres), that genres are always changing, and that genres are inseparable from their social and historical contexts. Other studies of genre have been in poststructuralism, contemporary feminism, and writing pedagogy. Cohen, influenced by traditions of Jewish scholarship and study, has assimilated into the American academy and society while remaining devoted to the Jewish community. While I will not discuss it in this essay, his genre theory may be viewed as carrying some of the values discussed by the other literary scholars treated here.

2. Chaya Shoshana (L Lee Knefelkamp), "Living in the In-Between," in Evelyn Torton Beck, ed., *Nice Jewish Girls: A Lesbian Anthology*, Beacon Press: Boston, 1982, pp. 91–99.

3. Thanks to Kenneth Schultz, who having returned from several stays among the Abayudaya, shared his observations and his research with me

4. In *Anti-Semite and Jew* (1948), Jean-Paul Sartre wants to distinguish the "inauthentic Jew" as one who wishes to deny his Jewish identity Yet the term "inauthentic Jew" is itself a problem because who is in a position to judge what authenticity is when it comes to claims of Jewish identity?

5. Freud Quoted in Yosef Hayim Yerushalmi, *Freud's Moses: Judaism Terminable and Interminable*, (New Haven: Yale University Press, 1991), p. 41. Yerushalmi quoted it from George S. Viereck, *Glimpses of the Great*,: London,: Duckworth, 1930, p. 30.

6. Susanne Klingenstein, *Jews in the American Academy, 1900-1940* (New Haven: Yale University Press, 1991). Klingenstein describes how Jews entered elite institutions in other subjects much earlier than they did in English literature.

7. One such instance is Evelyn Beck's volume, cited above, note 2

8. Hazard Adams, ed, *Critical Theory Since Plato*, Wimsatt and Beardsley, The Intentional and Affective Fallacies, 1949.

9. A few years ago, this view was contradicted by Norma Rosen and by Anthony Julius Rosen wrote "On T. S. Eliot: Geniuses and Anti-Semites," in *Accidents of Influence: Writing as a Woman and a Jew in America*, Albany NY: SUNY Press, 1992; Anthony Julius wrote *T. S. Eliot, Anti-Semitism, and Literary Form*, Cambridge, Cambridge University Press, 1995. Cynthia Ozick in her long essay "T. S. Eliot at 101" in the 20 November 1989 issue of *The New Yorker* (119–154) analyzes how Eliot's significance as a poet rose and fell in the academy. Although she recognizes that she once was in awe of him, she

offers that "it is now our unsparing obligation to disclaim the reactionary Eliot." (154)

10. Note 9, above Whether Norma Rosen, Anthony Julius, and Cynthia Ozick will find sympathy for their arguments from the general public is a different question, however.

11. Here is one statement of Jewish messianism that represents the feature of it I am citing:

> The Messianic hope is wider than the emancipation of the Jews, it is more comprehensive than the establishment of a Jewish, politically independent State It participates in the larger ideals of humanity, the ideals of perfection for the human race, but it remains on Jewish soil, and retains its peculiarly Jewish significance. It promises universal peace, an age of justice and of righteousness. . . .

(from Julius H. Greenstone, *The Messiah Idea in Jewish History*, Philadelphia: The Jewish Publication Society of America, 1906, pp. 278–279).

12. Lionel Trilling, "T S. Eliot's Politics," in Diana Trilling, ed., *Lionel Trilling: Speaking of Literature and Society*, Harcourt Brace Jovanovich: New York, 1979, pp. 156–169.

13. "Making Men More Human," in Diana Trilling, ed, op. cit., pp. 220–223.

14. I did not change the use of the male pronoun in citing both Trilling and Rosenblatt

15. Which subsequently became *The Partisan Review* The essay in now found in Diana Trilling, ed., *op. cit.*, pp. 50–76

16. In Diana Trilling, *op cit.* pp. 343–360.

17. "The Person of the Artist," in Diana Trilling, ed, *op. cit.*, pp. 285–294. (1957)

18. These method-prone critics include Norman N Holland, Wolfgang Iser, and Hans Robert Jauss. Each proposed a fixed formula for looking at reading: Holland sought an individual's fixed "identity theme" that governed all that person's readings; Iser thought that all readers "fill in gaps" that all works have; Jauss sought each work's "horizon of expectation." These critics did not question the need for a repeatable disciplined "method" for the study of readers and reading.

19. Susanne Klingenstein, *op cit.* Her discussion of Trilling is in Chapter Five, pp. 137–198.

20. But one should remember later, more outspoken voices such as Shulamith Firestone, *The Dialectic of Sex* (1970), and Andrea Dworkin's *Woman Hating* (1974) Other Jewish voices of the seventies and after include Dorothy Dinnerstein's *The Mermaid and the Minotaur*, Nancy Chodorow's *The Reproduction of Mothering*, Robin Lakoff (see note 30), Deborah Tannen

(sociolinguistics), Jean Elshtain (political science), Gerda Lerner (history), Ruth Hubbard (biology), and many others.

21. Readers of Rosenblatt's work will note that there are many restatements of her themes, but that in the reading of her work, they do not seem redundant Rather, they cast the main themes in somewhat different light each time.

22. Another statement of this perspective in somewhat different language is: *Fundamentally, the process of understanding a work implies a re- creation of it, an attempt to grasp completely the structured sensations and concepts through which the author seeks to convey the quality of his sense of life Each must make a new synthesis of these elements with his own nature, but it is essential that he evoke those components of experience to which the text actually refers* (italics in original)

23. Madeleine R Grumet, *Bitter Milk: Women and Teaching*, Amherst, Mass., University of Massachusetts Press, 1988. Grumet details how, in the nineteenth century, the overtaking of school systems by male administrators in the indirect service of industrial needs, changed the meanings, values, and styles of teaching that had taken place in more diffuse, less rigid classrooms such as the one room schoolhouse. The dividing up of the curriculum into discreet subjects further encouraged this top-down approach to teaching. Rosenblatt's attention to response challenges this hierarchical arrangement.

24. In my *Readings and Feelings* (NCTE, 1975), in my discussion of "interpretation as a communal act" (Chapter Four) and in Stanley Fish's idea of an interpretive community, we continue Rosenblatt's early thinking Although awareness of collective interpretation is not distinctively Jewish, it is also plausible that, among Jews, the authority of the community was a more palpable social force than it has been in larger societies.

25. "The nature of the student's rudimentary response is, perforce, part of our teaching materials" (*Literature as Exploration*, p. 51)

26. Most recently, see Michael Steig, *Stories of Reading*, Baltimore: Johns Hopkins University Press, 1989

27. Honoring subjectivity is not a uniquely Jewish value However, Freud and Husserl, two Jewish men, have similarly *socially oriented* takes on subjectivity, to be distinguished, perhaps, from the views of Heidegger and Jung. Significant frustrations in the lives of both Freud and Husserl derived from their failure to conceptualize their intuitions about the social reach of subjective experience. However, the feminist critiques of psychoanalysis and philosophy did not have this frustration because they assumed that the personal was *not separate* from the public, the social, and the political. This latter view may be summed up by the terms self-inclusion and social purpose, discussed later in this essay.

28. Not that there is any hope of their success

29. One of the more dramatic instances of self-inclusion was that of Jane Tompkins in several essays written over the past decade, essays now gathered in her book, *A Life in School* (New York: Longmans: 1996) Tompkins is not a Jew; it is worth noting, therefore, that her discovery of the value of self-inclusion was so dramatic as to be unlike those of Freedman and Rich, (discussed later) whose attention was on *what* they disclosed rather than on the surprise of its good feeling. Tompkins's statements are moving and well-articulated, yet when I read them I am surprised at Tompkins's own surprise when she contemplates how much can be learned from self-exploration in public venues. Perhaps I should not be surprised: Tompkins grew up and lived in a culture in which the personal was actively suppressed and discouraged; she did not think it was legitimate to write on a more candid level of self-inclusion than she did.

30. In other fields, Jewish women played a key role in analogous attempts to broaden academic values and styles of work Robin Lakoff, for example, identified herself as a linguist, yet carefully included her personal perspective in her scholarly work, either as an introduction or part of the discussion itself. In consequence of her self-inclusion, the reader gets a truer sense of the weight and application of the linguistic considerations, especially from Lakoff's requirement that she *cannot* write about situations in which she has no stake. Perhaps just as significantly, Lakoff more often than not departs from an exclusively linguistic discussion, in order to provide an accurate sense of context for her attentions to language.

    Naomi Scheman, a philosopher, considers how being a Jew has begun posing more problems for her than being a woman. These issues are mixed in with her broader, discussions of gender in philosophy. Included in her book, *Engenderings* (1993), are accounts of her feelings as a Jew in alien contexts. She questions what it may mean that today knowing how to live as a Jew seems more obscure to her than knowing how to live as a woman.

    In each of these cases the autobiographical inclusions seem to create a new academic genre that is a combination of feminist and Jewish values.

31. Diane P Freedman, "Border Crossing as Method and Motif in Contemporary American Writing," in *The Intimate Critique: Autobiographical Literary Criticism*, eds. Diane P. Freedman, Olivia Frey, and Frances Murphy Zauhar (Durham: Duke University Press, 1993) , p. 13. Freedman's longer treatise in this vein is *An Alchemy of Genres: Cross-Genre Writing by American Feminist Poet-Critics*, (Charlottesville: University of Virginia Press, 1992).

32. In my essay, "Collaboration and the Pedagogy of Disclosure," (*College English*, January 1995) I discuss in some detail how these conflicting pressures played out in one of my courses, entitled "Literature and Jewish Identity".

33. Adrienne Rich, "Split at the Root," *op cit.*, pp. 89 and 90.

34. Adrienne Rich, " If Not with Others, How?" in *Blood, Bread, and Poetry: Selected Prose*: (New York: Norton, 1986), p 205.

35 "if I am not for myself, who will be for me?"

Chapter 4

Teaching and Learning in a Multicultural World: Who *We* Are

Linda Bliss

It is late summer as I write this. The days are getting shorter, the air feels cooler and once again I find myself looking forward to the beginnings of both the school year and the Jewish New Year. For most of my life this has been a time of introspection, a time for seeking and granting forgiveness for past misdeeds, a time of renewal and anticipation. It is a time for thinking about who I am and to whom and what I am connected. It is a time for wondering what opportunities the coming year will hold for me and how I should respond to them.

As part of celebrating the Jewish High Holy Days, I do not attend school on either Rosh Hashanah or Yom Kippur. When I was a child, growing up in New York City, I didn't think much about my doubled American and Jewish identity, perhaps because I was among so many other Jewish students and teachers in my public schools doing the same thing. Our absence from school was expected and accepted then; it was taken for granted. I echo Letty Cottin Pogrebin's comment about her New York childhood, "I didn't think about being Jewish because I didn't have to."[1] As a college student and later as a mother and teacher living in places where this was not so, these annual dual beginnings have led me to reflect upon the complexities of cultural identity in general and Jewish identity in particular in America today.

These reflections, and my elementary, secondary, and college level classroom experiences in places including a small town in the woods of Maine, in St. Thomas, (one of the United States Virgin Islands), and in the mountains of North Carolina eventually led me to a graduate program in Cultural Foundations of Education and my present work in teacher education. I was drawn to the program because teaching, especially teaching American History in these far-from-New York places had convinced me that I needed to better understand the dialectic between people's sense of their cultural identity and how they participated in important educational issues of pedagogy and curriculum.

It had become increasingly clear to me that my colleagues, and my educational theories and practices flowed from our responses to questions concerning our own and our students' identities. The questions I have in mind here are basic ones: "Who am I?" "Who are you?" "What is our relationship?" Based on our replies, we make pedagogical decisions, including: "What should I teach you?" "Why?"

It has also become increasingly clear to me that educators' responses should be thoughtful ones. They are our responses to contemporary problems and opportunities. Perhaps more importantly, at their core they relate to existential questions of meaning and purpose: Why are we educators? What sort of world are we working to create? How? Our replies to these questions concerning identity go beyond intellectual inquisitiveness; they reflect our sense of morality and spirituality and therefore demand our serious attention.

We ask them in a time that has been characterized as a "best of times, worst of times." This is a time of great advances in technologies that can help us communicate and have increased access to information. It is a time when the deadly secrets of modern plagues such as AIDS are being unlocked. At the same time this is also a time of alienation, cynicism, social fragmentation and economic dislocation. As David Purpel points out in *The Moral and Spiritual Crisis in Education*, this is a time of "massive injustice," "poverty, misery and exploitation," "estrangement and apartheid," and "increasing despair, a time when more and more people perceive themselves as victims and as powerless. . . ."[2] I join him in urging educators to respond to these challenges through our work.

After twenty-five years in these various classrooms, my recent graduate studies have given me an opportunity to reexamine my identity as an educator. When I began my studies, I expected this. I also found, quite unexpectedly, that I had an opportunity and support for reexamining my identity as a Jew. One result of this is that now my own response is centered around becoming more knowledgeable about the relationship between my Jewish identity (how I live, what I do because I am Jewish) and my pedagogy. In my studies, including in my dissertation, I investigated historical, sociological, and spiritual issues of Jewish identity. I came to understand how my own family's story fit into the stories of Jewish immigration and assimilation into American culture. My Jewish identity was enriched by Jewish ideals and values I learned from both the prophetic tradition and contemporary Jewish feminists. They helped me connect reflective pedagogy and working for social justice. It was liberating in the last chapter of my dissertation to speak about the need for changes in educational practices and goals explicitly out of my developing feminist Jewish consciousness.

And yet, such is the complexity of being Jewish in America, that I did not add the word "Jewish" to the title until the night before the oral defense of the dissertation. I finally did so despite the fact that I felt vulnerable bringing my imperfect and particular understanding of Jewish ideals and identity so explicitly into the current academic discourse about schools. There seemed little space for it, even in discourses about multiculturalism and diversity. Afterward, I still worried that this space I was helping create increased difference and distance where I sought common ground and connection with potential readers and employers. I still feared that I was contributing to the divisive Balkanization that identity politics so often produces.

A year later, these apprehensions remain, even as I affirm my belief that educators truly engaged in reflection and dialogue about who they are and how and what they ought to be teaching will undoubtedly deepen and enrich current educational discourses. We need such a discourse, one that will resist and transform the current ones that tend to be alienating, superficial, and overly concerned with either bureaucratic or technical matters that do not go beyond how we can increase standardized test scores or rancorous debates over canon, reading method, or classroom discipline. We teach in a time when Jonathan Kozol's stinging indictments of the *Savage Inequalities* in our schools make the best-seller lists, and have little discernible effect on social or educational policy. As Maxine Greene has repeatedly pointed out, we need a discourse that develops critically conscious, "wide awake" educators who both analyze contemporary situations and develop practices informed by a strong commitment to social justice. We need to find ways to turn toward each other and reach out in concern, empathy, and hope.

Soon I will distribute my syllabus to a new group of Appalachian State University students. They will be taking an undergraduate course in Foundations of American Education as part of their preparation for becoming teachers. Fitting the demographics at this institution, I anticipate that most of these students will be white, Protestant, young men and women who have grown up in North Carolina. Few will have had experiences in ethnically diverse communities or schools. Fewer will have knowledge of Jewish beliefs, customs, or history, or have had Jewish classmates or friends. Together during this semester we will critique past and present American schools and explore possibilities for our participation in their future. I will explain why they don't have class scheduled on my upcoming religious holidays—and our dialogue will begin.

Striving for dialogue is an important part of my pedagogy, despite the institutional barriers to establishing relationships in classrooms that enable dialogues to take place. I have come to believe that people engaged in dialogues are optimists; they are acting on their belief that there exists the possibility of being understood and understanding self and others. Dialogue requires a strong commitment to both ongoing self-reflection and taking responsibility for respectfully reaching out to other participants. People in dialogue are acknowledging diversity and difference in beliefs even as they are affirming their desire for connection and common ground. It is a respectful process, vital to the sort of society I envision myself working toward.

This is not to say that the process is easy; it is not. It usually takes a lot of time and energy. When you have something very important to say or when you find it painful to hear what someone else is saying, it is difficult to listen. When you don't feel articulate or when you are apprehensive about how your contribution will be received, it is difficult to speak. Despite the difficulties of engaging in dialogue, I am drawn to the reciprocity inherent in a process where each participant must be *both* speaker *and* listener, open to the other.

Another thing that makes dialogue such a complex process is that each person speaking and listening is doing so from "multiple positions"[3] or "multiple possibilities of choice and identity."[4] Contemporary understandings of identity emphasize its compound, open and contextual nature. In *Modernity and Ambivalence*, Zygmunt Bauman points out that each person today is considered to be a member of many cultural subsets, a unit of many meanings, an ultimately "ambivalent compound."[5] Thoughtful educators should seek to better understand those fluid connections to places, people, language, and values that shape their identities—and therefore their pedagogies and their lives.

My understandings have been helped by writer and social activist Letty Cottin Pogrebin's reflections about her "wandering we." She comments that because of this doubling of identity, "My priorities are forever shifting, upstaging each other, pulling me in different directions." Like her, I have felt that pull, even as I too often include family, Jews, women and Americans in my "wandering we". I also share her desire to integrate the sometimes competing interests of her "warring, wandering 'we' " in her work and her life.[6] Like her, I am well aware of the diversity that exists among Jews and our other "we's." I know that some of this diversity comes from the fact that "Jewish" is a "uniquely messy" sociological category encompassing both complex religious and ethnic aspects.[7] Like Pogrebin, I too am working to better make sense of how being Jewish (with connections to both aspects) informs my work. Finally, I join her in seeking to engage in work that protects the others in her various "we's" and fosters shared impulses to create a more humane world, finding ways to recognize the transcendent in ourselves and others.

Toward that end, I bring the writings of Pogrebin, Jewish sages including Hillel and Abraham Joshua Heschel, educators including Maxine Greene and David Purpel, and my own experiences and stories into my classroom dialogues. There, I frame my contemporary concerns about identity and action within Hillel's ancient ones. I also invite my students, few of whom are Jewish, to respond. Hillel's two-thousand-year-old questions are still relevant ones for us all to consider. He asked:

> If I am not for myself, then who will be for me?
> If I am only for myself, then what am I?
> If not now, when?

The urgency toward advocacy "for" self and other is still compelling. I hear echoes of these concerns in contemporary philosopher Cornel West's urging us to consider the "moral content" and "political consequences" of our conceptions of who we are.[8] Both West and Hillel remind me that how we define our relationships with others is part of how we define ourselves and that serious consequences flow from these definitions.

In recognition of my participation in the human search for communal as well as individual identity, I extend the "I" in Hillel's first question out to my "wandering we." Because I "belong" to different groups, it is sometimes not easy to know *where* to turn to meet the "deep visceral need" I share with all other human beings, the "longing to belong" West describes that sends us in search of others like us. We turn to those who help fill our desire for "recognition, association and protection."[9] We seek ways to bind ourselves to those who acknowledge us, those who hear us, those who make us feel secure. Together, we face others and the vicissitudes of life. In my classrooms, sometimes this means my standing beside others present because of some shared aspect of our identities (as in "we the good students" who want to share the benefits of education), and sometimes it means standing with others not present (as in "we the different/minority students" who have experienced marginalization in our society and schools.)

The impulse to support, protect, and be responsible for myself and those within my "wandering we" may be necessary for my/our survival, but for Hillel it does not stand alone as a good justification for actions or attitudes. It is necessary, but without also responding to the second question, it is not sufficient. "If I am only for myself, then what am I?" addresses my relationship with others who may be "Other" because of differences between us. As someone whose native birth, white skin, and middle-class economic standing often position her within the American mainstream, here is where I locate my relationship with the strangers, the outsiders to that mainstream. Such relationships concern me; I find myself often struggling with them in my classrooms, even where my being Jewish with New York City immigrant origins has made me the stranger and placed me outside the mainstream of the school community. I try to remember that while it is important to be an advocate for myself and the various and sometimes competing "we's" I claim, to only "be for" those like me is to abrogate other responsibilities I accept as Jew; responsibilities to seek justice for all, to remember the basic dignity all human beings deserve, and to engage in *Tikkun Olam* helping to heal and improve the world. As Leonard Fein points out in *Where Are We?*, his study of American Jews today, to continue to struggle with both of Hillel's first two questions is to live at the intersection between particularism and universalism, and to feel its "both-and" tension.[10] Despite the fact that this tension has sometimes been uncomfortable, maintaining it energizes me and helps me understand who I am. It provides the basis for a moral critique of educational practices that I invite my students and fellow educators to adopt.

Hillel's final question, (If not now, when?) compels me to action. Actually, in all the questions I hear a concern for how I (we?) ought to be in the world and how important human actions are to its future. The problem of my life, and my pedagogy, has been to understand and participate in current cultural dialogues in ways that help me survive and nourish my desire to help make the world a more humane place.

My struggle to better understand myself and my participation in the dynamics that play out within the first two questions and to envision ways to participate in this ongoing creation is part of what I contribute to my classroom dialogues—and I encourage my students to do the same. In our search for common ground, we share our stories and interpretations.

As part of my dialogue with readers here, I offer some personal reflections. Abraham Joshua Heschel has pointed out that too often, "We formulate and debate the issues while oblivious to, and alienated from, the experiences or the insights which account for our raising the issues."[11] My research into issues of identity and pedagogy has helped heighten my own awareness and I hope that sharing these reflections helps deepen your own understandings and reflections, and our dialogues. I am convinced that we should be more explicit concerning how we know what Roger Simon calls our own "autobiographical concreteness"[12] because our educational theorizing and conceptualizing (which inform how we come to meet each other) flow from these understandings.

When I was growing up, I always knew that I would become a teacher. In part this was because I liked children and I did fairly well in school. In my home secular education in general was encouraged. It was seen as an attainable, acceptable way for Jews to gain a firm foothold in middle-class American society. My family encouraged me to see teaching as a step up from my parents' white-collar office positions and two steps up from my immigrant grandparents' working-class jobs. Education was always presented as an excellent way to expand one's economic and social opportunities. Teaching was also presented as the ideal profession for women, because teachers might be home with their own children on school holidays. In addition, I was personally drawn to the notion that teaching was connected to improving the world, to helping people. Being a teacher seemed like a wonderful way to share; a way to help others learn about the opportunities possible in America. All the stories I had heard about education when I was growing up reinforced this view I developed of its manifold benefits. All in all, I was a fairly typical assimilated New York granddaughter of third-wave Russian Jewish immigrants. This belief in education might be considered a leitmotiv of the stories told by and about the approximately three million Jewish immigrants of the turn of the century third wave and their descendants.

In school I had learned to proudly claim as my own an American history that began with the Pilgrims and a Western history that went back to Greece. I was taught to be proud of a heritage that valued democracy, liberty, and justice and of a country that had been built by immigrants who became Americans. At home what little I learned about my Jewish heritage connected me to other Israelites, arising as *a people* seeking justice after four hundred years of living as oppressed strangers among the Egyptians. Informally I learned of a heritage of centuries of exclusions, exterminations, and exiles, eventually leading to the migration that brought my family to the United States. To my family, it appeared that in America inclusion and justice were real possibilities for Jews, possibilities to be treasured. Outside of school I was nurtured by both American television of the fifties and my grandparents' amazing stories about life in czarist Russia and turn-of-the-century New York. I claimed as my own both Howdy Doody and Hester Street. However, as I said before, I did not reflect on the complexities embodied in these positions while I was growing up. Such reflections began when I left New York City to live among people who did not share this heritage.

I attended a public college in a small town two hundred miles from New York City. There I decided to major in education with a concentration in social studies. This concentration allowed me to pursue my interests in both history and the social sciences. I wanted to know more about how people through time and across space have dealt with each other and with the tribulations of life. It seemed to be central to educational concerns. Some of this interest came from the tales of other times and places I had heard at home.

It was not until I began teaching that I began to realize that what is taught in schools under the name of "social studies" is often unconnected to, or even in conflict with what children learn at home about their heritages and who they are. Looking back, I am chagrined at how readily I accepted the traditional views of history and society I studied then, and how ready I was to pass this tradition on to my students when I graduated.

This is in spite of the fact that I was aware that the questions I encountered outside my classrooms in college seldom connected to my university coursework. The questions came mostly from students whose backgrounds were different from mine, or from those who were opposed to the United States's involvement in Vietnam. I slowly began to realize that they were important questions about what it meant to be a person of a particular heritage and how that might affect our interpretations of what it meant to be a patriotic American. These "extracurricular" questions raised many important issues for me; however I did not connect them all to "education." Along with many of my fellow students, I voted to close the university to protest our government's policy concerning Vietnam and our professors' disinclination to discuss this in class; we saw connections between ourselves and what universities ought to be concerned with.

At the same time, my nascent Jewish identity was developing along a parallel track. I struggled to answer my new non-Jewish acquaintances' questions about Jewish belief and the "why's" of Jewish holidays and rituals. In addition, hearing about different Jewish experiences from suburban Jewish class- and dormmates began to expand my own Jewish questions. There was no expectation that what I was learning in this area might be related to the official workings of the university, including calendar and curriculum. Neither did I anticipate the entire issue of my Jewish identity having much interaction with my teaching; I did not sense how alienating this situation was. In addition, at the time I was not aware of the absence of women in both these inquiries into human experience. Now it seems that this was yet another aspect of being assimilated into mainstream American society.

Perhaps because my subsequent teaching has included teaching American history in some out-of-the-way, isolated places, the questions raised by my experiences in school have had such a large influence on my pedagogy. The parochialism of my formal education became increasingly apparent to me as I moved around and taught. For the most part, my students had very different backgrounds from mine. Our disparate understandings of what it meant to be American reflected very different experiences and my attempts to engage them in dialogue involved continually reexamining my own assumptions. I have learned a lot about the histories of people who have not always fared well in America. I have not always known what to say to them, how to deal with our diversities, how to make room for all our stories, how to create a place where we all might become reflective about these heritages, and finally, how to work together to create humane schools and societies that support critically conscious people. Sometimes I think the most difficult thing has been straining to maintain a sense of optimism for such a future and seeking to imbue my students with it. I often sought to expand their choices, and they taught me of the limitations of choice. Not everything is open to choice; as West points out, identities "from above" limit, and heritages shape cultural identity choices.

A few examples from these teaching experiences might illustrate ways in which these issues have been part of my career as an educator. My first teaching position was in 1979, in a public junior high school in St. Thomas, where I taught American history. My West Indian students there were almost all poor and working-class young people of color. I learned much about the African roots of American history that year, as they were an important part of the official curriculum. Unlike the program I had studied ten years before, this school curriculum began in Africa, and then proceeded to the indigenous cultures in the Western Hemisphere that existed in the time before European expansion and conquest. Then the European story was added, like the third leg of a stool, to support the entity known as "American history." The curriculum, and the students in St. Thomas, provided me with a new lens with which to see America's history. The old one has seemed woefully inadequate ever since.

My students heard about my America, the great land of bounty and promise. I learned to see racism and imperialism I hadn't seen before. My learning often happened when I tried to answer my students' questions about their ancestors' places in the story or about the general history of black people in America. One of their thorniest questions had to do with the Civil War. It took place over a decade after the governor of the Danish West Indies (including St. Thomas) freed the slaves in response to their peaceful revolt. My students wanted to know why, given the pattern of manumission throughout the Western Hemisphere, white people in America still fought to keep black people in slavery. Their questions about American racism were troubling and made me analyze my own whiteness as I not done before. Heschel says that "knowing is not due to coming upon something, naming and explaining it. Knowing is due to something forcing itself upon us."[13] That year I came to know of some of the insidious effects of racism that I had been able to ignore before. The inclusion of disturbing racial aspects of American history was very powerful; it made me search very hard for "our" America. Finding common ground with these young people was often difficult. I was unprepared to teach them. In my teacher training I had not learned to ask of my students, "Who are you?" or to ask of them and myself, "What can I teach you? What should I teach you?" Ultimately, convincing many of them that it was possible for poor people of color to do better economically and find social justice in America proved beyond my limited "new teacher" abilities. Frustrated, I left the school at the end of the year.

Today, I am thankful for much that I learned there. While teaching at this school, I learned about some of the choices for people who attended a school where books were hard to come by, supplies almost nonexistent, and the academic failure rate consistently around 80 percent. It was a school where the level of violence was usually at the simmering point. I learned in a very visceral way about how such surroundings can shape people's understanding of their choices and chances for changing their lives.

My experience teaching at this school also gave me a deeper understanding of how important it is for a school curriculum to include information about and affirmation of the variety of peoples in America. I support this primary point of multicultural education today. However, it troubles me that there was little psychic space in this school for me to affirm my support for multiculturalism by affirming a strong Jewish identity. Considering people primarily as members of almost homogeneous groups whose members share a skin color not only ignores important differences that people experience within those groups, but also leaves little room for inclusion of other aspects of our human variety. I am also concerned that affirming *only* group identity of any sort also squeezes the individual, with all his or her uniqueness, out of the discussions. Both help strengthen stereotypes and weaken opportunities for building community across groups. They make it more difficult to recognize potential "we's." In addition, I believe that our critiques of race, racism, and the European conquest would have been enriched by inclusion of both the 1492 forced expulsion and confiscation of wealth of all the Jews from Spain and the nineteenth-century transformation of Southern and Eastern European immigrants into "white people" in the United States. Within these critiques we might also have found more common ground than we did.

Years later, my mostly working-class, white, Appalachian students in a North Carolina high school knew very little about either the heritage of my former West Indian students, or my own, equally foreign New York Jewish (immigrant) one. Many of my students in this rural mountain community spoke about an American identity that did not stem from immigrant ancestors. They saw their ancestors as Americans, not immigrants to America. Immigrants have come since the nation was started by those Americans, however, and if I chose to consider myself the descendant of immigrants then that was my decision. They preferred that I not pursue this line of questioning, however: it put distance between us when I was trying to create community.

I came to this school still believing in the power of education to improve people's lives. However, my struggle to make this condition, this offer, a real part of my students' lives continually brought home to me how closely their receptivity was tied to the connections they felt to me. For example, it was difficult for these students to consider me part of their "we." Many of their immigrant ancestors had arrived as the United States was forming as a nation. As Bauman points out in *Modernity and Ambivalence*, the building of modern, nontribal nations depends on the residents being redefined as *friends*, and then these friends being redefined as *natives* and *patriots*. Connections, rights, and privileges are extended to the other native/patriots, but no further. Foes are to be opposed, and strangers are to be convinced to either become friends, or be declared foes. I often got the feeling that my decision to position us all as the descendants of immigrants reinforced both their view of me as stranger and their own as natives instead of providing us with a common identity. The harder I tried to reveal the complexities I saw within the development of the American nation and American culture, the harder it seemed for them to accept me as a friend/native and my theories as reasonable and patriotic ones.

Equally alien for them was my emphasis on the multiethnic nature of American history and contemporary society. The school was located in a strongly homogeneous Protestant fundamentalist community, and my being Jewish also made me a social stranger in their midst. This went beyond their feeling sorry for me because I didn't celebrate Christmas. It meant that, unless I saw the error of my (Jewish) ways, I was going to hell. I am thankful to the student who actually talked to me about this. He was troubled by this idea, and wanted to find out what I thought about it. He spoke out of concern for me and I appreciated both his candor and his concern. His comments indicated both a distance that appalled me, and a caring that touched me. I will always remember with gratitude his willingness to reach out and engage me in this conversation about something so important to him. In a sense, he was asking important questions about identity, relationship, and the content and goals of education. In our ongoing after-class discussions that ensued, I got a hint of what good education in a democracy of diverse people might include.

At that school, however, more typical were distances related to being different. My accent, style of communication, and language revealed my Northern roots. I quickly found out that even my use of the term *Civil War* rather than *The War Between the States* emphasized my non-Southerner Otherness.

This war was the defining moment in American history for these young men and women, but for different reasons than for my previous students. As white Southerners they often saw themselves as the descendants of people who lost their noble struggle for freedom and self-determination. When I questioned their sense of resignation or their pessimism about bringing about positive change through united popular effort, they often told me, "That may be the way things happen in New York, Mrs. Bliss, but let me tell you about how things work around here." And then they would tell me of how the wealthy people had always run things around here. I felt that too often, the way they "knew" their history disempowered them and my attempts to help them change that understanding made me even more of a stranger in their midst, thus making it more difficult for them to believe anything I said.

As I taught history, my students' and my "American" stories rubbed against each other. Sometimes the resulting sparks illuminated sides of America we hadn't seen before; the similarities and differences in our heritages were brought into sharper focus. The longer I have taught, the more strongly I believe that it is crucial for us to seriously struggle with these issues in our schools. My experiences have also taught me that this is a very difficult task. Our cultural differences in classrooms sharpen the struggle at the same time they make seeking a humane, supportive common ground even more important.

My own search took me into teacher education. My first college positions were as a social studies methods instructor and general student teacher supervisor. These roles, in turn left me discouraged at the overwhelmingly technical and bureaucratic nature of educational endeavors and discourse I found myself participating in. Too often the institutional emphases seemed to be on developing efficient lesson plans; learning approved curriculum, grading, discipline and attendance guidelines; and helping new teachers fit into existing schools. Student evaluation was based on competence demonstrated in these areas.

There was too little time, space, or institutional support for reflection, questioning, and dialogue about what ought to be taught and why. Once again, I found myself questioning my goals as an educator, and becoming frustrated at my own ignorance of alternatives and inability to change conditions.

These recurring questions and frustrations led me back to graduate school. It was important to me to find a place where I felt that these concerns would be seriously addressed. I sought a safe, supportive place for this rather daunting midlife identity reexamination. I was ready to respond to an invitation to be analytic, critically questioning, and introspective. When I had started teaching, I had a rather simple, naive sense of optimism and possibility. My experiences "in the trenches" had discouraged and disoriented me. I sought a more mature, knowledgeable, powerful sense of commitment and possibility. I was open to suggestions about how to become an educator whose theories and practices both integrated and strengthened her connections to her diverse students, communities, and heritages. I looked for a place where the faculty and other students would be understanding, supportive, and interested in engaging in dialogue with me about what sort of world we were creating and supporting through our work as educators. I found this in the cultural foundations of education program in the University of North Carolina at Greensboro. One of the most unexpected pleasures of my life is that Jewish ideals and experiences were included in these dialogues.

In general, we students were encouraged to become more knowledgeable about the grounding for our understandings of important issues including how we understood our relationships to these issues. We were encouraged to question our hitherto taken for granted worlds, to value being critically conscious about how we live our lives, to consider alternatives. The program was dedicated to helping us (students) become "wide-awake" to the underlying moral dimensions of social and educational issues. We were challenged to commit ourselves to seeking social justice in part through engaging in principled educational practices. It was not acceptable to exclude questions of purpose and meaning or to limit the discourse to technological and bureaucratic matters. Considerations of what was good and right, what was compassionate and just, were always appropriate.

As I deepened my analyses and understandings, one of the most significant and far-reaching things I took from this extraordinary experience was a stronger language of critique and possibility. An integral part of this language seeks to affirm and strengthen the modern democratic ideals of justice, freedom and equality that undergird so much American rhetoric and so many of its dreams. My immigrant grandparents were impressed with the degree to which they were included in these promises. In part, because I share their gratitude, I seek ways to work with others toward social justice. I recognize that these ideals are complex concepts whose definitions and explanations are contested between the left and the right in our society today, but I am ultimately hopeful that some agreements across political orientations can be forged around an understanding that, to quote Henry Giroux, these "principles and rights embodied in the democratic revolution that has progressed in the West over the last three centuries" are rooted in "the capacity of individuals to be moved by human suffering so as to remove its [social and economic] causes. . . ."[14]

This Enlightenment heritage affirms that human relationship and sense of agency are integral to democratic movements. It acknowledges individual and communal responsibility for improving existing social and economic conditions. More pointedly, I believe it acknowledges that the injustices and inequalities in our society cause unnecessary human suffering and demands that we take action to change this situation. As educators, through our lives and our labors, we should be advocates for education dedicated to the development of both analytical and technical skills *and* the feelings of empathy that will move people to use these skills toward the establishment of a more democratic, equitable society. I believe that in such a society the participants in the cultural dialogues about how the ideals of justice, freedom, and equality might be further integrated into our schools and society should reflect the society's diversity of ethnic heritages and economic situations. In such a society these democratic ideals are not conflated to capitalism's marketplace needs.

As Giroux points out, this calls for educators to be social analysts who have an opportunity to publicly exhibit "moral courage" and be "transformative intellectuals," making "organic connections with the historical traditions that provide them and their students with a voice, history, and sense of belonging."[15] Educators know this is not an easy task. I continue to find that my ability to make these "organic connections" is related to my ability to recognize or re-create shared "historical traditions." In my present work this means that I find it easier to make these connections with my students when we discuss our desires to be involved in "doing good" in society and to reproduce in our classrooms the best of our own educational experiences. It is much more difficult for me to make these connections when we discuss how people's experiences in school are affected by their racial/ethnic/religious identities. Most of my present students are white, Protestant, working- and middle-class young people who have grown up in fairly homogeneous small towns of North Carolina. Ethnicity is a foreign concept to them, and they tend to exoticize both the differences and the people who claim ethnicity as part of their identity. Sharing and analyzing my experiences as a Jew in America and in the public schools becomes problematic in this setting. I do so, knowing that I am often disrupting rather than supporting the historical and contemporary cultural understandings these students bring to my class. I do so, proposing and articulating new understandings, because it is important for my students to feel that they are also participating in their naming and shaping. I am challenging these future teachers to think about how they might reinterpret their/my/our history and culture to be more pluralistic. I am calling on them to relate the democratic ideals they aver to me, and to others who are also somehow different from them; especially those whose differences make them easier to marginalize and exclude from the American mainstream. I am challenging them to listen for the experiences of people who are suffering and inviting them to be empathetic to these strangers. I am calling on them to recognize our shared humanity. I also encourage them to imagine participating in democratic, nurturing schools and belonging to a more humane society that didn't consider our society's tendencies toward intensive competitiveness, excessive consumerism, and increasing sense of alienation and hopelessness as either inevitable or acceptable. I urge them to consider ways of acting on their responsibilities as educated human beings and members of a democratic society.

For many of my Appalachian students, these are extremely challenging things to consider. They seem unrealistic options, too far removed from the authoritarian world they know to be seriously considered. It is difficult to ask new questions and change how we fundamentally perceive our places in the world. Through films, readings, and classroom discussions and exercises that invite review and revision I work to help these future teachers consider these interpretations and alternatives to be both viable and attractive.

Such imagining and planning requires both rigorous critique and a sense of possibility and hope. The critiques often reveal privilege and pain, and the injustices we inflict on each other. Giroux rightly points out, anyone engaged in this "critical pedagogy" must explore:

> in programmatic terms a language of possibility that is capable of thinking risky thoughts, that engages in a project of hope, and points to the horizon of the "not yet." A language of possibility does not have to dissolve into a reified from of utopianism; instead, it can be developed as a precondition for nourishing convictions that summon up the courage to imagine a different and more just world and to struggle for it. A language of moral and political possibility is more than an outmoded vestige of humanist discourse. It is central to responding not only with compassion to human beings who suffer and agonize but also with a politics and a set of pedagogical practices that can refigure and change existing narratives of domination into images and concrete instances of a future which is worth fighting for.[16]

As I presently seek to develop such practices, my language of possibility in the classroom is grounded in both these democratic ideals and a rich, fundamentally optimistic prophetic Jewish tradition. The latter reminds us that all human beings, through their daily actions, affect what sort of world we live in. This gives us both great responsibility and great opportunity. Despite the fact that being human means that we are fallible, imperfect, and sometimes prone to forgetting our power for good, I draw strength from the knowledge that we are also beings capable of participating in *Tikkun Olam*, helping heal the world, helping create a more just, peaceful world, a world characterized by a sense of wholeness where people's actions reflect their compassion for themselves and each other.

Soon I will meet my new students. Any language of possibility we speak will have to be mutually intelligible, if we are to develop educational praxes that will meet the ongoing challenge we all face as Americans to extend the ideals of "liberty and justice for all" and the challenge we all face as human beings to help create a world of justice, harmony, and peace. In order to communicate my vision, in metaphors and examples my students can appreciate, I will have to listen closely and carefully to theirs. Toward creating a place where they feel safe enough to undertake the difficult work of critique and creation, I will work on developing a sense of "we." From my own classroom experiences I know this is not going to be easy, or always even possible. In addition, I know that educational researchers such as Ellsworth have eloquently described the difficulties they have encountered in doing so in today's college classes.[17] However, as Buber points out, in order for us to "say *we* with one another," I must strive to meet them on terms that will allow for the possibility of us "saying *Thou* to one another."[18]

When we can do that, perhaps we can become educators who help the people of the United States find ways to recognize our general human and specific commonalties (such as our support of democratic ideals) and find ways to work together across our regional, racial, and religious differences without denying those differences. Perhaps we really can help create a place and time where people turn toward each other and rise to the challenge of Hillel's third question: If not now, when?

Notes

1. Letty Cottin Pogrebin, *Deborah, Golda, and Me: Being Female and Jewish in America* (New York: Doubleday, 1991), p. 146.
2. David Purpel, *The Moral and Spiritual Crisis in Education* (New York: Bergin & Garvey, 1989), pp. 111–112.
3. Cornel West, "A Matter of Life and Death" in *October*, 61, 1992, p. 20.
4. Sara Bershtel and Allen Graubard, *Saving Remnants: Feeling Jewish in America* (New York: The Free Press, 1992), p. 8.
5. Zygmunt Bauman, *Modernity and Ambivalence* (Ithaca, NY: Cornell University Press, 1991), p. 95.
6. Pogrebin, op. cit., pp. xi and xvi.
7. Bershtel and Graubard, op. cit., p. 99.
8. West, op. cit., p. 20.
9. Ibid., p. 20.
10. Leonard Fein, *Where Are We?* (New York: Harper & Row, 1988), p. 193.
11. Abraham Heschel, *Who Is Man?* (Stanford, CA: Stanford University Press, 1965), p. 32.
12. Roger I. Simon, "Being Ethnic/Doing Ethnicity: A Response to Corrigan" in *Breaking the Mosaic: Race and Ethnicity in Education*, ed. J. Young (Toronto: Garamond Press, 1987), p. 32.
13. Heschel, op. cit., p. 109.
14. Henry Giroux, "Introduction" in *Postmodernism, Feminism and Cultural Politics*, ed. H. Giroux (Albany, NY: State University of New York Press, 1991), p. 11.
15. Ibid., p. 53.
16. Ibid., p. 52.
17. Elizabeth Ellsworth, "Why Doesn't This Feel Empowering? Working Through The Repressive Myths of Critical Pedagogy" in *Harvard Educational Review*, 59:3, 1989, pp. 297–324.
18. Martin Buber, Between Man and Man (New York: Macmillan, 1965), p. 175.

Chapter 5

On Singing the Lord's Song in a Foreign Land

Alan A. Block

Emma Is Singing . . .

My eldest daughter is seven years old and is enrolled in the second grade; thus it is that I have now attended two Winter Sings at her public elementary school. It never ceases to amaze me how wonderfully the children perform, how happy they seem to be before the parents and friends whom they love and who love them. The children stand literally aglow sharing the celebration of the season. Emma, my daughter, stands amidst them, singing.

But I am deeply concerned by the single voice that I continually hear in the school program. I listen to my daughter and some of her classmates, and I am painfully aware that they are not present in the celebratory community of the Sing. When these children sing *they* are not present in the act. I am not saying that they do not participate and that their voices remain silent; even from the rear of the crowded auditorium I hear Emma's crystal voice and see her shy smile. Rather, my daughter, and others like her, is silenced by an exclusion of her life from the activity. She, and others like her, is not a part of the words and melodies that she is asked to voice and to share. These acts are not part of her culture, and they hold dubious, uncertain meaning for her. We do not celebrate Christmas; as Jews we celebrate Chanukah. But on the night of the Winter Sing, the symbols that surrounded my daughter, and others like her, and the songs that she was asked to sing and which she enthusiastically sung, excluded her. The songs were not about her life; they did not acknowledge the rich and wonderful heritage in which she partakes. The songs and activities of which the program was comprised excluded her voice and her culture, equally as viable and beautiful as the one represented during the evening. When my daughter sang she could not hear her self. Santa Claus never comes to our house; Christmas will not offer my daughter the opportunity to retrieve her two front teeth. On the first night of Chanukah, we will light the candles that celebrate the successful revolt of the Jew against tyranny and the rededication of the symbol of their faith—the Temple.

. . . is Singing

It is Easter morning. Coincidentally (to some but not to others!) it is also the fourth day of Passover. Emma and I are returning movies we rented the previous evening from the local video store. It pleases her to enter the store alone and drop the tapes into the slot for return. It gives her a sense of independence and agency. I sit in the car and watch her prance.

Emma returns to the car and with a pensive look on her face. She says, "Dad, the lady in the store wished me a Happy Easter. I wanted to wish her a Happy Passover. But I didn't." "Why didn't you?" I ask. "I don't know," she responds, "she probably wouldn't understand what I was talking about." No, I agree, I do not think she would have understood. Emma and I have had this conversation before; she once said that she wished there were more Jews in our town so that other people would know what Chanukah is and would celebrate it with her.

Emma . . . Is Singing a Song of Shabbat

It is June in Wisconsin. Spring arrives here late if it arrives at all. Today, the first day of summer—and Emma's birthday—spring finally is present. A minyan gathers in our backyard for Shabbat services. We live on four acres, but behind those four sit eighty acres and woods. Though we have neighbors, they are few and are mostly out of hearing. We are out of sight and presumably outside hearing.

We sit in a circle and the Torah sits on a table in the midst of our group. A Mifgash summer retreat is meeting at our house, and as part of the weekend activities we hold Shabbat services. We are praying, men and women in tallit and yarmulke. *Shema Yisrael, Adonai Elohaynu, Adonai Echad,* we sing. Emma sits in the circle of fifteen people, three of whom are Rabbis, and joins in song. I hear her. She stays for the Torah discussion (today's portion concerns the rebellion of Korah in the desert of Sinai). In the d'var Torah, Miriyam discusses her conflicted feelings for Korah. When she was younger, she says, she identified with the rebel leader, but now she is less certain with whom her sympathies lie. I note in my d'var Torah that for the first time in this Torah portion, God speaks directly to Aaron, calls on him specifically. This interests me because the reference occurs right after Korah's rebellion in which Aaron's position has been threatened. God seems to offer assurance to Aaron by speaking directly to him and not to him through Moshe or with Moshe present. Emma sits quietly and intently listening to the prayers and the discussion until the final strains of Adon Olam fade into the woods behind our house. I see her mouthing words. She is trying to sing. Shabbat Shalom, Emma.

I feel particularly sensitive to Emma's situation because I grow aware that she and I endure a similar dilemma. We both struggle with being Jewish; rather, not with *being* Jewish but with being able to speak as a Jew. The assumption in this community, as I believe it is in most communities, is that we are—and, therefore, speak—as Christians. Christianity here, as most elsewhere, is the language of the realm. A friend once advised me that he had long ago renounced Christianity, that it played no part in his life, and that I alienated him in our relationship by my insistence on being Jewish. I responded that even if he renounced Christianity, the citizen would always assume that he were Christian; if I renounced my Jewishness (as I did for many years) the citizen would always assume that I were Christian (as they did, for many years—as they still do though I try to speak as a Jew in the halting language of the learner). I am and have been a teacher for twenty-five years in the public secular arena; I have not spoken as a Jew because I did not have and was not offered a language with which to do so. That is, I taught as the *Judeo*-**Christian** world (their term) taught me to teach; I used the texts I was given, and they were always Christian texts; I did not know there were alternatives. As Leslie Fiedler reminds me, those texts taught as "our heritage" were really "their heritage—which is to say, Christian and therefore necessarily anti-Semitic."[1]I learned to speak and even to love a language that not only excluded me but gave voice to hatred of me. Now I help others learn how to become educators, and I discover I am using the language with which I was taught; I did not know there was another language. Yet . . .

I read in the Torah that God created the world with his voice—with words. "When God was about to create the world by His word, the twenty-two letters of the alphabet descended from the terrible and august crown of God whereon they were engraved with a pen of flaming fire. They stood round about God and one after the other spake and entreated: 'Create the world through me!'"[2] I learn from midrash that God created the world based upon a model he read in Torah, the existence of which actually preceded that of the world. How else, the Rabbis ask, would God have known how to make the world? The world itself in Rabbinic thought, I amazedly discover, is an interpretation of a text! Rabbinic thought prioritizes the act of interpretation and not the interpretation itself. I have spent my entire life reading and interpreting texts. Textual interpretation is, of course, a primary principle of the critical pedagogy I practice. I did not know it is a tradition based in Rabbinic thought. When I rebelled from the Greek hermeneutical tradition, I did not know that I entered the Rabbinic tradition; I did not know that what is Greek and what is Rabbinic in language and textual practice are not necessarily synonymous. Yet, Susan Handelman writes, "With the deceptively simple words 'In the beginning God created the heavens and the earth,' the Hebrew Bible begins. In fact, however, the statement was (*long before Derrida,* emphasis added) a supreme challenge to the entire classical tradition of Western metaphysics . . . to assert that matter was not eternal, that the world had a temporal origin, that substance came into being through divine fiat, indeed through divine *speech* . . . threatened the foundations of Greek ontology (emphasis in original)."[3] Rabbinic thought, unlike that of Plato with which I have spent my life, held that the world could not be perceived through Reason because there were no natural laws that could be rationally explicated or logically deduced: everything could have been otherwise, the Rabbis taught. Rather, according to the Rabbis, reason might be a human construct and not the manifestation of natural order. Indeed, the Rabbis suggest that God created several other earths before finally settling on this one. Whereas Rabbinic thought saw the world created out of nothing, Greek thought, in which I have been immersed throughout my education—indeed, which has defined itself as education—posited a *logos* that preceded the word.[4] There is meaning, Plato suggested, and it must be found. From this Greek foundation, Western pedagogy derives.

The search for meaning for the Jew and the Greek—textual interpretation—are two very different processes. Western education has traditionally been founded on the belief in meaning and the possibility of the proper search for it. For the Greeks, logos is that which we can articulate in words; logos is, thus, behind the words and inevitably may only be incompletely expressed by them. For the Greeks words could represent things—though not be them—and, therefore, there were always things outside the words. I learn, however, that Rabbinic thought teaches that words can never be exhausted by things. I learn that contrary to Greek philosophy, in Rabbinic thought there are always words outside the things, indeed, even outside other words themselves. I learn that for the Rabbis there is always another use of and an interpretation of text because what is at stake is not final knowledge but practice.

I have learned and learned again that American education has been centrally founded upon Greek metaphysics: American education has always sought what knowledge is of most worth. It would seem that a great part of American education does not know philosophers before Plato. "The first proponents of intellectual education were the Greek philosophers Socrates, Plato, and Aristotle," writes John L. Elias in his recently published text *Philosophy of Education: Classical and Contemporary.*[5] There are in his text no references to Rabbinic thought or Jewish educational practices; it is as if the Greeks invented the Western educational tradition. Well, indeed, they have. But, as Walter Benjamin (Jewish) has said, "There is no document of civilization which is not at the same time a document of barbarism. And just as a document is not free of barbarism, barbarism taints also the manner in which it was transmitted from one owner to another."[6] Perhaps I may attribute the dissatisfaction perennially expressed about education to its foundation in Greek ontology; our continual sense of educational failure stems from a stubborn adherence to logos, to meaning. Richard Rorty claims that

> . . . our Glassy Essence [intellectual soul] remains with us . . . [A] sense of moral failure mixes with a sense of grievance that philosophy—the discipline supremely concerned with 'the higher'—has not made us more aware of our own nature. That nature, it is still felt, makes its distinctive character most clearly felt in a certain sort of knowledge—knowledge of the highest and purest things: mathematics, philosophy itself, theoretical physics, anything which contemplates universals. To suggest that there are no universals—is to endanger our uniqueness.[7]

I recognize in Rorty's listings the standard curriculum of the public schools—at least that of the privileged—but that is another story. For here it is significant to recognize that the Greek model upon which much of American education was founded denied the very foundation of Jewish teaching that might have offered an alternative perspective and educational practice. The Platonic concept of the Real—real concepts and real ideas—a belief in mind that could grasp these concepts and ideas through reason persists, I might suggest, in an effort to deny not only the Jewish voice itself but to deny the suppressing and silencing of the Jewish voice in the discourses of education. Socratic teaching/learning is at the heart of most progressive and even some less progressive prescriptions for schools but not the Rabbinic method wonderfully displayed in the Talmud. There conversation may be defined as readaptation and reinterpretation of the Book to meet the kaleidoscopic changes in the Jews' situation. The Talmud is the written story of interpretation, of making of bylaws, and of adding to the store of Jewish legislation. It is a way of thinking about how to live in the world based upon an ethical ontology. Emmanuel Levinas[8] writes that "Obedience, not knowledge, is the attitude called for by the Word of God, which cannot separate men as theories do. The Word of God is ethical. It is openly so." The question in Talmud is how might the ethical word be obeyed. There are no singular solutions. The Rabbis debate but they do not resolve. A joke—for in our suppression, we speak, as Freud suggests, in parapraxes and jokes:

> The master sits in front of his class of young students. He begins his lesson: "Class, can any one tell me why the first book of the Bible, *Bereshit*, begins with the letter **gimel**?" The class is silent. From the back of the room a timid hand goes up. "Yes," asks the teacher sternly. "Can you tell why the first book of the Bible begins with the letter **gimel**?" And in a hushed and tentative voice the child responds, "But, teacher, the first book of the Bible doesn't begin with the letter **gimel**, it begins with the letter **bet**." "Well," says the teacher looking at the student sternly, "that's one answer!"

The Greek logos on which Western education is based premises a right and wrong, a correct and an incorrect knowledge. Allan Bloom, who was Jewish says, "A life based on the Book is closer to the truth, that it provides the material for deeper research in and access to the real nature of things."[9] It is not the Torah to which Bloom refers when he speaks of the book; his search for the real nature of things belies Rabbinic thought. Rabbinic thought prioritizes a multiplicity of meaning, offers not knowledge but ways to it. But the language of the schools excludes Rabbinic thought; I have spent my entire life in schools. What language was I speaking? Or more appropriately, whose language had I heard, learned, and now employ?

It is, of course, a rhetorical question: I then spoke and perhaps yet speak a Christian tongue. In America at least, how else could I have achieved the small modicum of success I have? How else would I have been understood? I wonder now, when we Jews sing, whose songs are they that we sing? "How can we sing the Lord's song in a foreign land?" asks Psalm 137. And I ponder that query now in this chapter. For even in secular public schools populated particularly by a Jewish population, these songs are rare. Christmas programs are still *de rigeur.* School events are almost always held on Shabbat. The academic world still functions by the Christian calendar; there is no point in asking if Emma's soccer games will be held on Saturday or Sunday mornings.

And more to the point and for me specifically, what does that song that is Jewish sound like? How can we hear and learn the Lord's song in a foreign land? If the Jewish tradition has been so long suppressed, how can I rediscover it that I might learn to speak it? If there are alternative voices in the Jewish tradition—if the Jewish voice is alternative by its very nature—and if I understand my political stance as alternative to the present ideologies of education steeped as they are in traditional Western metaphysics,[10] then how can I recognize what is Jewish in that voice and learn to speak it as a Jew? What is Jewish about education? What in education is Jewish? I learned to read history against the grain; perhaps I did so aware of my position *as a Jew* outside the academy. I know perhaps what language I used, but what language might I use now? "How can we sing the Lord's song in a foreign land?" As a Jew, Emma is coming to recognize that her voice is silenced—that if she is to speak it must not be as a Jew. Emma would be Jewish. She is helping me learn to speak as a Jew.

The Most Difficult

In his *Tales of the Hasidism,* Martin Buber recounts a story of Yaakov Yitzhak of Pzhysha (The Yehudi). "It's no great trick," says the Yehudi, "to be a worker of miracles, a man who has reached a certain spiritual rung can shift Heaven and earth—but to be a Jew, that's difficult!"[11] I know there are differing interpretations, all equally viable, regarding the difficulty of being a Jew. The long history of persecution and discrimination that culminates in the Holocaust bears testament to this difficulty. Central to the Yom Kippur service is the tale of the ten martyrs who died for Judaism under the Roman persecution. I have lived my entire life with the knowledge of the eternal persecution of the Jews and with knowledge of the Holocaust. Perhaps it was this knowledge that led me into alternative paths; clearly Western Christian ethics were not really vital in the modern world. I suspected that history must be read against the grain, but I found no language with which to express myself; indeed, the only texts I had to use were Christian ones in which Jews were at worst, hated, but at best simply excluded. I used them as I could in a limited and perhaps halting way. To be a Jew in a Christian world *was* difficult.

And I learned as well when I was younger and I lived in almost wholly Jewish communities, that to be a Jew was to follow halachah—to know the laws and to keep them. There were, I learned, 613 of them. This rigor too was difficult. The laws of kashruth were difficult; we owned two sets of dishes and silverware though we ate out religiously at the Chinese restaurant every Sunday. The regulations of Shabbat were intricate and difficult to obey, especially in the secular Christian society. There was, of course, no support outside our community to be Jewish; after all, almost all Little League games took place on Saturday mornings; school events were always held on Friday evenings and Saturday mornings or afternoons, and the mall (a new phenomenon then) was open on Saturdays but closed on Sundays. Being Jewish was extracurricular and was not a part of my regular schooling: I went to Hebrew school every afternoon and Sunday morning to learn Hebrew. I never did.

Grossbart, in Roth's "Defender of the Faith" gives some voice to this difficulty in being Jewish. Desiring to attend what he claims is a belated Seder offered to Jewish soldiers by his aunt, Grossbart is beset by institutional and administrative difficulties that prevent his participation. As he comes to realize, the social world is not organized to make access to Jewish forms and customs easy. "It's a hard thing to be a Jew," Grossbart acknowledges. "But now I understand what Mickey says—it's a harder thing to stay one."[12] In the army, obeying halachah was impossible. But neither is there support in contemporary society for such an endeavor: the majority of schools in the United States still do not close for the Jewish Holy Days. How can we sing our songs in a foreign land? Yes, Grossbart, to be a Jew was and still is difficult. J. D. Salinger's great hero is a compleat WASP; *The Merchant of Venice* was required reading; I do not remember one author identified as Jewish in all of my early education. I remember Fagin; I remember the witch's broth that contains the liver of blaspheming Jew; I remember T. S. Eliot's jew under it all; I remember "that Jew" Robert Cohn in Hemingway's *The Sun Also Rises*. I read Plato and Dewey and Sartre and so much educational history and theory; there was no Jewish language in all of my readings. I searched in vain for evidence of Jewish thought.

The Yehudi seems to understand that what is difficult about being a Jew concerns activity in the world. Having achieved a certain spiritual level, one may leave the world, so to speak, but Judaism seems to require not asceticism and isolated spirituality but rather seems to entail engagement with and integration in community. Judah Halevi writes "that the individual [must] recite the prayers of a community, and if possible in a community of not less than ten persons, so that one makes up for the forgetfulness or error of the other."[13] That is, prayer seems to require community for its efficacy and for its completion. Then what are we to do when the language in which we speak is foreign to the community, is anathema to it, and is denied utterance? Indeed, when the language of the community denies the voice of the Jew, the Jew has no option but to speak the language of the realm and thereby lose agency. Where in the academy can we find these ten persons to ensure that we make up for the forgetfulness or error of the others? I think language is what largely encodes the world for human beings; there may be other means of representation, but if we are to communicate with each other, we must finally use language. Perhaps that is why the Bible notes that in the beginning was the Word. God *said*, Let there be light. It is language that creates the world.

What makes being Jewish difficult for me now is the lack of voice or, rather, the silence of the Jewish voice—its ultimate failure not only to be spoken but to be heard. On the one hand I recognize that voice as one spoken within the Jewish community; it is contained in Jewish texts that are guardedly maintained in Jewish institutions and spoken of with great respect and even adoration amongst ourselves. Levinas cites a text reportedly written from the doomed Warsaw Ghetto resistance: "I love him, but I love even more his Torah. And even if I were deceived by him and became disillusioned, I should nevertheless observe the precepts of the Torah."[14] It is in the word, of course, that belief resides, especially in a world where God has forsworn all aids to manifestation. The texts and their language are to be loved even more than God. Those texts are absent from public discourse.

I am a professor in a mid-western university in a department that includes education studies. I look at the calendar for the academic year and I note that school is in session for Rosh Hashanah and Yom Kippur. Indeed, on the academic year calendar these holidays are not listed. How do I celebrate the holidays? How do I be Jewish when the assumption is that I am not and all the forms and practices deny my practice? How shall I speak?

I am a professor in a mid-western university in a department that includes education studies. It is the presumption that I am Christian. When I speak, therefore, I speak as a Christian. How do I speak as a Jew? I have never thought of that issue! All my teachers have been Christian, even the Jewish ones. That is, the literature of education hardly mentions the "J" word; Jewish writers never mention their being Jewish. The presumption, of course, is that they are Christian. And yet somehow education and language rest at the core of Judaism. I always believed that it was *I* who spoke; but over the past several years, I have begun to interrogate the Jew in the "I." That interrogation was also a search, for the language I speak in this mid-western university—and which I think may be a similar language across the United States geography—is a language that excludes Jews. Can it be that in my struggle to invent myself I have used language that denies me? I recall the argument of the feminists who write that language excludes women and that to use it is to attempt to be present in a form that excludes the speaker. Yet I am and have always been Jewish. Who am I speaking?

I am a professor in a mid-western university in a department that includes education studies. For twenty-five years I have spoken in the public educational environment. I am and have been silent. I am struggling to find a voice with which to speak.

Talk to him. You speak shellfish.
Alvy Singer

You will recall that, in Woody Allen's film *Annie Hall*, Alvy Singer meets Annie after a game of tennis at a New York City downtown indoor court. She has showered and changed into what is now recognized as the Annie Hall look;[15] he declares that he never allows himself to be naked in the presence of another male. In a flirtatiously awkward bit of repartee Annie offers to drive Woody Allen uptown and then invites him to her apartment for a glass of wine. Standing uncomfortably on the rooftop terrace of her apartment exchanging empty conversation, Annie suddenly turns to Alvy and says almost ingenuously and certainly unashamedly, "Well, you're what Grammy Hall would call a real Jew." Now there has been nothing in the previous dialogue that would suggest that religious preferences have been part of their introductory conversation; certainly given Alvy's paranoia[16] it is doubtful that his friend Max would have introduced the subject to Annie.[17] And so it seems to me that Annie surmises Alvy's

Jewishness from the quality of his voice. Alvy *sounds* Jewish. It must then be through the quality of his voice that Annie is able to define Alvy Singer.[18] It is that voice that both defines and excludes—a voice seemingly ridiculed for its quality but ignored for its content: it is the voice Emma and I would like to learn to speak. I am listening for the voice in education and I cannot hear it, only evidences of its silences. I desire the privilege to be recognized as a Jew by my language.

I think that this silenced voice might speak to matters of curriculum and education. In this chapter I would like to briefly and incompletely begin an exploration of the significance of that voice—its several silences in the worlds I have lived. Those silences, of course, are mine, and this writing is a beginning to give some voice to them. Because I would like to suggest that the Jewish voice not only has been silenced from curriculum studies (we cannot hear a particularly Jewish voice—a voice speaking as a Jew) but also is absent from the curriculum in the school (our myths and stories are all Christian—even the Jewish ones), or at least so they are read. I would like to suggest as well that the return of this voice might bode well for thinking about and implementing curriculum in the United States for the twenty-first century and beyond.

Problematizing the Jewish Voice: Making it Illegitimate

Now, I really do not know what Jewish sounds like; having had it pointed out, a linguist, I am sure, could identify its rhythms and meters and lexicons; I am not a linguist and why these rhythms and meters and lexicons are considered Jewish, I do not think anyone can know. I know only what the Jewish voice has come to sound like—Hyman Kaplan; Jackie Mason; Fran Drescher, the Nanny; even Stinky the plant, on Sesame Street. I am certain that it is defined not by any one known characteristic and that it comes to be recognized more by the hearer than by the speaker. That is, the Jewish voice has been defined in its difference from the voice of the non-Jew and accepted as a sign of demarcation by both non-Jews and Jews. This is not only true in its physical voicings but its philosophical and psychological soundings as well. The Jewish voice functions to separate the Jew from mainstream society. Alvy Singer, for one, is very conscious of the difference between his language and that of Annie Hall: he says affectionately to her, "Who would even think I'd be going out with someone who says 'Ladedah'!" Of course, we do not know what is different about 'ladedah' or why Alvy would never say it, but we are informed by him that it is foreign and different from his own voice that has already been defined—and self-defined—as Jewish.[19] That Jewish voice announces difference: at the least it declares its position outside normal social linguistic conventions and is adjudged as a result and by the non-Jewish as well as the Jewish world to be illegitimate for serious discursive communication within society. Annie has defined Alvy by his voice; Alvy seems to already have his own anti-Semitic caricature of the Jew: upon casual, almost disinterested, conversation with her and hearing her dissertation topic he says pointedly and sarcastically to Alison Portchnik about her own cultural milieu; "So what are you telling me? New Jersey Jewish left-wing liberal intellectual Central Park Brandeis University Socialist Summer Camp . . . father with the Ben Shahn drawings . . . really strike-oriented." Reduced to a cultural stereotype and rendered powerless because of this positioning, the Jew is situated outside the dominant Western Christian culture even by other Jews. In large part, I think that this occurs as a result of the quality of the voice.

That is, the Jewish voice positions the Jew as outsider, and even by the Jew him/herself; positions the Jew as the stranger, the one who calls into question the very foundation of order upon which contemporary society is founded. The Jewish voice threatens the social order because it violates social mores, social boundaries, and social discretions. Philip Roth's Alexander Portnoy[20] complains of his thoroughly Jewish parents: "No, you don't have to go digging where these people are concerned—they wear the old unconscious on their *sleeves!*" That unconscious is revealed in the Jewish voice, and it belies the order and civility of the modern world; the Jewish voice is not the voice of reason. Revelation of the unconscious calls the dominance of reason into question and threatens the order of the modern world.

That the world is so ordered is derived, perhaps, from the Christian Enlightenment myth of Reason, itself a product of Greek thought. This myth narrates that human progress is a product of the application of reason to explorations in the external world. Human reason orders the world. Western Greek metaphysics argues that to know is to represent accurately what is outside the mind. It is the method of science; but, says Handelman, Rabbinic thought and language develops "a highly sophisticated system of interpretation based on uncovering and expanding the primary concrete meaning, and yet drawing a variety of logical inferences from these meanings without the abstracting, idealizing movement of Western thought."[21] I am reading the argument in Chapter VII of *Bava Metzia*; I cannot begin to explain the intricate and convoluted paths the Rabbis take in their discussion. There seems to be no order nor resolution to the discussion though there is explication of the text. I am thrilled. I have spent my life in books. I have never read anything like this before. I learn from Emmanuel Levinas that

> The pages of the talmud, mischievous, laconic in their ironic and dry formulations, but in love with the possible, register an oral tradition and a teaching which came to be written down accidentally. It is important to bring them back to their life of dialogue or polemic in which multiple, though not arbitrary, meanings arise and buzz in each saying. These Talmudic pages seek contradiction and expect of a reader freedom, invention, and boldness . . . we are in the presence of allusions made by hypercritical minds, thinking quickly and addressing themselves to their peers. They do not proceed in the manner of those who would justify their deductions by appealing to the authority of a revealed and forced letter of the text.[22]

Would that my classroom foster such freedom, invention, and boldness! I think there is much to be said about classrooms and education—its practice and substance—in the language of Chapter VII of *Bava Metzia*. I think I would like to learn to speak this language.

Rabbinic thought, I learn, denies the metaphysics that founds the Western philosophical positions upon which I have stood. Rabbinic thought threatens the foundation of order. Rabbinic thought jeopardizes the Western foundations upon which education has grown. No wonder its silence has been so well effected and preserved. I am turning fifty myself this year; I read in Plato of the ends of education: ". . . when they are fifty, those who have come safely through and proved the best at all points in action and in study, must be brought at last to the goal. They must lift up the eye of the soul to gaze on that which sheds light on all things; and when they have seen the Good itself, take it as a pattern for the right ordering of the state and of the individual, themselves included." The true, the good, and the ordered are the result of education, itself an ordered process; it is upon this foundation that traditional Western educational philosophy has been based. It is founded on a belief and trust in order. I am not comforted. As a Jew I learn that I am not part of that order; as a Jew I do not believe in that order nor feel a part of it. I am a stranger to it—and partly to myself. I stand on precarious ground. Zygmunt Bauman writes that "Modern existence is both haunted and stirred into restless action by modern consciousness; and modern consciousness is the suspicion or awareness of the inconclusiveness of order."[23] Outside that order, it is held, is not another world but, rather, the horror of chaos. The ordering principle of modernity is the categorization of the world into known units in the desperate attempt to escape uncertainty. This categorization invents order: order invents the world: there is nothing outside that order. Yet indeterminacy seems central to Rabbinic Jewish thought: the Jew, whose language threatens that order, threatens the foundation of Western civilization. Schools are central to the civilization. Jews speaking as Jews must be kept out of them for the sake of civilization.

The Jew as stranger, who is neither friend nor enemy, and who is heard and recognized in her language denies the easy categories that structure the social order; the stranger threatens the discrimination between inside and outside—friend and enemy—a discrimination that enables what Zygmunt calls "sociation." And because the stranger threatens the opposition between friend and enemy and thereby questions the whole social order s/he must be dealt with: assimilation is both means and end product, though assimilation is ultimately a blind alley. Assimilation—the practice of molding, in this case, a bit of "Jewish" material into a meaningful pattern—is a paradox; the rules by which assimilation are accomplished are set by those friends within the structure for those strangers without it. Those within define only those behaviors they themselves practice and validate and thereby leave intact what clearly belonged to the stranger; assimilation is always incomplete. Secondly, the stranger who desired to assimilate was always suspect, adopting behaviors—in this case linguistic practices—that were not natural to him/her: they could therefore always be suspect. Yet it also appears that this is the voice the Jew cannot actually lose and through which s/he can speak and be believed, though the Jew may not speak in proper society. That is, only when the Jew speaks as a Jew will s/he be believed; but the Jew may not speak in society as a Jew if s/he desires to be heard. John Murray Cuddihy quotes Freud's Jewish joke, even noting Freud's sterilization of it:

> The doctor, who had been asked to look after the Baroness at her confinement pronounced that the moment had not come, and suggested to the Baron that in the meantime they should have a game of cards in the next room. After a while a cry of pain from the Baroness struck the ears of the two men: "*Ah, mon Dieu, qui je souffre!*" Her husband sprang up, but the doctor signaled to him to sit down: "It's nothing. Let's go on with the game!" A little

> later there were again sounds from the pregnant woman: "*Mein Gott, mein Gott, what terrible pains!*"—"Aren't you going in Doctor?" asked the Baron.—"No, no. It's not time yet." At last there came from next door an unmistakable cry of "*Oy vay iz mir!*" The doctor threw down his cards and exclaimed: "*Now* it's time."[24]

The joke is based upon the curious paradox spoken of above: on the one hand it suggests that under the cultural artifact—in this case, the assumption of a language of culture—a Jew may be discovered. That is, when a Jew speaks, the truth is hidden when it is spoken in the use of anything but its Jewish voice. The conclusion might be reached: Jews are deceptive and assimilation fails. But the joke suggests as well that the Jew may be understood only when it speaks as a Jew—that is, when s/he speaks in a recognizable Jewish voice. And then, of course, it is the voice of the stranger and it can be dismissed. Assimilation is impossible. To want to speak like the Other is to acknowledge the power of the Other and to broadcast to that Other its power—thus for the sake of order and continued dominance—or for a mistaken hope for power—the Jewish voice is minimized. And rendered invalid.

The Jewish voice has always been suspect and it has, perhaps, always denoted the Jew as stranger. The Jewish voice has functioned to demarcate the Jew from society. It has been made to do so by the categorization, reinscription, and usurpation of that voice by Western and Christian philosophies. Sander Gilman writes that the Jewish voice ". . . becomes a sign of one's difference, of the dis-ease of being Jewish."[25] And so the Jewish voice in the history of Western civilization is absent except in its illegitimacy—a subject of derision and satire; when we speak of cultural models and products it is a Western Christian culture of which we speak. And to do so we must employ a Christian voice; it is, we have learned, the only legitimate voice that can speak the truth.

Gilman remarks, in fact, that the movement of the Gospels is the movement toward the denial of Jesus's Jewish voice: Whereas in the Gospels of Matthew and Mark Jesus's last words are written in Aramaic and require translation into the vernacular, "In Luke and John there is no need for translation or interpretation. The language of the passage is completely transparent to the Christian reader of the Gospels. The reader of the passage in Luke and John understands that Jesus speaks the same language as the reader; in the former Gospels Jesus's language is not transparent: he speaks another tongue."[26] That is, in the latter Gospels Jesus no longer *sounds* Jewish and his words, therefore, need no translation. Gilman writes that "The Jew who sounds Jewish, for some American Jews, represents the hidden Jew within, the corrupt Jew of the Gospel, the mark of difference which offends even after the Jew is integrated into mainstream of American culture."[27] It is this voice that requires secrecy and inspires suspicion and derision; that voice contains the stereotype that defines the Jew as outsider, as stranger. It is Fran Drescher's voice that differentiates her from the clearly WASPish house in which she serves as Nanny, the ultimate joke on the position of the stereotyped Jewish princess, who in this case achieves her central and powerful household place as an unmarried servant. It is the voice that Annie Hall hears spoken by Alvy Singer.

It is this voice that the Jew attempts to lose in order to assimilate. That voice has been silenced in those efforts of North American Jews to assimilate. Leslie Fiedler writes that it was only when he had returned to Italy at the age of seventy that he realized that he might finish the essay "What Can We Do About Fagin?" that concerned anti-Semitism in the canonical literature and that he had unsatisfactorily begun at the age of thirty-five. "It was only at that point," he writes, "I realized that to do the job right I would have to incorporate into my original piece the doubts that first assailed me in Urbino: doubts about whether assimilation into the traditional High Culture of the West did not mean for me—offspring of plebeian Eastern European Jews—a kind of apostasy, a falsification of my very identity."[28] I, too, have spent my life in the Western canon desiring to belong to it; whose language did I speak? What did I say? Sander Gilman writes that the demand that the Bible be read as a precursor to the coming of Christ reinscribes the Jewish voice. "The entire story of the Jews is reduced to a preamble to the coming of Christ" and silences the voice of the Jew, reinscribing the story in an alien milieu.[29] Thus, the Jew who sounds Jewish, Gilman argues, is the counterimage of the hidden language of the Jew; the silent Jew maintains his difference in his silence. As John Murray Cuddihy and others note, this "return of the (y)id" creates antisocial behavior and must be transformed. It might be possible in studying the usurpation of the Jewish voice that we might begin to understand how my voice as student and educator—how the voices of my students—has been effectively silenced by and in the discourses of education. To read history against the grain would be to discover the hidden voices of Jewish traditions, beliefs, and practices in education; to read history against the grain would be to hear the

Jewish voice in traditional pedagogical discourse and to reveal the suppression and translation of that voice; to read history against the grain would be, perhaps, to expose to American education an alternative pedagogy that might be truly transformative.

Articulating Moments: On the Silence of the Jewish Voice in Curriculum Studies

Thus it can be said and for my purposes here that this socially recognizable yet socially illegitimate Jewish voice has been effectively silenced in the schools—except as stereotype—and is veritably absent from curriculum studies. When I presently speak about curriculum in my classes, when I practice curriculum, I am constrained to enter the Christian conversation about curriculum theory and employ the language of that realm. I speak from a position of silence; I would now like to briefly articulate some of those spaces of silence. It is my beginning. It is my hope that those spaces may soon be filled with song.

For example:

William H. Schubert, in his synoptic text on curriculum, traces the history of curriculum, as do so many authors, back to the Greeks. He writes that "The primary origins of curriculum today can be traced to ancient Greece."[30] Perhaps this is so; I have been educated in a Western Greco-Christian voice. Schubert makes no mention, however, of the influence of the Hebrew on the Greek, and in this denial he suppresses the Jewish influences on American education and perpetuates the long silence of the Jewish voice. Nor does Schubert make mention of the contempt with which the Greeks held Jewish thought and textual practice and how Greek thought developed in opposition to Jewish praxis. That is, the structures of Western education sit atop a silenced, unacknowledged, Jewish foundation. That silence given voice offers the possibility of change. Excluding Jewish thought was necessary in the reinscription of the world by the Greeks and the early Christians to justify their worldview; the Jewish voice threatened the unity to which the Greek aspired and that the Christian sought. Thus, Emmanuel Levinas understands that the process of translating the Talmud into the idiom of today is a process of translating the Hebrew into Greek and the Greek into Hebrew; I must learn to read both Hebrew and Greek. Thus far I have been taught only the latter not learning its relationship to the former. I must teach myself Hebrew. It is only then that I may begin to speak.

Schubert proceeds: "The educational curriculum of the Middle Ages was indisputably Christianity . . . To gain perspective on curriculum thought and practice in the Middle Ages, one must begin with the origins of Christianity."[31] Though not exhaustive, Schubert does present the development of Christianity and its developing relation to the Western world. Yet what is not part of Schubert's discourse is how Christianity delegitimized, usurped, and reinscribed the Jewish voice and therefore altered forever pedagogical purpose and practice. The origins of Christianity in Schubert's account do not note, for example, how Paul's insistence on personal mediation (Jesus as mediator) replaces the textual mediation of Jewish practice. For Christianity, faith in Jesus substitutes for the immediacy of textual authority and the primacy of interpretation. Handelman writes that "In place now of textual mediation is personal mediation through the figure of the new redeemer, whose presence has ended the long metonymy of Jewish history . . . ."[32] For example, in Romans 10:4, Paul writes, "For Christ is the end of the law, that everyone who has faith may be justified." Interpretation is ended with Jesus's word; the text is made flesh, and meaning is based in acceptance of his meaning. The whole pedagogical process that will become the Talmud and its methodology is denied.

Interpretation is constrained by this textual practice. For if faith in Jesus replaces faith in the text, then the concern is for the meaning of Jesus and his words and not for text. It is what Jesus meant and not what I interpret the text to have said that is paramount. To be understood Jesus told stories, but these stories had specific and finally knowable meaning; Matthew writes (13: 34–35) that "In all this teaching to crowds Jesus spoke in parables: in fact he never spoke to them without a parable. This was to fulfill the prophecy of Isaiah . . ." Thus metaphor, in which meaning derives from a linguistic arrangement that is based in a denial of difference and in which the letter of the text is meant to be transparent, comes to predominate in textual practice, and the possibility of meanings is constrained. Jesus remarks that parables are easier to understand than the complexities of law; the people, he complains, "look without seeing, and listen without hearing or understanding."[33] The true meaning of the text and one that only Jesus knows lies behind the letters; meaning is teleologically constrained for words are not things but may only point to them. It is the personal mediation of Jesus that interprets text; it is the teacher who knows and the student who learns.

A certain pedagogy results from this interpretive stance that assumes specific meaning that is beyond text and that requires an interpreter for comprehension. For example, Paul (Hebrews 3:15–17) writes in the letter to Hebrews that "When Scripture says, 'Today if you hear his voice, do not grow stubborn as in those days of rebellion,' Who, I ask, were those who heard and rebelled? All those surely, whom Moses had led out of Egypt. And with whom was God indignant for forty years? With those, surely, who had sinned . . ." Paul makes the metaphorical leap: the sinners who in the desert refused to believe may be equated with those Hebrews of Paul's time who refuse to accept Christianity. Textual meaning is constrained and the Jewish voice illegitimized: "For indeed we have heard the good news, as they did. But in them the message they heard did no good, because it met with no faith in those who heard it. It is we, who have become believers, who enter the rest referred to in the words, 'As I vowed in my anger, they shall never enter my rest.'" The Hebrews of Paul's time are made equivalent to those in Sinai in order to convert nonbelievers. The text is read to ensure consistency with belief. I have often stood with those who heard the good news but could not believe it.

Metaphor constrains meaning in ways that the metonomyic practice of Rabbinic thought does not. Consider the opening lines of Nathaniel Hawthorne's canonical text *The Scarlet Letter:* "The founders of a new colony, whatever Utopia of human virtue and happiness they might originally project, have invariably recognized it among their earliest practical necessities to allot a portion of the virgin soil as a cemetery, and another portion as the site of a prison." Readers of the novel might discuss what these structures tell us about the founders, but there is no illimitable possibility implicit in the choice: the possible meanings are constrained by metaphor. Compare, however, this story in Talmud (*Bava Metzia*, 85b):

> Elijah used to frequent Rabbi's academy. One day—it was New Moon—he [the Rabbi] was waiting for him, but he failed to come. Said he to him [the next day]: "Why didst thou delay?"—He replied: "I had to wait until I awoke Abraham, washing his hands, and he prayed and I put him to rest again; likewise to Isaac and Jacob." "But why not awake them together?"—"I feared that they would wax strong in prayer and bring the Messiah before his time."

I find in the Talmud no interpretation of the story as in Paul; indeed, this particular story is set between two accounts of eye disease and trouble and in a chapter that is originally concerned with questions of the rights of the laborers' working day. The process of discussion by which this story is told, the placement of the story, and the refusal of interpretation offer freedom that Pauline metaphor denies. Yet it is the latter that has dominated education since the Greek emphasis on logos and has been based in Christian practice. Schubert gives no expression to the delegitimization of the Jewish voice by Christian belief; he effects and enforces the silence of the Jewish voice. He acknowledges that Jesus "took away the ritual of Hebrew church law and dogma[34] as well as the Greek and Roman deification of reason and worldly knowledge and granted each person the right to a life sustained by personal communication with God,"[35] but nowhere does Schubert discuss what that Jewish law and dogma might be. Nor does he address the pedagogical implications of this linguistic and legalistic shift. None of this is in his text.

Schubert does state that Augustine "moved in a more reconciliatory direction by attempting to join the teachings of Plato with those of the Church"[36] but never acknowledges a) how Plato's own philosophy can be distinguished from Jewish philosophy or b) how Augustine interpreted Jewish practice as idolatry. According to Augustine the Jews wrongfully took signs for literal things and did not look beyond those signs; they could not, thus, believe in Jesus. Christian practice, following Augustine, interpreted the sign as "elevating them to the things they represent." Entire curricula, certainly in reading, were constructed based on this position, but the alternative Jewish tradition that Augustine branded heretical is never given voice and remains absent from curriculum history and discursive practices. Schubert's silence continues the expropriation and delegitimization of the Jewish voice, and yet his text is a synoptic curriculum text that purports to historicize the field. "My primary purpose," Schubert writes, ". . . is to convey the character of curriculum knowledge to those who will need to use it. Clearly, it is addressed to those who plan to be curriculum leaders in schools as well as to scholars."[37] This book does not acknowledge the suppressed presence of a Jewish voice; curriculum and curriculum study have become a Christian enterprise.

Gerald Gutek, in *A History of the Western Educational Experience*, situates the beginning of Western education with the Greeks. He then goes on to acknowledge that "The history of Western education clearly reveals, however, that American educational developments were not isolated culturally from events occurring elsewhere. There was a continuous interaction between American and European educators from the first days of colonial settlement."[38] Gutek links the tradition of American education with that of European culture and yet remains particularly silent regarding the effective silencing of Jewish voices in education. If the suppression of the Jewish voice is part of the European cultural tradition, then it must be acknowledged as a central factor in American education as well. Clearly a Jewish voice has been effectively silenced. Indeed, as Leslie Fiedler reminds me, our heritage is really their heritage and is decidedly anti-Semitic.

Eminent historian of education Lawrence Cremin situates the origin of American education, too, in the Greco-Christian tradition. Cremin writes that "[Horace] Mann's resolution was not without its theoretical difficulties. He was attracted to the naturalistic pedagogy of the Swiss reformer Pestalozzi, but like Pestalozzi himself, was deeply committed to moral instruction. How does one free a child and shame him at the same time? The problem goes back to Rousseau, and ultimately to Plato. Rousseau of course, never solved it."[39] In Cremin's account the problem of education begins with Plato; Jewish voices are once more silenced and absent. The restoration of that voice means that Jewish culture and values be given voice as culture and value embedded in history and economics and community. How might I then speak? How this might change the educational agendas of our nation's schools!

Herbert Kliebard's excellent history of education, *The Struggle for the American Curriculum,*[40] portrays the contested field as the struggle among separate interest groups: humanists, child developmentalists, social efficiency proponents, and social reconstructionists. Each contingent advocates for a curriculum premised on a particular vision of society. But in Kleibard's text the absence of a clearly Jewish voice announces that whichever society is promulgated within educational discourse must be, as it were, Christian. That is, the voices in Kleibard's text often speak eloquently, but in the silences it is acknowledged that they do so as Christian voices. If there is a Jewish voice in the text, it is a silent one. Daniel and Laurel Tanner write that "The history of the curriculum reveals repetitive periods of reform and counter-reform reflecting the shifts in sociopolitical tides."[41] That may be true, but it is also true that the Jewish voice has been censored and self-censored and therefore silent in those shifts in political tides.

In a remarkable and thorough book called *Understanding Curriculum: An Introduction to the Study of Historical and Contemporary Curriculum Discourses* in the chapter "Curriculum as Theological Text,"[42] the word *Jew* appears only in relationship to immigration and in the term's ubiquitous incarnation *Judeo-Christian*. There is no Jewish voice identified in all of the book's eleven hundred pages. Yet there are in this chapter whole sections on Liberation Theology and its contributions to curriculum theory, on the influence of hermeneutics on curriculum study, but not the Jewish practice of midrash or Talmudic interpretation—a Jewish influence on hermeneutics. In this chapter the entire relationship of curriculum development is discussed in a Christian context; it is the story of the relationship of the churches to the public schools and to the public sphere of educational practice. We are told that "Christian concerns regarding the value content of public school curriculum are legitimate; concerns regarding their religious freedom are understandable." There are Jews in the book; but if a Jewish voice is present in curriculum studies and deliberation, it is not spoken in this book. And this is a book of voices.

William Doll in his widely popular *A Post-Modern Perspective on Curriculum*, acknowledges that postmodernism, which calls into question "the sweeping changes affecting art, literature, mathematics, philosophy, political theory, science, and theology—changes questioning the basic epistemological and metaphysical assumptions in those fields—will play themselves out in education and curriculum. . . ."[43] Doll never doubts that the changes will be great. What Doll does not acknowledge—perhaps because he cannot know—is that postmodernism might be directly linked to the thought of Rabbinic Judaism, that postmodernism is couched in Jewish thought and language; the entire cultural tradition that is called into question by postmodernism is the Christian voice that has usurped and suppressed the Jewish voice. Doll situates the postmodern curriculum perspective in the developments of science and especially chaos theory, but this postmodern curriculum may actually be first heard in that silenced Jewish voice. Thus Susan Handelman, drawing relationships between Rabbinic thought and Derridean textuality, says that "If Judaism is the experience of the infinitely other, it is precisely this irruption of the totally other that threatens the Greek logos, and the Christian holy family as well. Like writing, the Jew is historically the castigated other, intruder, threat, scapegoat, exile, idolater, and it is surely no accident that those who take up arms against the paternal logocentrism of Western thought would be Jews . . ."[44] I begin to wonder whether I might not understand that the vituperative critiques against poststructuralists and their language—and the threats that these discourses make to traditional social patterns—can be understood as inherently anti-Semitic and consistent with the historical suppression of the Jewish voice?

Poststructuralism might be understood as a retranslation of traditional Rabbinic (Jewish) interpretive practices. Jonathan Culler situates poststructuralist deconstructive practices in the structuralists of the 1960s. "Enterprises now deemed post-structuralist, such as critiques of the sign, of representation, and of the subject, were manifestly already under way in the structuralist writings of the 1960s."[45] But I am discovering that such enterprises preceded the 1960s by more than a few years and were practiced early in the Rabbinic tradition of Judaism. In the same year that Culler's *On Deconstruction* was published, Susan Handelman explored how Rabbinic thought (and pedagogy) prioritized "the infinity of meaning and plurality of interpretation" that were anathema to Christian thought. Paul's proselytizing had replaced the multivocality of text—which is the focus of poststructural explorations—with the certainty of the Body and is founded on the desire to "escape the deferral and mediation of the text and language for a communion of pure presence." Jewish thought, however, seemed based in polysemy and difference. Jewish thought and hermeneutical practice were denied in the attempt to make the word flesh. Paul writes to the Hebrews (10:1–11):

> For the law contains but a shadow, and no true image, of the good things which were to come; it provides for the same sacrifices year after year, and with these it can never bring the worshippers to perfection for all time. [For this Jesus's body is required.] First he says, "Sacrifices and offerings, whole-offerings and sin-offerings, thou didst not desire nor delight in"—although the Law prescribes them—and then he says, "I have come to do thy will." He thus annuls the former to establish the latter. And it is by the will of God that we have been consecrated, through the offering of the body of Jesus Christ once and for all.

And James writes that "He who disparages a brother or passes judgment on his brother disparages the law and judges the law. But if you judge the law, you are not keeping it but sitting in judgment upon it. There is only one lawgiver and judge, the One who is able to save life and destroy it (4:12)." Meaning is constrained and resituated in faith in Jesus. This is antithetical to Rabbinic practice. Yet this is the voice of Western educational practice.

Poststructualism argues for polysemy, but it is the denial of difference that organizes Christian language practice and meaning making: meaning in Christian tradition is singular and embodied; education seeks the one, true answer. Rabbinic thought, Louis Finkelstein writes, holds that ". . . the text is at once perfect and perpetually incomplete; that like the universe itself it was created to be a process rather than a system—a method of inquiry into the right, rather than a codified collection of answers . . ."[46] In the Talmud appears the following:

> Rab Judah said in the name of Rab, When Moses ascended on high, he found the Holy One, blessed be He, engaged in affixing coronets to the letters. Said Moses, "Lord of the Universe, Who stays Thy hand?" He answered, "There will arise a man, at the end of many generations, Akiba b. Joseph by name, who will expound upon each tittle heaps and heaps of laws." "Lord of the Universe," said Moses, "permit me to see him." He replied, "Turn thee around." Moses went and sat down behind eight rows [and listened to the discourses of law]. Not being able to follow their arguments he was ill at ease, but when they came to a certain subject and the disciples said to the master, "Whence do you know it?" and the latter replied, "It is a law given unto Moses at Sinai." He was comforted.

Though the law had been given Moses he did not recognize its exegesis in Akiba's practice but is comforted in the identification of the text as the books he had written down. No authority is authoritative; the process is all. This is not part of Doll's text.

Rabbinic Jewish practice, as does its descendant, deconstruction, insists that interpretation is endless and implicit in the text. Rabbinic practice denies authority in interpretation:

> Reb Eliezer said to the other Rabbis "If the *halachah* agrees with me, let it be proved from Heaven!" Whereupon a heavenly voice cried out: "Why do you dispute with R. Eliezer, seeing that in all matters the *halachah* agrees with him." But R. Joshua arose and exclaimed [quoting from Deuteronomy, XXX, 12): "*It* [by which he means, I take it, the decision] *is not in heaven.*" What did he mean by this?—Said R. Jeremiah: That the Torah had already been given at Mount Sinai; we pay no attention to a Heavenly Voice, because Thou hast long since written in the Torah at Mount Sinai, *After the majority must one incline.* (Ex. 23:2)

Despite the politics of this final phrase, which is intentionally misquoted from the Torah by the Rabbis for their own purposes, the textual authority is not established but exists, rather, in the interpretive process. Rabbinic thought denies the answer for the investigative process. If postmodernism, which as Doll suggests has fostered a poststructuralist (deconstructionist) method, has its antecedents in Rabbinic thought, why has this remained unvoiced? How have these roots been severed and conjoined elsewhere? Indeed, in Pinar and Reynold's text *Understanding Curriculum as Phenomonological and Deconstructed Text,*[47] Derrida's work in deconstruction is linked to the phenomenogical tradition and to Heidegger and not to the Rabbinic tradition of Judaism.

Sara Horowitz writes that "consistently, the Jewish voice—or more appropriately, Jewish voices—has been silenced, except insofar as it mimics or reproduces the voice of normative culture and modulates itself in timbres pleasing and non-threatening to the large society."[48] That is, Jews speak in and about the classroom but they must not speak as Jews if they wish to be heard. This assimilationist desire has often placed the Jew in the camp of the educational conservatives who argue in advocacy for canonical definitions of curriculum. These are the arguments of Diane Ravitch, for example, whose advocacy for national standards determines her language and denies a Jewish voice. She writes, "To many the movement for national standards and assessments seems a startling turn of events, a development unprecedented in American history. The fact is that American education has a long history of standard-setting activity, sometimes overt and purposeful, at other times implicit and haphazard."[49] Nowhere does she acknowledge that this call for standards is founded in the Christian philosophical tradition that has consistently denied the Jewish voice, indeed, deemed it blasphemous and evil. For example, regarding standards Rabbi Raphael said: "Measured behavior is a dreadful evil. It is a dreadful evil when a man measures his behavior to his fellow-men. It is as if he were always manipulating weights[50] and measures." How different American education might have been if Raphael's voice had been included in Ravitch's conversation.

But in denying that voice, I believe we also deny the culture and wisdom that might effectively change the nature of curriculum and help us in restructuring schools. As it is now, our attempts to speak as Jews must appear as it were as jokes and parapraxes. Freud tells another story of the man whose desire to join proper society led to his public renunciation of Judaism by conversion. It is a story of the Jewish voice. Nevertheless, the man felt an emotional tie to Judaism and at an appropriate time told his baptized sons about their Jewish heritage.

> One day while we were sitting at tea with our otherwise friendly hosts, the lady of the house, who had no inkling of her summer guests' Jewish ancestry, launched some very sharp attacks on the Jews. I ought to have made a bold declaration of the facts in order to set my sons the example of "having the courage of one's convictions," but I was afraid of the unpleasant exchanges that usually follow an avowal of this sort. Besides I was alarmed at the possi-

> bility of having to leave the good lodgings we had found and of thus spoiling my own and my children's . . . limited holiday period, should our hosts' behaviour towards us take an unfriendly turn because of the fact that we were Jews. As however I had reason to expect that my sons, in their candid and ingenuous way, would betray the momentous truth if they heard any more of the conversation, I tried to get them to leave the garden "*Juden* [Jews]," quickly correcting it to "*Jungen* [youngsters]." In this way I enabled the 'courage of my convictions' to be expressed in a parapraxis.[51]

That is, to speak as a Jew requires subterfuge, in which case we are always misunderstood: if we want to engage in the conversation we must soon correct our discourse; or, conversely, we must speak as a Jew and risk our securities. It would seem that it has been the exercise of Western Jewry to deny their Jewish voice for the comfort of assimilation. At a 1977 conference sponsored by the Melton Research Center for Jewish Education entitled *From the Scholar to the Classroom: Translating Jewish Tradition into Curriculum,* the following introduction is made: Professor Joseph Schwab "has made a major contribution to the scholar-curriculum problem in general education . . . We asked him to open the conference with a discussion of the many problems related to the application of the fruits of scholarship and research to elementary and secondary curricula . . . ." Interestingly, Professor Joseph Schwab, who is Jewish, does not situate any of those problems in the Christian Western tradition of philosophy or educational traditions. He does however say:

> The means by which scholarly materials are adapted to the purposes of education are quickly told but only slowly mastered. The means are easily understood but difficult to use. They are difficult because they require collaboration by men of five different bodies of experience, each such body of experience being alien to the possessors of the others bodies of experience. The collaborators, then, must first learn something of the concerns, values, and operations which arise from each other's experience. They must then, and this is harder, learn slowly to honor these various groupings of concerns, values, operations, and adapt and diminish each his own values to make room in this thinking for the others. Finally, they must bring these partially coalesced bodies of judgmental factors to bear on the body of scholarly materials.[52]

It is possible that this method might be understood to have been situated in Rabbinic tradition and that the Talmud presents us with its exemplar. Nowhere in his essay—nor in the other seminal work that Schwab wrote on curriculum—is this tradition noted. Rather, Schwab is situated in the Christian Western discursive tradition. The Jewish voice has been effectively suppressed and/or denied in discourses of education. For the sake of curriculum—for the sake of my voice—it must be recovered. There are those who are concerned with how the Jew must be educated; I am concerned with what is centrally Jewish about education. I did not know to listen. I did not know how to sing my song in a strange land.

For example: I have argued extensively that curriculum might be understood as a getting lost.[53] I have always looked to Christian voices—alternative though they may be—in my learning. Thoreau, for example, tells us that to get lost is the easiest of events: one has only to turn about once in the world with the eyes closed to lose one's sense of place so as to be enabled to find it again. And I discover that this notion may also be founded in Judaism. Perhaps we might consider curriculum as Teshuvah, a return from lostness. Martin Buber defines Teshuvah as a turning to the world in order to redeem it and, of course, ourselves. It is still the finding of self after a lostness, but it may now be defined in a Jewish context. "Teshuvah," Buber tells us, "is the name given to the act of decision in its ultimate intensification; it denotes the decisive turning point in a man's [sic] life, the renewing, total reversal in the midst of the normal course of his existence."[54] That is, Teshuvah is the decision to change one's life. I think there is no way to look at Teshuvah except as a curricular issue. "One hour of return in this world," Buber quotes the Pirke Avot, "is better than the entire world to come." The return—Teshuvah—is a process and it is engagement in *this* world. If curriculum might be understood as Teshuvah, and if Teshuvah is a return to the world, then from where are we returning? from what might we be returning? to what do we return? who are we in that return? I think the pursuit of these questions might be understood as the subject matters comprising curriculum. Buber's Teshuvah, return, the name given to the act of decision to engage the world in deed in order to perfect it, is curriculum: it is to engage with the world with the hope of redemption. I have dealt elsewhere (Block, forthcoming, b) with the idea that curriculum is the engagement in lostness and foundness.[55] Teshuvah is the decision to raise shehkinah that, Buber argues has fallen into the world in dispersion (not unlike the Jewish experience of Diaspora), to reunite the dispersed with the divine, but which can only be accomplished by raising the conditioned to the unconditioned—by making the human like God. In this way the human achieves divinity and divinity becomes human, the unity to which Buber aspires becomes realizable. In this sense curriculum is a turning to the world to redeem it and ourselves. Curriculum is to engage in *tikkun olam.* That is, curriculum is redemptive: in it we become God and God becomes us. The world is healed by our own healing. The relevance of a Jewish voice begins to emerge.

Martin Buber notes that what the Western world has come to know as the Age of Enlightenment might have meant for the Jew "the Age of Exile," an era of "barren intellectuality, an intellectuality that, far removed from life and from a living striving for unity, fed on bookish words, on interpretations of interpretations; poverty-stricken, distorted, and sickly, it subsisted in a climate of idea-less abstraction."[56] That is, the voice of the Jew was subsumed by the legitimate voice of reason—it was a Western, Christian voice and its language derived from the Western Christian experience. Hannah Arendt attributes this move to a period when the Jews' own secular learning had been minimal. Thus, culture came to mean non-Jewish culture: the intellectual abandonment of Judaism "resulted in a situation within Judaism in which the Jewish spiritual heritage became more than ever before the monopoly of rabbis."[57] Dry scholarship resulted. In education Jews did not speak as Jews; they could not speak and still be heard. The Jewish voice became illegitimate for educational discourse.

I read in Cornel West that the grand spiritual godfathers of pragmatism are Thomas Jefferson, Ralph Waldo Emerson, Abraham Lincoln. In his book *The American Evasion of Philosophy,* West claims that his version of pragmatism hearkens back to the Jewish prophets who brought urgent and compassionate critique to bear on the evils of their day. But then West goes on to say that his prophetic pragmatism is located in the Christian tradition. I wonder, What happened to the Jewish prophets? Was it merely their actions—critique—to which he hearkens, or is there not also substance in their voice? "American pragmatism is a diverse and heterogeneous tradition," West writes.[58] But that tradition does not seem to include Jewish culture and wisdom. West writes that his kind of prophetic pragmatism is Christian because "on the existential level, the self-understanding and self-identity that flow from this tradition's insights into the crises and traumas of life are indispensable *for me* to remain sane. It holds at bay the sheer absurdity so evident in life, without erasing or eliding the tragedy of life . . . Second, on the political level, the culture of the wretched of the earth is deeply religious."[59] I might suggest that this tradition, despite West's claim otherwise, might derive first from a Jewish tradition. Hillel wrote, "If I am not for myself, who will be? If I am only for myself, who am I? If not now, when?" Have the spiritual godfathers of pragmatism glossed over the Jewish prophetic voice? If Dewey had read the Jewish prophets they do not appear in his bibliography. Indeed, we note that Dewey defines language "in its widest sense, a sense wider than oral and written speech. It includes the latter." But Dewey makes no mention here of what is heard and given legitimation. Dewey doesn't seem aware of the Jewish tradition that two Torahs were given at Sinai, the written and the oral one. There is no Jewish speech in Dewey's language.

I am, of course, interested in the profound silence of educators regarding the Jewish tradition that seems to me to have direct links to what is known as American pragmatism. Buber writes that "It is characteristic of Judaism that it can be content neither with truth as idea nor with truth as shape or form, neither with the truth of a philosophical theorem nor with the truth of a work of art. Its goal is truth as deed, and the striving toward this truth is its meaning and lasting significance."[60] For Buber the deed is always defined by its engagement with the world: "The deed . . . is dragged into the mud as soon as it enters the world and becomes visible." But it is not Buber we read in schools, except perhaps his more secular *I-Thou*; rather, we study Richard Wilbur's poem "Love Calls Us to Things of This World," which speaks on the same theme. It is, perhaps, a Christian translation of a Jewish theme. That is typical. The roots of American pragmatism that has figured so prominently in American educational discourses may run to Jewish sources. Recovering those voices would be a fascinating archeology and would change the nature of the world in which we live. Curriculum is redemptive. I must learn to speak.

On Poetry and Punch

Emma's class is having a special event. Called *Poetry and Punch,* it is advertised as an oral presentation to the parents of work—poems and jokes—learned by the children. Following the short presentation, there will be cookies and punch served. Emma has been excitedly practicing her piece. When the invitation arrives, I realize that *Poetry and Punch* is being held on Yom Kippur. I search the school calendar but cannot find the day listed. Yom Kippur is not noted on the university calendar either. Emma is sad she will not be with her classmates for *Poetry and Punch,* but she looks forward to shul. We will sing and she likes the singing. I am not satisfied with her disappointment. I am not satisfied with our silence.

Notes

1. Leslie Fiedler, *Fiedler on the Roof: Essays on Literature and Jewish Identity* (Boston: David Godine, 1991), p. 16.

2. Louis Ginzberg, *Legends of the Bible* (Philadelphia: Jewish Publications Society, 1956), p. 2.

3. Susan A. Handelman, *The Slayers of Moses* (New York: State University of New York Press, 1982), p. 27.

4. Emmanuel Levinas argues, "This marvelous coincidence of obedience and commandment, subjection and sovereignty [which the Jew feels in faith], bears a well-worn but handsome name: reason . . . Rationalism does not menace the Jewish faith." Emmanuel Levinas, *Difficult Freedom: Essays in Judaism*, trans. Sean Hand (Baltimore, MD: The Johns Hopkins University Press, 1990a), p. 144.

5. John L. Elias, *Philosophy of Education: Classical and Contemporary* (Malabar, FL.: Kriefer Publishing Company, 1995), p. 5.

6. Walter Benjamin, *Illuminations*, ed. Hannah Arendt, trans. Harry Zohn (New York: Schocken Press, 1969), p. 256.

7. Richard Rorty, *Philosophy and the Mirror of Nature* (Princeton, NJ: Princeton University Press, 1979), p. 43. Rorty doesn't seem to know or want to acknowledge that his pragmatism or conversational edification might be steeped in rabbinic thought. Rorty himself is not Jewish.

8. Emmanuel Levinas, *Nine Talmudic Readings*, trans. Annette Aronowicz (Bloomington, IN: Indiana University Press, 1990), p. 114.

9. Allan Bloom, *The Closing of the American Mind* (New York: Simon & Schuster, 1987), p. 60.

10. As far as I can tell, most philosopohy of education texts begin serious investigation with the Greeks. Thus, Edward J. Power writes, "Over the centuries educational philosophers have been in the habit of writing directions for education, so illustrations of a prescriptive educational philosophy of work are fairly easy to find. The persuasive deductive logic of Aristotle started education in this direction." Edward J. Power, *Philosophy of Education* (Prospect, IL: Waveland Press, 1982/1990), p. 10.

11. Martin Buber, *Tales of the Hasidim, The Later Masters* (New York: Schocken Press, 1975), p. 232.

12. Philip Roth, *Goodbye Columbus* (New York: Bantam Books, 1969), p. 135.

13. Judah Halevi, *The Kuzari: An Argument for the Faith of Israel* (New York: Schocken Books, 1964), p. 156.

14. Emmanuel Levinas, *Difficult Freedom: Essays in Judaism*, trans. Sean Hand (Baltimore, MD: The Johns Hopkins University Press, 1990a), p. 144.

15. In its confident diarray and potpourri of style, it is definitely not a Jewish look.

16. You will recall Alvy's original conversation in the film: "I distinctly heard it . . . he muttered under his breath 'Jew' . . . We were walking off the tennis court and you know, he was there and his wife and he looked at her and they both looked at me and underneath his breath he said 'Jew' . . . I pick up on those kind of things."

17. Max actually accuses Alvy of this paranoia: "The failure of the country to get behind New York City is anti-Semitism . . . every time someone disagrees with you it's because of anti-Semitism."

18. A colleague suggested to me that perhaps Annie's identification of Alvy Singer as Jewish derives from his New York citizenship. However, Alvy's friend Max is also a New Yorker. It is he who is responsible for introducing Alvy to Annie and yet it is Alvy whom she calls "a real Jew."

19. I have my thoughts: 'Ladedah' seems to express a flippant unconcern to which the Jew can never aspire.

20. Philip Roth, *Portnoy's Complaint* (New York: Random House, 1969), p. 97.

21. Handelman, op. cit., p. 19.

22. Levinas, *Nine Talmudic Readings*, op. cit., p. 5.

23. Zygmunt Bauman, *Modernity and Ambivalence* (Ithaca, NY: Cornell University Press, 1991), p. 9.

24. Freud's laundering of the punchline has the suffering woman scream out "Aa-ee, aa-ee, aa—ee!" John Murray Cuddihy, *The Ordeal of Civility* (New York: Basic Books, 1974).

25. Sander Gilman, *The Jew's Body* (New York: Routledge, 1991), p. 31.

26. Ibid., p. 28.

27. Ibid., p. 28.

28. Fiedler, op. cit., p. 7.

29. Gilman, op. cit., p. 18.

30. William H. Schubert, *Curriculum: Perspective, Paradigm, and Possibility* (New York: Macmillan Publishing Company, 1986), p. 56.

31. Ibid., p. 59.

32. Handelman, op. cit., p. 84.

33. It is not a far cry from these words to the regular description of contemporary students by the harsh critics of education.

34. I am shocked at the reinscription of the synagogue into Christian discourse.

35. Schubert, op. cit., p. 12.

36. Ibid., p. 60.

37. Ibid., p. 3.

38. Gerald Gutek, *A History of the Western Educational Expeience* (Prospect, IL: Waveland Press, 1972/1987), p. 5.

39. Lawrence Cremin, *The Transformation of the American School* (New York: Vintage, 1964), p. 11.

40. Herbert Kliebard, *The Struggle for the American Curriculum* (New York: Routledge & Kegan Paul, 1987).

41. Daniel and Laurel Tanner, *Curriculum Development: Theory into Practice* (Englewood Cliffs, NJ: Presntice-Hall., Inc., 1995), p. 295.

42. William F. Pinar, William Reynolds, Patrick Slattery, and Peter Taubman, *Understanding Curriculum: An Introduction to the Study of Historical and Contemporary Curriculum Discourses* (New York: Peter Lang, 1995), p. 614.

43. William E. Doll Jr., *A Post-Modern Perspective on Curriculum* (New York: Teacher's College Press, 1993), p. 3.

44. Handelman, op. cit., p. 173.

45. Jonathan Culler, *On Deconstruction* (Ithaca, NY: Cornell University Press, 1982), p. 25.

46. Handelman, op. cit., p. 40.

47. William F. Pinar and William M. Reynolds, *Understanding Curriculum as Phenomenological and Deconstructed Text* (New York: Teacher's College Press, 1992).

48. Sara Horowitz, "Jewish Studies as Oppositional? Or Gettin' Mighty Lonely Out Here" In *Styles of Cultural Activism*, ed. Philip Goldstein (Newark: University of Delaware Press, 1994), p. 155.

49. Diane Ravitch, *National Standards in American Education* (Washington, DC: The Brookings Institute, 1995), p. 33.

50. Buber, op. cit., p. 130.

51. Sigmund Freud, *The Psychopathology of Everyday Life*, ed. James Strachey, trans. Alan Tyson (New York: Norton, 1960), p. 93.

52. Joseph Schwab, "Translating Scholarship into Curriculum" in *From the Scholar to the Classroom* (New York: Melton Research Center for Jewish Education, 1977), p. 1.

53. Alan A. Block, *Occupied Reading* (New York: Garland Publishing, 1995); *I'm Only Bleeding: Education as the Practice of Social Violence Against Children* (New York: Peter Lang, 1997); "Curriculum as Affichiste: Popular Culture and Identity" in *Curriculum Identities*, ed. William F. Pinar (New York: Garland Publishing, forthcoming).

54. Buber, op. cit., p. 67.

55. Alan A. Block, "Curriculum as Affichiste: Popular Culture and Identity" in *Curriculum Identities*, ed. William F. Pinar (New York: Garland Publishing, forthcoming).

56. Ibid., p. 29.

57. Hannah Arendt, *The Jew As Pariah*, ed. Ron H. Feldman (New York: Random House, 1978), p. 22.

58. Cornel West, *The American Evasion of Philosophy* (Madison, WI: University of Wisconsin Press, 1989), p. 5.

59. Ibid., p. 233.

60. Buber, op. cit., p. 110.

Bibliography

Arendt, Hannah. *The Jew as Pariah*. Edited by Ron H. Feldman. New York: Random House, 1978.

Bauman, Zygmunt. *Modernity and Ambivalence*. Ithaca, New York: Cornell University Press, 1991.

Benjamin, Walter. *Illuminations*. Edited by Hannah Arendt. Translated by Harry Zohn. New York: Schocken Press, 1969.

Block, Alan A. *Occupied Reading*. New York: Garland Publishing, 1995.

———a. *I'm Only Bleeding: Education as the Practice of Social Violence Against Children*. New York: Peter Lang Publishing, forthcoming.

——— b. "Curriculum as Affichiste: Popular Culture and Identity." In *Curriculum Identities*. Edited by William F. Pinar. New York: Garland Publishing, forthcoming.

Bloom, Allan. *The Closing of the American Mind*. New York: Simon & Schuster, 1987.

Buber, Martin. *On Judaism*. New York: Schocken Books, 1995.

———. *Tales of the Hasidism, The Later Masters*. New York: Schocken Press, 1975.

Cremin, Lawrence. *The Transformation of the American School*. New York: Vintage, 1964.

Cuddihy, John Murray. *The Ordeal of Civility*. New York: Basic Books, 1974.

Culler, Jonathan. *On Deconstruction*. Ithaca, New York: Cornell University Press, 1982.

Doll, William E. Jr. *A Post-Modern Perspective on Curriculum*. New York: Teacher's College Press, 1993.

Elias, John L. *Philosophy of Education: Classical and Contemporary*. Malabar, Florida: Krieger Publishing Company, 1995.

Fiedler, Leslie. *Fiedler on the Roof: Essays on Literature and Jewish Identity*. Boston: David R. Godine, Publisher, 1991.

Freud, Sigmund. *The Psychopathology of Everyday Life*. Edited by James Strachey. Translated by Alan Tyson, New York: Norton, 1960.

Gilman, Sander. *The Jew's Body*. New York: Routledge, 1991.

Ginzberg, Louis. *Legends of the Bible*. Philadelphia: Jewish Publication Society, 1956.

Gutek, Gerald. *A History of the Western Educational Experience*. Prospect, Illinois: Waveland Press, [1972] 1987.

Halevi, Judah. *The Kuzari: An Argument for the Faith of Israel*. New York: Schocken Books, 1964.

Handelman, Susan A. *The Slayers of Moses*. New York: State University of New York Press, 1982.

Hawthorne, Nathaniel. *The Scarlet Letter*. New York: Signet, 1959.

Horowitz, Sara. "Jewish Studies as Oppositional? or Gettin' Mighty Lonely Out Here." In *Styles of Cultural Activism*, edited by Philip Goldstein. Newark: University of Delaware Press, 1994.

Kliebard, Herbert. *The Struggle for the American Curriculum*. New York: Routledge & Kegan Paul, 1987.

Levinas, Emmanuel. *Difficult Freedom: Essays on Judaism*. Translated by Sean Hand. Baltimore, Maryland: The Johns Hopkins University Press, 1990a.

Levinas, Emmanuel. *Nine Talmudic Readings*. Translated by Annette Aronowicz. Bloomington, Indiana: Indiana University Press, 1990b.

Pinar, William F., and William M. Reynolds, editors. *Understanding Curriculum as Phenomenological and Deconstructed Text*. New York: Teachers's College Press, 1992.

Pinar, William F., William Reynolds, and Patrick Slattery, Taubman, Peter. *Understanding Curriculum*. New York: Peter Lang, 1994.

Power, Edward J. *Philosophy of Education*. Illinois: Waveland Press, 1982/1990.

Ravitch, Diane. *National Standards in American Education*. Washington, D.C.: The Brookings Institution, 1995.

Rorty, Richard. *Philosophy and the Mirror of Nature*. Princeton, New Jersey: Princeton University Press, 1979.

Roth, Philip. *Portnoy's Complaint*. New York: Random House, 1969.

———. *Goodbye, Columbus*. New York: Bantam Books, 1969.

Schubert, William H. *Curriculum: Perspective, Paradigm, and Possibility*. New York: Macmillan Publishing Company, 1986.

Schwab, Joseph. "Translating Scholarship into Curriculum." In *From the Scholar to the Classroom*. New York: Melton Research Center for Jewish Education, 1977.

Steinberg, Milton. *As a Driven Leaf*. New York: Behrman House, Inc., 1939.

Tanner, Daniel, and Laurel Tanner. *Curriculum Development: Theory into Practice*. Englewood Cliffs, New Jersey: Prentice-Hall, Inc., 1995.

Waskow, Arthur. *Godwrestling Round 2*. Woodstock, Vermont: Jewish Lights Publishing, 1995.

West, Cornel. *The American Evasion of Philosophy*. Madison: University of Wisconsin Press, 1989.

Yerushalmi, Yosef Hayim. *Freud's Moses*. New Haven, Connecticut: Yale University Press, 1991.

Chapter 6

". . . the word in the world, the world in the word, ourselves in the word": Literature/Jewness/Pedagogy/History

Miriyam Glazer

Reading creates selves. . . our selves come into existence—acquire agency—reading, in the acknowledgment of the word in the world, the world in the word, and of ourselves in the word. (Alan A. Block, *Occupied Reading*)

The task I see for feminist theory in education just now is one of making conversation with our professions and with our history within them. We can theorize our vulnerability as practitioners of our disciplines and as teachers, speak our exile, and, in doing so, resettle our disciplinary communities. (Jo Anne Pagano, *Exiles and Communities: Teaching in the Patriarchal Wilderness*)

Rifling through my files, I come across a letter I wrote to my parents from Kibbutz Ein Hashofet, near Haifa, Israel, in 1964, five days before my twentieth birthday. I was readying to leave the kibbutz ulpan and return to Antioch College for my senior year.

It's like a dream come true. Studying and working here for almost six months in Israel; learning Hebrew; living a completely new way of life. How beautiful the Sabbath is, our one day of rest. We cleaned up and longed to light candles. Here Judaism has a new meaning—one can be proud to be identified with the Jewish people here, rather than with nouveau riche, I-have-a-bigger-car-than-you-values; this is a new identity for me—I am learning so much.

And my purpose as a human being—if we human beings have a purpose—has become more stable, more solidifed, having been in this new world these last few months. To say I want to teach literature at a small college

> *in the States is not just an empty few words for me now—it is something I know I must do.* And to bring back to the States a firmer belief in our obligation to create a better society based on an ideal of social justice—I don't think I'll be as hesitant to stand up for what I believe even if I must be in a minority.

Thirty-two years later, in my study in Santa Monica, the letter so amazes me, I read it over and over again. Yes; over the years, in my intermittent reconstructions of things past, I did remember that the kibbutz experience had transformed my sense of my own "jewness." The excitement of studying Hebrew, picking grapefruit, and even scrubbing toilets with young Iranian, South African, Romanian, Italian, Australian, and Uruguayan Jewish men and women who had come to Israel . . . the coming-to-know the kibbutzniks themselves, who, unlike any Jews I had ever known, celebrated Shavuot solely as a harvest festival, and whose life choices challenged the assumptions of my familiar bourgeois social order, forcing me to think in a new way—

> *We came to Palestine not only as Zionists but also as socialists. We came not trained as agricultural workers but as doctors, teachers, and lawyers. We came not because we wanted to set up a retreat from the world based on poetic feelings for agriculture, but because we wished to create a Jewish homeland. We wanted to farm the land but we believed that farmers need not be peasants. Anyway, whoever decided a lawyer was higher than a chicken farmer?* (Moshe Barzalai, Lecture to the Ulpan, Ein Hashofet, copied into my notebook, November 1964)

—all of that I remembered. But I did not remember—have never, ever, remembered—that the experience of the kibbutz ignited a sense of vocation for me. I did not remember my determination to become a literature professor at a small college, committed to "our obligation to create a better society based on an ideal of social justice." And to stand up for what I believed.

I am amazed and humbled, partly because I realize now that what I am today is what I set out to be thirty-two years ago, a literature professor at a small college, and partly because I've so long imagined such a different narrative of why and how I got here. In the narrative I've told, it's political upheaval, history, happenstance, circumstance, a fluke of fate, the need to earn a living, that turned me into a teacher. According to *that* story, I fled the political and intellectual turmoil of graduate school with my master's, tried working at the *New York Review of Books* while moonlighting at Liberation News Service, got beaten up at the Pentagon, and finally, in confusion and despair, having read Malcolm Cowley's *Exiles' Return*, gave up on America to live abroad as a neo-lost-generation ex-patriate "just until the Vietnam war ended." But while e.e. cummings and Gertrude Stein and Ernest Hemingway went to Paris, in 1968 my version of the expatriation narrative led me to follow my older sister Alyne to exotic, post-Six-Day War Jerusalem, the Prague of the times, where thousands of other young people from all over the world were gathering. I was not, I insisted, a "new immigrant," I had no intention of "making *aliyah*" to Israel. Like the protagonist of Israeli writer Nurit Zarchi's short story "Madame Bovary in Neve Tsedek,"[1] I arrived in the country on "feet with no soles." Jerusalem was an interlude, a quest-romance, an adventure, at once a liberating "exile" from my quotidian American self, and a "return" to a place in which I would be, mythologically, spiritually, temporarily, at "home." In that "city of cities [where] you can hear God breathing,"[2] I could both relish the cosmopolitanism that came from mingling with the cultures of the world and experience another self, "deeper," ahistorical, transhistorical, romantic. I would no longer wear my jewness uneasily, as I had in America, but rather become a "daughter of Jerusalem," "dark and comely" like the Shulamite of the Song of Songs; a Middle Eastern woman-self who confirmed her womanhood by, in Marianna Torgovnick's phrase, "going primitive."[3] I wore Palestinian peasant women's embroidered dresses and Bedouin earrings. I hung a camelsaddle bag on the wall of my one-room flat, sipped cups of bitter coffee in the Old City, and wrote poetry in sidewalk cafes. But then, went my narrative, I ran out of money, so I applied for a job at the Hebrew University. A letter came back saying that Hebrew University didn't hire faculty with only a master's degree, but would I be interested in teaching literature in the brand new English Department at the then fledgling University of the Negev? I *was* interested, and beginning in 1968, except for the two years I went back to the States to earn my doctorate, I simply, claimed the narrative, "landed up staying" at Beersheva for eleven years.

How much easier it has been to claim Chance rather than Purpose, to see myself as swept along by the romance of expatriation and the demands of *parnasa* rather than as pursuing a destiny. My narrative ignored my determined choices. My passion for teaching. My passion for teaching *literature*. As my narrative wrote itself over the years, I deleted the intensity with which I believed, as a young woman, that teaching literature could change the world. And most of all, the narrative eliminated the interconnectedness of that passion with the experience and figuration of being a woman, a Jew, and a woman-Jew. Only in recent years, as the narrative wound on to include the way (quirky, fortuitous) I came to leave Israel, settle in Los Angeles, and eventually find myself again creating an undergraduate Literature Department; again engaging in this polyvalent enterprise of educating young Jews, have I reimagined purpose and destiny playing a part. I have found myself writing Torah commentaries these days; re-reading that letter now from 1964 makes me feel like Jacob on his journey, who fell asleep, dreamed, and then abruptly awoke to discover *God was in this place and I knew it not* (Gen. 28:16).

When I think back—think back to when I forgot that I was doing with my life just what I intended to do with my life—it occurs to me that the first blow that paralyzed the neurons of purpose fell in the wake of a war. Or perhaps that is when my nerve centers were first shell-shocked, numbed. For the outbreak of the Yom Kippur War in 1973 traumatized the country, dissolved its self-confidence, caused many of its assumptions to unravel. Fifteen years ago, I wrote that "the ambivalent luxury of separating personal and public lives has never been a possibility in Israel. The public destiny resonates in the bones and nerves when one wakes up in the morning."[4] Though that was by way of introducing my anthology of Israeli women poets, the "one" I was describing was me. The shock of the war, and the tumult that reigned in Israel after the war, turned my assumptions upside-down and inside-out. When along with all the other dislocations a woman's movement arose, challenging the religious and civil laws, the customs, practices, beliefs, and the accommodations of our lives, I found myself troubling not merely the mortar and bricks with which I had constructed my own life, but the whole architecture.

The Yom Kippur War was to the 1970s in Israel what the Reign of Terror had been to the Romantic poets I wrote about as a scholar; though for them it had been "bliss in [the] dawn" of the French Revolution "to be alive," and being "young was very heaven!",[5] the blood-bath after the Revolution plunged the young English radicals into despair. The war was what the Kennedy and King assassinations were to Americans in the 1960s, what the Rabin assassination would be in the nineties. It was an irruption signaling the collapse of exultation, the voiding of the illusion of victory, however tenuous, over the inertia and horrors of history. It was a moment of hope destroyed.

Before the war, in the heady days of 1968–70, when most Israeli Jews were still exulting in the military triumph of '67[6] and the newly expanded borders of the country, traveling down Hebron Road on the West Bank to Beersheva was for me a great adventure. Once we were out of Jerusalem and past "Rachel's Tomb" on the outskirts of Bethlehem, I used to gaze out of the window of the *sherut*, the intercity cab, at the terraced hillsides dotted with stoney Palestinian-Arab villages, at the sight of a wizened old man in a *keffiyeh* riding his donkey along the tortuously winding road, a lone woman bent over the grapevines in her small family plot—a Middle Eastern version, for me, of Wordsworth's "solitary highland lass." Huddled in the *sherut*, I experienced the scenes along Hebron Road less as a conflicted present, less as an occupied territory disrupted by this rumbling black vehicle bearing the license plates of the Israeli victor, than as an ancient, poetic, picturesque "past." I felt as if, safely encapsulated, we passengers had been scooped into a time-warp and would reemerge into the present only after abruptly entering the desert city.[7] To be sure, it was not the same present as the one we had left; poor, mostly Mizrahi, Beersheva was a ramshackle town compared to sophisticated, more "cultured," more Ashkenazi, Jerusalem, but it was still the present. Arriving at our makeshift storefront "classrooms," I felt exhilarated, energized, by the enthusiasm of the students who had eagerly awaited the coming of an English Department to the Negev. In my politically, intellectually, and emotionally more unconscious narrative of those days, I saw myself fulfilling my mission as a Jew by leaving the comforts of the city even for two days a week to heed David Ben Gurion's call and, at least intellectually, "make the desert bloom."

Teaching in Beersheva was an existential solution for me as an American Jewish woman, alienated both from an America wrenched apart by the Vietnam war and from a Judaism that seemed to have no place for me and in which I could imagine no place. Like many Israelis, living in Israel I had come to equate "real" Judaism with the repressive, masculinist, way of life represented by the ultra-Orthodox. Like Diaspora Jews who come to Israel to feel part of a "people," I had found a way to embrace jewness free of the burden of Judaism. As a secularist like the kibbutzniks at Ein Hashofet, I would help build the country. They planted citrus groves. I would plant literature.

It did not occur to me then that teaching English literature was an odd way to do it, any more than I was conscious of exoticizing and thus psychologically and politically erasing the realities along Hebron Road. Young, yearning for purpose, wanting to have *something* to give, shielded by my professional role from my own silenced sense of *not* belonging as an English-speaking newcomer, I did not see to see.

I could not have imagined that, in traveling through the West Bank to the Israeli desert to carry out the same curriculum that the British had imposed in the universities of their empire, I was enacting a complex intellectual colonialism, serving as another unwitting spokeswoman of the European imperial project. After all, like most Western-educated Diaspora Jews, I myself was a "sort of half-breed of colonization," in the words of Albert Memmi.[8] On the one hand, as I had learned in childhood from Hebrew School, synagogue, and at home, emotionally and mythographically Israel was "mine"; once I was there, the very contours and colors of the landscape seemed to speak to my soul. Despite their presence to me only as the object of my gaze and the vehicle of my projected desire for an "authentic," still inchoate, womanhood, I thought myself bonded more intimately to those peasant women in the fields than to most other Americans. On the other hand and simultaneously, like thousands of other Jews educated in literature in the universities of the West, I had internalized the illusion that the literary heritage I should claim as mine—I, the granddaughter of poor Russian-Jewish immigrants to Brooklyn, daughter of parents whose *mama-loshen* was Yiddish—was mostly British, male, and Protestant. In college and in graduate school, to be "literary," "educated," "cultured," had meant acquiescing to a complex exile, a multiple abandonment. The prerequisite for academic success was an obliteration of my lived experience as a woman, Jew, and woman-Jew, who had grown up in the newly "American" home that I'd grown up in. What Memmi writes of the consequences of a colonialist education was true for Diaspora Jews as well as for other ethnic and racial minorities in the States: The "memory which is assigned [to the student] is certainly not that of [her] own people. The history which is taught [her] is not [her] own."[9] I was to leap over a shadowy chasm and identify with a nearly exclusively male gentile British culture in which my existential knowledge was invisible, with a "book of myths," as Adrienne Rich writes in her poem "Diving into the Wreck," "in which/our names do not appear."[10] The English Literature book of myths was one, moreover, whose construction of women and whose pervasive if often subtle antiSemitism I consented, like the professors I learned from, to ignore. What if Fagin is a Jew? If Shylock's daughter Jessica despises her heritage and can't wait to convert? Isn't it enough that Shylock cries, "Hath not a Jew eyes?"?

Perversely enough in light of their lingering hatred of the British mandate days, my students wanted that culture, too. But perhaps "perverse" is the wrong word; their privileging of English was rather to be expected given their ideological milieu. For though I had been raised in the Diaspora and they, in the "homeland," we all were all seduced by the self-proclaimed and assertive power, the deceptive attractiveness, of the gentile West. Raised to aspire in the melting-pot era, I had learned to denigrate my own ethnic and class context in return for the promise of an elusive, sophisticated, intellectual elevation through the study of English literature. I never even considered an immersion in Jewish texts. Israel, too, was a nation of immigrants dominated by the social paradigm, if illusion, of the melting pot. Through a Eurocentric, Ashkenazi-dominated Zionist education and culture, the Israeli students had imbibed not only an insistent identification with the West, but also a simultaneous rejection of the Levantine cultural context from which many of them had nevertheless sprung and in which Israel is geographically situated. The "West" was "modern." The "West" was power. The "West," above all, was *not Arab.*[11] So two days a week I lectured enthusiastically on Shakespeare, Spenser, and Milton to retired Army officers, intellectually hungry wives of pilots stationed in Beersheva, kibbutzniks, avid young elementary school teachers, and upwardly mobile new immigrants from India and Eastern Europe trying to carve out a decent life.

Then I climbed into the diesel-powered sherut and was driven back to Jerusalem, the sole woman in a taxi crammed with six other sweaty *professorim*, at the end of the day.[12]

I took a leave of absence from 1971–73 to complete my doctorate at Brandeis on one of radical visionary William Blake's more impenetrable prophetic poems. I blinded myself to his call to "the Jews" to "Take up the Cross . . . & follow Jesus"—I literally did not see it—while, in ways that foreshadowed my own later pedagogy, I paradoxically also struggled to articulate how his poetry was designed less to "create a System," than to sensitize readers to their own interpretive acts.[13] I arrived back in Israel in October with my neatly bound dissertation clutched under my arm, to a blacked-out Lod airport, in the midst of the Yom Kippur War. Eight hours after my arrival, an air raid siren bled through the Jerusalem air. As we all huddled in the shelter, memories suddenly arose in me of childhood Take-Cover! drills, of crouching in the chalk-dust under our school desks to shield ourselves from atom bombs. How real the threat of attack was now, and how unreal that childhood scene had been, I kept feeling, how unreal. With what illusions had we been raised! Had anything in America ever been real? Had anything I ever learned at school been real? What did William Blake and all of English Romanticism have to do with any of this? What did literature? What did teaching literature?

Like the rest of the country, after the Yom Kippur War I was in shock. Five thousand soldiers were killed in the *mechdal*, the debacle, the screw-up, as the war came to be called—ten times more than had fallen in 1967.[14] The country was traumatized; the economy crippled, the people devastated by the losses and enraged by the unreadiness of the military. The much-vaunted impregnability of the "Bar Lev" line in the Sinai had been a failure. In the north, the Syrians had broken through on the Golan, and it took weeks for the Israeli army to regain the lost ground. Fear and distrust were swept into the corners of the national psyche once occupied by exultation. In my dazed state, I wrote letters to friends in the States to pour out my own grief, keep sane:

> *Something has happened to Israel since the war. Death was always a part of life here, young men were always being buried—if not because one of the intermittent Big Wars, then because of the War of Attrition, or a terrorist attack, or an unexpected border skirmish—but since the Yom Kippur war, death has seeped into Israel's veins. There was too much death, much of it because of bungling by the military authorities. The blood of all those dead soldiers has poisoned the blood of the living, poisoned the life-blood of the country. Bitterness. Anger. Waste. Mothers accused Moshe Dayan of killing their sons. Dayan, the great hero of the Six Day War. The country is torn and bleeding.*[15]

Golda Meir's government was forced to create a commission of inquiry to investigate. Then the elections, originally scheduled for October but disrupted by the war, were finally held at the end of December. Though Labor managed to piece together a government by forming a coalition with the National Religious Party, the right-wing Likud under Menahem Begin, which insisted that the Arabs wanted to annihilate Israel and thus Israelis must hold on to the territories with "a strong hand and an outstretched arm," increased its power. Still a "temporary resident," not yet a voter, I spent New Year's Eve 1974 in my local polling booth as an observer for the new, leftist, Citizens' Rights Movement. The CRM startled everyone, including the party itself, by winning three seats, the third of which went to American-born feminist Marcia Freedman who, new to politics, was abruptly catapulted into the Knesset. Freedman immediately initiated what became clamorous and heated national debates about women's rights.

Later, when the Agranat Commission published its devastating critique of the government's behavior during the Yom Kippur War, Golda Meir was forced to resign. Yitzhak Rabin became Prime Minister.[16]

Terror and tumult continued all of 1974. In May, while spring flowers burst into life all over the country, three terrorists—and with them thirty children—were killed in Ma'alot, in the north, when at Moshe Dayan's command Israeli soldiers stormed the schoolbuilding the terrorists had occupied. People demonstrated in front of Meir's house and in the Knesset, demanding that all the Palestinian terrorists in Israeli jails be killed and the death sentence be passed on any terrorists that were caught. When Kissinger arrived, a huge rally was held in downtown Jerusalem against "surrendering Kuneitra" ("GO HOME NIXON'S JEWBOY"; "THIS WEEK KUNEITRA, NEXT WEEK JERUSALEM"; "NO VIETNAM PEACE FOR ISRAEL"). Tanks were poised in front of the YMCA to guard him in the King David hotel. Katyusha rockets aimed at the center of Jerusalem were found by an Arab who reported his discovery to the police. After Ma'alot, I sat through dinner conversations with friends who wondered obsessively about how they would know which child to save first if they opened their front door and faced terrorists ready to shoot them.

At the height of this postwar anxiety, bitterness, and tension, the universities reopened. The atmosphere worsened as bureaucratic conflicts tore the institution apart. The rector in Beersheva forced the faculty to sign a statement agreeing to any change in any working conditions—hours, wages—because of "the war effort." Now, too, sorrow, loss, death, rage, memories of dead children, burned-out tanks and slaughter, were in my classroom; heavy hearts, horrified souls. Among my students were war-widows, mothers whose sons had been taken prisoner, returning soldiers constantly having to leave their studies to go back for reserve duty. How was I to teach? What was I to teach? Was I supposed to pretend there were no shrouds hovering in the corners of the room?

The English department had been established under the auspices of the Hebrew University. After the war, the outgoing chair, from Jerusalem, urged me to move to Beersheva and assume the leadership of the department, though doing so would mean my confronting the same sense of difference and isolation she herself had experienced as the University's only woman academic department chair. But moving into the chair's position for me meant also seeing our literature curriculum in a new light. I soon found myself questioning why the Beersheva curriculum was merely a repetition of Jerusalem's. What was the rationale for teaching what we taught? Did we serve the same population? Who, actually, were we? Though the whole country had just been through a war, many of the twenty-five English department faculty were recently arrived immigrants who spoke Hebrew haltingly, and had no history in the country. What were our words in the wounded world of this nation? What were the worlds in our words? Where were we, where were our students, in the words? In the anguish of the times, could literature—English literature—and the traditional formal pedagogy of the curriculum, help us? Could it heal, help us all understand, speak to the woundedness?

Standing in front of my students, I found myself asking the same questions. "What are we doing here, studying this literature? What should we be doing? Is the function of studying English literature only to help us all escape?" Spoken softly, sadly, tentatively, hungrily, their answer was "yes." Yes. To continue doing what we were doing was not to help make the desert bloom. It was merely to offer a palliative to the war-weary Israeli students, one linguistically, culturally, historically, aesthetically, spiritually, divorced from the all-too-knotted reality we all lived.

But it was too painful to me to consign literature to the margins of experience, nor could I shrug my shoulders and content myself—make sense of my own life—teaching what was just a diversion. Though the price I had paid for entree into the promised land of literature-in-academia had been the exile of my own embodied experience, I was only beginning to discern a grammar for that loss then. Like the "poet-prophets" of Romanticism whose work I taught, and perhaps like more than one Jewish scholar of Romanticism, in the absence of religious belief, literature and the human imagination were the source of the sacred to me, just as the kibbutzniks, celebrating May Day complete with giant posters of Karl Marx, sacralized Socialism.[17] Through the sensual, aesthetic, and intellectual pleasures of language and literary form, of writing, reading, and thinking-in-words, I had sought agency, to borrow Block's term in *Occupied Reading*, seeing and perceiving the world through the literary word. The lenses I'd learned to see through had never taken the measure of my own eyes, but they were the lenses I wore in order to create narrative sense of my world. After the war, the narrative was unraveling. I needed a new prescription.

In the context of the traditional pedagogy reigning in those years not only in Beersheva but also throughout Israeli universities as a whole, even to encourage students to question our curriculum was to break ranks. Even to speak as a *we*. The classroom setting itself discouraged it; describing myself earlier as "standing in front of my students" was not a figure of speech. While I had been in the States writing my dissertation, the university had moved out of the old storefronts to its new campus. Now the University was a barricade of massive poured-concrete buildings in which were housed a few cramped faculty offices never intended for meeting with students, along with someone's idea of real classrooms: In each, a raised platform faced parallel rows of long formica tables with attached seats, the whole bolted down into place. This arranging of students "in rows, all eyes facing front, directly confronting the back of a fellow's head, meeting the gaze only of the teacher," as Madeleine Grumet has pointed out, "deploys the look as a strategy of domination."[18] The new classrooms were the architechtonics of a pedagogy that asserted the elevation and isolation of academic authority, the "mastery of [the] teacher over the student."[19] Mastery over, domination. The students were like the Palestinians I had gazed at through the window of the Israeli sherut that rumbled through their towns, invasive and untouchable; they were both rendered objects.

Implicit in such a classroom structure is the assumption that education entails the acquisition by students "of predefined forms of knowledge," rather than the "generating, enacting, and embodying [of] living relations between a text and its audience or actors," as Susan Handelman has suggested.[20] Though I could not have put it into words then, in retrospect I perceive my discomfort with the classrooms as an extension of my uneasiness with an educational mission that held fast to "predefined forms of knowledge," as if I as professor had the keys to the kingdom the students could acquire if they only listened silently and well. But more than academic arrogance was woven into that position. In such a setting, where teachers are expected "to know and, in that knowing, to confer knowledge and power" on the students, the implicit pedagogical model, from a Lacanian perspective, is exclusively phallocentric, as Grumet argues. The lecture platform is turned into a proving ground for an endless reenactment of the oedipal drama: preoccupied staking their own claim to the symbolic order, professors "wrench the text away from the parent, the law, from phallic authority."[21]

Like the pedagogy, the curriculum also objectified the needs of professors more than those of the students. Claiming "universality" and denying its own historical contingencies, the curriculum authorized the desire of immigrant English-speaking Jews, who had been ironically transformed by Israeli nomenclature into "Anglo-Saxons" they/we never were in their/our native countries, to occupy a privileged position in Israel by acting as its representatives (though when and how had English literature represented *us*?). Buttressing that privilege was curricular aloofness from the complex social and cultural milieu in which literature was taught. Within the context of those classrooms, to engage my students in dialogue about our curriculum of studies, to share my own doubts and my own anguish with them, to stimulate questions about the appropriateness of reading, teaching, learning English literature the way we had read, taught, and learned English literature in the past, felt subversive. The rigid formality of the classroom space had been designed to elevate authority while hindering if not entirely occluding informal dialogue, conversation, relationality—including that of the students with one another. In those rooms the students could face only the teacher. Never each other.

It was at the modest Art School of Beersheva that I discovered a very different model. One of the teachers, the late Joyce Schmidt, had emigrated from Chicago. "I knew if I were going to settle here," she told me, "I'd have to be open to doing art differently, doing a different art." Hoping to establish, along with the students, a cottage industry that would support the work of the school, Schmidt studied the process of hand-making paper out of indigenous Negev plants. Moved by her determination to relate to the environment she had come to live in, by the transformative process of paper-making itself, and by the textural richness and beauty of the paper that emerged, I came to see her work as a metaphor for the kind of curriculum I could believe in and that I wanted to teach. The real task before us was, as Adrienne Rich writes in her poem "Leaflets," "how to use what we have/ to invent what we need."[22]

What did we have? To evolve a living curriculum that stepped down from the lecture platform and engaged our students'—and our own—real lives, we needed to see who our students were in their own terms, and where we were actually situated. Beersheva was not Jerusalem, and by a long shot not Cambridge or Oxford either. We were living in a desert that was trying to grow a city. Long a center for nomadic Bedouin, an Arab town until the War of Independence, Beersheva was an ancient settlement where five-thousand-year-old figurines had been unearthed. It was a Biblical crossroads with a site marked "Abraham's Well," the remnants of a camel market on Thursdays, an

Ottoman Turk downtown, a British cemetery from World War I, and, most recently, an influx of Russian Jews alongside a culturally diverse, multilingual population who had immigrated from dozens of other countries. A curriculum alive to its milieu would not merely *present* English-language literature, it would reflect on and critique the aesthetic, intellectual, cultural, and religious assumptions of that literature. Particularly in light of the signature of British imperialism on the Middle East, the curriculum would consider how English literature imagined the Levant and Levantines, as well as how it constructed the "foreigner" (Jew, Arab, immigrant, among them). Crucially, too, it would critically examine the role of English in non-English-speaking countries and offer comparative studies of English and *Hebrew* literature.

Many of our students already were, or wanted to become, elementary or secondary school teachers of English. A curriculum responsive to the reality of its students would include the literary works they would one day teach, and reflect on the process and problems of teaching those texts in the Israeli context. It would recognize that the presence and power of America was increasingly being felt in Israel, and so empower our students to "read" America critically in order to grasp the complexities of its intensifying impact on Israeli culture.

Stranded between cultures and paradigms of education, educated to leave myself out but feeling pressingly the need to bring us all in, I also began to ask why we "secular Israelis" acted as if we were not *Jews*. Had the totalizing narrative of the gentile West been so seductive that we had all assented to read as if it were "not ourselves," as if we were talking about "anything else,"[23] when we came across lines like T. S. Eliot's:

> *The rats are underneath the piles.*
> *The jew is underneath the lot.*
> *Money in furs?*[24]

What did we make of Fagin and Shylock, or for that matter of George Eliot's noble Zionist, Daniel Deronda, or Joyce's wandering Jew, Leopold Bloom? And what did I do with William Blake's cry for building Jerusalem "in *Englands* green & pleasant Land"?[25]

At the core of this drive to see, name, engage, who and what was really present in the classroom, this drive to demystify text, audience, actors, was more than the war. It was also the destabilizing discovery that the source of the estrangements I had always felt was only partially that I was a Jew growing up in assimilationist America, and much more fundamentally that I was a *woman*. In the critical climate of the 1990s, when gender, along with ethnicity and class, are so readily acknowledged as shaping our apprehensions, it may be difficult to recall what an upheaval, a disruption, a transformative revolution in consciousness, the naming of gender increasingly entailed. While I was in the States plodding away on "The Altering Eye" in "the torments of Love & Jealousy" of Blake's *Four Zoas*, I had first been introduced to the feminist movement, to the first glimmerings of how woman's presence in culture and literature had been constructed or erased. "Most women who have awakened remember having slept, *having been put to sleep*," writes Helene Cixous. A woman awakening begins to see how "the 'dark continent' trick has been pulled on her: she has been kept at a distance from herself, she has been made to see (=not see)." To begin to see how I had been taught to "see (=not see)"[26] and to open my eyes *as woman*, was to begin to make connections, to see others as well, men *and* women, students, teachers, curriculum, the now, the here, the actual presences in the actual classrooms. It was to face that, like most positions of power in the country, like the university as a whole, our habits of pedagogy as well as our curriculum were what Peggy McIntosh has called "womanless."[27] No wonder I wandered on, off, and around those lecture platforms. In the fissure of bewildered apartness I had always repressed or leapt over through acts of abstract intellect and intuition was my own isolation: the predominance of male-derived and male-defined knowledge, the near absence of women's, and professionally, of other women.

In awakening to feminism I wasn't entirely alone. After the Yom Kippur War, women's issues also began tumbling onto the national agenda. During the war, the economy had come to a halt while most able-bodied men served in the army. Civilian women determined to contribute to the war effort had not become Rosie the Riveter; we/they were limited to knitting balaclavas, sending homemade cakes to husbands and sons on the front, and serving as "hostesses" in military hospitals and soldiers' rest homes.[28] Along with outrage at the unreadiness of the army and the slaughter that had ensued, women discovered that the sexism of Israeli society meant being rendered nearly superfluous when the survival of the nation was at stake. Even public transportation had ground to a halt; the bus companies had always refused to train women as drivers.

As a result, after the war an Israeli woman's movement began slowly to be born.[29] In 1974 I attended a groundbreaking national feminist conference in the Jerusalem forest that addressed inequities in labor laws and in employment practices; the difficulties of legal abortion; the realities of domestic violence and sexual abuse; oppressive laws governing personal status in the control of the Rabbinate, and the suffering of *agunot*, "chained" women who cannot remarry because they are anchored to a husband who either will not or cannot issue a Jewish writ of divorce—in some cases, because though the husband had been declared "missing in action" in the war, his body was never found.[30] In the Knesset, Marcia Freedman proposed a liberalization of the abortion law. Heated debate on the proposed changes took center stage for months. But any liberalizing of the abortion law was opposed by the National Religious Party, which Labor needed for its governing coalition. Two years after that first feminist conference, at the height of the feminist agitation that increasingly pitted the demand for women's rights against the entrenched sexism of Israeli society as a whole and the ultra-Orthodox religious authorities in particular; during a period of social, political, and religious tensions that within a few months would come to a climax with the toppling of the Labor government, I went on a journey to the then-remote Sinai desert with a group of artists. They went to hike and draw. But I had a different agenda. Seeped in years of studying how the Romantic poets spiritualized landscapes, I envisioned this journey to the foot of the legendary mountain as a spiritual test. If the poet Else Lasker-Schuler could hear "God breathing" in Jerusalem, at Mount Sinai, the mythic site of the covenant at the core of Judaism, I could "have it out" with Judaism's God. In contemporary terms, it's as if as a newly born feminist, I went to Sinai to deconstruct the landscape-as-patriarchal-spiritual-text.

Sometimes a dried river bed is only a dried river bed. But for me, then, rising before dawn and walking hour after hour through the stone-strewn wadis of the Sinai, facing the massive boulders and crags of sheer rock in the overwhelming heat and stillness, I felt as if I were witness to aftershocks of God's voice cracking through history, as if the moment of the Revelation at Sinai had left, at heart, a broken sun-seared landscape of scarred ruins. The nothingness terrified me. Back at the field study school in the evening, as our guide described the subterranean volcanic processes that had created the jagged mountains and boulders, I melted his words into metaphor. If the mountain had been claimed by Jehovah, the Father God, I told myself, the magma seething below the surface of the earth was the hidden, explosive, energy of the feminine. The magma was the mythic Great Mother, raging ever since she had been perceived as a dangerous pagan goddess by the ancient Hebrews and banned from Judaism forever. Generations later in the modern state of Israel, her daughters still suffered from that banning. In my own search for meaning and purpose in those troubled and chaotic postwar days, Sinai had become the site of a psychomachia between power and powerlessness still being played out in everyday life.

We were abruptly thrust back into here-and-now history at the Tel Aviv airport upon our return. Soldiers crowded around us pouring out news of the hijacking and rescue at Entebbe. But in the weeks and months that followed, in the underground streams of my own psyche, I knew I had to translate my experience of Sinai into literature, into life. I wanted to understand what had happened to the Great Mother. I had gone to Sinai a woman-in-conflict; I returned a determined feminist.

Slowly I began to grasp that the spiritual value of the feminine in a culture is revealed not through religious worship, but through the treatment of women, childbirth, and women-as-mothers. Wounded by the decimation of the Shoah and by the losses suffered in war, Israeli culture was obsessed with motherhood. But that very obsession could often instrumentalize women and, in devastating ways, denigrate them. In the women's group I came home to after Sinai, we were all either desiring pregnancy or already pregnant. So we organized ourselves into the Beersheva Women's Health Collective and, after hearing rumors of women's mistreatment, asked permission to investigate the conditions in the gynecological and obstetrical wards of the local hospital.

During the days and nights we subsequently spent there as part of our investigation, we saw what happens when women in childbirth are turned into landscapes of pain and threats. The Mother I sensed in Sinai was in the labor rooms and the birthing rooms, left alone and uncovered for hours, screaming *Ba'ali, mah asita lee?* ("Husband, what have you done to me?"), threatened with Caesareans for "not behaving." Bedouin women, instinctively trying to squat to give birth, were mocked as *Chayot Ha'Negev*, "Negev animals." A mother who had birthed twenty-three children pleaded for a tubal ligation and was refused because she "didn't have the husband's permission." The head doctor had a sideline restitching hymens so brides could pretend to be virgins on their wedding night. He confessed to us that his ideal birthing scenario would be a woman who read the newspaper while he pulled her baby out with forceps.

We submitted a report, demanding changes; there was a brief national scandal. But to the credit of the Director of Health Services for the Negev, many of our recommendations began to be instituted. As a result of our investigation, several women from our group entered women's health professions. Both figuratively and literally, I went across the street from the hospital to the university, and then took a step that Israelis considered so radical I became notorious as a *feministit*, the national radio station called for an interview, a women's magazine asked me to become a columnist, and requests to speak at women's groups poured in. I launched the first "Women's Studies" university course in the country.

How tame it was by American standards! "Women in Literature" looked at how women had been constructed in literature by men and how American women novelists and poets had constructed themselves. But when I asked the students to compare contemporary Israeli women poets to their counterparts in the States, the possibility of doing so jolted them. Their secondary school curricula had included the supposedly "personal" lyrics of the pre-state poet Rachel and, in some cases, a poem or two of the modernist Leah Goldberg. They had dipped into Dahlia Ravikovich and heard a poem of the Hasidic Zelda read at the funerals of soldiers. But who *were* the other Israeli women poets? What did they write? How did they write it? My students didn't know. Nor could I help them, for neither did I. I had assigned the project because I wanted to learn too. The result was that we undertook the research and reading together.

We went on reading when the semester ended. We moved out of the classroom into my home. We went to Tel Aviv to meet poet Yona Wallach; to Jerusalem to meet Hedva Harekavi and Zelda. We kept on meeting every week for over a year. Eventually, yearning to bridge my American and Israeli worlds, I compiled and edited many of our translations into *Burning Air and a Clear Mind*, the first anthology of Israeli women poets to be published in English.

The ambivalent luxury of separating personal and public lives has never been a possibility in Israel. The public destiny resonates in the bones and nerves when one wakes up in the morning. Yes. The Labor government fell on December 21, 1976—but not because of feminist agitation, or the proposed abortion laws, but rather because the National Religious Party resigned from the coalition to protest Labor's allowing the United States to deliver four Phantom jets on the Sabbath. As a result of the new elections, and for the first time since the establishment of the State, Labor was forced into the opposition. In what became known as the *mahapach*, the upheaval, the right-wing Menahem Begin became Prime Minister.

Begin called a press conference immediately to alert journalists that from that day on the occupied territories of the West Bank would be called by the Biblical names, "Judea" and "Samaria." The secular-political "state of Israel" turned into the politically charged and mythically infused "Greater Land of Israel." Though those of us on the left had long been chagrined by the political compromises, nepotism, and corruption of the Labor Party, the rise to power of the militantly nationalistic Likud, justifying expansionism under the banner of the Bible and Judaism, were sources of sorrow, if not despair. The schism tearing Israel apart today was bound onto the wheel of fire then: The schism between militantly religious and right-wing nationalists, on the one hand, and, on the other, liberal secularists and that tiny minority, observant Jews in support of an accommodation with the Palestinians; between those for whom Israel must remain defiantly "a nation that dwells alone," and those eager to become a nation-among-nations.[31]

The tenor of the country changed. For the first time in the history of Israeli cinema, for example, films began to portray mental breakdowns, as if liberal Israelis "were beginning to collapse under the strain of disillusionment. . . ."[32] With the right wing in control, Arab lands being quickly confiscated and settlements of militant neo-Zionists proliferating, my own sense of alienation deepened. Zionism had always been conceived as what David Biale has called an "erotic revolution," the building of a Judaism "with muscles," the creation of a "virile New Man."[33] Now we entered another act from the same play. The same *mentaliyut* that denied women's civil and religious rights also denied the rights of the country's other "Others." The seeds of the contemporary crisis in Israel were sown then: With increasing frequency today women in Jerusalem are physically harassed if they are "immodestly dressed" by ultra-Orthodox standards, while the anti-Palestinian fanaticism of the right wing is intensifying. Like so many other young middle-class Jewish American women, I had once searched for my own womanhood in Jerusalem, imagining myself the dark "Shulamite" American culture could not conceive. Today, Israel is being used to "redeem" Jewish American male sexuality. Among the most religiously self-righteous and settlement-obsessed are Jewish American men, reborn as skull-capped cowboys who brandish their Uzis at Palestinian

Indians. Proclaiming Jewish hegemony on the West Bank frontiers of "Judea" and "Samaria," they wrench themselves from the humiliating stereotype of the feminized *nebbish* that marked them in the America they left.[34]

How shall we sing the Lord's song in a strange land? asks the Psalmist (137:4). With a troubled sense of irony, the strange land of the psalm now felt more and more to me like Israel. Not that I knew what "the Lord's song" was; only that in that question was enfolded mine. How can one sing of the values one most deeply cares about in a tonal system in which one's very notes seem alien? With the rise of ultra-nationalism, I began to feel by contrast how essentially Diasporic, how American, my own consciousness was, how deeply rooted in the desirability of Jews "sharing space with others,"[35] of a society committed to pluralism, at least in law. I imagined leaving.

But I might never have left had not the dean of the university unexpectedly dropped by my house one morning to tell me that I had been chosen to be a Visiting Scholar in Los Angeles. "You have no idea what you're doing to my life," I murmured, as if I already sensed how the story would end.

Deciding to remain in the States was a painfully fraught decision that at the time bewildered my family, friends, colleagues, and me as well, for I could not then fully articulate why I felt so strongly that the Israeli chapter of my life was over. Nearly two decades later, I look back and see that in struggling, studying, teaching, translating, huddling in a shelter, hiking through the hills, restively searching, becoming a mother, I came of age in Israel. Living there changed the meaning for me forever of what it means to me to be a woman, an academic, and a Jew. But by living there I also learned that I am too Diaspora a creature to feel at home in a "homeland" where religion and politics so intimately and destructively mix. I am too respectful of my own Jewish womanhood to be willing to endure the hammerlock on both Judaism and women's rights that the ultra-Orthodox impose on Israelis, or to be drawn to the Israeli alternative, a secular jewness that has turned vacuous in this post-Socialist, post-Zionist age.

Still. Without those years in Israel, would I also have been freed of the comparable vacuity, the life of cultural and spiritual assimilation I see among so many Jews in America? Had I never lived in Israel, what content would my jewness have today? How would I ever have come to discover that I am both too Jewish and too feminist to believe in the severance of "literature" and "life"?

Re-reading that letter that I wrote to my parents from the kibbutz, it's strange to me that at nineteen I almost had it right. I have long known that living in Israel gave me gifts I have wanted to share in America. But when I was nineteen, I didn't know that the "small liberal arts college" in the States that I'd want to teach in would a Jewish one. Nor could I have imagined that the core curriculum of that college would be a restless negotiation between "Jewish" and "Western" civilizations, as restless a negotiation, indeed, as my own. When I was nineteen, too, the gender issues at the heart of so much of our educational enterprise today had not even been named.

I did not know that the literature I would one day teach would be both Jewish and gentile, American and British, Israeli and Arab, and that it would fully include works by women as well as by men. In fact, when I was nineteen I certainly didn't know that the curriculum and pedagogy of a university Department of Literature could reflect the astounding richness of the many faceted narrative I'd also choose to live.

Notes

1. In *The Mask Maker* (Tel Aviv, Biton, 1993), pp. 59–68 (in Hebrew). My translation of this story will appear in *Dreaming the Actual: Israeli Women Writers at the Turn of the Twenty-First Century*, Albany, SUNY Press, forthcoming).

2. Else Lasker-Schuler, *The Land of the Hebrews*. Trans. Yehuda Amichai and Dennis Silk. In *Retrievements: A Jerusalem Anthology* (Jerusalem, Israel, University Press, 1968), p. 153.

3. Marianna Torgovnick, *Gone Primitive: Savage Intellects, Modern Lives* (Chicago, University of Chicago Press, 1990). See especially "Imagining Us," pp. 11–12.

4. In *Burning Air and a Clear Mind: Contemporary Israeli Women Poets*, ed. [Myra] Glazer (Athens, Ohio, Ohio University Press, 1981), p. xv.

5. William Wordsworth, "The Prelude," Book xi, ll. 108–109. *English Romantic Writers*, ed. David Perkins (San Diego, H arcourt, Brace, Jovanovich, 1967), p. 252.

6. Most, but not all. Immediately after the Six-Day War, on June 30, 1967, an ad appeared in the newspaper *Ha'aretz* signed by members of the far-left party Matzpen and, most notably, by Prof. Yeshayahu Leibovitz and cartoonist, ex-Palmachnik, Shimon Sabar, urging Israel recognize that "we are not conquerors" and should withdraw from all the conquered territories, including east Jerusalem. Leibovitz in particular warned for many years of the social, moral, and psychological price Israelis would pay for remaining military occupiers of the territories. I am grateful to Uri Talil for recounting this history of the times to me.

7. As I describe this sense of the scenes along Hebron road as being part of an eternal past, a kind of still-life, I think of Mary Louise Pratt's essay, "Scratches on the Face of the Country; or, What Mr. Barrow Saw in the Land of the Bushmen," *Critical Inquiry*, 138–161, in which she argues that the "portrait of manners and customs" fixes "the Other in a timeless present," textually producing "the Other without an explicit anchoring either in an observing self or in a particular encounter in which contact with the Other takes place."

8. In *The Colonizer and the Colonized* (Boston, Beacon Press, 1965), p. xvi.

9. *The Colonizer and the Colonized*, p. 105. See also Leslie Fiedler's remarks on the consequences of this Christianized education for the Jewish-American writer and the whole tradition of modernist Jewish-American writing in "The Christian-ness of the Jewish-American Writer," *Fiedler on the Roof: Essays on Literature and Jewish Identity* (Boston, Godine, 1991), pp. 59–72. The

eventual result, as Yosef Hayim Yerushalmi claims, is the whittling away of Jewish memory and a consequent "meager" Jewish past inscribed in contemporary Jewish-American writing. In *Zakhor: Jewish History and Jewish Memory* (New York, Schocken, 1989), p. 99.

The need to find sources of identification with the "British, male, Protestant" tradition is seen particularly in the field I originally chose, Romanticism, among the Jewish professors whose lead I emulated in eliding any suggestion of anti-Semitism. In college it was both a relief and an embarrassment to me to discover Lionel Trilling's 1950 essay "Wordsworth and the Rabbis"—a relief because the essay connected this Romantic figure with Jewish tradition, an embarrassment because Trilling was tacitly revealing himself to be a Jew. As William Galperin notes, in that essay Trilling "stresses, in ways that might seem beside the point but presumably were of great urgency to the author himself, the link between the Rabbis in their stance to the Torah and Wordsworth in his stance toward Nature." See William Galperin, "Romanticism and/or AntiSemitism," in *Between 'Race' and Culture: Representation of the 'the Jew' in English and American Literature,* ed. Bryan Cheyette (Stanford, Stanford University Press, 1996), pp. 16–26, and p. 185 n. 3.

10. In *Diving into the Wreck* (New York, Norton, 1973), p. 24.

11. Indeed, as both recent Israeli history and more and more voices are pointing out, this valorization of the West at the expense of the Levant points to a profound, historical, social, political, and cultural tragedy of Israeli life. See especially the crucial study by Ammiel Alcalay, *After Jews and Arabs: Remaking Levantine Culture* (Minneapolis, University of Minnesota Press, 1993). See also Shulamith Hareven, *The Vocabulary of Peace: Life, Culture, and Politics in the Middle East* (San Francisco, Mercury House, 1996), particularly her chapter "Israel: The First Forty Years," pp. 95–124. Hareven claims that "positing Israel as a country of Western culture" is an "absurdity"; "one [suspects] that perhaps our vaunted Westernness is really only a form of anti-Easternism and anti-Arabism-unabashed racism" (pp. 111–112). Both also point to the price paid by the Hebrew language itself (and thus Hebrew literature) for being uprooted from its Semitic context. "Our language is becoming impoverished and unidiomatic, and in part it is simply translated from English," she writes (p. 117). See also her chapter, "On Being a Levantine" (pp. 81–87: "Peace with our neighbors is the lifeblood of language-struck types like me," writes Hareven, "because we wish to return the language to its Semitic roots-in other words, rescue it from extinction. For us, as secularization progressed, our Hebrew deteriorated and became shallow and devoid of cultural resonance, a language out of context. Here, because of our exposure to the West rather than the Levant, people sometimes write American books in Hebrew, or Russian books in Hebrew. . . . We have come to accept the fact that our newspaper articles contain ten measures of linguistic and cultural ignorance; that our educated class, which in every civilized country is the standard bearer of language, prefers to write in English-not even good English, but sociologese" (p. 86).

12. But *not* on Hebron Road. Though traveling back to Jerusalem on the "old road," that is, within the Green Line, took much longer, at night Hebron road was considered too dangerous to travel because of the risk of terrorism. The illusion of the placid picturesque gave way, in the darkness, to uncomfortable truths. How strange it is to me, in retrospect, to realize how inured we had become to the "danger," how we took it for granted, how we never, in all my years traveling that road, questioned it.

13. William Blake, "To the Jews" *Jerusalem,* Plate 27: 112 (London, Oxford, 1952), Foreword by Geoffrey Keynes. Blake's line, "I must create a System, or be enslaved by another Man's" (*Jerusalem,* plate 10:20) was used by redoubtable critics like the late Northrop Frye to "read" Blake by creating a symbolic "System" supposedly designed to explain Blake's. Just as I argued then that such accounts ignored the *actual experience* of the reader wading through Blake's poetry, so later I was to argue against the mode of formal pedagogy that eliminated the student's actual engagement with the text as part of the teaching process.

14. For this statistic, and for the political history of this period, I am grateful both to Uri Talil and to Marcia Freedman, *Exile in the Promised Land: A Memoir* (Ithaca, New York, Firebrand Books, 1990).

15. In 1994 I went to see the play "Gorodish" by Hillel Mitelfunkt, which opened at the Tel Aviv Cameri, November 20, 1993. Playing to a packed house, "Gorodish" was a scathing exposé of the political corruption before and during the Yom Kippur War. Those grim, rapt, faces in the house—had they been soldiers in that war, parents who lost their sons in the war? The "Golda" of the play had little in common with the tough-love grandma from Milwaukee that the American Jewish disneyfied imagination constructed.

16. The Agranat Commission's report has not been consigned to the dustbin of history. Former commando, military chief of staff, foreign minister, and present Labor party leader Ehud Barak is quoted as warning Netanyahu about "his split with the military establishment." According to the *Jerusalem Report,* Barak said: "Before the [Jerusalem Old City] tunnel, I said to [Netanyahu]: 'I tell you from experience, talk [to the Palestinians] on every subject.' He gave me some kind of smooth answer, and I interrupted: 'Mr. Prime Minister,' I said, 'you'd better listen very carefully. Clear a few days on your schedule and read very carefully all the heavy volumes of the Agranat Commission report on the 1973 Yom Kippur War, including the one about the political echelon.' To be prime minister of Israel is no laughing matter." *Jerusalem Report,* November 14, 1996, p. 18.

17. Compare Dahlia Ravikovich's line, "If not for Labor movement values/Men would eat each other alive," in "Unusual Autumn," translated by Chana Bloch, *Dreaming the Actual: Israeli Women Writers at the Turn of the Twenty-First Century,* (Albany, SUNY Press, forthcoming).

18. In *Bitter Milk: Women and Teaching* (Amherst, MA, 1988), p. 111.

19. Paolo Freire quoted by Block, *Occupied Reading*, New York, Garland, 1995), p. 200.

20. See "The 'Torah' of Criticism and the Criticism of Torah: Recuperating the Pedagogical Moment," in *Interpreting Judaism in a Postmodern Age*, ed. Steven Kepnes (New York, 1996), p. 231.

21. See *Bitter Milk*, pp. 126–127. In ways that accord with my own experience and thinking, Grumet draws on the work of Nancy Chodorow to argue that the Lacanian model excludes the "the mimetic, maternal, and semiotic identifications . . . established in preoedipal experience." Still, she says, "Lacan's narrative of our origins" should be read as a "reasonable rendering" of the psychoanalytic process enacted in "the pedagogy of the academy" (p. 125).

22. Adrienne Rich, "Leaflets," in *Leaflets: Poems 1965-1968* (New York, Norton, 1969), p. 56.

23. Adrienne Rich, "Trying to Talk with a Man," *Diving into the Wreck*, p. 4.

24. In "Burbank with a Baedeker: Bleisten with a Cigar." See the analysis of Eliot's anti-Semitic discourse in Anthony Julius, *T.S. Eliot: anti-Semitism and Literary Form* (Cambridge, Cambridge University Press, 1995).

25. In *Milton*, 1:16. *The Poetry and Prose of William Blake*, ed. David V. Erdman (New York, Doubleday, 1965), p. 95. My emphasis.

26. Helene Cixous and Catherine Clement, *The Newly Born Woman*. Trans. Betsy Wing (Minneapolis, University of Minnesota Press, 1986), pp. 66, 68.

27. In *Interactive Phases of Curricular Revision: A Feminist Perspective* (Wellesley, 1986), quoted in William F. Pinar *et al*, *Understanding Curriculum: An Introduction to the Study of Historical and Contemporary Curriculum Discourses* (New York, 1995), p. 368.

28. Obsessively baking cakes: "During and after the Yom Kippur War, when men were mobilized for six months and women found themselves very lonely and powerless, a flour shortage occurred: The women were baking too many cakes, and continued to do so even when the shortage was made public!" Regine Waintrater, "Living in a State of Siege," *Calling the Equality Bluff: Women in Israel* (New York, Pergamon, 1991), p. 118. In this otherwise excellent academic collection, the "equality bluff" is called in many areas of Israeli life, but interestingly enough, not in academia.

29. Or, rather, reborn. The early women *halutsot* had believed in sexual equality and thought that once in Palestine "there would be no distinction between men and women." They were soon disavowed of their optimism. See Lesley Hazelton, *Israeli Women: The Reality Behind the Myths* (New York, Simon and Shuster, 1977), pp. 15–21.

30. The *agunah* has been a recurrent figure in Hebrew and Yiddish literature; her problematic and ambivalent status has served as a locus for social, cultural,

and religious criticism. See the sensitive and important study by Miriam Weisel, "The Bruised Heart: An Analysis of the Image of the Agunah in Biblical through Contemporary Literature," Unpublished M.A. Thesis (University of Judaism), 1994.

31. Is Israel fated to catapult back and forth between those images? After ousting the Shamir government - the avatar of the narrative of a "fortress" Israel—the late Prime Minister Rabin announced at his inaugural that "Israel will no longer be 'a nation that dwells alone' but will join the global community." Since the assassination of Rabin and the election of Netanyahu, the polarization has only intensified. According to commentator Ze'ev Chafets, in 1996 "you can't turn on a radio talk show . . . without hearing dire warnings that Israel is on the brink of a religious civil war. . . . We are not one, but two peoples, with the fault line running between those who want to be ruled by the Torah and those who want to live in a modern democracy...We can fight over this country, make one another miserable at best and destroy another at worst. Or, we can do what logic dictates and separate. There is enough land, people and resources for two Hebrew states—Judea and Israel." An ironic "two-state solution" far different from that movements like Peace Now have envisioned See "A Two-State Solution," *Jerusalem Report,* November 28, 1996, p. 22.

32. Ella Shohat, *Israeli Cinema: East/West and the Politics of Representation* (Austin, University of Texas, 1989), p. 233.

33. See David Biale, *Eros and the Jews: From Biblical Israel to Contemporary America* (New York, Basic Books, 1992), pp. 177–203. See also Hazleton's chapter, "Zionism and Manhood," *Israeli Women,* pp. 91–111.

34. On the "nebbish" trope, see Harry Brod, "Of Mice and Supermen: Images of Jewish Masculinity," *Gender and Judaism,* ed. Tamar Rodofsy (NY: 1995), pp. 279–293. For a sardonic portrayal of these fanatically religious- nationalistic American Jewish men *and* women in Israel, see Tova Reich's *The Jewish War* (New York, Pantheon, 1995). Even more disturbing than the men, however, are the Jewish women in Hebron. Ultimately, writes Netty C. Gross, "theirs is a harsh ideology, in which suffering redeems- in which the God who honored the barren, sorrowing mothers of the Bible with children, will likewise reward this generation of Hebron mothers for their female tenacity." "Women on Both Sides of the Hebron Breakdown," *Jerusalem Report,* November 28, 1996, pp. 12–13. What psychic drama is being enacted when they are willing to risk the life of their family, their own life, as well as the lives of soldiers, so that they can live under the Jewish hegemony near the *graves* of the Biblical mothers?

35. Though I borrow the phrase from Daniel Boyarin and Jonathan Boyarin's "Diaspora: Generation and the Ground of Jewish Identity," *Curriculum Inquiry* 19 (Summer 1993), p. 713, I want to distinguish between the experience for Jews of Diaspora in the United States and Diaspora as it was experienced in the past in most European countries. The suffering and persecution suffered by Jews all through European history the authors, it seems to me ignore.

Chapter 7

Being Jewish: A Narrative of Cynicism and Joy

Barry Kanpol

> Testimony is a very hard spirit to convey in a written text . . . it struck me that dialogue was one of the ways where the sense of mutual witness and testimony could be made manifest. I link that sense to regular communion service in the Black church at Yale where we would often stand in a collective circle and sing, "Let us Break Bread Together on our Knees," and the lines in the song which say, "When I Fall on my Knees with My Face to the Rising Sun, Oh Lord Have Mercy On Me." I liked the combination of the notion of community which is about sharing and breaking bread together, of dialogue as well as mercy because Mercy speaks to the need we have for compassion, acceptance, understanding, and empathy[1].

Introduction

The above quote from bell hooks perhaps adequately characterizes the struggle one may have in personal and collective testimony. Tied to this struggle is the realization that, indeed, struggle can be lonely; it can be cynical; it can be joyful; it can be unified with others. Ultimately, personal testimony is hard as well as deep and committed work that crosses over to the political. Thus, when I stand in front of my undergraduate and graduate foundations classes, I usually "tell" my students that education is invariably about who you are and what you believe in, and this is often conveyed in both overt and covert ways. Concurrently, I elaborate on the significance of personal narrative as a starting point to examine what education means in the community at large. There is no doubt in my mind, that a part of this personal narrative is reaching deep down into the gut of one's personal faith (or in some cases, no faith) in order to answer these particular questions: Is or can my faith be connected to the everyday life world of teaching and learning? If so, how do I keep true to both my faith and a rapidly changing "postmodern" world? In short, I ask students at least implicitly to think about their particular testimony, their story, the sense of the world they inhabit. I make it clear to students that being vulnerable is part of opening up to one's history, beliefs, and prejudices, etc. This is precisely what has been asked of me as I contribute to this volume. Not to be vulnerable and elaborate on personal narrative or at least a part of my testimony, or to shy away from this project would have been to commit an injustice to my students as well as myself, particularly as the critical theoretical frameworks I have been operating out of for nearly a decade beg this type of personal reflection! With that in mind, in this essay I will quickly summarize one aspect of a critical theory framework as being couched within what I denote as a politics of cynicism and joy. I then recapitulate personal narrative on experiences both as a child and as an adult that connect directly to my Jewish experiences. I analyze these experiences in light of the theoretical framework developed in the first section. Finally, I conclude with the ramifications of the identity issues raised and the theoretical frameworks analyzed for the practice of an enlightened education.

Some of the Literature: The Politics of Cynicism and Joy

I have argued at length elsewhere[2] that the educational left, particularly those aligned with what has now become commonly known as the "critical pedagogy movement," have yet to generate a language that speaks to and with multiple sets of audiences. I have also argued that pouncing on the postmodern bandwagon has plainly become another avenue for one-upmanship and rush to publication[3], a form, I would argue, of academic nihilism: In short, more of the same old academic jostling for position and political game. Frankly, I have become exceedingly bored with all this.

In my mind, the time has come for the educational left, particularly those involved with what is commonly thought of as the critical pedagogy movement, to come to terms with the profound theological possibilities and implications of its work. With the advent of Jonathan Kozol's devastating descriptions and critique of inner-city schools in the United States[4], critical pedagogues in the educational arena have offered much deconstructive analysis of structural school issues around race, class and gender, most of which have suggested hopelessness and despair. Ultimately, to ask the question, *to what end* is all this deconstruction needed, has to be continuously asked inorder to gain political ground.

In the larger philosophical picture, educational postmodernists have negated *T*ruth and have concentrated on the particular[5]. Within this value of difference as a marker, a lot of good has happened in critical educational circles. We view ourselves as pioneers in a new educational movement, rallying for "critical multiculturalism"[6], "feminism" and its multiple formations[7], as well as "gay" rights[8] and other claims to personal and public space involving the marginalized and oppressed[9]. Critical educational history is too cumbersome to go into detail here, yet if I were to describe where it is leading us, I would encapsulate the postmodern "stuff" as both **cynical** and **catch 22**, yet necessary for a liberating agenda that the part of the most emancipatory form of modernism[10] and being Jewish promises for me!!

It is important to note that critical theorists in general, myself in particular, have carried an air of cynicism into their work for many years now. For me, cynicism, or the cynic is one who is inclined to investigate the sincerity and goodness of people's motives and actions, or the value of living, one who highly questions the material interests of individuals. Let me be clear here. I am *not* arguing that cynicism, as defined above is necessarily a bad or evil thing. Critical theorists in education have understood for some time that there are very good reasons to be significantly suspicious of a society whose institutions like schools claim democratic virtues, yet in the everyday life-world espouses an often contradictory capitalistic market logic[11], often resulting in race, class and gender inequities[12].

Theoretically, the cynicism I am talking about grows out of a "catch 22" logic that educational theory in general has found itself in. Put differently, how does one escape the dialectic? This was highly questioned in Willis's now notorious work in education, where the inevitability of cultural reproduction weighed heavily against the backdrop of the culturally productive aspects of counter-hegemony within a capitalistic framework[13]. Unable to escape this dialectic, educators have since grappled with the inevitability of this logic[14]. In my educational foundations classes for instance, teachers are at pains to counter the damning oppressive structural constraints imposed on them by the state-mandated curriculum, intensification of labor, and deskilling, etc. Concurrently, as they see and feel emancipatory hope, counter-hegemonic forms raise their ugly heads, and thus, my in-service teachers are at once cut back by other constraints and forced into some other form of oppressive conformity. Because of this one-step forward, two-step backward syndrome, they become cynical, and find little solace in ways out of the cultural nightmares they find themselves in, despite the sincerity that structures their original criticisms and feelings of despair. No less can be said of those criticalists who argue that it becomes impossible to become the Other - those marginalized and oppressed[15]. This dualistic and often oppositional logic, also cynical, while sincere in intention, and often but not always correct in the everyday life world[16], denies the theoretical and practical possibility for fusion with Other in an intercommunicative dialogue of liberating struggle and possibility. To me, cynicism, then, becomes *a necessary but not sufficient* condition for social transformation. Its positive and emancipatory intent is often contradicted by the logic of opposition and excessive competition and is thus constraining and accommodative to dominant and oppressive ideological forms. As a response to this confusion, I have in the past fused modern and postmodern theoretical constructs as a possible avenue out of this theoretical web. This has also been attempted by others as well[17], and will be alluded to later in my analysis of my "Jewish" narrative.

There is another side to critical educational theory that is often left by the wayside. To me, social transformation must be inclusive of "joy" both as a spiritual and /or philosophical position and in the world of the everyday. Connecting to a politics of alliance and liberation, Michael Lerner asserts in a conversation with Cornel West:

> This is a perfect moment for the alliance of Blacks and Jews to advocate Politics of Meaning that explicitly takes seriously the most fundamental "traditional value": Love your neighbor as yourself. A progressive Politics of Meaning would reclaim the biblical value of caring for others that was Central to the Torah and Jesus. In fact, these biblical ethics stand in sharp contrast to the ethos of selfishness, enshrined in the politics of Newt Gingrich, Rush Limbaugh, and the very *un-Christian* Christian right[18]

A politics of meaning, *joy* is politically loaded to mean alliance, commonality, and what Lerner describes in his own work as "renewal." He comments, more spiritually, connecting joy to ethics:

> Reclaiming a sense of celebration and joy at the wonders of creation is another sense of Jewish renewal . . .What is unique about Judaism is that it entwines this sense of awe, wonder, amazement, and this spiritual reality that

> surrounds us, with a vision of God who not only created the universe but also is the force that makes possible an ethically guided universe[19].

For Lerner as well as West, joy connects ethically to renewal as a Politics of Meaning in which liberation from oppressive social forces becomes a guiding motif - despite, I might add, their differences in faith. Joy, thus understood, is a healing process or *Tikkun*, which in Hebrew means to repair and/or heal. The bond of commonality entered by Lerner and West, as an act of solidarity has enormous philosophical implications as related to joy.

The way I am using cynicism and joy should not be seen as a static dialectic. As a process of common democratic struggle, joy must be seen within cynicism and growing out of cynicism as a necessary condition for human liberation. For example, in his book on Deleuze, philosopher Michael Hardt argues for commonality as a basic form of joy. He relates how workers in the novel by Nanni Balestrini *Vogliamo tutto* (We want Everything) struggle for group solidarity. This is interpreted by Deleuze as an

> attack on their essence as workers. They arrive at a moment when they are able to go beyond, to discover a terrain of creation and joy beyond the worker[20].

Hardt' emphasizes that workers in this novel recognize their commonality and,

> their expression in collective action take the form of a spatial or social synthesis, composing an expansive and coherent body of desire. As the body of workers expands, their will and power grow. The synthesis involved in the workers' collectivity is an internal return of the will . . . precisely when the workers actualize their critique, then they pass into action in the factory and in the streets, they achieve the constructive moment of joy and creation. The actualization of the workers is a practice of joy[21].

Hardt's central point here, I believe, is to locate a philosophy of joy which is necessarily tied directly to a philosophy of practice, a suggestive argument linking commonness or common behavior and /or common desire to a practice of joy. Commonness can and should be related to what Laclau and Mouffe term, a "democratic imaginary"[22]. Here, political struggles and/or antagonisms are connected by their commonness to end various forms of alienation, subordination and oppression. Cynicism that leads to joy as commonness as solidarity, is only a part of this philosophical treatise.

Hardt goes on to argue that for Spinozian practice, joy must be entwined with a speculation that leads to an *affirmation* in order for an ethic of "democratic political practice"[23] to be established. It is joy within affirmation and vise versa that leads Hardt to argue that indeed a critical political practice is an ethic that includes "the affirmation of speculation and the joy of practice"[24]. The movement from speculation to practice, and from affirmation to joy is, I would argue, a political moment that includes critique or cynicism of the existing structures in which we work as cultural workers, which in essence furthers this democratic imaginary that commonly bonds social actors attempting to end various forms of alienation, subordination and oppression. Put differently, cynicism as a necessary condition for social transformation cannot exist alone without affirmation and joy as part of this common transformation process. I might add, that despite the problematic of commonness (note the constant bashing of critical pedagogues on each other), joyful passions are embedded within a common critical goal. This commonness is an affirmation of joy. The leap from cynic to joy is a body-being-politic implies that commonness is sought across distance and time as well as locally if possible. This leap also suggests that "the passage for passive joy to active joy involves substituting an internal cause for an external cause; or, more precisely, it involves enveloping or comprehending the cause within the encounter itself"[25].

The above short theoretical treatise has suggested that cynicism and joy are part and parcel of a critical educational position. There is also no doubt in my mind that my politics has been informed by own particular history. With that in mind, I want to turn to narrative as a way be which to bridge my own history to the theory discussed in this first section.

Some Personal Narrative

Probably a defining moment for any critical theorist is their personal understanding of the oppressive structures they formerly or presently live in. As a critical pedagogist, I too have a micro narrative, life stories replete with instances where I could feel forms of personal alienation, oppression and subordination subjecting me as well as I acting as a protagonist. These instances, in some part, form a cornerstone of my politics. They are a part of my construction of a "critical" pedagogical position. This involves a political response to the conditions of everyday experiences, to the values that embody me and the culture I presently live in. With that in mind, this section will focus on areas of my own narrative. I do this, in part, to vulnerably share some of my history so that others may begin to either understand or empathize. I do this, perhaps therapeutically as well, so that I can better understand the dialectic of cynicism and joy I earlier theorized over.

I was born to two very proper folks, in Melbourne, Australia. My father was/is an extremely hard working man. My mother was/is a devoted wife. She was always around when I needed her, invested in my daily activities which included school work and outside interests such as my sporting concerns. She was raised within an Orthodox Jewish tradition, while my father grew up as a Zionist, still respecting and holding to Jewish traditions. My mother's Jewish lineage consisted of the conservative religious sort. I often recall at her mother's house, the rigid Saturday rituals—no lights or T.V. on Saturday, a clear understanding of which dishes to use (milk or meat) and what side of the sink to clean these dishes as well as hands, etc. As I grew up, the division of labor in my parent's home was very clearly divided gender inflicted. My parents seemed content with that lifestyle. It was predictable and I felt safe in both their particular and social set-up.

Both Mum and Dad had found their ways to Australia differently. In short, Dad had come through China (by way of Russian parents) and Mum through Poland. For various reasons they were both in Israel when they met, Dad through the Israeli Independence war and Mum on a personal visit. They found each other and eventually, their way to Australia and lived there for 20 years. As Zionists they returned to Israel in 1973, with the two children, and still live there.

Growing up in Australia was easy. While my parents struggled financially, particularly early in their marriage, through discipline, motivation, desire, and a little luck, my father became an entrepreneur and moved into middle class. I never felt materialistically in need. If my parents struggled financially and/or personally, I never knew about it. I grew up with that privilege, recalling fleeting times when Dad would be upset when business wasn't going well.

Perhaps my childhood could be divided into at least two significant areas: School and Religion. I vividly recall attending a private Jewish day school. Two pronounced things happened to me during that time. School was both a bore and very competitive. There was no substantive vision for why we were to receive an education, only that it would land a more prestigious job one day, thus providing upward social mobility. I have described elsewhere in detail how this process was one of hegemonic control[26]. But, there is another part to this story about schools for me that has been left out publicly, which also has serious ramifications. Even though I grew up in a traditionally kept Jewish home (which Mum always tried to ritualistically keep through Friday night candles, observance of High Holidays, Kosher food and more), little mention was made of this impact on my life, particularly as it relates to everyday teaching experiences. I recall many instances of my Jewish upbringing that remain profoundly with me today. *In part*, this also forms a cornerstone of my politics, of who I am in the present educational context.

Like others[27] religion was as I felt at the time, forced upon me through prayer and ritual. I recall having to recite certain prayers every morning as well as attend Hebrew classes twice daily. I distinctly remember my Hebrew teacher of grades 2, 3 and 4. While I do not recall that she liked me, I was put off by the endless vocabulary lists that hounded me through 6th grade. After 6th grade, Hebrew classes became one big joke. I rebelled in school and made it a point with other male conspirators to make our Hebrew teachers cry. We were not going to be forced to learn an alien language, especially if it had no relevance to our daily lived experiences. At least, this is why I rebelled. Yes, I was resentful of anything that was authoritatively taught and denying me freedom of thoughtful expression.

Despite my personal struggles in this Jewish school, being "forced" to learn for Barmitzvah rituals was still rather enjoyable. I wanted to make my parents proud and I would be able to showcase my talents. And, I did. My Bar-Mitzvah to this day remains etched in my memory in a number of ways. I fondly recall the week-end celebrations, with me as the center of attention, with family and friends gathered from all over the country. I guess entrance into Jewish "manhood" was a big deal. So, I played on, although I was never told why this was important, only that it was. I was the good kid and acquiesced to what was required of me, this even though I disliked the methods of forced Hebrew instruction in my school. And, despite the centrality of my Barmitzvah to Jewish experiences of the community, I was concurrently bogged down personally with academic requirements. Unfortunately, I lied before my Barmitzvah as to the grade I received for a test and about the fact that I had taken a test two days earlier. Yes, despite the glory and symbolic significance of this Jewish ritual I wondered even then, if a part of this ritual included fear of performance, testing and living up to expectations. Who was I chanting in synagogue for? I didn't understand what I was singing even though the Rabbi made a point of telling the congregation that he felt that "Barry sang as if he knew what every word meant." When he said that, I knew I had good acting qualities in me! It was after my Bar-Mitzvah, that I suddenly shot up in height and as it was also a time of adolescence, I began to seriously think about my role as a member of society. Personal identity was questioned, particularly with my impending immigration to Israel.

Going to synagogue grew to be a forced commitment I began to resent, particularly after my entrance into "Jewish manhood." While I was growing up, I realized that synagogue symbolized not only a place of prayer/worship, but more specifically, of social mobility and/or a social outlet. I have fond memories at synagogue, particularly as a six year old, playing with my grandfather and receiving his personal attention. In the long run, however, I attended synagogue to meet friends, and socialize by talking football with my "mates" or to see girls who seemed interested in me. Eventually, I attended synagogue rarely, mainly on the high holidays. And, it was a chore. When living in Israel, I never attended synagogue. I was told that as I was Jewish and living in Israel, a Jewish homeland, not attending would be O.K. What a distortion of a spiritual life!!! In general, it seemed weird to be told to pray twice or three times a year for forgiveness of one's sins, particularly on Yom Kipper (Day of Atonement). Why should I atone when I felt I was being shafted by a system where I was defined by my principal in my Australian school as a failure who should be a "barber," and who falsely accused me of "smoking drugs and womanizing all the time," this despite my sporting prowess and virginity. So, while I may have personally "sinned" (not even knowing what these sins were, so I didn't know why or what I was atoning for), so did the institution I was living in!!! What about the other 364 days of the year I would think to myself as I do now. Besides, when I attended synagogue at the time, I couldn't understand the Hebrew and the hymns sung, even though they were repetitively drummed into me over the years. Actually, I couldn't wait to sing these hymns. They signified the end of services! Little sense was thus made over mandatory services.

I really don't want to remain cynical. For not all is that negative. I warmly recall reading Old Testament Bible stories late into the night in my bed before I would doze off. I would read these stories over and again—stories of Creation, Adam and Eve, Cain and Abel, Noah,

Abraham, Isaac, Sarah, Jacob, Moses, Miriam, Pharaoh, David, Saul, Jonathan, Samson, and Ruth, etc. I learned what miracles in the desert were, a covenant, yes, God's promises, etc. I believed it all. I was fascinated. Would I ever have a personal covenant like Abraham and Moses? Could I ever be like those Biblical heroes? They were larger than life figures! Today, I often reflect on how those stories brought and to some degree still bring me safety and joy, especially to a questioning today and troubled child spirit then. I even remember, as I write now, the smell of the pages those stories were written on. They are etched in my memory forever. Often, when visiting my parents in Israel, I return to those stories and muse through them nostalgically recalling fond memories of childhood!

I joyfully recall Passover and the Jewish New Year, and even the various rituals celebrated with my family. Even though I wasn't taught so much what the profound symbolic ramifications of these rituals were, they were nonetheless the stuff that held families together, and I appreciated them then, as I do now. What really fascinated me were stories of escape, justice, freedom, martyrdom and commitment to a "promised land," etc. Perhaps that's why my parents are in Israel today! And, perhaps that is why I'm in the field I'm in today—justice, freedom, escape, etc.

Very sadly, I was met with a fair amount of anti-semitism as a child/boy growing up. "Dirty Jew" and "Jew boy" were often flung at me in discriminating and humiliating ways. Playing competitive sports for non-Jewish teams was never easy because I often felt left out, different and at times "less than," despite personal success. I would try to hide my identity. And, while I didn't go out of my way to tell my non-Jewish friends "who" I was, everyone still found out that I was Jewish. Relatedly, and **just as important**, I grew up in a closed Jewish community who *also* discriminated against non-Jews. I would often hear the words "Those Goyim (Non-Jews)" as a statement of Jewish retaliation to "those Jews or dirty Jew," particularly by my parent's friends. And, in the street where I lived from 8–17 years of age, many people didn't speak to my sister or I, or many kids weren't even allowed to play with us because we were Jewish. Today I still ***despise both forms of discrimination—Jewish and non-Jewish.*** Most sadly, I grew up with both guilt and shame at being Jewish—an interesting dualism, since I was always taught to be proud of my Jewish heritage. I would often walk to synagogue on the Day of Atonement and have to pass a public school. I would see kids staring at me; at my suit and tie.

Or was I paranoid? I quickly learned to walk across the street from the school so as to avoid more shame. My hiding had deeper ramifications, all of which is still very difficult to make sense of today.

As I grew up through my formative years, I learned that **TRUTH** was supposedly a Jewish thing. There was no mention of meaning making beyond the Old Testament. I grew up not knowing that there was the possibility of Part 2 to the Bible. I grew up not knowing the difference between Jew, Gentile or Christian, or about the appreciation of difference in general. Joy and love again were supposedly Jewish things. This contradicted my personal experiences; forced religion, authoritarian school structure, the discrimination of both Jews and non-Jews that I always experienced (as the discriminated and discriminator), and the feelings of guilt and shame I had, etc. Who needed this stuff I would always inwardly retort!

Since those days, life's experiences have had a way of humbling me. A struggling immigrant in Israel for 10 years (more forced Hebrew and illiterate in the dominant language), a failed marriage and eventually a career that sits entrenched in theoretical nihilism and despair (given many of the postmodern viewpoints I have often adopted) have sometimes rendered me quite sarcastic, hopeless and sorry in the face of social and cultural structural nightmares. And, this despite my privileged social position. My politics has often been confusing. No wonder! Despite postmodern theoretical suavities, I often have wondered what meaning I can take out from my youth and present life that makes story telling so powerful, so profound, and so real, that a politics of hope **can** rear its head. So, I feel that I **must** take those biblical stories of joy and seek every emancipatory moment out of them. And, I must challenge traditional Jewish ways, as I always did as a boy, and then read the New Testament as well, and again etch out emancipatory possibilities. I cannot be discriminatory to others' view of the Bible, otherwise I would be guilty of the same discrimination I grew up with. These culminating experiences and thoughts are part of what Sharon Welch[28] describes as "dangerous memories," instances that rear liberation hopes in the face of some personal oppression, alienation and subordination.

Talking Back and Breaking Bread

In a recent publication of mine[29], I argued that in order for the educational left to make inroads into the dominant culture, a new language would have to be produced that would be more inclusive of the dominant culture. I openly admitted that the left (critical pedagogy in particular) was bereft of a spiritual language, lost in its social causes and general cynicism and despair. To what end do we critique? This is a question that must be asked over and over again, to check where it is we are headed, and why we are going there. It is our moral responsibility to constantly reflect on this question.

My history, some of which has been narrated above, begs this question: How does one build alliances within difference that has as its core a normative "modernistic" platform of a personal and social emancipatory nature? Feeling many times personally alienated, either because of my "Jewishness" or where I was living at any particular moment (particularly Australia, but also in Israel), critical pedagogy has meant a method by which to reclaim, challenge, alter and move within one's historically constructed identity. Given the various forms of discrimination by both Jewish and non-Jewish people I encountered as a child and as I still do as an adult in assorted manners, critical pedagogy has also meant struggling to fashion the modernist ideals of enlightenment that I read "into" the Bible as a kid growing up, as well as meaning making that can forever be "postmodernistically" deconstructed!! Perhaps, more importantly, critical pedagogy has personal meaning to me, one which Giroux describes as "border crossings"[30], but more profoundly, perhaps, a spiritual border crossing in the name of a progressive politics of alliance. Thus, the imagery of **talking back and breaking bread** symbolizes the ability to challenge forms of oppression as well as dialogue over emancipatory possibilities.

The above image is seen in the book by Lerner and West[31]. They come together across religious and spiritual differences, yet etch out similarities of history as related to alienation, oppression and subordination. Comments Lerner:

> Yet, this is a perfect moment for an alliance of Blacks and Jews to advocate a Politics of Meaning that explicitly takes seriously the most fundamental "traditional value.": Love your neighbor as yourself. A Progressive Politics of Meaning would reclaim the biblical value of Caring for others that was central both to the Torah and to Jesus. In fact, these biblical ethics stand in sharp contrast to the ethos of selfishness, Enshrined in the politics of Newt Gingrich, Rush Limbaugh, and the very *Un-Christian* Christian right . . . It is precisely because both our communities already have a foundation for this alternative way of thinking, in the Torah, in the New Testament, and in some more humanistic trends of Islam, that it becomes possible to imagine a real working together that is neither patriotizing nor self-negating[32].

As a child, I was never taught to "talk back" or "break bread," despite the Passover imagery and breaking bread together as a family. Only today, I realize that I am talking back by challenging oppressive structures.

In their book **Breaking Bread**[33], bell hooks and Cornel West take on the imagery of sitting together and dialoging across differences, much like West and Lerner. West and hooks come together in a spirit and compassion as well as testimony and solidarity. In their conversation, hooks and West inform readers of the power of faith; for them, Black and Christian. For them breaking bread also images "serious talk about coming together, sharing, participating, creating bonds of solidarity . . . linking some sense of faith, religious faith, political faith, to the struggle for freedom"[34].

Personally, Breaking Bread first brings to mind the image of the Jewish festival of Passover, celebrated for Jews in solidarity throughout the world. In breaking the traditional Passover bread, Jews are reminded that a central message of Passover is one of freedom, hope and humility of a God that helped free a nation of slavery. Second, the image of breaking bread takes me back to Jesus in the New Testament. He broke bread with his disciples in a bond of solidarity, a common understanding about freedom, in this case, a freedom of and belief in a savior. No matter the interpretation, a rudimentary and profound message is clear. To break bread is to be humble. To "dialogue across difference"[35] is to concede and understand, incorporate borders of theoretical knowledge into a common moral and faithful vision for freedom and democracy **with** our non-Jewish brothers and sisters. To some, this may mean understanding what Paul's struggle in the New Testament was about—jailed because of his belief of the highest moral and faithful order, or Martin Luther King's message of "I have a dream" meant, or falling back to Romans 12, 2 when connecting spiritual sides of faith to political transformation:

> And be ye not conformed to this world: but be ye transformed by the Renewing of your mind.

An appreciation of such transformation may be viewed by Abraham's rejection of his father's idolatrous life (note a sense of rejecting excessive materialism here) or a deep appreciation of what sacrifice may have meant as in Abraham's willingness to sacrifice his son because of his belief and conviction to a higher order. It is as if Abraham, in his rejection of his father's values, was as bell hooks decries in *Talking Back*:

> Moving from silence into speech is for the oppressed, the colonized,
> The exploited, and those who stand and struggle side by side as gesture
> Of defiance that heals, that makes new life and new growth possible.
> It is that act of speech, of "talking back," that is no mere gesture of
> Empty words, that is the expression of our movement from object to
> Subject—the liberated voice[36].

Personally, that liberated voice moves between the dialectic of cynicism and joy. Breaking Bread and Talking Back metaphorically signifies a breakdown of the cynic and a movement to joyful possibilities as a starting point to understand how social and cultural transformation may be viewed, how borders of theoretical understanding may be negotiated with this end in mind: a vision of moral and ethical responsibility that seeks an emancipatory and normative framework, despite historically constructed faith differences.

The above utopian vision (perhaps modernistic here) suggests a sovereign of possibility. In part, my Jewishness has meant a deeper understanding of dialectical thinking (cynicism and joy) with an emancipatory common struggle that travels beyond Jewish boundaries for survival. Theoretical, spiritual and practical borders of difference that centers on what Purpel and other liberation theologists[37] describe as a search for a vision of possibility that has its roots in connection with a higher belief in Spirit or God must be sought as an alternative to **but not negation of** difference. For West, this struggle for meaning and ultimately democracy, "is an ethical implication of the Christian conception of what it means to be human, how we understand democracy, what is its content, its substance"[38]. For hooks and West, this struggle is rooted in faith and commitment to a higher moral vision, tied to a belief in God that "is understood in relation to a particular context, to specific circumstances"[39] and a commitment to enduring one's faith despite the suffering one might occur within that belief, or the particular circumstances one may find themselves in. Jewishness too, with all its history of oppression and alienation has personally meant an understanding of the "Other" and the common bond of joy to be that Other, concurrently being cynical of how that Other has been co-opted into the dominant culture.

Stories have a way of humbling me, simply by reminding me of the complex world we live in. While I personally believe and have adopted many of the postmodern arguments, I am still led and driven to interrogate the moral fabric of many nihilistic postmodern theorists who lack a unified vision for a common good, a vision of faith, or a vision of order to repair or represent the common hopes and dreams of ordinary people. These hopes are entwined within the stories we tell and the profound symbolic meaning we attach. It is here where the cynic and joyful Jew I represent can be found, still deeply struggling over meaning and interpretation of how faith both personally and generally can be connected within a postmodern world to an enlightened modernistic set of ideals and ethics.

Conclusions: Implications for Teacher Education

I do not stand infront of my classes and force the relationship of faith to social practice down anyone's throats, even though this has become a major issue in policy decision making (note the harsh and sometimes volatile debate over Outcomes Based Education between the extreme Christian Right and those who support OBE) and vitally important to me. But, I do tell my story. I do relate those areas of cynicism and joy to my students that have engulfed my life. Students in turn tell me their stories, their narratives (as much as they choose). I do believe that faith is connected to social practice **but not** in the evangelical sense that some would believe.

Indeed, to speak the language of the dominant culture is to find a language that speaks to and with others. Thus, as a critical pedagogist, it is my duty to seek out emancipatory possibilities by talking the language of the dominant culture. There is nothing wrong, in my opinion, to talk of teachers as prophets. I ask students to envision themselves as prophetic figures with a moral mission. There is nothing wrong, in my opinion, of asking students to think of their classroom as holy. What does a holy classroom look like? There is nothing wrong in my opinion with thinking of education as a sacred ideal. What does a sacred education look like is something my students have to grapple with. There is nothing wrong, in my opinion, in looking at education as creating a fusion of spirit and practice. What does a spiritual classroom look like? I appeal to in- and pre-service students' good sense, their ethical nature, their initial desires as to why they became teachers in the first place. In telling my personal story in various snippets during the semester, I invite students to bond dialectically in cynicism and joy in a postmodern world with the sincere modernistic quest to achieve human emancipation as an end in itself. Thus, the connection of my Jewish identity to practice and an answer to the question: To what end do I do what I do?

Notes

1. See bell hooks and Cornel West, *Breaking Bread* (Boston, MA: South End Press, 1991), p. 1.

2. See Barry Kanpol, "Critical pedagogy and liberation theology: Borders for a transformative Agenda." *Educational Theory* 46, 1, pp. 105–119, 1996.

3. Ibid., for more of these arguments.

4. See Jonothan Kozol, *Savage Inequalities* (New York: Crown, 1991).

5. See Jean Francois Lyotard, *The Postmodern Condition* (Minneapolis: University of Minnesota Press, 1984) and Michael Peters (ed.). *Education and Lyotard* (Westport, CT: Bergin & Garvey, 1994) for more on these arguments.

6. Barry Kanpol and Peter McLaren (eds.) *Critical Multiculturalism: Uncommon Voices in a Common Struggle.* (Westport, CT: Bergin & Garvey, 1995).

7. See Lynda Stone, *Feminism in Education* (New York: Routledge, 1994) for the many and various theoretical arguments.

8. See a recent issue of *Harvard Educational Review* 66, 2, Summer, 1996 for various arguments around gay rights.

9. For a brilliant analysis of youth culture as the marginalized and oppressed see, Henry Giroux, *Fugitive Cultures: Race, Violence Youth* (New York: Routledge, New York, 1996).

10. For more on the emanacipatory form of modernism, especially as related to teachers, see Barry Kanpol, *Towards a Theory and Practice of Teacher Cultural Politic* (Norwood, NJ: Ablex, 1992).

11. For a deeper understanding of this contradiction, see Svi Shapiro, *Between Capitalism and Democracy* (Westport, CT: Bergin & Garvey, 1990).

12. See Michael Apple, *Teachers and Texts* (London: Routledge, 1986).

13. See Paul Willis, *Learning to Labor* (Lexington: D.C. Heath, 1977).

14. See Ibid., Jean Anyon, "Social class and the hidden curriculum of work." *Journal of Education* 162, pp. 66–92, 1980, Shapiro, *Between Capitalism and Democracy*, Henry Giroux, *Theory and Resistance in Education* (Westport, CT: Bergin & Garvey, 1983) and Barry Kanpol, *Teacher work tasks as forms of resistance and accommodation to structural factors of education*, *Urban Education* 23, 2, pp. 173–187, 1988 for more on the dialectical logic of resistance and accommodation, especially as related to education.

15. See Ellizabeth Ellsworth, "Why doesn't this feel empowering" Working through the repressive myths of critical pedagogy" *Harvard Educational Review* 59, 3, pp. 297–324, 1989, for more on this.

16. See my reply to Ellsworth, in *Harvard Educational Review* 60, 3, pp. 363-365, 1990 for more on this.

17. See Kanpol, Op. Cit. 1992.

18. See Michael Lerner and Cornel West, *Jews and Blacks: Let the Healing Begin* (New York: G.P. Putnam's Sons, 1995), p. 272.

19. Michael Lerner, *Jewish Renewal*: (New York: G.P. Putnam's Sons, 1994), p. 96.

20. See Michael Hardt, *Gilles Deleuze* (Minneapolis: University of Minnesota Press, 1993), p. 46.

21. Ibid., p. 47.

22. See Ernesto Laclau and Chantal Mouffe, *Hegemony and Socialist Strategy* (London: Verso, 1985) for more on this.

23. See Hardt, Op. Cit., p. 122.

24. Ibid., p. 59.

25. Ibid., p. 98.

26. See Barry Kanpol, *Critical Pedagogy: An Introduction* (Westport, CT: Bergin & Garvey, 1994) for more on hegemonic control.

27. See Peter McLaren, *Schooling as a Ritual Performance* (London: Routledge, 1993) for more on the connection between religion, schools and student resistance.

28. See Sharon Welch, *A Feminist Ethic of Risk* (Minneapolis: Fortress Press, 1990) for more on dangerous memories, particularly pp, 103–180.

29. See Barry Kanpol, *Teachers Talking Back and Breaking Bread* (New Jersey: Hampton Press, 1998).

30. See Henry Giroux, *Border Crossings* (New York: Routledge, 1992) for more on border crossings.

31. See Lerner and West, op. Cit. 1995

32. Ibid., pp. 272–273.

33. See hooks & West, op. Cit. 1991.

34. Ibid., p. 34.

35. See Nicholas Burbules and Suzanne Rice, "Dialogue across differences: Continuing the conversation." *Harvard Educational Review*, 58, 3, pp. 280–298, 1991.

36. See bell hooks, *Talking Back* (Boston, MA: South End Press, 1989), p. 8.

37. See David Purpel, *The Moral and Spiritual Crisis in Education* (Westport, CT: Bergin & Garvey, 1989) for a summary of liberation theology as related to education. Also, see Cornel West, *Prophetic Thought in Postmodern Times* (Monroe, Maine: Common Courage Press, 1993), David Ray Griffin, William Beardslee and Joe Holland, *Varieties of Postmodern Theology* (New York: State University of New York Press, 1989) for more summaries and Analysis of liberation theology.

38. See West, op. Cit. 1993, p. 225.

39. See hooks and West, op. Cit., 1991, p. 9.

Chapter 8

Mathematics, Critical Pedagogy, and the Jewish Question

Stephen Lerman[1]

> *A professor of zoology at Harvard some years ago asked his graduate students, among whom were several foreigners, to write papers on the elephant.*
> *A German student wrote: "An Introduction to the Bibliography for the Study of the Elephant."*
> *A French student wrote: "The Love-Life of the Elephant."*
> *An English student wrote: "Elephant Hunting."*
> *An American student wrote: "Breeding Bigger and Better Elephants."*
> *There was also a Jewish student in the class. He wrote: "The Elephant and the Jewish Problem."* (Nathan Ausubel, A Treasury of Jewish Folklore)

This little story is taken from a favorite childhood book, *A Treasury of Jewish Folklore*. It was compiled in the United States in 1948. I must have borrowed a copy from my grandfather's bookshelf and made it my own. We were an extended family; grandparents, children, and grandchildren living within a stone's throw and many other cousins within another stone's throw. My grandfather was the center of the extended family, the patriarch, and seder nights would see perhaps forty relatives seated with him at the head of the table. He died when I was nine and my grandmother became the center of the family, the matriarch. The generation preceding my grandparents had come from Poland and many of their children had been successful enough in business, the *shmatte* trade, to be able to move from the East End of London in the 1930s to the suburbs. I think it was unusual for families to move out of the East End and still live closely enough, geographically, to experience the richness, some might say claustrophobia, of an extended family. Of course in the East End that would have meant living in neighboring houses or perhaps the same house. The suburb in which I grew up is still Jewish, although now the very orthodox stand out sharply where we made an effort to be as invisible as possible.

I used to read and reread the stories and jokes from the *Treasury* and still today I find that a word or an event reminds me of a story. The one above captures Jewish self-obsession, the foreignness of Jews and the prevalence of the racial/national stereotype. I hesitated to give this writing a Jewish title; indeed I was surprised and bemused when invited by Svi, the editor, to contribute. In all other aspects of my life I am an involved and active Jew, but in my work in education the fact of my Jewishness only arises, and then just occasionally, when I am together with other Jews in my field. At least that was my immediate reaction to the invitation. As I thought more, and began to talk to some of my Jewish colleagues, my story changed. My Jewishness plays a much greater part than I recognized. But how does it manifest itself, and where was the initial denial coming from?

In the first part of this piece of writing I tried to open up thoughts, feelings, and memories, my stories, as they occur to me, in a fairly free flow. Subsequently, perhaps, it may be possible to build a story of generalization and explanation. I have used 'piece of writing' where I usually write 'chapter' or 'paper' because this feels different to my usual academic writing.

Contradictions

I think the task of uncovering the role of my ethnicity in my life in education is made harder by being a British Jew. Our unwritten code as children was to become as English as possible, to keep our Jewishness discrete and out of sight, and to emulate the English upper middle classes. In my late teens I rebelled against that restriction but retained, and retain today, the contradiction. I both desire to admit, even announce, my Jewish identity and seek to hide it. I refuse to be constrained by my childhood "Shhh, you don't have to tell everyone" reaction when I want to speak publicly about something connected with being Jewish, but I am constrained, I do lower my voice, and I do look instinctively cautiously around. I reject stereotypes of Jews yet make a point of being first to pay my share of any restaurant bill, for example, often paying more than my share, which buys into the stereotype. I identify with communities suffering oppression and racism but know that Jews are not free of being oppressors; we are seen as rich, successful exploiters of others. I reject that positioning at every opportunity but am also constricted within it.

I am a white, European, middle-class, heterosexual male, but hey it's OK, I'm a Jew and I know what it's like to be oppressed too. To be Protestant in addition to all the rest of that privilege must be just the pits.

I cannot understand anti-semitism at the level of 'me'. I can offer some explanations of it as a social phenomenon, as a macro- and even a micro-response, as a learned reaction from parents or peers, or as a religiously-inspired reaction to the Jew, but I cannot understand how anyone might hate me, wish to throw me out of their country, perhaps even kill me, without knowing me, because I am a Jew. At the same time I am powerfully conscious and almost fearful of these possibilities, despite never having encountered direct, strong, anti-semitic behavior or language. Not so my daughters. They have no hesitation in pronouncing their ethnicity. Perhaps that fear will die with my generation?

The School Teacher

I studied mathematics at university and had no doubt that I would become a teacher. Looking back, I see now that I was following my cousin who was the first grandchild, a grandson. In a significant picture of us as children he is seated next to our grandfather and I am on my cousin's other side, holding his hand, looking up. When he studied mathematics and became a teacher there was no doubting what I would do.

Being actively Jewish has always been a part of me even when I laid it all aside for a brief time after returning to England following attempted emigration to Israel. Six months after arriving back I ignored the festival of *Yom Kippur* in 1973 to find, on visiting friends that evening, that war had broken out in Israel; I felt as though I was being punished for having lasped from my Jewishness. I'm not claiming that the war was my fault, but chaos theory suggests that the flap of a butterfly's wings on one side of the world can cause a storm on the other side of the world, so who knows? The problem was that I could not identify with my perception of Anglo-Jewry as a people concerned with business, conservative, and desperate to keep a low profile about their Jewishness. There was no opportunity for the community to find a positive forward-looking identity for Jews outside Israel, no growing Jewish culture or program of Jewish education. At that time I was proud of those few Jews who were in the Labour party or other groups involved in left wing activities. I was not in the slightest bit interested in being in business. I did not want to be that kind of Jew. My role model wasn't Lord Sieff of Marks and Spencer but the Jewish councillors in poor London communities, working for everyone's welfare.

To an extent, being a radical schoolteacher of mathematics was for me a preemptive defense against the possibility of anti-semitic action against me although I recognized, when I thought about it, that being a radical educator would not ultimately offer any protection. As I saw it, as a teacher I played a role in turning children into adults. Schools were the site of potential revolution; change education and you change society. Make children aware of injustice and they will bring about a peaceful revolution. Specifically, I felt that I had it within my compass to help children to know what it is like to be oppressed, whether by virtue of gender, class or cultural identity, to understand how it appears in social relations, and to choose not to oppress. Consequently, in my classes I chose to be frank about being a Jew.

A particularly unruly twelve year-old in my mathematics class, Stephen, needed a refill for his pen. After wandering around asking, unsuccessfully, all the other children, he turned to the whole class and said, "You are all Jews, noone will give me a refill." I said, "Stephen, there is only one Jew in this class and that's me." I then spent some few moments explaining why the word 'Jew' appears in the Oxford English dictionary as a synonym for 'mean' and asked them to give me other examples of the use of 'Jew.' "A Jew is someone who bends down to pick up a penny" was just the first response.

This is an example of my reaction to such events. But I was active too. I created situations where I encouraged children to say what they thought or had heard about Jews. It was important to me to enable and encourage children to say those things in an environment where they felt it was safe to do so and where they would get a reply that would contextualize those prejudices. This particular school was an inner London Church of England school. There were no Jewish pupils and there was only one other full-time teacher who was Jewish. I elicited some strange comments and questions as well as familiar ones. "Why are Jews mean?" was often asked; just once I was asked, "Why do Jews walk with their feet turned out?" In the staffroom too I could not resist any opportunity to raise people's awareness of oppressive stereotypes.

The head of science, taking his turn to tell a joke one lunchtime, said "Do you know how to encourage the birth of a reluctant Jewish baby? Wave a penny between the mother's legs." I chose not to ignore the joke but tried to explain how it made me feel, using examples of other minority ethnic 'jokes' to make the point. My response was received with incredulity. It was only a joke after all, I was told.

A young geography teacher, who came from mid-Wales and had been brought up in the Baptist tradition, confessed to me that she had walked behind my chair when I was sitting in the staffroom on the first occasion on which she had found out that I was a Jew, just to check that I did not in fact have horns growing out of my head. She said she knew that it was ridiculous, but had been told this fact by her Baptist minister, and she just had to check. We talked about religion and its role in encouraging and producing anti-semitism and other prejudices.

There are many similar experiences that I could recount and I was fortunate never to have encountered a more strong or violent anti-semitic prejudice. I would certainly be much more cautious in inner London schools today.

It seemed to me at the time that part of the role I chose for myself as personal-example-educator against prejudice necessarily led me into engaging with other social issues too, as a union representative, by standing out against corporal punishment, and in many other small ways. I would discuss social problems with my pupils, a dangerous thing to do in a school where the moral values were firmly in the care of the Church and its representatives. I saw myself as continuing the tradition of the radical Jew, in part because social revolution would lead to emancipation for Jews too and in part because Jews knew what it was like to suffer oppression and persecution and hence should take the lead in fighting against it.

The Researcher

I started my doctoral studies while looking after my young children in a role swap. I gained a place at Cambridge—the inner sanctum of the upper middle-class England that English Jews strive for. I felt excited, I had made it, but overwhelmingly I felt alienated, an outsider. I was Jew the Obscure, knocking on the walls of class and Englishness, even though I was nominally inside. At our first meeting my supervisor gave me a glass of cold dry sherry and we talked about trivialities; then he pointed me in the direction of the library and said, "Come and see me in four weeks time and show me what you have done."

This is where radical mathematics enters my story. My dissertation would do nothing less than revolutionize the teaching of mathematics in schools. Mathematics was seen by children and adults as cold, abstract, unrelated to life and to emotions; it offered no room for creativity or pleasure. My dissertation would uncover the social and intellectual roots of those perceptions, misperceptions actually, and overturn them. Teachers and consequently children would view mathematics differently as a result of my dissertation. The first title for my thesis was "The Philosophy of Mathematics Education." Of course in the end, several years, supervisors, and universities later, the dissertation was completed but the focus of the study was rather more narrow. Nevertheless it still had an element of a Messianic ideal in it. I wanted to show that if teachers adopted a social view of mathematical knowledge, rather than a platonic view, mathematics teaching became open-ended, creative, and imaginative, and pupils and teachers would co-construct mathematical knowledge together. This was, sociologically, a rather naive approach but supervisors in mathematics education were not very familiar with sociology at that time and I did not come across any challenging literature.

I obtained my PhD seven years after we made the role swap. One of the 'congratulations' cards I received was from my mentor, my cousin, saying that I had overtaken him for the first time in our lives. This was almost as much of a shock as being called Doctor.

The University Lecturer

Until recently in my academic career I have rarely mentioned that I am a Jew, except to other Jews. Somehow I saw other identities, female, black, working-class, as legitimate and utterable, but not Jew. When I thought about it I felt sure that both being in education, rather than some other profession, and taking a critical, progressive stance was connected with my Jewishness, but it was much too difficult to think about. It seemed clear that one's identity as a woman, as black, or as working-class was constitutive of the selves who work in academia (and elsewhere of course), but I was reluctant to articulate how my being a Jew was constitutive of the way I perceived education. Nevertheless I was active in issues of emancipation and equity within mathematics education and published a number of papers addressing some of these issues, my first being in 1987 and my most recent an invited plenary address on social and political aspects at the most recent British Congress on Mathematics Education (1).

I think now that my confusion was strongly influenced by events in the Middle East. I was a doctoral student and a beginning lecturer, attending my first conferences and presenting my first papers, when

Israel invaded Lebanon and the *intifada* began. A critical issue in the international mathematics education community at the time was whether to allow South Africans to attend conferences. Most people felt that mathematics and mathematics education had nothing to do with politics and this was precisely the issue that I addressed in my dissertation. I was part of the radical group, pressing for an open debate and a vote, and I was acutely embarrassed to find that the Israelis stood by the South Africans. I confronted them, demanding to know why Jews, of all people, could not stand up for an oppressed nation who were second-class citizens, even non-people, by virtue of their ethnicity. I was told, "If it's the South Africans being banned today it will be the Israelis tomorrow." The Israel thing has been a significant element in my silence. Not that I was confused about Israel: I was angry with Israel's treatment of the Palestinians through many decades but I had no doubts about the need for the State of Israel. But my Zionist connection was certainly a silencing element for me. Except, I have to say, when confronted on it. I met with some colleagues once with whom I had been involved in critical pedagogy issues. One of them compared the behavior of Israel to white South Africa, with which I reluctantly almost agreed, and Palestinian refugee camps with Nazi concentration camps, with which I could not agree. I was very angry and very upset, particularly in having to confront the area in which I had been silenced, with those very colleagues with whom I did not wish to discuss my Jewishness. Interestingly the one other Jew in the group remained silent. I realized then that my silence was essentially empty.

I suppose that in the United States where Jews are seen as among the most powerful ethnic groups politically and economically, once again the Jew is seen as the oppressor by disadvantaged others. That is not a strongly held image in the United Kingdom.

Interestingly, one good friend with whom I have discussed my Jewishness and the time I spent in Israel, including six months in the Israeli army, is a Palestinian community worker from Ramallah, Munir Fasheh. We were both members of a small group of mathematics educators invited to South Africa in 1993 to meet at an ANC-sponsored conference to discuss a unified curriculum for the coming post-apartheid era. I learned a great deal of painful information about life under Israeli military rule from Munir.

I found and continue to find common ground with radical educators, critical of governments, concerned and angry about disadvantage, active in one context or another. There is a 'criticalmath' group inspired by the work of Paolo Freire. There is also a growing body of research in ethnomathematics, which is a view of mathematical activities as being sociocultural in origin. These activities are sometimes frozen into traditional art and craft forms, and of equal value to academic mathematics, seen itself as another ethnomathematics. The criticalmath group puts the two words together to make connections with the ethnomathematicians. I have strong ties to both groups, although I have some reservations about the theories.

Today

Now I am not silent about my Jewishness. Why? One reason is the passing of years including some time in analysis. I can now accept the various elements in my personal story and be open about my strengths and weaknesses. Another is the growth of postmodern and feminist literature and research which encourages the placing of one's stories into one's work.

To be comfortable about being Jewish, I now believe, is to accept living with the contradictions. They are tensions, but they are constructive. For a start Israel is flawed. I grew up with a utopian vision of Israel, that it would be a light unto the nations. The conflicts with its Arab neighbors were temporary, the Jewish experience of prejudice, of being hated, of being denied equality would lead them to make a just and fair resolution with the Palestinian Arabs. Well, that's not the way it is. The Jewish people are as flawed, as torn with weakness and prejudice as anyone else. But Israel is there, and it should be there. I, we, have to live with that. Where else is perfect? So why should I expect Israel to be perfect? My attempt at *aliyah*, emigration to Israel, was to a *kibbutz*, a socialist community which was itself a light unto that nation. I found that it too was flawed. I left because I couldn't live with fallibilities; I was searching for resolutions, not constructive tensions.

I wrote above: "Somehow I saw other identities, female, black, working-class, as legitimate and utterable, but not Jew." That denial of my self has silenced me. It is accepting that the identification 'Jew' is a less important one than 'person of colour', or 'woman'. But at the same time I have an embarrassed awareness that the Jewish part in the history of culture, science, and commerce is hugely disproportionate to the numbers of Jewish people. Both sides of this particular tension elicit silence. I feel now that this is both my problem as well as everyone else's. There is a dialectic here, as in all these tensions. Historically the fear for one's life, as a Jew, has been a huge stimulus to a desire to succeed, to be the best. To be rich and of low profile is very dangerous, but to be the richest, known and needed by the powerful, may, just may, provide safety. It's the same with intellect and with creativity. I believe the drive to education and to achievement that is typical of Jewish families is in large part motivated by that historical tension, being convinced that one is less than others but more than others at the same time, and striving to reach the latter. So it's my problem. And it's everyone else's problem since that contradiction is part of who we Jews are in the world.

The Holocaust too leaves us pulled in two ways. It was such a horror that we cannot put it down. I still cry at the old newsreels of the opening up of the camps, I still feel a triumph at our survival, and I also still feel the bewilderment that we were seen to be a lower order of humans, subhuman, deserving of destruction. I can't stop talking about it. But I also don't speak because those non-Jews who are around me feel guilty and, I fear, tired of the story. When the British government first heard about the concentration camps from Jewish escapees and resistance fighters their reaction was, "It's those whining Jews again." I can hear people say (although noone has said it) "You aren't the only ones who suffer. Because of your skin color you don't stand out in Britain today." And it's true, of course.

There has been a catalyst in my realization of the tensions in my Jewishness, Lev Semyenovich Vygotsky, who was born one hundred years ago today, as I write these particular words. In my academic work I came across his theories in 1991 and immediately became attracted to them. In education, and particularly in mathematics education, we have always turned to psychology in order to theorize about teaching mathematics (2). I think this is largely because mathematical knowledge has traditionally been unchallengeable as the underlying description ot the way God created the world. The history of mathematics was largely seen as the unfolding of knowledge, the discovery of mathematical truths. True mathematical knowledge needs no sociology, only incorrect mathematics. Thus we could only look to theories that told us how to teach this knowledge, not to theories that engaged with what that knowledge is and how it develops. We were dominated by behaviorism in the first half of the century, realized particularly in drill and practice and positive and negative reinforcement. We have been dominated by the individualism of Piagetian psychology since then. Although I too was a constructivist in the 1980s I was always concerned about the individualistic, even solipsistic, stance and particularly with Piaget's backgrounding the role of language in learning. I drew on Wittgenstein's argument against private languages in a critique (3) of the particular version of Piaget's constructivism that has become dominant in mathematics education, particularly in the United States, radical constructivism.

Lev Vygotsky's two books (4) were a revelation. He argued that human consciousness was constituted through communication and by the mediation of cultural tools, by analogy with the Marxist idea of material tools changing the world and transforming people. Cultures are constitutive of people. His development of a Marxist program for psychology was particularly attractive to me just when socialism seemed to be dying around the world, both from the onslaught of postmodernism and the death of meta-narratives, and with the end of the totalitarian regimes that nevertheless had started as socialist dreams. Only some time later when I came across a biography of Vygotsky did I realize that he had been brought up in an orthodox, Jewish, extended family in the Pale. His theories fell into place. His work focused on how consciousness is constituted in culture and he sought an explanation for it in terms of internalization. To the best of my knowledge his Jewishness did not appear overtly in his writings. He was involved in literary and artistic circles after the revolution and he entered the field of psychology in 1924. There is some considerable discussion in the literature about Vygotsky's limited view of cultural development in contrast to his rich interpretation of the function of language in the constitution of individual consciousness. I suppose it would not have been appropriate to focus on cultures in an ethnic sense given the opposition of Marx, Lenin, and Stalin to nationalism. Class was the ultimate structure, others being just consequences. Given the situation of Russia and the other countries of the Soviet Union in the early decades of this century, for Vygotsky it would also have been clear that culture had to mean progress, industrialization, civilization and in particular literacy (5). It's ironic, however, that his historical-cultural method offers an explanation for people being products of their time and place, their multiple cultures, when his image was of a unidirectional cultural progress. Similarly it's ironic that Vygotsky's method accounts for the construction of individuals within culture, in particular his own Jewish experience, yet he does not specifically refer to it. The discussion arises from the confrontation of versions of relativism, whereby we refuse to ascribe different values to different cultures, although we can certainly speak of development within cultures since otherwise the whole educational project is meaningless. But that discussion is a modern one.

My research and writing has been strongly influenced by Vygotsky and his followers ever since and that has played a part in legitimating my Jewishness—almost a 'coming out'—in my academic life.

Conclusion

I cannot say anything about Jews as a whole, nor am I suggesting that this applies only to Jews of course, merely what feels to me to be connected to my Jewishness. I hope the various strands in my story indicate the connections.

I am in education because I am Jewish. Learning is a richness in itself to be pursued throughout one's life, as the rabbis teach us. As an educator I can, perhaps, encourage that view of learning among my students. It also affords me the chance to continue learning. I consider myself very fortunate to be in an environment where ideas, reasoning, research, reading, and culture are highly valued. While I feel also that 'business' is a typical Jewish enterprise, I find myself saying that I'm not that kind of Jew.

I am a critical educator because I am Jewish. While I no longer believe that schools can revolutionize the world, I am sure that teachers are important persons to children and we can play a small but significant part in the formation of their perceptions of others and in their learning about social relations that take an equitable account of others. The Jewish people have suffered badly over the centuries and should therefore play an active part in fighting prejudice and discrimination. I do believe that we should be better than others in being antiracist ourselves and I am angry when I come across Jews for whom this is not their view.

I am a critical mathematics educator because I am Jewish. For the most part I have to say that mathematics is simply my chosen field, although the extent to which it was a choice I have talked about at the beginning of this piece of writing. I will say, though, that mathematics offers a particular challenge because it is generally seen as the field of human intellectual activity that is most separated from concrete reference, particularly anything associated with people. Its value is seen in its distance from emotions, needs, purposes, and applications. It *is* applied to practical contexts but 'application' is how it is seen. As I have said above, much of my work has been in opposition to this perspective. I will write here something about the key issues of a criticalmath perspective and some of the problems associated with it and then I will come back to considering connections with being a Jew.

Criticalmath

I have written a number of papers on mathematics and values and on antiracist mathematics and I find that I am continually being asked to explain how mathematics can have anything to do with values, or how it can be racist or ant-racist. Some years ago (6) there was a question used in a national school mathematics examination for sixteen year olds that asked students to read information from a pictogram showing the expenditure on armaments of NATO and Warsaw pact countries. After a number of typical statistical questions the final part asked the following:

> The money required to provide adequate food, water, education, health and housing for everyone in the world has been estimated at 17 billion a year." (New Internationalist 1980)
> *How many weeks of NATO + Warsaw pact military spending will be enough to pay for this?*

Reaction in some conservative newspapers was immediate and strong—this was the blatant introduction of politics into school mathematics. Another question from the year before (7), shortly after the Falklands/Malvinas war between the United Kingdom and Argentina, which appeared in the national examination for seventeen year-olds must have been deemed nonpolitical since it received no negative comments in the press. It read:

> A pilot flying an aeroplane in a straight line at a constant speed of 96 m/s and at a constant height of 2000m, drops a bomb on a stationary ship in the vertical plane through the line of flight of the aeroplane. Assuming that the bomb falls freely under gravity, calculate,
>
> (a) the time which elapses after release before the bomb hits the ship,
> (b) the horizontal distance between the aeroplane and the ship at the time of release of the bomb,
> and
> *(c) the speed of the bomb just before it hits the ship.*

It could be argued that this differential interpretation is absurd but that all it implies is that no examples from 'real life' are safe to be used in mathematics, so none should be. That would lead to mathematics education being completely divorced from everyday life, making its learning even harder than it is now. More fundamentally, I would point to the completely different spatial/geometrical concepts of non-Western nations (8) or the different ways of calculating areas used in other cultures. Since one cannot say *a priori* which is correct, or indeed what 'correct' might signify, it is merely an instance of Western hegemony.

The challenge of being a critical pedagogue also stems from the uncomfortable fact that success in school mathematics is a key to many doors, although there is no intrinsic reason why it should be so. There is a considerable amount of pressure on the community of mathematics teachers and researchers to 'produce the goods', to raise standards of mathematics in schools. On the one hand, one must question the sources of those demands and their consequences. In the United Kingdom, international comparisons of mathematical achievement are used as means of regulation of teachers and schools. On the other hand, since mathematics is a key to employment and status, we owe it to children to help as many of them as possible gain that key. This is somewhat akin to aiming to bring everyone above the average, since the measures of success and failure are intended to exclude.

I have treated the terms 'progressive' and 'critical pedagogue' unproblematically in this piece of writing thus far but I will briefly examine their use. The Conservative British government consistently attacked the term 'progressive' from when it came to power in 1979, identifying it with 'beliefs of the 1960s' and blaming it for just about every perceived problem, particularly in education. Reason enough to hold onto the label! In the last year or so the term has also come under attack within mathematics education from some writers and an analysis of the positions that they are establishing through their attack would be very revealing. Specifically, 'progressive' is generally identified with a child-centered view as realized in individualized teaching or work in groups with the teacher encouraging children to construct their own mathematical knowledge. As I discussed above, I have reservations about that view of learning (9) but I choose not to attack the label, both because it suggests an identification with the Conservative position and also because I still wish to consider myself progressive. The word may need reinterpretation though, and here I use it in the sense that I want to see progress toward more students gaining confidence and enjoyment as well as certification in their school mathematics. Outcome is important; the earlier sense of 'progressive' ignored what happens to children and in fact laid the blame for their failure on the children themselves for their lack of readiness in development (10). In relation to the term 'critical' I have mentioned that there is an international criticalmath group. This is not the place to rehearse the debates over Habermas and postmodernism. Like many others I find myself wanting a way out of the postmodern trap of an apparent inability to critique across discourses but I do not find the answer in critical theory.

These are issues about which I care passionately. That they arise for me in the context of mathematics education rather than some other curriculum area or in social policy is certainly a result of my childhood and the subsequent choices I have made. But I also want to say that there is for me something that resembles *torah* and *talmudic* study in mathematics. I studied quite a lot of *torah* and a little *talmud* as a child and teenager and always wanted to spend more time on it but as I did not remain orthodox I never managed to create the opportunity; I may do so one day. First I should point out that the mathematics problems we struggle with are not of the kind that fit the common perception, namely that there is an appropriate method and a right answer. The issues are more complex and disputable. Is this a good way to tackle the problem or that? The heuristics have their own rules which must be followed, like *gematria*. There may be a number of proposed solutions that differ from one another. Does the problem resemble another, can that approach or solution be used here, and might the solution to this problem be used in other problems? One solution may be more elegant than another—a criterion whose manifestation makes sense to mathematicians. The structures of analysis in mathematics themselves become objects of analysis. The meanings and referents are metonymic, found within mathematics itself. The style of mathematical work is similar too. There is an excitement and absorption when one puts aside the administration and the marking and one argues with colleagues about a difficult mathematics problem, which recalls the style of talmudic study. I don't want to push this too far but for me mathematics offers something that I may have experienced in *talmud*.

I will end by saying that I enjoy teaching, in fact I enjoy teaching mathematics and mathematics education. The perceived importance of mathematics has certainly kept me in a job. This reminds me of another story:

"If I were Rothschild," said the melamed of Chelm, "I'd be richer than Rothschild."

"How is it possible?" asked a fellow citizen.

"Naturally", answered the melamed, "I'd do a little teaching on the side." (11)

Notes

1. My thanks to Miriam David, Gaby Weiner and Peter Winbourne for conversations that helped me a great deal, and to Louise Fox for her insightful comments at an early stage of writing.

Bibliography

Apple, M. (1995) 'Taking power seriously: New directions in equity in mathematics education and beyond'. In W. G. Secada, E. Fennema & L. B. Adajian (Eds.) *New Directions for Equity in Mathematics Education* Cambridge, UK: Cambridge University Press.

Ausubel, N. (Ed.) (1948) *A Treasury of Jewish Folklore* New York: Crown.

Lerman, S. (1989) 'Constructivism, mathematics and mathematics education' *Educational Studies in Mathematics*, 20(2), 211–223.

Lerman, S. (1996a) 'Mathematics teaching for empowerment and equity: an achievable goal?' *Proceedings of the Third British Congress of Mathematics Education*, 1, 17–30.

Lerman, S. (1996b) 'Intersubjectivity in mathematics learning: a challenge to the radical constructivist paradigm?' *Journal for Research in Mathematics Education*, 27(2), 133–150.

LREB (1985) Additional Mathematics (A/O) paper, London Regional Examinations Board, Pure Mathematics and Theoretical Mechanics.

LREB (1986) Ordinary level Mathematics paper, London Regional Examinations Board, SMILE mathematics.

Pinxten, R. (1986) *Towards a Navajo Indian Geometry* Ghent: Boeken Reeks.

van der Veer, J. (1996) 'The concept of culture in Vygotsky's thinking' *Culture and Psychology*, 2(3), 247–263.

Vygotsky, L. (1978) *Mind in Society: The Development of Higher Psychological Processes* Cambridge, MA: Harvard University Press.

Vygotsky, L. (1986) *Thought and Language* (Revised Edition, A. Kozulin (Ed.)), Cambridge, MA: MIT Press.

Walkerdine, V. (1988) *The Mastery of Reason* London, UK: Routledge.

Chapter 9

On Being a Jew and a Boston Braves Fan: Alone and Afraid in a World I Never Made

David E. Purpel

I. In the Beginning

Much of my family's story is achingly and painfully familiar, part of the narrative of Jewish experience that allows one to use the words routine and tragic in the same sentence. Both my parents were born in the same shtetl in what is now Ukraine, just south of Kiev and each of them witnessed the murder of a parent by bandits in the chaos and tumult of the Russian civil war. Both fled in terror and made their individual ways as teen-agers across Europe by the grace of luck, grit, bribes, some kind people, a network of Jewish agencies, and God knows what else. They eventually arrived in Boston in the early twenties, got married, and settled down to a life of poverty, struggle, fear, and grief.

Their life spans coincided with World War I, the Bolshevik revolution, the Red scare, the Depression, the rise of Fascism, the New Deal, World War II, the Holocaust, the Atomic age, the Cold War, McCarthyism, the establishment of the state of Israel, the Korean war, the Civil Rights Movements, the war in Vietnam, the Watergate scandals, and the assassinations of Archduke Ferdinand, Leon Trotsky, Mohandas Gandhi, John Kennedy, Martin Luther King, and Robert Kennedy.

Politically, they were basically radicals but their commitment to socialism was always delimited by their fear of Stalin and the traditions of virulent Russian anti-Semitism. They adored FDR but were tempted to vote for Norman Thomas, they were strong supporters of the labor movement, and they thought that government was there to protect us from big business. They almost always voted and followed political campaigns with great interest and acumen.

They had read Gogol and Tolstoy in Russian, Shalom Aleichem and the brothers Singer in Yiddish, and Dorothy Parker and Philip Roth in English. They had seen Menashe Skulnik, Maurice Schwartz, and Molly Picon on the stage, in the movies, and on television and heard them on the radio. Likewise Mary Martin, Helen Hayes, and Paul Newman. They loved Sid Caesar's comic genius, were scornful of Milton Berle's vulgarity, and were much more devoted to *Playhouse 90* than to any sitcom. They never went to a proper school.

They did this in between the frustrating and backbreaking tasks of running a small grocery store, beset with a shrinking clientele and ferocious competition from the "chain stores' and the overwhelming chores that come with parental responsibilities. They had five children (one of whom died from a ruptured appendix at the age of two) each one of whom provided them with opportunities for pride, aggravation, hopes, and disappointments They had their share of existential crises, marital disputes, major illnesses, and probably less than their share of joys, triumphs, and celebrations.

They were indeed complicated folks, often loving and generous, sometimes mean-spirited and spiteful; always worried and fearful; usually secretive and guarded; capable of genuine gaiety and laughter, and yet ultimately presenting a morose image of themselves as victims, surviving with poignant dignity but struggling to control their demons of terror, fear, and despair. They were very intelligent, even wise; well-read; politically sophisticated; sort of open -minded but also wary and skeptical of change. Their attitudes toward their Jewish and American identities were complicated, full of fierce loyalties but laced with ambivalence, ambiguity, and paradox.

They certainly wanted their children to be Jewish but their modes of acculturation were irregular and unfocused. For one thing, and probably for reasons much more psychological than ideological, they purposefully decided *not* to live in a Jewish neighborhood, which gave us all the opportunity to interact with a predominantly Irish Catholic, working-class community one which at best aspired to and occasionally reached attitudes of strained toleration toward "kikes." My parents put heavy stress on Yiddishkeit, were only mildly observant although strict on some issues (no mixing of dairy with meat, no pork or shrimp, no school on the Holidays, at least most of the time), and although they were both quite knowledgeable about religious practices and traditions they expressed a skeptical if not cynical attitude towards religious institutions. They were apprehensive, suspicious, and patronizing of *goyim* and contemptuous of assimilating and socially ambitious Jews, whom they called "all-rightniks." They taught us to read Yiddish authors but not the Torah; they discussed/argued political and social issues with us but not theological ones; and they insisted that we remember and revere our heritage as Jews even as they disavowed the Jewish God.

I went to Hebrew Schools four days a week (after public school and on Sundays) and became a bar mitzvah. That was the only formal Jewish education I ever had and although I learned to read and write Hebrew it was a very threadbare education at best. And yet I have become convinced that with all the mixed signals and missed opportunities, and all the other craziness in my home, my parents provided me with some critically important and energizing notions that have helped to shape my worldview, one that clearly has a strong Jewish flavor.

In retrospect these Jewish influences that came from my childhood seem to have influenced my professional work more than they did my personal life. (But that's another story.) In some ways my professional foci(citizenship education, critical thinking, clinical supervision, critical pedagogy, moral education) even as they shifted all seemed to have common resonance with some of the more visible Jewish values. However, this did not become clear to me till I came to write *The Moral and Spiritual Crisis in Education* the work that best represents my professional concerns and value commitments.

I have to confess that I often felt inspired while I was actually writing this book. By that I emphatically do not mean that the book was ghostwritten by some divine author but rather that I sensed that I had entered a different kind of space, a mysterious space made special and exciting because it seemed to be sacred. I do not believe that I would have been open to this experience had I not just read Abraham Joshua Heschel's monumental work *The Prophets* which is truly inspired. When I read it I was afraid I would hyperventilate, so powerful, so profound, and so compelling was it to me. I knew that the paradigm of prophetic thought focusing on a God of history, justice, and mercy striving in covenant with humanity to create a loving and just community that Heschel so eloquently and passionately describes was and is the one for me. What was so extraordinary was the way Heschel's book was simultaneously familiar and new to me. The substantive elements were all new to me; in truth, up to that point I had zero idea of the significance of the Prophets—who they were, what they did and said, and what they represented. And yet the essential message seemed to be in harmony with my intuitive sense of what constitutes the ultimate meaning and purpose of life. What was annoying to me was that it had taken me so long to find this paradigm. What was mysterious to me was how I had somehow come to resonate with this basic language in spite of my unfamiliarity with the particular literature.

What was also inspirational was that I was struggling with something far more important and worthwhile than my usual limitations and constraints, nothing less than the opportunity to write within that sacred paradigm. How successful or unsuccessful I was in this responsibility is not totally clear to me but one thing did became apparent to me, namely that I had discovered what had always been there, i.e., an essential part of the moral and spiritual grounding of my work. The exciting thing was that this came to me in such a mysterious way and the embarrassing thing was that I didn't really know very much about this grounding.

This only partially explains why the book that eventually emerged, while certainly stressing the centrality of the prophetic tradition, does not speak directly to the Jewish sensibility that permeates it. It took me a long time to fully recognize what some of my colleagues told me early on, namely, that I had written a Jewish book without saying so. It took me much less time to recognize that if I indeed had written within Jewish traditions, I had done so as an amateur. Hence my agenda became clear. I needed to know a lot more about this grounding and so I have read and continue to do a lot of reading and studying of traditional Jewish sources. I am finding it to be both exciting and frustrating, both accessible and opaque, simultaneously compelling and remote. I also realized that I needed to be a lot more explicit about my Jewish orientation and have made some tentative and modest steps in that direction in my writing and teaching.

I have taken the time to write about my parents and my personal background partly to highlight the difficulty of factoring out the Jewish dimension of my life from the myriad of other influences and factors, be they psychological, historical, sociological, or characterological in nature. It is easy enough to say that my parents were Jewish, that I grew up in a Jewish home, and that I consider myself to be a

Jew. After that it's very hard. Not only is it excruciatingly difficult to explain what I mean by what I have said about my Jewish background and identity but it is also exceedingly difficult to sort out and explain the enormously complicated dynamics of the matrix of personal, cultural, circumstantial, contingent, and societal events that shape my consciousness. Indeed, it is this complexity that makes this writing assignment so challenging, so difficult, and so risky. Furthermore and significantly, when it came time for me to begin to work on the assignment, I realized that my customary professional discourse and writing style were not going to be of much help and more likely would be counterproductive in addressing the questions of the integration of my personal and professional lives.

The task would seem to require serious self-interrogation, a process that I have so far assiduously and successfully neglected and avoided. Indeed, I have been so successful that I've had to think hard about a different approach that would at least enable me to make a good faith effort at writing this essay. This led me to understand that even though until fairly recently I had largely avoided careful, systematic self-examination of my Jewish identity, my Jewish consciousness has surely not evolved randomly nor is it disconnected from my persona nor from my work. Rather, it is expressed in my attitudes, behaviors, and sensibilities and lodged in the crowded, messy, and unswept compartments of my interiority.

In order to bring some order to this clutter I decided to rely on of all things, you should excuse the expression, my intuition. My intuition told me that I would have to dig deep to find some gems but, happily, these gems are stored in places that are dear and accessible to me. These places turn out to be the vast treasure of Jewish stories of all varieties, be they legends, tales, jokes, anecdotes, allegories, or midrashim. More particularly, the richest source of self-insight would be those stories that I especially love to read, hear, and tell over and over again. My intuition driven reasoning is that I can learn a lot from those specific stories precisely because I continue to tell them, i.e., their very persistence in my nervous system indicates that they resonate with my innermost sense of meaning. Therefore, the technique I will employ in this essay is simply to tell a few of these stories and then reflect on their meaning and significance for me.

Before I tell these stories I will need to add a few more bits of autobiographical information that can help to describe and explain the interpretative orientation that I bring to the process. I now believe that one of the most revealing if not formative events of my life was my experience with the Boston Braves during the 1940s. This was a time when there were only sixteen major league baseball teams and when Boston had franchises in both leagues, one of them the incomparably more popular and more talented Red Sox; the other, usually referred to as the "hapless Braves," was a team with little or no talent and with few paying customers. As vaunted and revered were the Red Sox as a team of destiny and redemption, the Braves were derided and dismissed as a source of shame and embarrassment. The Red Sox were celebrated, the Braves barely tolerated; attendance at spiffy Fenway Park would range from twenty to thirty thousand while the faithful who made their way to dingy Braves Field rarely numbered more than eight or ten thousand; Red Sox fans were braggarts and arrogantly demanding just as Braves fans were humble and easily satisfied; and if the Red Sox failed to finish first in the standings it was considered a miscarriage of justice while it was considered to be a moral triumph if the Braves finished sixth in an eight team race. I was to become a devoted Braves fan.

How I got to be a Braves fan is fairly clear. One day during summer vacation I walked down to the local park and noticed that a man was passing out cards to other kids. Intrigued, I sidled over and made myself available, hoping that I might be included. it quickly became clear that the man was not discriminating and was pleased to give me or anyone else one of these cards. The card offered the holder free membership in the Boston Braves Knothole Club which entitled members to Pavilion admission to any weekday game for the price of thirty-five cents instead of the regular ninety cents. (I didn't know what Pavilion meant except that it was better and more expensive than the sixty cents bleachers.) That's what led me to what was to be the first of countless visits to shabby, very uncrowded Braves Field.

However, the reason for the constancy of my loyalty in the face of continuous humiliation and disappointment remains elusive although less mysterious than it once was. Although I surely "liked" the Braves, I can't say that I admired them nor was I an adoring fan of any particular player. I can't say that I simply enjoyed going and listening to the games for I became very emotionally involved with whether or not they won (which they usually did not). If they won I would be elated but always aware that the happiness would be of very short duration and when they lost, I would be completely unsurprised but disconsolate nevertheless. I also have to admit that I secretly "hated" the Red

Sox and their fans and nothing was sweeter in those scary wartime days than to read the newspaper on a day when the Braves won, the Red Sox lost, the Allies advanced, and the Nazis were repulsed.

I was also mystified by some of my friends who actually chose to root for teams outside of Boston (e.g. the New York Yankees or the St. Louis Cardinals) and appalled by the fact that their choice was based on the undoubted, but to me irrelevant, reality that these were talented and winning teams. Not only did I believe that this was disloyal but I thought it was a violation of the rules.

It is easy enough to attribute this strong identification, loyalty, and bonding to the developmental processes of early adolescence but even with greater age and maturity I continue to feel connected and to believe that my well-being is somehow related to the fortunes of the various incarnations of the Braves from Boston to Milwaukee to Atlanta. Moreover, this has also come to be true for all the other Boston sports teams (including the Red Sox whom I've come to forgive and embrace). The truth is that I still care a lot about how these teams fare even as I realize how silly and dumb all this is and even more as I realize how well nigh impossible it is for me to disconnect from these relationships for try as I might, I cannot be indifferent to the fortunes of these teams.

In some ways the questions and quandaries concerning these connections are similar and parallel to the ones regarding my Jewish identity. Did I choose to be a Braves fan any more or less than I chose to be Jewish? Why is my loyalty to the Braves and Jews independent of anything Jews or Braves believe, do, or say? If the recruiter for the Red Sox Knothole Club had been at the park a day earlier, would I have become a Red Sox fan? Was my initial bonding to the Braves a matter of obsession? a genuine symbiosis? an instance of self-indulgent pride and chauvinism? Or was it an example of true and profound commitment? Am I Jewish only because of the happenstance of birth and do I have any more capacity to renounce my Jewish identity than I did to reject my Braves fandom? Did I continue to support the Braves because they were, presumably like my perception of Jews, oppressed, despised, and pitiful? Or was it *vice versa*? Did I resent the Red Sox because they were a metaphor for the smug, entrenched, and powerful *goyim*? Perhaps my two major identities were related by dint of their affording me the opportunity to have a unique identity in my neighborhood and/or to be oppositional; perhaps they both represented my status as marginal and minority; perhaps they reflected a concern for justice and mercy for the oppressed, or perhaps they both allowed me to wallow in martyrdom and victimization.

II. The Stories of My Life

As I have indicated, my plan is to continue this analysis primarily through the use of stories that are dear and compelling to me that seem to contain important insights into issues of Jewish identity. I have no intention of trying to define, explain, or analyze the concept of story, or the importance of stories to Jewish experience, or even the importance of narrative in a post-modern world. This is because (a) I don't know how to, (b) it's not relevant to my purpose, and besides, c) it's story time.

A. The Mother and her Son the Physicist

The mother of a renowned physicist , proud as she is of her son, feels frustrated that she doesn't really understand what he does, and asks him if he would explain Einstein's theory of relativity to her. The son, the physicist, has mixed feelings about this-he is touched by the gesture but fearful of the difficulty, the inevitable frustration, and the consequences of failure. Nonetheless, he proceeds cautiously and patiently and miraculously the mother slowly but surely begins to understand more and more until she not only fully comprehends but is able to carry on a sophisticated dialogue with her son on theoretical physics. The son is ecstatic and feels good not only about what his mother has accomplished but also about the implications for science education. The mother is also very proud and happy but it is clear that she remains a bit puzzled and skeptical in spite of her achievement. She decides to share her uncertainty with her son and during a dinner-time conversation, as he is yet again summarizing the major elements of Einstein's theory of relativity, she abruptly interrupts him. "Okay, okay," she insists,"I understand the theory fine, but, just tell me one thing Sonny: Is it good for the Jews?"

This is a very old story and obviously gets subtly changed with the telling but its shocking punch line has remained the same. There are some interesting and revealing dimensions of the story as told: the relationship between an adoring mother and an achieving son (Jewish jokes rarely speak of achieving daughters); the patient yet anxious son warily trying to please the insatiable demands of a clinging mother;

and the paradox and ambiguity concerning the mother's level of intelligence and sophistication. However, the story's power would seem to pivot on the extraordinary reductionism in which sooner or later everything comes to be seen through the vulgar prism of Jewish chauvinism.

I love this story—I find it to be very funny in both its irony and its exaggeration but I also love it because it has come to mean much more to me than a good gag. For one thing, there is within the story the strong suggestion of the angst and insecurity that is so much part of Jewish experience, for the mother's question could easily be changed to "Is it going to be bad for the Jews?" The concern derives from a consciousness shaped by the requirement to be constantly alert to the possibility of danger including, if not especially, from seemingly benign sources. Paranoid Jew would seem to be a redundant term and one cannot but identify with the courage of this woman to give voice to the kind of suspicion and wariness that many if not most Jews nervously and embarrassingly feel about the unfamiliar. When we laugh at this woman we are no doubt reflecting our own difficulty in distinguishing absurd from genuine threats since we know that there are plenty of both in the land as we try to simultaneously protect ourselves from looking silly and being victimized. The mother in this story plays it safe—better we should ask, lest we get lulled into a false sense of security by the distractions of family ties and academic thought. In this instance, politics triumphs over concerns for both relationship and scholarship.

It's at this point that the smile weakens, the laughter begins to fade, and the anger and resentment starts to appear. We are now back in touch with the reality that a whole people has come to be consigned to the condition of feeling constant and justifiable dread, a condition that speaks to centuries of enduring intolerable injustice, pain, and suffering.

There is additional wisdom here that is obscured by the mother's extreme ethnocentrism, for the story is a powerful statement about the inevitability of subjectivity, partisanship, and perspective. The mother is clearly single-minded in her interests, seemingly obsessively focused, seeing virtually everything only from the perspective of what contributes to the welfare of Jews. However, nowadays philosophers could easily term such phenomena as hermeneutical while psychologists might call it projection, cultural critics could mark it as an instance of a particular interpretative narrative, ideologues might refer to it as bias, and pundits as spin control. To that extent, the mother's response is prototypically human but, of course, its highly exaggerated form takes it to the level of absurdity and exquisite irony. However, the story does teach us about the relationship between the external and the internal, while providing us with a lesson on the problematics of subjectivity, particularly of the dangers of zealotry and chauvinism.

So what does my fascination with this story tell me about my Jewish identity? The fact that the story is immediately accessible and understandable to me says already that I have a close affinity to some kind of Jewish community. I have to confess that I can both identify with and be repelled by the mother's paranoic obsessiveness and to that extent the story tends to have an alienating effect on me. In spite of this, the story also has within it the roots of quite a number of issues that are at the center of my work. As I've already indicated, the persistence of the fear and dread is so strong and vivid to me that I find it both impossible either to accept or to deny its implicit horror. It is no surprise to me that my teaching and writing is marked by continuous references to the unacceptable presence of enormous unnecessary human suffering and to the assertion that the educational process ought to be seen primarily in its relationship with the struggle for social justice.

This story has also required me to scrutinize my attitudes toward the mother, for even as I am embarrassed by her narrowness, I am moved by her sincerity and earnestness as well as the poignancy of her concerns for a loving relationship with her son and the well-being of the Jewish people. It is surely possible and important to be critical of her attempt to manipulate her son and to distort science but it is also important on a personal level to understand her perspective. We need to celebrate her commitments when we give her the benefit of the doubt and to at least forgive her parochialism when we can't. The importance of giving the benefit of doubt, of affording understanding and compassion to people , and of searching for moral transcendence in "ordinary people" are themes and values that have intrigued and haunted me as I try to figure out the place of empathy, compassion, and affirmation in my notions of a redemptive education.

More critically, I value the story to the extent that it shows how piety and self-righteousness can mask self-serving, blind, and knee-jerk partisanship. The reaction of the mother in this story is to me a metaphor of a very common attitude among any number of strongly committed folks who so deeply identify with their group or cause that they can get carried away into excessive self-absorption and neurotic xenophobia. Surely this story could be easily adapted to the excesses of other beleaguered groups struggling for recognition and survival. There have been many, many times when I've wanted to tell this story in the context of having to listen to revisionist harangues which place a heretofore neglected group in the number one spot on the victim-list and into the very epicenter of what is most vital in the universe. A sensitivity to political correctness (and worrying about how this would reflect on Jews) usually prevents me but the devastating punch line is always there waiting only for the set-up: Tell me, at the core of things, is postmodernism (or existentialism, or critical theory) good for Women? or for African Americans? or for Gays? or for the Rain Forest? or for that matter, the Boston Braves? Just fill in the blanks.

Tell me, is this funny or not? Tell me, Ma is this part of the Jewish tradition?

B. The King and the Poisoned Grain

This story is not from the world of jokes but from the realm of Hasidic lore and it is my understanding that it was originally told by Nachman of Bratzlav. However, I have recast the story from the two written versions I have seen and the many I have heard.

In a country long ago and far away, the prime minister comes breathless to the king with disturbing information. "Sire," he says, "I have the most dreadful news to report. The new crop of grain that our people have just completed gathering has been found to contain within it a poison of such power that it makes those who partake of it utterly mad. Since this crop is our only source of food, it is certain that all the men, women, and children of our kingdom will in a very short time become mad." The king is mortified to hear such grievous news and buries his head in his hands, sobbing with great bitterness and pain. "Do not despair, my king," says the prime minister, "for I have other information that surely will ease your pain and that is that there is still some of last year's harvest left in the royal granary. Indeed sire, there is enough for you and me to carry us through until the next harvest."

The king looks up, dries his tears, and speaks softly but firmly to the minister, "No, this will not be done as I do not wish to be a sane ruler of a mad kingdom. Therefore, you and I will both eat of the new crop and we will become mad like everyone else. However, before we eat of the poisonous bread, we will each paint a red dot on our foreheads. In this way, we shall always know and remember that we are mad."

To me this is primarily a story about the importance of confronting and accepting both harsh realities and compelling responsibilities. The king is fully aware of the cruelty and the tragedy of the situation and in this desperate situation, does not grasp for straws and nor does he seek a personal escape hatch. The king's watchful minister also confronts reality head-on and accordingly has performed his bureaucratic functions well—he has assembled the facts, assessed the available resources, developed options, and has a plan of action. What he lacks, however, is the king's wisdom and vision that extends beyond political survival to what is required for a long and difficult struggle for the kingdom to regain its sanity. What is minimally required is a recognition of the patent suffering that is sure to follow as well as of the limitations that will face the community in its struggles. Beyond that, the king knows that the responsibility of leadership rests with full membership in the community, not just politically but spiritually and existentially. The denial of the opportunity for special privilege not only affirms the king's solidarity with and compassion for his people, but his insight that he must experience and share their suffering if he is to presume to lead them.

The king is also wise enough to know about denial and the tendency to sentimentalize. He realizes immediately that even the powerful and wise will need to be reminded of what really is, what once was, and what might yet be. There is in this story a poignant message of the importance of awareness, memory, and vision and a hint at the dangers of denial, forgetting, and co-optation. The king is not worried about preserving the memory of nostalgia but about the preservation of the memory of lost capacities and aspirations. He seems to fear that the people will blur what they must face with what they might still transcend, thus forgetting in their confusion the memory of hope and possibility. In this story, realism and vision are not contradictory but complementary, not conflicting but synergistic, not a matter of forced choice but an opportunity for partnership.

I believe that this aspect of the story helps me to understand why I have been so wary if not contemptuous of educators who are so optimistic and gushy about the latest research finding, innovation, or change. I continue to be amazed at the cheerful hubris that surrounds the claims for the importance of new insights and the possibilities of the latest educational remedies. Don't they know that things usually *don't* work out and that in the long run Murphy triumphs? Don't they know how devilishly complicated human behavior is and how little we actually know about it? I guess such alienation and pessimism is part of the legacy of a Jewish Braves fan.

I also continue to be startled by the way we (I) continue in our lunatic educational practices, for not only do we persist in engaging in professionally sanctioned yet morally suspect behaviors but we are also active in perpetuating and validating them. It is hard for me to accept the fact that intelligent and good people do such destructive and corrupting things as grade students, compete for academic honors, participate in selective admissions, and develop merit pay schemes. One popular Jewish response to such determined forgetting, which is often expressed with an exaggerated shrug accompanied with a "Nu, so what can you do?" at least offers some recognition of the seriousness of the situation but its inherent passivity is troubling. Another Jewish way, as reflected in this story, is the path that I have found to be more productive and that is the one of humility and agency in which we definitely act but in the full awareness of our limitations and restrictions. Consequently, I find myself frequently quoting both in my teaching and writing the wonderful Talmudic adage that: "The task is not ours to finish, but neither are we free to take no part in it".

Others see also in this story a major emphasis on the king's iron determination to maintain the Jewish community and his strong bond with the Jewish people, hence the story can be seen as a powerful affirmation of solidarity, community, and peoplehood. Although the story clearly is meant to be about Jews, the community of this story is not explicitly defined or delineated by reference to religious beliefs or cultural values. The king loves and identifies with these people, it would seem, primarily because he feels very strongly that he is one of them and they are part of him. Hence the very difficult question of distinguishing roots from meaning; to what degree do I value my Jewish roots because I value Jewish traditions and beliefs and to what degree do I treasure Jewish values because I cherish my Jewish roots? This tension between concern for the universal and connection with the particular, although by no means a monopoly of Jews, is perhaps at the center of the struggle represented in this book to integrate Jewish identity (concrete and particular) with the traditions of the Enlightenment (abstract and universal).

There are, in addition, some dimensions to this story that continue to cast dark shadows for me. What are we to make of the king and the kingdom if we are to interpret them respectively as metaphors for

God and for Israel, as is often the case in Hasidic stories? Is God seeking even closer involvement with His people and/or does He seek to offer hope and support only in times of profound crisis? Is there a suggestion here that the whole world has gone mad and that only God retains the power of choice? Are the people of Israel being asked to accept that madness comes with the territory and that they are destined to a Sisyphean life of struggle to find God's way? Perhaps all God gives us is that red dot and the rest is up to us. Perhaps the story asks us to have faith in the wake of all these uncertainties and fears and in spite of cruel realities and bleak futures.

At times I confess that I could easily interpret the story as telling us that we are indeed already mad but have forgotten by choice or default that we are. As an educator and a Jew, however, I reject that view as I have come to believe that our most important function is to resist despair and promote hope. I embrace the tradition that insists that it is a sin for a Jew to despair and accept the wisdom of the red-dotted king in reminding us of our madness for as upsetting as that acknowledgment might be, it can very well serve as the first step in the struggle for redemption.

In any case, my own work is constantly informed by the issues of the face-off between the forces of harsh reality and the dreams of liberating visions. There surely are compelling reasons to ground an educational program in the task of preparing people to grapple with the world seen as if it were inhabited with lunatics who occasionally aspire to be sane. I am, however, also attracted to the educational tradition that sees the world as if it were peopled by angels struggling to avoid being evil. I wind up in what I gather to be a characteristically Jewish position of embracing paradox and accepting uncertainty but, nonetheless still insisting on the necessity of human agency. This orientation is brilliantly encapsulated in Reinhold Niebuhr's succinct characterization of the moral significance of the Biblical Prophets as being rooted in their "confidence that life is good in spite of its evil and that it is evil in spite of good. In such faith both sentimentality and despair are avoided."

C. The Rabbis and their Sons

The son of an American rabbi delights his father by deciding that he wishes to follow in his father's footsteps and announces his intention not only to become a rabbi but to go to a yeshiva in Israel for his training. The father is overjoyed and pledges his total and unswerving support. The father's joy is to be short-lived, for just two years into his son's studies he receives a phone call from Israel in the middle of the night.

It is from his son who is in a very agitated state, his voice full of excitement and nervousness. The son has had an extraordinary epiphany and has converted to Christianity! He speaks of a newly found joyous sense of peace and fulfillment, yet is fearful of alienating his parents, yearns for his father's understanding, and begs for his blessing. The father is too shocked and bewildered to respond coherently and asks his son to allow him time to absorb the news.

The father is deeply shaken, racked with guilt, anger, sorrow, and apprehension. He prays, he anguishes with his wife, he reflects, he goes over any number of explanations and while this process helps, he is still tormented by doubt and pain. He says to himself, "I have been an observant and God fearing Jew and raised my son to be the same, always believing in the goodness and mercy of the Almighty. What have I done to deserve this?"

He is also deeply embarrassed about his son's conversion which prevents him from sharing his pain and getting help with his anguish. Finally, he summons up his courage and decides to confide in his closest friend, also a rabbi, for whom he has the greatest respect as a wise and pious person. He goes to the friend, tells him the story and asks him, "How could it be that such a thing could happen to a pious and observant Jew like me?" The friend listens intently to the story, turns pale, clasps his hands to his face and gasps. He gathers himself together, gives out a long sigh, and answers, "Funny you should ask. I also have a son who likewise went to Israel to become a rabbi and he too became a Christian and I also was too ashamed to tell anyone."

The two friends sit in stunned silence, their pain deepened and their consternation now greatly magnified. When they speak it is with humility and near desperation that they look to each other for some explanation, some way to find meaning in their experiences. They both quickly come to the realization that in such difficult times, only a direct appeal to God Almighty would suffice. Knowing full well the dangers and risks of what they are doing and with great apprehension and reverence, they speak directly to God and beg for some divine inspiration or sign that would provide them with answers to their troubling and heart-breaking questions: "Oh God in heaven, we are two pious Jews who have faithfully and lovingly followed thy will. We both have sons whom we sent to

Israel to become rabbis and both of them have forsaken their heritage and become Christians. Why did this happen?"

When they finish their prayers and beseechments, there is a hushed and tense silence. The two men united by their parenthood, vocation, and pain, wait in a state of agitation and anxiety. Soon, there is a rustle in the room followed by the faint rumble of thunder and the appearance of a most pleasing glowing light. Then, much louder thunder and more powerful light and the unmistakable sound of a voice being cleared. There is the sound of a long sigh followed by a voice that says, "Funny you should ask. I also have a son whom I sent to Israel to become a rabbi and . . .

Again there is pathos and pain and again there is irony and mockery with added dashes of fatalism, victimization, and loss of control. This is a story about good people in bewildered pain and about a God who knows all too well about human anguish. Yet we are left as unsure about His attitude toward it as we are about His ability to do anything about it. However, there are also in this story intimations of struggle, hope, yearning, and aspiration, all aspects of the quintessential human impulse to search for meaning and harmony in the universe and on earth. The story also references the peculiarly Jewish tradition of humans challenging God, insisting on the individual's right to question Him, demanding that God meet His covenantal responsibilities. In addition, the God in this story is not quite as remote and mysterious as other representations and indeed this God seems to empathize and even mirror human vulnerabilities. It is this kind of dialectic of divine inspiration and human responsibility that has prodded me to find ways to accommodate revelation, agency, and mystery in my work. To me a proper education needs to makes space for the mystery and glory of moral and spiritual imagination just as it needs to nurture the knowledge, skills, and insights that give those flights of imagination concrete expression.

In addition there are other overtones that connect to me, namely the references to America and to Christianity. There is the obvious pride that the fathers feel about their sons' decision to emigrate to Israel, presumably a sign of more profound commitment than even that of rabbis in the Diaspora. At the same time, the fathers have remained in America presumably prospering and thriving such that they have the fruits of freedom, autonomy, and choice. The story reminds me that my life is also informed and shaped for better or worse by my American consciousness and my immersion in a Christian culture.

The connection to Christianity is indicative of the hesitance, ambiguity, and ambivalence that marks my own attitudes toward the tangled and tragic history of Jewish-Christian relations. I certainly bear the pains of anti-Semitism ranging from the subtleties of innuendo and condescension to the raw experiences of violence and hatred and I share in the anger and bitterness directed at those who would harm and kill Jews in the name of a religion grounded in unconditional love. In addition, I have also suffered from experiencing the disdain and contempt that many Jews have for most Christians. Moreover, I have been drawn to the teachings of the historical Jesus that seem to resonate and complement my notions of what constitutes Jewish ethics, namely a profound commitment to participating in the continuing creation of a world of peace, love, and justice. This affinity has produced significant disapproval over the years not only from my family but from some of my best Jewish friends fearful that I might become an apostate and give aid and comfort to the enemy. I am not at all pleased with this disapproval as it feels constricting and parochial and it is in such times that I am likely to tell the story of the Mother and the Physicist.

Having said that, I also feel the poignancy of the sons' conversions not only because of the disappointment for the parents but because the conversions represent a rupture in family tradition and, implicitly, a threat to Jewish survival. I very much value the continuity of family, tradition, and community that is so celebrated by Jews and can therefore easily empathize with the fathers' anguish. Yet, I certainly very much value and honor modern notions of individual autonomy and choice, evidence of the powerful influences of Enlightenment thought on my life.

Hence, this ambivalence has both political and theoretical implications for me. Politically, it means that I must address the questions of identity; do I identify myself as unambiguously, if not partisanly, Jewish? Is my strategy toward dealing with Christians (as well as with other communities) to be one of competition, coexistence, or ecumenism? Is my strategy toward dealing with Jews on non-Jewish views to be one of mediator, translator, or apologist?

As a professional I need not only to figure out how these matters impinge on my teaching and writing, but I also need to address the compatibility of Jewish and Christian (as well as other) orientations since my work is vitally concerned with the moral grounding of public education in a multicultural society. I continue to take the position that it is necessary and possible to forge some kind of vital consensus of what might constitute a spiritual and moral basis for an education directed at creating communities of peace, love, justice, and joy within the framework of a diverse and democratic American society. It would seem that this task is both a personal and a professional one in that I need to wrestle with the integration of the various strands that shape my own life as I engage in the larger political and ideological struggles for moral cohesion.

There are, of course, many other stories that are dear to me and many other interpretations of the ones I have told. However, I believe that what I have presented is indicative of much of my thinking on these matters. Writing this essay has enabled me to clarify a number of issues but it has also left me riddled with lots of ambivalence and uncertainty. I find it especially difficult to sort out the effects of my Jewish background and experience from the other influences on my professional life but I have just about decided that this concern is not only likely unanswerable but ultimately it is more interesting than it is important. What I believe is more pertinent to this essay is the question of the degree to which I intentionally and systematically work to frame my professional life within a Jewish tradition.

There are a number of serious obstacles to doing this, not least of which is my inability and reluctance to identify with any particular Jewish tradition. In addition, there are the complicated political, cultural, and institutional problems involved with teaching in a public, secular, nonsectarian university established expressly for the purpose of serving a particular community and its diverse population. There is no question that I am drawn to certain traditions of Jewish learning and prayer that conjure up for me a very appealing fantasy of being in an interpretative community that requires and affirms serious study, reflection, contemplation, and debate. However, this fantasy is different from the vision of Enlightenment academic life for it involves study and dialogue in a shared discourse that is centered on questions of ultimate meaning, cultural practice, and social survival rather than the disparate, multidisciplinary, and poly-dimensional discourses involved in the metaphor of the free marketplace of ideas. I am strongly attracted to a life rooted in grounded study, dialogue, and reflection but I can also be critical of such a life to the extent that it distracts us from the responsibility to act in and on the world and to the degree that it is enabled through the oppression of others. Still, study is sweet and to study in the Jewish tradition of doing so in community with learned and wise companions is sweeter still, especially if the sweetness is an important ingredient in the making of larger meaning. This seems to be a Jewish teaching that is consonant with my professional identity, i.e., the faith that there are communal educational processes that actually do contribute to the creation of a just and loving community and that that function is, in fact, *the* most important purpose of education.

As a faculty member in a modern public university my task involves working with students from a very wide range of orientations and backgrounds. There are certainly intellectual and ideological connections that I share with my students but they are broader, more procedural than substantive, and in any case they are not about being Jewish. Indeed, the discourse of my teaching emerges out of the traditions of Liberalism and the Enlightenment with its emphasis on individual expression, autonomy, openness, and free inquiry. I affirm and support this approach even as I wonder how it would be to study and teach not within the flexible and forgiving framework of permissive liberalism but rather within the stricter parameters of Jewish traditions of study.

Beyond that lies the reality that as a child of the Enlightenment and a product of American culture I find that some extremely important commitments of mine become somewhat problematic within the context of Jewish traditions. My being is in large part defined by commitments to totally inclusive democracy, radical equality, and unconditional love, which are in considerable tension with the hierarchy, sexism, racism, and violence that often permeates Jewish thought. I am frankly impatient with the labored efforts that it takes to find support for democracy, equality, and unconditional love in the Torah, especially when there are other secular or non-Jewish sources where such affirmation is proudly and unequivocally presented.

However, let me quickly add that this ambivalence and hesitation, as real as it is, is incomplete, for I also have come to a place where I can clearly affirm myself as a Jew much beyond the point of doing so by default. What is clear to me is that I very much want to learn more about Jewish thought and experience and to deepen my still evolving Jewish consciousness. More to the point, this affirmation has significantly manifested itself in my current teaching and writing.

III. Affirmation

I entered education in part because I believed that greater understanding and knowledge were the keys to making a better world. This notion expanded to the belief that critical rationality in the Socratic traditions of probing skepticism, careful analysis, and precise thinking are the ultimate weapon against prejudice, oppression, and authoritarianism. I still highly value these traditions and indeed, my teaching style continues to emphasize tough questions that are intended to make students squirm a little and think a lot. (Never mind that the reverse often happens.) Although I have always felt some disquiet about this orientation it took me a long time to understand that what was unsettling about it was it had no grounding except itself. It seemed to me that either the educators seriously interested in significant social reform were basically saying that it is good to think critically for its own sake or that they were reluctant to be explicit about what they believe to be morally right. It finally dawned on me that what was utterly lacking not only in Education but in all of Academia was moral affirmation, a rather startling omission, particularly for those educators committed to creating a better world.

Again, it is Heschel who speaks to me: "Socrates taught us that a life without thinking is not worth living. Now, thinking is a noble effort , but the finest thinking may end in futility. . . . The Bible taught us that life without commitment is not worth living; that thinking without roots will bear flowers but no fruit."

My professional work is totally concerned with grounding educational policies and practices not in critical thinking and not in creative expression but in moral commitments. To pursue critical thinking and creative expression for their own sakes is self-indulgent at best and idolatrous at worst. I certainly believe that these processes can be vital resources in the struggle to create a life of meaning but without a framework of meaning they are only neutral techniques capable of enabling good or evil. This makes the affirmation of a framework of meaning the prime requirement of any educational orientation worthy of serious consideration. Once I came to that conclusion I had no choice but to make my own moral affirmations and framework of meaning as clear as possible, or to use a religious phrase, to profess my faith.

With all this said, I can now make it clearer how at least in two very important ways my Jewish experience is deeply embedded in my professional concerns. Firstly, I am dedicated to moral commitment and to meaning before anything else, before critical thinking, before creativity, before reading, before great literature and art, even before Einstein's theory of relativity. I see the value of education to the extent that it serves the good (I believe that this is what religious Jews call being obedient to God's will); anything else is a bonus. Notions of the good and of the meaningful should provide the criteria for determining the appropriateness of educational policies and practices and for measuring their efficacy. Such a position seems to me to be deeply Jewish since my view is that the most urgent and basic message of Torah is that in spite of a lot of contrary evidence we must operate in the faith that life has meaning, direction, and purpose.

Secondly, to paraphrase Will Herberg: My faith emerges from my affirmation of the history of the Jewish people as my redemptive history and I have appropriated it as my personal background history making it the foundation of my existence. If this history is the foundation of my existence then it inevitably is the foundation of the work that serves to define me.

The stories I have told and discussed surely reveal that this faith is constantly being tested by complex and troubling issues and that a great deal of uncertainty, ambivalence, and ambiguity remain. However, writers like Alasdair MacIntyre have helped me to accept this confusion and move on from there by pointing out the value of identifying with a particular moral tradition and community as well as the danger if not impossibility of pursuing the moral life without such identification. What I find especially helpful is MacIntyre's characterization of a moral community as "an historically extended, socially embodied argument." MacIntyre goes on to say that a critical dimension of such a community involves participants arguing about what should constitute its moral commitments. I fully intend to continue participating in that "historically extended, socially embodied argument " and to integrate the moral commitments of that living tradition into my work with passion, care, and reverence. The nature of my involvement will probably continue to resemble that of a lover's quarrel, a process of loving affirmation and critical skepticism, occasioned no doubt with moments of indifference, even hostility.

As an instance of how this process is going, I cite the following excerpt from a paper I recently wrote on the relationship between education and spirituality, in which I discuss issues related to my Jewish identity. Much of what I say reflects Jewish traditions but I also have to say that I would not be offended if some of it does not; however, I would greatly value critiques of it from any number of Jewish perspectives. This is what I wrote in the Spring of 1996:

"I affirm traditions that not only recognize that humans are fated to create our world but believes that above all we are called upon to create a world resonant with divine intention—a world of peace, justice, love, community, and joy for all. These are traditions that accept as givens the potentials of human abilities as well as the limits of human fallibilities; they posit our capacity to be generous as well as to be selfish; to be angelic as well as demonic; compassionate as well as cruel; wise as well as foolish. Such traditions revere knowledge but only as it is tempered with the wisdom that advances justice and mercy; a perspective that acknowledges the enormity of the task but dismisses human despair as sinful; and one that represents a consciousness of outrage in the wake of cruelty and injustice but always in the faith that witness, confession, and healing offer the possibilities of transcendence and redemption. What is absolutely crucial to redemption is human responsibility and human agency since these traditions require that we act as God's agents, dedicated to constructing and sustaining communities based on joy, love, peace, and justice."

IV. Epilogue

As I expected, the process of writing this paper has clarified some issues, confused others, and raised brand new ones for me. Perhaps the issues all come under the heading of the problematics of choice. I did not choose to be a Jew, I do not believe that I can choose not to be a Jew, I am absolutely clear that among other important things, I am a Jew, and I have no problems with any of this. As the adage says, one does not choose to be born or to die or, as George Santayana said,"No one speaks language, everyone speaks a particular language," or, as the saying goes, "Everybody has to come from somewhere." Frankly, I don't know if it would be better if I could have chosen or what I would have chosen if I could, but in any case the issue is moot to me.

Of course, I have much more choice about how I express and manifest my Jewish identity and the fact that I have such a lot of choice stems in large part from the happenstance of my living in twentieth-century America. As I navigate between the freedom and autonomy that comes with the territory of the Enlightenment American style and the commitments that come with the territory of Jewish traditions, I struggle with several questions. Is it O.K. for me to pick and choose the Jewish traditions that are appealing to me and resonant with my work? (I sort of think it is but I need some help with this.) Is it all right to see Jewish sources as, to use Roger Simon's term, fertile grazing areas for finding support for my ideas? Should I define myself as a Jew living in exile or as an American "who happens to be Jewish"? Should I become more attached to a particular Jewish tradition and work to deduce its relevance to American education? Is my work as an educator about encouraging *goyim* to be more Jewish or better informed on Jewish thought or both or neither? Perhaps I should accept and even embrace a life of multiple and shifting professional identities, moving from one paradigm and context to another. As a matter of fact, can I just give up fussing over these issues and forget all about this identity thing?

The most complicated question for me personally, however, has to do with my realization that, as with my connection to the Boston Braves, my deepest and strongest ties are at base irrational. In a very real sense, these bonds have absolutely nothing to do with the content of Jewish history, nor its religious teachings, nor its literature, as much as I love and treasure them. I came to treasure them because I am Jewish; I did not become Jewish because I treasured them. I know this kind of visceral bonding resonates with the consciousness of the physicist's mother, but there it is and I remain very, very puzzled by it all. As far as my work is concerned, would it have had a similar orientation if I were born an Episcopalian or if I were a fourth-generation Jew? or if I were an Israeli? I'm not even sure I need to know.

I find myself at the end of this essay with even more questions than I had when I began, which reminds me of a story.

Two people, one a Jew, the other not, are having a long and heated conversation. One of them, in a moment of frustration, asks, " Why is it that every time I ask a Jew a question, they always answer with another question?" The Jew replies: " So what's wrong with asking questions?"

References

Herberg, Will. *Faith in Human Theology*. Philadelphia: Westminster Press, 1976.

Heschel, Abraham. *God in Search of Man*. New York: Farrar, Strauss, and Giroux, 1955.

Heschel, Abraham. *The Prophets* (2 vols.). New York: Harper and Row, 1962.

MacIntyre, Alasdair. *After Virtue*. Notre Dame: Univ. of Notre Dame Press, 1981.

Purpel, David. *The Moral and Spiritual Crisis in Education*. Granby: Bergin and Garvey, 1989.

Purpel, David "Moral Outrage and Education" in Kane, Jeffrey, *Education, Information, and Transformation*. Prentice Hall, forthcoming.

Chapter 10

A Curriculum of Courage, A Pedagogy of Inclusion: A Jewish Woman Makes Her Way Through Academia

Mara Sapon-Shevin

Introduction

It was five o'clock in the afternoon, and I had returned to my university office after a late afternoon class. My last few weeks had been filled with planning and organizing a Human Rights' Conference focusing on the Holocaust, a project initiated after rumblings of anti-Semitism on our campus. My activities and my presence as a Jew had been widely publicized—television and radio interviews, a short article in the newspaper. On the floor of my office I found a piece of paper. It read: "Shut up and get out of here or your reproductive capacity will be sharply diminished." On the back, the paper said, "Holocaust—destruction of the Jews." Stunned, I read and reread the paper and then destroyed it, trying hard not to acknowledge what I had found and what it meant that this had been left in my office. It was not until the next night, returning from Synagogue services, that I finally told my husband what I had found, and, in the telling, allowed the meaning of the note to sink in. I called my Dean. She was distressed and sympathetic and conveyed her commitment to hold a departmental meeting to talk about building security in general and support for me in particular. The next day, after the meeting was announced, my colleague in the next office—male, white, Christian, 250 pounds—said to me, "You know, if I were you, I wouldn't take it personally."

This chapter is about my taking it personally. It is about living my life as a Jew, as a Jewish woman, as a Jewish woman academic without borders. This chapter is about transforming a rich legacy as a Jew as well as experiences of exclusion and isolation and the complexities of being Jewish in a Christian world, into a set of principles and commitments that infuse my teaching and thinking, my being in the world.

This is a very hard chapter to write. There is no shortage of things to say, no dearth of passion. What is the obstacle? It is fear of visibility. Why would that be a problem? I teach, write, and publish extensively, generally welcoming visibility and sharing my ideas. But this book is about making our Jewish selves visible in academia, about speaking not as curriculum theorists but as Jewish curriculum theorists, about claiming our voices as Jewish voices.

Historically, many Jews have remained safe by "passing," by "fitting in," by not appearing or acting "too Jewish." This book in general, and this chapter in particular, is about breaking that silence. Not a silence of voice, but a silence of Jewish voice, nuanced, accented, scattered with Yiddish expressions and cultural references. When I mention what I am writing to a non-Jewish colleague, and mention some of the other coauthors, she remarks, "Oh, I didn't know he/she was Jewish." A Jewish colleague looks surprised at the list of authors and says the same thing. It is as though noticing who is a Jew and who is not is somehow inappropriately tribal, chauvinistic, or prideful. In academia, aren't we supposed to be past such clannish identifications and affiliations? I sense occasional feelings that being asked to be in this book is perceived as somehow receiving an "unfair advantage" unavailable to people who are not Jewish, as though somehow I have used my status as a Jew to secure a publication—"You know those Jews, they hang out together!" From such anticipated censure comes some of my reluctance.

But there is also great joy and excitement in breaking this silence. Finally, all of me. An end to bifurcation, trifurcation, the multiple identities that I sometimes hide or disguise. I always wear my chai necklace, but only occasionally do I wear it outside my clothes rather than tucked in close to my heart. This chapter is a chance for me to make sense to myself and readers how my pieces fit together. As I work on writing, I alternate between time spent at the computer and time spent practicing my haftorah and preparing a d'var Torah for Sabbath services in three weeks. At long last, I get to talk about all parts of my life, without the typical editing and self-censorship. In this writing I have an opportunity for wholeness.

Other Jews have noted fear of breaking the silence. Mimi Orner, in a paper entitled "Surplus Visibility and the Jewish Identity: The Case of the Jewish Mafia"[1] expands on Daphne Patai's concept of surplus or excessive visibility.[2] Patai argues that for members of minority groups there is no middle ground; we are forced to choose between invisibility and surplus visibility, "between silence and the accusation that we are making excessive noise." The surplus visibility in some ways reinforces the invisibility—keep quiet, or you'll be accused of being too loud, too noisy. This concept is not limited to Jews, but extends to every group whose presence threatens people's conceptions of what is normal and typical; lesbians holding hands in public are accused of "flaunting their sexuality," African Americans wearing kente cloth are viewed as trying to be "ethnic" and somehow un-American.

Certainly a whole book about Jewish academics constitutes making a lot of noise; one both hopes and fears that it will be hard to miss. If safety for Jews has come from staying quiet, small, and nonthreatening, then this is a major departure. Will I become targeted as a result of my openness? Accused of being self-serving or self-indulgent for talking about issues of anti-Semitism and Jewish oppression? Should I, like my ninety-two-year old Grandma, tell everyone, "Really, it's okay. Don't worry about me, I'll be fine." Or dare I speak from the heart and name my truths?

In this chapter I discuss the ways in which my Jewishness and my identity as a Jewish woman have helped to define my work and my worldview, shaping both what I teach and how I teach. I will talk about some of the critical incidents that helped to shape my Jewish consciousness and the times and places and ways in which I can myself recognize how my Jewish history affects and guides my work in education. I want to examine the ways in which the positive, admirable qualities of my Jewish background and identity have helped me to act powerfully in the world and in my work and have given me particular sensibilities that infuse my life projects. But I also want to discuss how Jewish oppression and other pains experienced as a Jew in this culture are also enacted in my work; the glimpses that I have of how my work sometimes subtly, sometimes blatantly, reflects my fears and my hurts as a Jew as well as my rich religious and cultural heritage. I will conclude by talking about several instances in which I have attempted to address directly issues of anti-Semitism and Jews in the academy and the lessons I learned from those experiences.

I make no pretense here of relating a definitive autobiography, or even the most thorough account of the events I describe. The limits of my writing about my life and work are numerous and humbling; I am confident that there have been many defining moments that remain opaque to me. Similarly, I'm sure there are numerous manifestations of my identity in my work that remain invisible to me at the same time that they are probably blazingly obvious to others. Because I often do not disassociate "Mara the Jew" from "Mara the professional," it is impossible for me to present my story as though it were the merging of two identities. The story of my life, like all lives, is both seamless and a patchwork. There are parts of it that make great sense to me and other pieces, which I struggle to integrate and comprehend. I describe my life with a powerful awareness of the limitations of my own narrative and the ways in which my story both frames me and blurs my boundaries.

I was born in Columbus, Ohio, and grew up in Ohio, Massachusetts, Spain, Scotland, California, and upstate New York. I was raised as a Jew in a family that, although not strictly observant, was undeniably defined as Jewish. I went to Hebrew school all the way through high school, had a bat mitzvah at thirteen, celebrated with dreidls and latkes at Chanukah with one present for each of eight nights, dressed up as Queen Esther for Purim, and recited the four questions at Passover seders with other Jewish families. I married a man I had met at age fourteen in Hebrew School, had a Jewish wedding, and have two daughters, Dalia and Leora. I am what others label "a practicing Jew"; I go to services almost every Shabbat, celebrate all of the major Jewish holidays and some of the minor ones, wear a chai around my neck and identify myself openly (and frequently) as Jewish in most settings in which I find myself. I bring a menorah and dreidl cookies to work, talk to my students about things Jewish, explain to the man at the post office why Chanukah seems "early" this year and why my presents have to reach my nieces, and include references to my Jewishness in every keynote I give and workshop I present.

But my self-definition as a Jew has not been as constant or unequivocal as the above narrative might indicate. There have been clear times when I have "felt" Jewish, noticed my Jewishness more, or asserted myself as a Jew with more forcefulness. Woven in through the warp threads of "being Jewish" are woof threads of "defining moments of Judaism" that hold the fabric together. As I interrogate those moments, I notice that I am most likely to be aware of my Judaism when I am in the minority (one smaller than the typical minority for Jews), or when I feel threatened as a Jew. And many of these defining moments have become part of my understanding of oppression and social justice and have guided my broader work in education and curriculum building. I describe here those particular moments in time as well as the ongoing backdrop of my Jewish life.

Defining Moments

Being Jewish in Spain

When I was six years old, my family spent a year living in Barcelona, Spain. I attended a Spanish-speaking school (all-Catholic) and had little association with other Americans. I also attended an after-school Hebrew school in the small Jewish synagogue in Barcelona, a building unmarked on the outside because of the risks and dangers to Jews during this time of Franco's Spain. I learned to read and write Hebrew with the instruction in Spanish. I remember moments of both great warmth and connection with the other Jewish families and also a deep foreboding and secrecy that hung over the Jewish community. This was, perhaps, my first real sense of the "dangers" of being Jewish, the definition of Jews as "outsiders," marginalized, not quite belonging, of the need to "pass" to be safe. If we were safe, then why didn't our synagogue have a sign and a Jewish star on it like at home?

From ages ten through high school, I lived in Rochester, New York, in a suburb that was approximately 50 percent Jewish. I was no longer a minority, and, although the outside culture occasionally made me painfully aware of my difference, my day-to-day experiences were Jewishly relatively easy. College at the University of Rochester, with a significant Jewish population, and then teaching jobs in Madison, Wisconsin, and Cleveland, Ohio, followed. In each of these settings, I identified myself as Jewish and was involved in synagogue and faculty activities, and generally felt comfortable as a Jew. At both the University of Wisconsin and Cleveland State, there were other Jews on the faculty, and a general acceptance of Jews within academic circles.

My children attended Jewish preschool programs and my older daughter attended kindergarten at a private, Jewish day school.

A Jew in North Dakota

In 1985, we moved to Grand Forks, North Dakota, where I accepted a teaching position at the University. The sense of Jews as outsiders, as not full members, as somehow endangered was revisited most prominently by this move. After living in many places as an adult (Rochester, New York; Kalamazoo, Michigan; Madison, Wisconsin; and Cleveland, Ohio), I suddenly found myself in a place where I was, for many people, their "first Jew." One of my colleagues at the University actually told me he was surprised to find out that there "still were Jews." He said that he had learned about "the Hebrews" in Sunday School as a child, but "didn't know there were any left." I felt myself seen as a dinosaur, a fossil of an earlier time, an atavistic throwback to some earlier era.

My understanding of academia as a place populated by Jews (my father having been a university professor) was suddenly disrupted. There were very few of "us" and we were identifiably different in many ways from the Norwegian Lutherans and German Catholics that constituted the town and the University. I was unable to find anyone who was able to cut my daughter's curly dark hair; the hairdresser said she wasn't used to "that kind of hair." Ritual foods had to be specially ordered for Passover, there were no Jewish greeting cards in the drugstores. Our house stood alone as undecorated at Christmas time, the only one on the street that looked plain and somewhat barren. Our family was "exotic."

This sense of otherness, of difference, of life on the margins was not, however, entirely painful or negative. Many non-Jews expressed genuine interest and concern for learning about Jews and Judaism, some of the children's teachers went out of their way to accommodate and make my children comfortable around holiday time, and the Jewish community itself was extremely close and connected. When the local newspaper did an article on Chanukah, our family was featured prominently. My husband and I were often invited to local churches and schools to teach about Judaism. When major news broke in Israel, we were often called by the newspaper to comment on the situation. After many years of being "just another Jewish family" in Cleveland, suddenly we were in the spotlight as "The Jewish family", or one of several Jewish Families. But there was a definite sense of "otherness," a need for Jews to remain vigilant in the face of anti-Semitism and challenge.

I have never hidden my Jewishness and have always claimed the identity proudly and often visibly. Nonetheless, my experiences at the university surprised and upset me. When I first came to the institution, a colleague took me out for lunch. She was warm and welcoming. During lunch we swapped stories of children and teaching and she concluded by telling me that she thought she'd like me, because I "wasn't like other Jews" she'd met. She then proceeded to tell me about pushy, arrogant, loudmouthed Jews she had known.

Two years later, when I received an equity adjustment in my salary (I had been the lowest-paid Associate Professor in the department), this same colleague was furious. She accused me of having threatened to resign, of having torn up my contract in the Dean's office (neither was true) and said, "That kind of pushy behavior may work for you and your kind back East, but it doesn't work here in North Dakota."

It wasn't entirely clear what "kind" she was referring to, but it was definitely the "kind" they had more of back East. Interestingly, as Geoffrey Tabakin[3] points out in a paper on anti-Semitism at his midwestern institution, the question "Are you from New York?" is actually a code in the midwest, associated with "You're from the East Coast, aren't you?" that identifies foreigners and Jewishness in particular. (This would, of course, be interesting and surprising to the millions of New Yorkers who are African American, Puerto Rican, Catholic, etc.). In any case, I had become clearly established as an Other, as different.

A sense of vigilance and watchfulness extended to my children as well. My younger daughter, Leora, came home one day from the second grade (a day close to Easter) upset to have been harassed by classmates. The children had told her that the Jews had killed their Lord, and that since she was a Jew, it was her fault. Just four months ago, my older daughter told me that while we lived in Grand Forks (this being six years ago), a whole gang of children had knocked her off her bicycle, yelling at her that she was a "dirty Jew." When I was shocked and said, "You never told me that!" she replied, logically, "I knew you'd be upset." My reaction proved to her that she was right.

After six years in North Dakota, we moved to Syracuse, New York, where I currently teach. There is a large Jewish community, and there are other Jews on the university faculty. There are many Jewish students and a genuine commitment to thoughtfulness about diversity issues, even if these are not enacted perfectly. We belong to a small, Conservative synagogue, and although I still often feel "different" from other Jews (my participation in actions in support of Arabs on the West Bank is not well received by more mainstream Jews), I am increasingly connected to the Jewish life of my synagogue and community.

The Nazis Are Coming

The most powerful recent experience feeling my Jewishness, both in its richness and its terror, occurred three years ago when a group of neo-Nazis announced a march in the neighboring town of Auburn.

They made public that they had scheduled their march for Yom Kippur and that the march would go from the Auburn town hall to Harriet Tubman Square, clearly an event scheduled to be as offensive as possible to both Jews and African Americans. For weeks, a small group of community activists met, trying to decide the appropriate response to such a demonstration of hatred and prejudice. There were some who favored doing nothing, arguing that the best way to discourage such behavior was to have it met by silence and lack of attention. The organized Jewish community was unanimous in its decision to do nothing about the march, as was the African-American community. Unfortunately, media attention had already created a situation in which the chances of "nothing" happening were small. It seemed inevitable that the event would be well-attended (if only by onlookers) and that there would be considerable news coverage. The decision of this adhoc group of activists, finally, was to assemble as a group, as a "visible presence" (as we called ourselves) and to hold signs that said, simply, "No." Members of the group each wore one of the symbols of those persecuted by the Nazis during the Holocaust—yellow stars, pink and black triangles, green triangles and so on. Another group of people appointed themselves as "peacekeepers" committed to maintaining the peace and keeping things from becoming violent.

The period of planning for the march was a tense time for me. I was upset by the fact that there were Nazis marching and, as a Jewish woman, I felt particularly vulnerable and frightened. But my feelings were stirred even further by the fact that my then-fourteen-year-old daughter, Dalia, wanted to be part of the demonstration. Part of me, as a parent, was proud that I had raised a child who was willing to take a stand, a child who went to thirty hours of meetings as well as ten hours of nonviolence training over two weekends. And another part of me, of course, was terrified that I was somehow agreeing to let my precious child be somewhere where she could get badly hurt. I wrestled with this through many sleepless nights, and was only somewhat reassured by the many people who made personal pledges to look after her and keep her safe throughout the march.

Although people on the planning group thought well about many aspects of the upcoming march and the necessity for a powerful response, there was little attention given to the Jews who lived in Auburn, where there was a small synagogue. When I raised the issue of what Kol Nidre services would be like for that congregation (the night before the march), I was reassured that the "police would provide any necessary protection." But I was not happy with that. As a Jew, I want to know that when the Nazis come, the people from my community, my allies, will be there standing by my side, not simply the police. After considerable discussion of this topic, a group of non-Jews organized a candlelight vigil, which they held outside the synagogue during services. My husband and I and our daughters, and two other Jewish friends from Syracuse, attended Kol Nidre services at the Auburn synagogue while thirty to forty people stood in silent, protective vigil outside the synagogue. When the services were over, every member of that congregation went out to thank the vigil keepers, many of them commenting that they had never felt as supported or cherished as much as by that act.

The march itself was relatively uneventful. A small group of neo-Nazis appeared on the courthouse steps, brandishing flags with swastikas, but they were frightened off by the large number of protesters and by a small group of demonstrators (not our group) who pelted them with metal nuts and bolts. The Nazis took a police escort and left town.

I found the size of the turnout impressive and reassuring and the power of the group energizing. As one of the few Jewish members of the Visible Presence group, I felt deeply connected to those who had stood by my side and was heartened that were the Nazis to appear at my doorstep, there would indeed be people there for me and my family.

But my biggest lesson came from my younger daughter, Leora. Leora, at eleven, did not come to the march. We had decided that she would spend the day with Robin Smith, a friend of the family, attending synagogue with Robin in the morning. Because Leora worries a lot about the people she loves, we hadn't shared every detail of the march with her. Riding in the car two days before the event, I said to Leora, "I just want to tell you what's happening on Saturday: Papa and Dalia and I are going to go to Auburn to march and you are going to spend the day with Robin." Leora immediately began to cry. "Why are you crying?" I asked. "Because I'm scared," she responded. "What are you scared of?" I pushed. "I'm scared you'll get hurt," she replied.

I reassured her as well as I could that we were committed to nonviolence, that we would take every precaution and that we would leave if the demonstration got violent or difficult. Leora began to cry again. "Now what?" I asked. She looked at me plaintively and asked, "Why are they doing this?" I took a deep breath. My experience has always been that when children ask a question, they want a real answer. They don't want research or statistics or an article to read, they want an immediate, simple answer. "Well," I ventured, "I think they are confused people who think that only white people should live, and that anyone who is black or Jewish or gay or lesbian or disabled or an immigrant shouldn't be allowed to live." She looked at me, paused for moment and then, shaking her head, offered, "Picky, aren't they!"

Leora's characterization of race hatred and a politics of violence and exclusion as "picky" is both laughable and yet completely on-target. When and where did those folks learn who was "in" and who was "out," who was acceptable and who was unacceptable? And what are the risks of failing to teach children a more positive response to difference? My commitment to the role of education in creating decent human beings was intensified.

There have been, of course, many more stories. Stories of connection and friendship, allies found in unlikely situations and tales of learning to be safe in unsafe-feeling places. It is difficult to separate "defining moments as a Jew" from defining moments as a parent, or an educator, or an activist, or simply as a human being. How can I separate the pieces of my history and label this one "Jewish" and this one "other." Nor do I make the assumptions that all Jews have similar experiences or even interpret the same experience similarly. My husband's Jewish family—low-key, quiet and reserved—was as different as could be from my own noisy, passionate and intense Jewish family. So I do not claim "the Universal Jewish experience" nor wish to imply that defining critical incidents for me as a Jew would have affected other Jews in the same way. Some Jews in North Dakota, for example, made very different accommodations to the pervasively Christian culture, and made different decisions about how to "be Jewish" in non-Jewish spaces. But when I think of my work as an educator, there are several themes pervading my thinking that seem directly linked to early and continuing experiences as a Jew.

Making Sense of My Work

My work can be summarized as paying attention to how society responds to diversity issues and struggling for belonging, safety and respect for all people. I remain hypervigilant to the many ways in which schools and other societal institutions use their power to silence and eliminate differences, and, although many of my differences have brought me recognition and status in addition to pain and isolation, I will continue to notice the unfairness of the system and not just the effects of that system on me.

Much of my work focuses on the establishment of caring, nurturing communities, both within individual classrooms and within schools and larger groups.[4] I see community building as central to all educational and curricular reform; attention to the ways in which people treat one another is the starting point for all of the work that I do. One of the key characteristics of a community, for me, is a certain measure of safety. This includes physical safety and also emotional and behavioral safety: the safety to be oneself, to reveal all aspects of personality, strengths and weaknesses within a context of support and nurturance. The connections between a theme of safety and my individual and historical identification as a Jew seem clear: Jews have often not been safe, and it is up to me to make the world safe for all people, including Jews like me.

The other major theme of my work in education has centered on strategies for addressing diversity issues in ways that are inclusive. Through my work in multicultural education, prejudice reduction, cooperative learning, and the full inclusion of students with disabilities, I have sought ways to prepare teachers to deal with difference without excluding or "othering" those often marginalized or perceived as different.

My strong belief in these principles comes from many places. When I look for the connections between my Jewishness and my current work, some of the sources of my thinking and beliefs are positive—the ways in which my religious traditions and teaching have taught me to honor certain precepts. But deep self-reflection allows me to also see that some of my beliefs and commitments come from areas of deep hurt, often hurts as a Jew, related to these same areas. The answer to "How has your autobiography as a Jew shaped your work as an educational academic?" then, is a complex one, worthy of unpacking. While one would never claim that Jews are the only ones with commitments to social justice and education, the question is "Do my commitments in these areas look different because I am Jewish?" "What are the Jewish threads within my work?" While I would not want to be portrayed as a person whose painful childhood oriented her to a pathologically-shaped commitment to community and inclusion, neither would it be honest to deny the ways in which experiences of terror and isolation have shaped my understanding of the world and my commitments to make it better.

There is an inclination, when writing one's autobiography, to make it seem somehow wonderfully integrated and logical; this decision followed this event, this early thread was manifested later here, this theme was pervasive, that belief consistent over time. But my thinking on the relationship between my Judaism and my work is not neat. It is all tied up together in an untidy package—pieces of string hold some of it together, masking tape, patches to cover holes. Because I would like my narrative to reflect that untidiness, that sense of both integrity and mixed conglomeration, of thoughtful collection and a junk drawer, I have decided to frame this portion of my text by first describing principles or values that seem powerful in my work, and for each of these sharing the ways in which aspects of my Jewish roots, training, education or past become manifest.

Social Justice/Arguing

The positive contributions of my Judaism to this belief are numerous. I was raised within a tradition that had a strong commitment to social justice. But what constituted justice and how things should be resolved were not passed down as concise rules or dogma. Rather, there was the sense that social justice was actively constructed by the participants through a process of debate and discussion. There were long conversations at the dinner table about ethical issues and the "right" thing to do. I loved that aspect of my Torah study and religious education that involved talking about ethics and values. I remember with great fondness a discussion in Hebrew High School about the *siags* (or fences) which are made around certain laws and precepts in order to guard against wrong behavior. I loved the argumentation, the debate, the passion and the energy. I thrived on discussions that were grounded in text but did not stop with text. I was encouraged to question,"What if", to wonder, to look for inconsistencies, incongruities, contradictions and missteps. I learned to think critically and to argue, with text, with teachers, and with classmates.

This passion for argument, this recognition of the power of words to persuade, this honoring of debate has become manifest to me in the work that I have done as an expert witness in due process hearings. Because of my strong commitment to the full inclusion of children with disabilities in regular classrooms and schools, I have been called on a number of times to serve as an expert witness in due process hearings, typically ones in which parents are seeking fuller membership for their child in the classroom or school community and the school district is unwilling to include that child. My task has been to go in, meet the child and the family, survey the school situation, documents, teachers, etc., and then testify what might be happening for the child other than the segregated programming now provided or proposed.

The process is always antagonistic, often overtly hostile, and typically exhausting. The lawyers for the school district attempt to discredit my testimony and often me personally. How dare I make this statement? What is my background? Am I not an advocate for a particular position (this being seen as inappropriate within this framework)? There is always considerable back and forth between lawyers, tense moments, tricky questions, attempts at entrapment. It is like a prizefight, ducking blows, looking for weak spots to attack, maintaining firm footing in the face of fear and possible defeat. I am called on to share my vision of a more inclusive present and future for that child.

It is work that I love, work that I am good at, and also work that makes me "feel Jewish." There are two aspects of the work that connect for me Jewishly. First, there are the intellectual and verbal skills that I acquired as part of my Jewish upbringing, which serve me well in this setting. I argue well, I listen carefully for inconsistencies, I respond (sometimes) cleverly, and make good points. I track long narratives and lines of questioning on the part of "the other side" and figure out where they are going and how not to fall into their intellectual and legalistic traps.

Second, there is the clear sense of taking on a social injustice and making a difference. The principle of *Tikkun Olam* (the repair of the world) was impressed on me strongly as a child. From an early age I responded, when asked what I wanted to do when I grow up, that I wanted "to make the world a better place." It was not simply a reflexive answer, but what I truly believed (and, parenthetically, assumed that all people believed!). I see this due process project as a setting in which I am actually able to make a difference; those hearings that we have "won" have made a significant impact not only in one child's life but in the lives of other children in that community. I strongly associate this kind of social justice work, scrapping for the underdog, with my Jewish heritage.

To be honest, there is a dark side of the above as well, a place in which that work is directly related to past hurts and oppressions. To be a Jewish woman in academia is to be accused, often, of being brash, too verbal, too powerful, too visible. And the due process work provides a situation in which that visibility, that power, and that verbal skill is not the occasion for labeling and derision but for valuation and honor. In the courtroom, my verbal fluency is for a good cause. I am not mouthy, I'm articulate. I'm not "argumentative, I'm fighting for a child's education and his right to stay connected to friends, family, and community. This is a setting in which I can be strong, relentless, and tenacious without fearing being labeled derisively as "pushy."

Passion/Taking a Stand

Part of my Jewish upbringing involved my exposure to considerable passion; my home was not a quiet place in which one spoke in turn. Rather it was loud and boisterous and energy and heat abounded. My religious education contained other kinds of passion: passion for the importance of being and staying Jewish, for learning, for justice, for studying hard.

When people refer to minority groups, the reference is generally to the relative numbers of various groups. But there is much more to being "in the minority." As a child and an adult, having the status as Jewish outsider, the one Jew among many Christians (and others) means that being "the only one" is, for me, not an unfamiliar feeling. "Everyone in the class will be celebrating Christmas this month, but Mara and her family will be celebrating a different holiday. Mara, would you like to tell us about your holiday?" Sometimes with great joy and pride and sometimes with significant discomfort and resentment, I have grown used to sharing who I am and what I believe. I have become used to being the one who sees things differently, whose experience is different, and who has different ideas or values. And so when I am the only one holding a certain position, I do not reflexively believe that I must, by definition, be wrong because I am in the minority.

There is little that I have written that has been "safe." I continually take on controversial topics and find myself in (often) lonely positions that I must then defend. But in many ways, my history as an "other," as "different," has prepared me well for that position, and while I do not always find it comfortable, it does feel familiar. Although I don't like feeling uncomfortable, neither do I back down nor shy away from potentially unpopular stands. I learned, early on, to stand my ground.

Some of my recent work in education has centered on the politics of gifted education.[5] I have argued that gifted programs as they are currently constructed and implemented in this country are meritocratic, elitist, and constitute a kind of educational triage. I argue that by removing those few students for whom the educational system is clearly dysfunctional, we leave intact and without critical examination, the majority of school structures and processes that are actually dysfunctional for most children. We leave unexamined rigid, lock-step curricula, passive pedagogy, hierarchical power relationships; we fail to prioritize the creation of nurturing classroom communities in which differences are embraced rather than scorned. I call, instead, for school and classroom restructuring so that all children's needs are met.

This has not been a popular position. Members of the gifted establishment have felt challenged and invalidated by my stance and there have been angry letters, reviews, and responses. I have been told that on one Internet bulletin board I am referred to as "the Princess of Darkness." When I appeared on a NPR talk show, callers uniformly phoned to disagree with my position and to argue for what I perceived as the rights of privilege, power, and meritocracy.

Most of the time, I stand my ground proudly, secure in my own thinking and relatively unruffled by the surrounding critique. I do feel strongly about what I believe, am willing to take difficult, counter-hegemonic positions, and do not assume that disagreement means that I am wrong.

But I also ask myself: Is this ability to situate myself and defend my position a strength gleaned from being in the minority and having to stand my ground? Or it is a now-embedded need to be different or "other," a recursive need to stand apart? While I like to think that my powerful stands are evidence of great personal courage and integrity, I also worry about another aspect of my position.

My commitment to equality of opportunity and social justice is indeed a manifestation of Jewish values and beliefs, but it is also the reaction of someone who has experienced "Jewish privilege" as well as "Jewish oppression." Jews have been disproportionately successful in academic settings and are well represented in gifted programs; this is a source of both great pride and an additional occasion for fear. Many years of defending myself against the accusation that Jews think of themselves as "the chosen people" (regardless of rabbinic interpretations of that phrase) have left me wary of positioning myself in favor of unearned or even earned differentiation *when there is not a solid base of social justice*. My threads as a Jew become tangled. Refrains of "Jews are better;" "Jews are different," now mingle with "Justice for all," "None of us is free as long as any one of us is oppressed."

How can I argue against acknowledgment and positive opportunities for my own people when we have experienced such discrimination and mistreatment in the past? How can I deny my own Jewish child the opportunity to be in a gifted program because of a strong commitment to justice and equality? These are not easy tensions to resolve, and I continue to wrestle with them, neither fully resolving them nor being content with my often-partial solutions.

Integration/Personal as Political

"Are you Jewish or American?" children used to ask me when I was a child and adults sometimes still do. "If you're Jewish, are you from Israel?" "Do you speak Jewish?" Is being Jewish a religion or an ethnicity? Are Jews a race? Is Zionism racism?

There is no limit to the confusions that abound about the ways in which Jewish identify is defined. Differences in self-definition, rabid anti-Semitism, incredible ignorance and fear all combine to make it difficult for both Jews and non-Jews to make sense of Jewish identity.

When my husband, Mayer, was three-years-old, a well-meaning relative, concerned that Mayer's Jewishly observant parents were "denying him Santa Claus" took him to see the department store's Santa and sit on his knee. When Santa asked Mayer what he wanted for Christmas, he confidently replied, "We don't have Christmas at my house—I'm an American!". He knew he was *something* that didn't celebrate Christmas!

Even my attempts to make issues of identity clear to my own children are often muddied by ignorant or insensitive outsiders. When my daughter Leora was three, Santa Claus came unannounced (to parents) to the day care center she attended. When it was her turn to sit on Santa's knee, the alert teacher, knowing that Leora was Jewish (it had been only several days before that Leora and I had presented Chanukah to her class) told Santa, who quickly altered his standard question and asked Leora, "What would you like Santa to bring you for Chanukah?" I was left with the difficult task of explaining to my daughter that no, Santa wasn't coming, Jews didn't celebrate Christmas, Santa wasn't for Chanukah, and, probably worst of all, she wasn't getting a Barbie doll.

But in spite of this confusing mix of identities, or perhaps because of it, the necessity and value of integrating multiple identities makes sense to me. As a hyphenated citizen ("Jewish-American") I have become accustomed to holding numerous, sometimes contradictory-looking or feeling labels or identities and somehow meshing these into an integrated, coherent self. The theory that all people hold multiple identities and see the world differently through their various lenses, the idea that "truth" or "reality" is socially constructed, often through struggle—all these components of a critical theory of education flow easily from my life experience.

The concept that the personal is political also emerged from my Jewish background. My Torah study taught me that everyday acts are infused with meaning and purpose. Learning the laws of kashruth and the Sabbath meant that yes, you are supposed to think about what you believe and who you are **all the time**. With every morsel of food you put in your mouth, you are supposed to think, "What is this?" "Is this something I eat?" "What will be the consequences of this action?" When you speak, you are supposed to think about the principle of lashon ha rah (hurtful speech) and to think about the repercussions of spreading gossip or untruths. There are Jewish laws for how to harvest your field, how to treat widows and orphans, how to support people in life and in death. There was never any shortage of prescriptions for "right behavior."

And so, the imperative that one's personal behavior should somehow link up with one's broader politics always made perfect sense to me. I readily accept the notion that all acts have meaning and that to imbue every behavior with purpose and thoughtfulness is to elevate that behavior to a higher plane.

It is not surprising, then, that my professional and personal/political goals are closely interwoven. I am active in peace politics. I teach about conflict resolution. I have participated in many gay/lesbian/bisexual support activities. I write about teaching children about differences. I march against militarism and war. I give workshops on "Teaching Children to Take a Stand." I sing in the Syracuse Community Choir, an inclusive group that sings songs of peace, justice and social concern. I lead singing at workshops I do, arguing strongly that everyone needs a voice. Our house is the gathering place for a wide assortment of people of all ages, sizes, sexual preferences, and abilities/disabilities; I research and write about building communities of acceptance and caring. The ways in which my life flows—professional/political/personal/social—all part of the same river has always been deeply satisfying to me. The opportunity to integrate all aspects of my life, to not have a "professional" stance different than my "personal" politics makes me feel whole.

Imagine, then, my surprise, hurt, and disappointment to be told during my tenure review at one institution, that "Mara's personal and professional agendas are too closely linked." "Wow," I felt like saying, after the sting was gone, "thank you for noticing the close alignment! This is something I have been working all my life to achieve!" Truly I have felt myself blessed to have a career that provides opportunities to integrate so closely what I believe and what I do. I don't have to do a job all day and then go engage in radical, political activism in my "spare time." Academia affords me the opportunity to teach about my principles, to act on my beliefs, and to expose many learners to different perspectives, books, experiences and opportunities relative to my agenda of social justice.

Do I read the critique of the commingling of my "agendas" as anti-Semitism? As antiwoman? As simply antipassion? It is hard to make a definitive judgment. The only thing clear to me is that one is expected by some in academia to separate, somehow, different aspects of one's life in the name of "professionalism," and that to be passionate and vocal, prominently radical or intentionally visible is often not valued. One should be an "enthusiastic teacher" but not a "flaming ideologue"; one may have strongly held beliefs, but should not be an advocate; it is appropriate to share one's visions, but one should not "indoctrinate." Clearly, not everyone shares my values about academia as a setting in which one can and should integrate all the pieces of life.

In addition to the general suppression of passion, there are also "taboo" topics within academia. At a recent curriculum conference, I organized a session entitled "Safety and Risk-Taking in Higher Education."[6] I asked participants to break the silence and talk about what it is they don't tell their students, don't share with their colleagues, or don't put in their syllabi. The session was emotional, challenging, and healing. Speaking the unspeakable, colleagues talked about issues of sexuality, religion, personal backgrounds and their own radical political agendas as topics they often don't share. Fear of reproach, of censure, of looking stupid, and of backlash or punishment kept many people silent, kept them from being fully present—as themselves—in their teaching and their work.

At this point in my life, as I reclaim more and more aspects of Jewish ritual practice, I have found that in many of the academic circles in which I travel, religion is a taboo topic. (I am sure this would be different in religiously-affiliated universities in which one is "supposed" to be religious.) In my institution, issues of sexual preference are much more likely to be discussed than of religious preference. People are more willing to tell you that they watch X-rated videos than that they pray. It is difficult to get colleagues to admit to religious practice or beliefs, and there is a way in which being religious is seen, somehow, as anti-intellectual, or primitive. Confessing that you are religious is a bit akin to acknowledging intellectual weakness and backwardness, like admitting you're superstitious or engage in weird rituals. Concerns about the separation of church and state, confusion about the differences between teaching about religion and forcing religious practice, and a general shyness about personally held beliefs about religion, God, and spirituality stand in the way of this particular integration for many people.

How do I deal with this taboo? I struggle against this convention by telling everyone that I am Jewish, by weaving my Jewishness into the work that I do. I give frequent keynotes on the topic of creating caring, nurturing communities in schools. And, as part of that presentation, I always tell the story of the Nazi march on Auburn (as a story about the dangers of exclusive thinking and the importance of teaching children inclusive stances towards difference) and I also claim myself as a Jew. I tell audiences that people have often said to me, "You know Mara, I never think of you as Jewish," and discuss with them the ways in which that is off-base and offensive. I explore with them what it means to tell me that; isn't it like saying, "You know, all the negative, stereotypical feelings I have about your group—well, I'll suspend them in your case"? And I tell them, "I am Jewish. Think of me as Jewish."

Two years ago, I was asked to give the Commencement Address at Nazareth College and was awarded an Honorary Doctorate. Invited by a Catholic college to give their commencement address, I focused my speech on *Tikkun Olam* (repair of the world) and spoke directly about the ways in which my Jewish background made that kind of active advocacy on behalf of the oppressed and disenfranchised critical. I have spent the last several weeks preparing my haftorah to read in synagogue, and I have taken it to work and chanted it for several colleagues and friends there, breaking the boundaries, challenging assumptions about who I am and how I am defined.

Sharing these things about myself is easier in some settings than in others. Speaking to a group of Jewish educators in Australia, it is easy for me to share the ways in which my Judaism is linked to my beliefs about inclusion and diversity. But when I speak to educators in Utah or Montana, knowing that I am the first or only Jew they have ever met, knowing that I am not surrounded by others who necessarily share a commitment to my safety and acceptance as a Jew, it is harder. I share my Jewishness both as an act important to me and as one important to my audience. And, not surprisingly, almost every time I speak (including my talk at Nazareth) a Jew approaches me and says, "You know, no speaker has ever said they were Jewish before, even when they were." So I continue to weave my Jewishness into my educational work, recognizing the feelings of terror when they arise (and they usually do) as evidence of the continuing need to speak this particular truth.

Inclusion/Building Safety

Like many Jews growing up in the 1950's and 1960's, my childhood was lived in the shadow of the Holocaust. There was little said about the Holocaust in my own house, but like a thick smog that hangs in the air, there were always the pervasive messages: Jews are not safe anywhere, Jews are in danger, if you look closely enough, most non-Jews are anti-Semitic, and, perhaps most damaging, don't ever get too complacent or let your guard down. Stories of Anne Frank filled my childhood; a little girl, like you, brown hair and eyes like you, just a little older than you, was killed by the Nazi's. Why? Because she was Jewish—like you.

Stories of the ways in which Jews have been excluded over time (from schools, neighborhoods, clubs), singled out for oppression because of their religious practices, appearance, thinking or beliefs were everywhere. Stories of relatives who couldn't get jobs because their last name was "Ginsberg," of my parents' exclusion from various clubs and organizations—these were some of the childhood stories I grew up with.

Issues of confronting exclusion and a lack of safety became critical issues for me. And, perhaps inevitably, as a reaction to my own history, creating safe, inclusive communities for all children, regardless of race, religion, disability, and family background has become my paramount concern.

I spend much of my time preparing teachers to work in inclusive, heterogeneous classrooms, learning teaching strategies that will enable them to meet the needs of a wide range of students without recourse to segregation and exclusion.[7] I adamantly defend the right of all children to be part of the typical learning community, making it incumbent on teachers and schools to change in order to meet the needs of children, rather than demanding that children reach some ideal standard of perfection or performance in order to earn their right to be included.

Although there are many other inclusion advocates, all of whom probably share some aspects of biography with me, there are occasional times and ways in which my work seems particularly linked to my Jewish roots and understandings.

In the summer of 1995, I had the opportunity to work with the Jewish day school teachers of Melbourne and Sydney, Australia, on issues of inclusion of children with disabilities. A large proportion of Jewish children attends Jewish schools in Australia, yet there has been little support for including Jewish children with disabilities in those schools. I was invited to work with teachers, principals, and parents in those cities to determine the kinds of curricular, pedagogical, and structural changes that would be necessary to fully include all Jewish children seeking a day school education within those settings.

At a meeting in Sydney with the heads of the Jewish community, principals of the involved Jewish schools and other *machers*, I was able to speak in ways that I could not have spoken if I were not Jewish. First, I was able to say, explicitly, that as Jews, we should know about exclusion and the dangers of exclusion and we should be painfully aware of the dangers of defining standards of perfection for inclusion that leave some people out. I was also able to talk about the principle of *Tikkun Olam* and the ways in which including all children is part of both my personal vision of a healed world and a model for students of communities of support and caring. I was able to make these connections because I was Jewish, because I had a shared history (if only through extension) with those with whom I spoke, and because I was able to make references to shared precepts and texts.

But, perhaps more significantly, I was able to make powerful statements about the ways in which the community should move, to chide the leaders for complacency and inaction, and to implore them to a more active stance because I could do so without being perceived as "anti-Semitic" or as a critical outsider. I was a critical insider, a role that stood me in good stead to leverage for change and action.

I think that, as a Jew, I understand the dangers of exclusion at a deep, gut level. To be excluded from school is to be cut off from one's community. And that kind of isolation is dangerous to all. It is within schools that we learn who counts and who doesn't, who constitutes a "classmate" and who can be considered "surplus population," to be ignored, derided or excluded from childhood friendship and community. But I see beyond the pain and damage to the excluded person to the risks to the whole community. Pastor Martin Niemoller's famous quotation from the Holocaust:

In Germany, they first came for the Communists, and I didn't speak up because I wasn't a Communist. Then they came for the Jews, and I didn't speak up because I wasn't a Jew. Then they came for the trade unionists, and I didn't speak up because I wasn't a trade unionist. Then they came for the Catholics, and I didn't speak up because I was a Protestant. Then they came for me—and by that time, no one was left to speak up . . . speaks of the need for solidarity and standing together, but it also speaks to the ways in which we must learn to become allies for one another and to the truth that none of us can feel or be safe when any member of our community is excluded.

In debates on the subject of inclusion, I have been identified as an "inclusion zealot" and as someone not willing to debate the rightness/wrongness of inclusion.[8] I am willing to discuss how we can include children thoughtfully and well, how we must support their teachers and their schools in developing inclusive programs and the kinds of curricular and pedagogical approaches that facilitate the inclusion process. But, like those who opposed slavery, I will not debate children's rights to be part of their classroom community.

Courage/Making a Difference

I was exposed consistently, as a child, to the idea that one person could make a difference, that courage was needed to fight against the evils of society, and that I came from a whole tradition of people who had been fighters—for social justice, against anti-Semitism and racism, for women's rights, and so on. And much of my work as an educator has focused on a process of *en-couragement*, that is, giving people the courage to make a difference. I have developed curricula related to teaching children to "take a stand" and have taught courses directly focusing on empowerment and social change.

I have attempted to make a difference in many ways. I have organized pro-choice marches, workshops on homophobia, inclusion, and antiracism. I have picketed at air bases, organized conferences on social justice teaching, and written about issues of oppression and prejudice. I have not, for the most part, concentrated on "Jewish" issues, but neither have I excluded them from my purview. I have chosen to describe here three specific attempts to make a difference relative to anti-Semitism and the lessons I learned from these attempts. I focus here on my attempts to take on anti-Semitism because I have found that taking a stand in this arena has been the most challenging and the most emotionally loaded. I think that examining my experiences in this area can reveal some of the reasons that many Jews who have been in the forefront of other liberation struggles have often found it difficult to either take that stand as Jews or to take stands about Jewish issues. These are lessons relative to social change in general and to Jewish oppression in particular. By examining where I have had a voice, I further understand my own power and my own silencing.

Holocaust Conference

When I was on the faculty at the University of North Dakota, a major donation was announced. Ralph Englestad, a UND alumnus, and then the proprietor of a gambling house in Las Vegas, Nevada, gave five million dollars to the University. Overjoyed, the University announced that they would rename the hockey stadium after Englestad. Shortly after the announcement of this donation, it came to light (in *The New York Times*) that Ralph Englestad had one of the world's largest collections of Hitler memorabilia, held birthday parties for Hitler, printed bumper stickers that said, "Hitler Was Right" and had T-shirts printed, in the tradition of rock tours, listing all the cities that Hitler had destroyed and the number of people killed in each location.

When this was announced, there was little outrage. In fact, there was little reaction of any kind. I, of course, was shocked and offended, but there was little public outcry. Some of the students were interviewed and said, "It's fifty years ago—what's the big deal?" After several conversations with the University president about what might constitute an appropriate response to this (seeming) dilemma, a "fact-finding" mission was sent to Las Vegas. Although I had suggested that someone Jewish, someone disabled, and someone gay/lesbian be sent as members of the delegation (these being people who had suffered in the Holocaust), this didn't happen. When the delegation returned, I approached one of them, a Christian faculty member in the Law School, and told him of my desire to talk to the President once again and ask that the University commit to an educational response of some kind, even if they didn't give back the money.

My Christian ally and I approached the President, who was very responsive. After considerable discussion and negotiation, it was decided that a one-year conference entitled "Human Rights and Wrongs" would be held. The first part was called "Lessons from the Holocaust" and the second part was devoted to other groups who had experienced oppression and genocide and their struggles (Native American issues, South Africa, etc.). As keynote speakers, Helen Altschuler, a survivor of Auschwitz, and Alfons Heck, a former member of the Hitler Nazi Youth party came to speak. Alternating stories, they described their lives—in 1933, 1935, 1937—with Helen detailing her family's exile, incarceration, and murder, and Heck describing his indoctrination to hatred and violence as one of the chosen youth, destined for leadership and greatness.[9] The presentation was powerful; the audience was huge and sat mesmerized for over two hours.

In addition to this activity, I also organized workshops and a film series on the Holocaust for the School of Education and participated in various panels and presentations. It was an exhilarating time and a frightening time as well. There was resistance from the secular community who thought this topic was too upsetting and dramatic (as well as too historical) but I learned the most from the resistance of the Jewish community. Although some members of the community were supportive of the project, others were worried and fearful. Some of the longtime Jewish residents of the community were prominent in the business community and had always felt like they "fit in" and belonged. Raising these issues now felt unsafe and risky to them. They worried that Jews would be targeted for discrimination, harassment, and acts of violence as a result of the attention given to the Holocaust.

Other than the piece of hate mail described in the opening paragraph of this chapter, I heard of no other incidents related to the conference, but I learned a great deal about the latent, deep fear that even these well-assimilated, long-term resident Jews felt. One Jewish man, whose family had lived in the community for several generations, confessed that he always keeps a bag packed, just in case he has to leave with his family in a hurry. So much for safety! I was stunned and chastened that even mature, established, financially successful, prominent Jews could still carry around that level of fear and distrust. The University kept the money and renamed the stadium after the donor, a fact which continued to cause me pain everytime I walked by the building.

Anti-Semitism in Higher Education

In 1992, following several conversations with Jewish colleagues who were concerned about anti-Semitism in their institutions, I organized a session at the American Educational Research Association. Although several of us had shared private stories over coffee and dinner, going public was tremendously frightening. We worried about how a session like this would be received. The session was called "You and Your Kind: Facing Anti- Semitism in Higher Education" and in the proposal for that session, I described some of the dilemma:

> The session begins from a base of stories: stories are seen here as both autobiographical reflection and a rich source of critical pedagogy, a way of sharing personal experience and of opening up such experience for public examination, analysis and critique. But which stories? How do we decide which stories we tell and to whom? Are there differences between the stories we tell our colleagues and those we tell our students? Between those we share with colleagues at other institutions but never to those in the next office? Embedded in these questions are issues directly related to anti-Semitism and internalized oppression: Why are these stories so difficult to tell? What are the implications of sharing them in a public form?
>
> In some ways, the same codes which maintain certain information as "Family secrets" also keep certain information within institutions. One of the barriers to breaking the silence about institutionalized anti-Semitism relates to the belief that "these things don't happen anymore." The belief that institutions of higher education are somehow above or removed from something as base as anti-Semitism makes such stories difficult to tell.
>
> Another impediment to sharing these stories is that, as academics, we have generally found it easier to talk about someone else's pain than our own. Some of us have become champions of other oppressed groups, but have found it far more difficult to talk about ourselves. The veneer of academic scholarship enables many of us to keep personal and professional issues separate. On those occasions when those boundaries are crossed, accusations of unprofessionalism and (often) anti-feminist attacks have made speaking out problematic and difficult. How can we speak out without being seen as whiny or self-serving? How do we ground our remarks in a way that enables them to have broader meaning and impact? How do we move beyond personal stories to more global understanding, analysis and action?[10]

This session was a first for AERA, and there was a large turn-out. Nearly one-hundred people came and listened while four Jewish faculty and two non-Jewish allies talked about critical incidents related to anti-Semitism from within their own institutions and served as "respondent/interpreters" to each other's stories.

The discussion was lively and passionate. After the panel members had dialogued, there was active and eager participation by audience members, many of whom wanted to share their own stories of pain and oppression in their own institutions. Several audience members spoke to the fact that the session had opened up a previously-unexplored, hidden area of their lives as academics. But the session also raised far more questions than it answered. Audience members did not agree on definitions of anti-Semitism and how it should or could be discriminated from "insensitivity." Some audience members were concerned about "crying wolf" about anti-Semitism at the risk of losing allies when they were really necessary. Other issues were raised as well: black/Jewish relations on campus and the need to form coalitions; the problems of faculty members with multiple identifies: lesbian and gay Jews, black Jews, Jewish women, etc.; concerns about Israel and the ways in which discussions of Israeli governmental policy provoked accusations of anti-Semitism; and concerns about who speaks for Jews on university faculties and how those voices are constructed.

Based on the success of this first session, and buoyed by the tremendous enthusiasm from the audience, many of them asking for follow-up, next steps, the formation of a Special Interest Group, etc., I organized a second session the next year. Entitled "Anti-Semitism in Higher Education: Educational Policy, Curriculum Theory and Coalition Building,"[11] the session was designed to go beyond the previous year's session and address directly issues of pedagogy, policy and action. The session was to be organized as multiple roundtables, enabling lots of conversations to go on simultaneously since our previous experience alerted us to the many people who had tales to tell.

What happened at this second session was startling and illuminative of the very situation that had made the group fearful to tell their stories in the first place. This follow-up session was scheduled at an early morning time, and thus we began with about twenty people in attendance. We arranged the chairs in a circle and had people go around and introduce themselves. Over half of the participants had been at the previous year's session and wanted to continue the discussion. A few others had heard about the first session and now wanted to join the dialogue. Also present was the husband of a former colleague of mine from North Dakota. His introduction was a hesitant, "I just want to see what's happening here."

The panel[12] began by telling brief stories and outlining the proposed format for the session. Before we could continue, the faculty member from North Dakota interrupted. "I just want everyone here to know that the stories Mara told last year about North Dakota were all lies. Those things never happened. She never found a note in her office. She made it up." We were stunned and wondered about how to go on. The panel members looked at one another, trembling. Other audience members were confused and didn't know what to say. There was silence. The panel attempted to continue, but we were interrupted again by accusations and verbal assault. I wasn't sure whether I should dignify his comments with a response, felt obliged to respond, and yet was conscious that this was a professional meeting and not a conversation in the hall. The rules of discourse were unclear. Emotions made thinking and responding difficult. The disrupter shouted that he had lived in North Dakota as a Jew for many years and none of those things had ever happened to him. If anything like that happened to me, it was because I brought it on myself. You could live as a Jew fine in North Dakota as long as you handled yourself correctly, and on and on.

Our worst nightmare was happening. One of the panelists, Geoff Tabakin, had begun the session with a discussion of the phenomenon of "jamais vu"—things which you have seen a million times which now feel scary and unfamiliar. Geoff now invoked this image for the session attendees; we have all been at AERA sessions before, we know how it's done. Suddenly we are in strangely unfamiliar and frightening terrain. The session became the enactment of voice and silence that we had agonized about. Was it safe to tell our stories? How would people respond? Why was a Jew responding with such anger and vehemence to tales of anti-Semitism? How could we, in the face of such passion and hurt, continue to talk analytically about issues so close to the bone?

The session ended roughly. The disrupter stayed to buttonhole participants and tell them, individually, that it had all been lies. Geoff, Mimi Orner and I escaped back to our hotel room where we sat and shook, cried and talked for hours, trying to figure out what had happened and what it meant about our organization, our session, our personal safety, and our identities as Jews in academia.

That experience taught me several things: First, that our terror of speaking up as Jews is not simply historical, but has, unfortunately, contemporary manifestations. We are not simply imagining the sanctions and reproach we might experience from breaking the silence. Second, and perhaps more distressing, other Jews collude with this silencing; many Jews have internalized the oppressive imperative to "suffer silently" and to avoid calling attention to our problems.

My most recent experience related to interrupting Jewish oppression held similar lessons for me. For approximately the last twelve years, I have attended a Curriculum Conference that is typically held in October. When I noticed when the Jewish holidays occurred for 1997, I became concerned about the timing of the conference. At the 1996 conference, I raised the issue with the organizers, asking when the 1997 conference was scheduled and expressing my concern that both Rosh Hashanah and Yom Kippur occurred on October weekends the coming year.

After some initial confusion and lack of information, it turned out that the 1997 conference had indeed been scheduled on Yom Kippur. I expressed deep concern and made clear my commitment to changing the dates. I went from that conversation to a session on Jewish Voices in Curriculum, which explored the ways in which Jews have been prominent in curriculum theorizing. At the end of that session, I raised the issue of the forthcoming schedule conflict in the context of the session. I stated that there were many prominent Jews active in the curriculum field, but the question was whether they presented themselves as "voices" or as "Jewish voices." I commented that I had been a vocal presence at these meetings for years, but now wondered, in the face of the disregard for the Jewish holidays, whether I had been present "as a Jew." I encouraged all the session participants (only a few were Jewish) to come to the general meeting that evening when the issue would be discussed, and added, parenthetically, that I sincerely hoped that this wouldn't be constructed as a "Jewish" issue. One Jewish colleague then responded, "I don't expect non-Jews to take this on as their issue."

Considerable behind-the-scenes discussions went on throughout the day with other Jews, allies, and leaders of the organization. At the meeting that evening, several of us who were very concerned waited with bated breath for the issues to be raised. At first, the topic was avoided; the next year's meeting dates and place were announced with no comments as to the possible conflict. Finally, several of us spoke strongly about the dilemma facing the organization. I stated that I didn't think discussions of "anti-Semitism" were useful at this point, although we might want to unpack later how such a situation occurred, why people didn't reflexively check the calendar when scheduling a September/October meeting. One non-Jewish ally raised the issue of the Christian hegemony of the calendar and the ways in which we don't notice others' oppressions. But the discussion was made complex by divergent messages from the Jews in the organization, including one who announced publicly that while he wouldn't come, he didn't see the scheduling as a problem. Another Jewish member was furious that the issue had been raised at all and, privately, verbally assaulted one of the Jews who expressed concern. The lines seem to have been drawn not only between Jews and non-Jews but between Jews as well.

After considerable discussion and some lobbying, the meeting date and location were changed so that they no longer conflicted with the Jewish holidays. The conference leaders were relieved that a solution was reached and there was a generalized reconciliation among those who had been concerned. I subsequently e-mailed the dates of the Jewish holidays through the year 2002 to the leaders of the organization.

I do not interpret this series of events as being about "anti-Semitism"; I do not for a moment believe that the conference planners deliberately chose a Jewish holiday for the conference date, nor that they were insensitive to the painful dilemma which arose. Rather the experience taught me about the difficulties of raising issues of Jewish oppression within academic, liberal, professional circles. Several people speculated about whose conflicts would likely be seen as an imperative for change, whose conflicts simply lamented. Others said, "Holidays don't matter to me. I wouldn't care if they scheduled it on Christmas," knowing full well, of course, that this would never happen. There were strong feelings all around.

My deepest lesson, sadly, was about internalized Jewish oppression; the "Don't make a fuss, you'll make the issues worse, it's not such a big deal" manifestation of silencing. The Jew who publicly announced that it didn't matter told me later, privately, that he doesn't expect non-Jews to be sensitive to his holidays or concerns. With these kinds of low expectations and the very real fears of censure and disapprobation (there were negative rumblings about having to change the date), it is not surprising that oppression of this kind continues. I kept asking myself: "Have I not been Jewish enough in this organization? What stands in the way of our speaking up as Jews and also for Jews?"

Conclusion: Doing My Work as a Jew

This last experience has brought me full circle. Must we always name ourselves as Jews in what we do? What happens when we do our work for social justice in the world and don't do it explicitly as Jews? Does that make our purview wider? Does it help us to form allies by avoiding the appearance of self-interest or chauvinism? Or, at some level, when we neglect to speak for ourselves, do we not only do ourselves a disservice but also make it more difficult for others to raise their own issues? Rabbi Hillel's famous words seem applicable here: "If I am not for myself, who will be for me? If I am only for myself, what am I? And if not now, when?" But I don't think the expression means only if I am not my own advocate, then no one else will be my advocate, but also "If I am not for myself, how will others be for themselves and how will we together seek common ground?" Perhaps standing up for ourselves both provides a good model and helps others to be similarly explicit and assertive.

When I look at how my own work has changed in the last ten years, it is clear to me that I have put myself "out there" as a Jew much more in what I write, present, and teach. I believe that speaking my truth as a Jew enables others to speak theirs. My silence does not build safety for others, rather it colludes with the oppressiveness of silencing in general. If all oppressions are linked, then working to eliminate any particular "ism" must be seen as connected to all others. The truest measure of any reform or justice imperative should be its effects on all marginalized and oppressed people. If there is not congruity, positive run-off, or reciprocity, then perhaps there is an error in design or implementation. I do not wish to relapse into the recursive refrain of my childhood, "But is it good for the Jews?" but neither will I conscientiously avoid that question in the name of multiculturalism, pluralism, or a distorted sense of political correctness.

Rereading what I have written feels frighteningly self-serving and rekindles my earlier fears about writing this chapter. Have I constructed myself as a person who does good things because she is Jewish? Am I saying, directly or subtly, that non-Jews don't or can't do the same work? Am I implying, even, that I do this work somehow differently than non-Jews who do similar work? And, of course, the major fear: Will I somehow be fueling anti-Semitism by what I write? Will non-Jews read this chapter as an insult or an assault on the work that they do? Will anti-Semites find in my work enough self-doubt and self-reflection to fuel their notion that Jews act out of places of great distress and are somehow irrational, less than fully professional, or too personally invested in what they do? Will other Jews find me "too out there" in ways that make them feel unsafe or which make them want to disassociate themselves from me—"Mara doesn't speak for all Jews."

I do not claim to speak for other Jews, in the sense that I believe my feelings or experiences to be universal or even Jewishly universal. I do know that my work feels different to me, more grounded, when I do it from a position of honest disclosure and am fully present within the work that I do. I want to battle against, "She was really _____ for a Jew" not by hiding who I am but by being explicitly Jewish in what I do. I will continue to work for social justice and to speak the truth about oppression and injustice. And I will do that work *as a Jew*, neither limiting my attention to anti-Semitism nor neglecting that perspective in the broader work.

I have come to believe that understanding the nature of my own oppression can help me to be more empathic and insightful about other struggles. My understanding of the nature of allies—those who stand with us and for us in our struggles—has been greatly enhanced by witnessing the behavior of those who have been my allies. My friend Beth promised me that if the police arrested my daughter, Dalia, at the anti-Nazi march, she would not let her be taken alone to jail; that is the kind of ally behavior that I now set as a standard for my own. Where will I put my body, my resources, my time, my energy when others are oppressed or in danger? Working actively against anti-Semitism helps me to work more effectively against other oppressions. To put anti-Semitism last, for fear of retribution, is to buy into the very oppression that I wish to resist. Victims don't make great freedom fighters.

Although I continue to broaden and deepen my connections with a wide range of people in the world, both Jews and non-Jews, I recognize and honor my "outsider" status and what it has taught me to notice. I hope never to become so assimilated or comfortable that I forget the pain of marginalization and the terror of the foreigner. The book of Exodus reminds us that "we were strangers in a strange land"; remembering that pain is critical to my continuing identification with others who find themselves on the outside, to my unrelenting commitment to dismantle walls and build bridges. And so I tell my friends and acquaintances, "Think of me as many things—woman, mother, peace activist, writer, educator, singer, freedom fighter—but always think of me as a Jew."

Notes

1. Mimi Orner, "Surplus Visibility and Jewish Identity: The Case of the Jewish Mafia," paper presented in a session entitled "You and Your Kind: Facing Anti-Semitism in Higher Education" at the meeting of the American Educational Research Association, San Francisco, California, April, 1992.

2. Daphne Patai, "Minority Status and the Stigma of 'Surplus Visibility', *The Chronicle of Higher Education*, October 30, 1991.

3. Geoffrey Tabakin, "Jokes," a paper presented in a session entitled "You and Your Kind: Facing Anti-Semitism in Higher Education" at the meeting of the American Educational Research Association, San Francisco, California, April, 1992.

4. See Mara Sapon-Shevin, "Celebrating Diversity, Creating Community: Curriculum that honors and builds on difference" in *Inclusion: A Guide for Educators*, eds. Susan and William Stainback (Baltimore: Brookes Publishing Co., 1996); Mara Sapon-Shevin, "Full Inclusion as Disclosing Tablet: Revealing the flaws in our general education system," *Theory into Practice* 35(1) (1996).

5. See Mara Sapon-Shevin, *Playing Favorites: Gifted Education and the Disruption of Community* (Albany: SUNY Press, 1994); Mara Sapon- Shevin, "Gifted Education and the Protection of Privilege: Breaking the Silence, Opening the Discourse" in *Beyond Silenced Voices: Class, Race, and Gender in United States Schools*, eds. Lois Weiss and Michelle Fine (Albany: SUNY Press, 1993) 25–44; Mara Sapon-Shevin, "Giftedness as a Social Construct," *Teachers College Record* 89(1)(Fall, 1987): 39–53.

6. A session presented at the Journal of Curriculum Theorizing Conference, Monteagle, TN, October, 1996.

7. See Mara Sapon-Shevin, "Including All Students and Their Gifts within Regular Classrooms," in *Controversial Issues Confronting Special Education*, eds. William and Susan Stainback (New York: Allyn and Bacon, in press); Mara Sapon-Shevin, "Building a Safe Community for Learning" in *To Become a Teacher: Making a Difference in Children's Lives*, ed. William Ayers, (NY: Teachers College Record, 1995): 99–112.

8. See "Can Inclusion Work? An Interview with Jim Kauffman and Mara Sapon-Shevin," *Educational Leadership* 52(4) (December/January, 1994–95): 7–11.

9. Alfons Heck, *The Burden of Hitler's Legacy* (Frederick, CO: Renaissance House Publishers, 1988).

10. From the session proposal submitted to AERA Participants included: William Ayers, Beth Blue Swadener, Mimi Orner, Goeffrey Tabakin, Wendy Saul and Mara Sapon-Shevin.

11. 1993 AERA session, Atlanta, GA, April, 1993

12. Mimi Orner, Geoffrey Tabakin and Mara Sapon-Shevin

Chapter 11

Election, Ambivalence, and the Pedagogy of Jewish Particularity

Roger I. Simon

> He has two antagonists; the first pushes him from behind, from his origin. The second blocks his road ahead. He struggles with both. Actually the first supports him in his struggle with the second, for the first wants to push him forward; and the same way the second supports him in his struggle with the first; for the second of course forces him back. But it is only theoretically so. For it is not only the two protagonists who are there, but he himself as well, and who really knows his intentions? However that may be, he has a dream that sometime in an unguarded moment . . . he will spring out of the fighting line and be promoted, on account of his experience of such warfare, as judge over his struggling antagonists.—Franz Kafka, *The Great Wall of China: Stories and Reflections*

If I were forced to order the fragments of my life into a narrative, it would be one of perpetual departures and beginnings. Too easily, I slip into an identification with those generations of Western Jews whose melancholic lives are depicted as a series of leave-takings and redemptive projects that set one in a perpetual state of dissatisfaction with one's place, with one's time—always being somewhat out-of-place, out-of-time. Twentieth-century creatures refracted through the contradictory discourses of modernism, they (I?) seem suspended in the empty space between a tradition left or denied and a mode of life that made settlement a false hope by narrowing the possible forms of intellectual and social propriety.

But this would be misleading, the narrative far too simple. No departure is ever complete, no beginning ever simply new. Memory is too demanding for that. So you must understand, I travel with an ancient book. If you open its pages your first impression will undoubtedly be that it is blank, but you will be mistaken. Its pages beckon the "waiting to be written" over the traces of what has been written. Each page is in fact, what Freud referred to as a "mystic writing-pad," similar to the treasured palimpsests of my childhood. Old enough to remember the red wooden stylus and the dark soft pregnable substance covered with thick (was it?) cellophane, I discovered here that all writing must remain haunted by the traces of writing past. If you looked hard enough, you could make out the impregnation of previous texts in between the letters of the new one. On the surface of a palimpsest all writing is new/old.

My book is a "book of wandering," traced through with the writing of multiple traditions; some Jewish, some not. This multiplicity has created the "material-discursive meeting ground"[1] which has shaped [and limited] my "knowledge production." As I write and erase/trace, my book thickens, Jewish/not Jewish at the same time. Theological, historical, literary, and social traces mix and settle/unsettle what I have to say and how I say it. My teaching and publications increasingly marked by this thickening, it becomes harder to pin down these performative modes of public participation. They become ambivalent and contradictory, perhaps in the process embodying a degree of typicality for North American Jewish academics moving toward postmodern modes of public Jewish identification.

There is very predictable biographical ground for this undecidable reality of assimilated/unassimilated Jew. My early Jewish education consisted of family ritual gatherings (holidays but not Shabbat) and the rite of attending three-day a week afternoon Hebrew school. Alternately compelling and boring, this education provided a childish Judaism unable and unwilling to help me address inevitable questions of a young Jew being drawn into America's suburban vision of modernity. These questions are aptly summed up in Danny Siegel's paradigmatic poetics: "If it's so wrong to play the pinball machines on Rosh HaShana a dozen counts of Jewish Law broken, at least—why did God let me win so many free games?" But not all was lost. The emotional resonance of this early education provided, if not a substantive framework of return, then at least the pull of collective affiliation, an affective force that has always been one moment of the now obviously unresolved dialectics of modernity. Wanting more, but refusing to displace "secular" commitments, my Jewish learning has become a patchwork of texts, parables, communal experiences, and sayings substantial enough to produce a realistic fear that (to reverse Benjamin) every second of time is a strait gate through which wisdom may enter and turn into cliché.

But there are further autobiographical gestures to make. The confusion produced by the too obvious limits on my social acceptance by gentile high school friends. The visceral demands of a dual national allegiance that posed questions that seemed unanswerable. The communal pride over Jewish support for the civil rights struggle of Black Americans expressed by those too ready to speak of their domestic laborers as "girls" and *schvartzers*. The recitation of the American mantra "liberty and justice for all" while wondering *Es iz gut far yidn*? I could go on but the story seems familiar, no?

As the history of many North American Jews of my post-Second World War generation will attest, such contradictions have produced rather indeterminate effects. At times they have led to the collapse of ambiguity through a assimilatory embrace or its opposite, a cultural/theological *chuvah*. Other times these contradictions seem implicated in the wildly vacillating commitments of adulthood. But most importantly, something new seems afoot; the reflexive recognition and embrace of ambivalence that, instead of being understood as confusion, is turning out to be the grounds for new diasporic practices of "doing Jewish." These practices are consistent with Levinas's statement that "the very fact of questioning one's Jewish identity means it is already lost. But by the same token, it is precisely through this kind of cross-examination that one still hangs on to it."[2]

With What *Nusach* Should a Jew Sing John Lennon's Imagine?

The Jew entered the modern university at a price that only recently has been called into question. That price was the privatization of "doing Jewish" and a sub-ordination of Jewish legal and moral commitments to nation-state law, ideals and universal human rights. Despite the cover of a liberal [i.e. personal] pluralism, this was an assimilationist bargain. Bauman makes the point succinctly: "Overt uniformity is all the easier to maintain as diversity. [Particularly..as it remains unobtrusive] it is increasingly recognized as the foremost of personal virtues; a duty and a pride."[3] A generation earlier, Lionel Trilling had already recognized the truth in Bauman's statement. "For me [he said] the point of honor consists in feeling that I would not, even if I could, deny or escape being Jewish. Surely it is at once clear how minimal such a position is . . . It is perhaps the position of most American writers of Jewish birth." Intellectual work intended for a Christian framed "secular" public sphere, though fed by the traces of Jewish experience, has taken the form of Benjamin's dwarf. It must be kept out of sight for the sake of propriety and the appearance of legitimization. I keep Talmud "in the closet", one Jewish academic confessed to me, even though [perhaps he meant "because"] it is the well-spring of my interpretive creativity.

But the times are changing. There is a substantive difference between being a stranger in a well settled native world, and a stranger in a world on the move.[4] In the first instance, it is clear what must be done to be accepted. Those long established in the spaces one seeks to enter embody the preferred, most acceptable ways to inhabit the social forms of institutionalized life. The stranger's capacities are alternatively quaint and exotic or parochial and shameful, but never central to established practices.

This was, but no longer is, an accurate reflection of the North American academy; "strangerhood" does not feel like a temporary condition much less than an unbearable one. Difference is being asserted in ways that bear no guilt or shame. The evidence for this lies in the proliferation of "ethnocultural studies," the acceptance and teaching of alternative epistemologies, the increasing diasporization of North America, and the openness to intellectual resources not codified as Christian. What is centrally different, compared to thirty years ago, is that now particularity is a treasured imprint rather than a stigma of difference. This has not resolved contradictions, only made them more public. The state of being distinct has turned into the only universal mark of the human condition, the postmodern mark of universal particularity. Yet this condition poses the challenge of figuring out how it is that only through setting oneself apart can one share in and respond to the predicament of others and live in a world integrated through its diversity, little worried by difference.

My concern in this regard is how might we (Jewish academics) rethink the bargain of the Enlightenment through a new assertion of Jewish pedagogical praxis while still steeped in progressive commitments to democracy, compassion, and social justice. I am aligning myself here with Boyarin's[5] evocation of the untranslatable Yiddish *yandes*, a practice of awakening "in and to history through an active and ethical engagement in the world in conformity with one's awareness of Jewish experience." This awakening requires recognizing that ambivalence is not a transitional state and that one must face its tensions head on.

What it might mean to face such tensions is contained in the seemingly bizarre postmodern conundrum: With what *nusach* should I sing

John Lennon's *Imagine*? While the term *nusach* originally referred to a pattern of copy or repetition of a text, it has come to refer to the melody, mood, and ornament through which a particular Jewish prayer text (although not all prayer texts) is chanted or sung. A traditional *nusach* creates an appropriate "sound" for a saying of a text. There are *nusachot* for specific texts and different *nusachot* for the same text sung in the context of different times/events in the liturgical year. Thus *nusach* is sensitive to its context of utterance, rooted in recognition that the infinite saying of what is said[6] is reflexively related to the communally shared presumptions of differentiated space/time. For example, the *nusachot* for the Days of Awe are not sung five months later during *Tu b'Shevat.*

Asking for the *nusach* by which postmodern Jews might sing *Imagine* rhetorically highlights one of the most difficult tensions within the project of engaging the world in conformity with one's *contemporary* Jewish experience. Lennon's anthemic peace song is a utopian vision of a united world, a modernist *Alenu* that celebrates the erasure of difference—including Jewish difference. I would be disingenuous to deny this song and its inter-texts has been part of the moral agenda that has animated my work in education. I cannot simply disavow its relevance. Yet might it begin to sound different if given a new tune? Perhaps the appropriate *nusach* would be the one with which a person chants the blessing before the recitation of a Torah portion: *Baruch atah Adonai . . . asher bachar banu mikol ha'amin v' natan lanu et Torato* (Blessed are thou *Adonai* . . . who has chosen us from the peoples and given us the Torah]. This *nusach* deliberately rubs against the grain of *Imagine*, filling out the musical rendition of its text in a way that may make us laugh but with nervousness and apprehension. No doubt it would be most appropriately sung during *Purim.*

As with all *Purim* jokes, there is a undercurrent of extreme seriousness in this musical suggestion. Its clash of motifs illustrates the great postmodern question of how to come to terms with Jewish particularity without denying that this particularity is rooted historically and theologically in the acceptance of one's designation as *am segulah*, a nation especially treasured by God. Richard Cohen points out that central to the price paid for an entry into modernity has been the disavowal or at least extended apologetics in regard to Jewish election or chosenness.[7] In these postmodern times where particularity is not to be effaced, must we not consider anew—in a mode linked to one's public participation as an educator/scholar—if there is a post-Enlightenment way for Jews to take seriously their own election? How might we seriously live amid our plural, ambivalent histories, while attempting (in the name of compassion and justice) to overcome history?

Election and Universal Particularity

There is little dispute that the concept of "chosenness" or "election" has been central throughout the history of Jewish thought. As Levy suggests, "it was and still is one of the most perplexing and controversial of concepts while being one of the most important and decisive for Jewish life and history."[8] The traditional warrant for the claim of election, of course, is Torah text; *li segulah mikol ha'amin.* For you are a people holy to YHVH your God, (it is) you (that) YHVH your God chose for him as a treasured people from among all that are on the face of the soil (Deuteronomy 7:6).[9] Henri Atlan[10] asserts one may interpret this passage as suggesting a perfect match or harmony between Israel and its god. In this frame, the concept of the chosen people points to a mutual adaptation between a particular people—a tribe of freed slaves whose existence as a people was inaugurated by the experience of liberation—and its god, who was revealed and defined only in that experience of liberation.

This "mutual adaptation between a people and its god" had, of course, the immediate effect of differentiating that people from others, separating it through the very act that established and defined it. Clearly this differentiation and designation as an elect nation of divinely treasured people has been a source of pride, unity, comfort, and hope for Jews through the long period of exilic persecution; a form of ideological compensation for the derision and discrimination of the diaspora.[11] But election and holding fast to particularities mandated by Torah also turned Jews into outsiders and not simply through Jewish xenophobia. Throughout Europe, Christian presumptions of supersession and the demonization of the Jews who as a people rejected this supersessionist claim, solidified the Jews' status as "a people apart." Jewish particularity became the mark of an anomalous position in non-Jewish societies.

There is of course much traditional and modern commentary regarding the meaning and consequences of Jewish election. However, no matter which interpretive emphasis one wishes to argue, the particularity of the Jewish people and the multifold aspects of Jewish civilization cannot be separated from the founding discourse of election. This discourse set the historical material terms for the production of Jewish particularity. Thus no matter what version of "Jewish identity" one affirms, this identity must in some way be bound up with the historicity of Jewish election. Virtually all facets of Jewish existence (material, cultural, spiritual, political) have been marked by these dynamics of differentiation. Whether one is observant or not, all forms of Jewish affiliation are elements of a multifold cultural formation marked by the historical event-ness of election.

The question then is what (if anything) is to be made of the event and historical legacy of Jewish election in practices of Jewish identification. No doubt, many Jews understood certain cultural achievements (low illiteracy, hygienic norms, a detailed moral discourse for the conduct of one's affairs, professional achievement) as evidence of a superiority made evident by the special love of God for Israel, a love manifest in the gift of Torah and the covenant made at Sinai. This tendency to self praise based on the particularities of a people's founding mythologies and historical experiences is clearly not unique. Neither is the tendency to transmute this praise into chauvinism. Within the long history of Jewish thought there have been those who have either sought to enhance (Halevi) or moderate (Maimonides) this tendency.

Given the emphasis on individuality and equality within the modern era, it is no surprise that within liberal Jewish discourse election became an anachronism. Hence, there have been many attempts to interpret election framed within a disavowal of any form of arrogant self-definition of superiority. Exemplary in this regard were redefinitions of election as the assignment of a Jewish "vocation" [Herman Cohen] or "mission" [Mordecai Kaplan] to be fulfilled through the exemplification of the moral message of Torah. But this framing has hardly solved the central question as to whether Jewish election must always be tinged with notions of a privileged relationship implying a unique, preferential status vis-a-vis other peoples. Thus the question remains: Is chosenness absolutely opposed to the unconditional respect of otherness?[12]

Perhaps this question might be approached through a postmodern lens that gives priority to the possibility of social relations in which the alterity of others is respected and responded to. In such perspectives, election might be understood as a founding moment of particularity that, in recognizing the infinite quality of all particularity, requires a disavowal of one's privilege or superiority. This seems to be a practice of Jewish identification (not identity) that Levinas was at pains to articulate, "one that speaks to Jews, opens the space of their difference, but does not speak only to Jews because as (a practice) it can at best open the space of pure difference and not only the space of Jewish difference. It is a Judaism, then, that speaks to all humanity, that teaches humanity its humanism, the absolute transcendence that opens up between people united ethically."[13] On such terms, the disavowal of chauvinism (ethnocultural *and* Torah chauvinism) is necessary. This obligates me to a truth that admits to its limits and repudiates its tendencies to violence without lapsing into moral indifference. On these terms there can be no *noblesse oblige* proceeding from nor constituting a form of moral authority based on Jewish election. I accept the alterity of others while being ready to defend the historical reality and future of my own particularity against those who wish to turn their commitments into hegemonic missionary projects. This requires, says Zygmunt Bauman, "abandoning the tendency to suppress other identities in the name of the self-assertion of one's own, while accepting, on the contrary, that it is precisely the guarding of other identities that maintains the diversity in which one's own uniqueness can thrive."[14]

This position reworks what Michael Wyschogrod[15] calls the mystery of Israel's election, the guarantee of the intimacy of God toward all peoples. It does not imply that gentiles learn they too are children of God by accepting that God's fullest relation is with Israel. It does imply God is related to gentiles through Israel as much as God is related to Israel through gentiles. God elects and we (in our human diversity) celebrate, critique, and make anew the specificities of our election without chauvinism *or* embarrassment. This is a form of Jewish survivalism based on the historicization of the concept of election. What interests me most about this position is that it assumes the historical obligations of the consequences of chosenness, the production of distinct modes of thought and sociality, without notions of mission or superiority.

Postmodern Pedagogy of Jewish Particularity

There are specific laws, *edot* (e.g. laws pertaining to Shabbat, Deuteronomy 5:13–15), that are crucial to Jewish particularity. Following David Novak, "the *edot* . . . testify to covenantal events by symbolic reenactment. They compose that part of revelation that gives tradition its historical intention and continuity. They are most directly concerned with the election of Israel . . . [and] . . . are modes of Israel's active, responsive experience of God's elective and ongoing love for her in the covenant."[16] The importance of Novak's observation is underscored in Nehama Leibowitz's precisely tailored study of the significatory status of Shabbat laws.[17] In the context of the presentation of Rabbinic commentary on *Parshat Ki Tissa*, in regard to Exodus 31:13, she contrasts the interpretations of Saadya Gaon and Ibn Ezra. The text in question reads: "For it [my Shabbat] is a sign between me and you, throughout your generations, to know that I, YHVH, hallow you." Saadya explains that those for whom the sign is intended are the nations of the world. Ibn Ezra presents an alternative. The sign is not a demonstration to the world, but intended to implant something into the consciousness of those who observe Shabbat, that we ourselves should know and be made aware of our election. If we take the laws to "keep Shabbat" as emblematic of the founding structure of Jewish particularity, from the standpoint of the historical legacy of election, both Saadya and Ibn Ezra seem correct. Shabbat mirrors the way a community understands its intimate personal relationship between itself and God,[18] a form of living memory of election. But the anachronism of "keeping Shabbat" among and in relation to the practices of other peoples also means that this living memory is a sign to others.

Embracing the historical realities of Jewish election requires a generalized practice of living memory, an active engagement with the present within a sense of responsibility for the ways the past informs us. From within a framework that disavows privilege or superiority, what might this practice become? In what sense can it/should it be a "sign" to others? Specifically, how might one practice a pedagogy in a postmodern space where separate identities stop short of exclusivity and take on the challenge of enacting the responsibility of each to the other through the specificity of particular histories and traditions? In other words, how might one accomplish a pedagogy of Jewish particularity that would participate in a public ethical project of cohabitation? Furthermore, what would this mean for our practice in those public spaces called schools and universities?

The pedagogy of Jewish particularity is not, at root, concerned with teaching about Jews and Jewish culture. It should not be designated a form of multicultural education, a project of presenting information that informs a diverse public about Jewish history, customs and beliefs (for a discussion of this agenda see *The Narrow Bridge: Jewish Views on Multiculturalism* edited by Marla Brettschneider[19]). Education about Jews and Jewish life has an important place in North

American education, however a stress on this concern misses the quite different radical force of Jewish particularity. While certainly "aimed at the renewal of Jewish intellectual life conceived of *as* social life"[20], a pedagogy of Jewish particularity begins with the question what difference Jewish difference can make in public discussions of how a populace might relate to each other and its shared physical world. This question subsumes not only the ways in which Jewish particularity might disrupt hegemonic practices that have historically privileged a specific cultural formation, but also what "newness enters the world"[21] by inserting new texts, terminology, and concepts into conversations about the substance and terms of the relations within which lives are lived.

This is a project of finding ways of explicitly inserting aspects of Jewish particularity (concretely the details of text, custom, and belief) into public, not exclusively Jewish, discourse for the purpose of critique and social transformation. It is this project that is animating [however crudely] much of my recent writing.[22] This project, at least to my mind, is not one that should be policed through a hypostasis of Jewish identity defined by authorities who wish to exclaim this—but not that—is authentically Jewish. Far more interesting are the actual details of a teaching practice that draws upon whatever resources are at hand for someone invested in the living memories of Jewish communities. This is precisely Boyarin's evocation of *yandes*, that awakening in and to history through an active and ethical engagement in the world in conformity with one's awareness of Jewish experience. What is *not* at stake here is a "Jewish approach" to the school subjects or university disciplines, "a series of signs, attributes, contents, qualities and values distinctly marked for comparison"[23] with other approaches to an issue. What is at stake is how the explicit adhesion to the specificity of Jewish culture and sensibility can participate in a redefinition of public discussion as to how, within plural democratic communities, life might become more joyful, just and compassionate.

The short essay "Reflections of Forgetting" written by Yosef Hayim Yerushalmi as a postscript to the Schocken Books edition of his *Zakhor: Jewish History and Jewish Memory*[24] serves as a useful example of a pedagogy of Jewish particularity. At a public conference on "The Uses of Forgetting," Yerushalmi theorizes the relation between remembering and forgetting through a discussion of three brief Talmudic texts. When I first read this provocative little essay, my reaction was one of shock. Academics who have been working in Jewish studies cannot, I think, appreciate the rhetorical force of this text for a Western intellectual discourse that has for centuries systematically purged itself of explicit Jewish particularity. Yerushalmi's essay is worth studying if for no other reason, precisely as an example of how Jewish specificity may simultaneously address its own concerns without being limited to this agenda. There are indeed a growing number of "proof texts" to study in this regard, work that ranges across philosophy, literature, law, education, and cultural studies. A survey of such work is beyond my purpose here, a limited aspiration of simply calling attention to a complex, multifold project and aligning my own academic efforts with it.

Amid Ambivalence Pitfalls Abound

A pedagogy of Jewish particularity is not without its dangers. Several years ago Alan Block and I began an uncompleted conversation regarding the appropriateness of a Christian Bible group in his city calling itself *Midrash*. My first response was positive, seeing this as an example of the way the historical particularity of Jewish text interpretation through the writing of *midrashim* might inform the way others approach the practice of reading, biblical or otherwise. This, for me, was no more than recognizing what has already begun as a pedagogy of particularity [of *midrash*] in work such as Handelman[25], and Hartman and Budick[26]. My worry was limited to a concern that non-Jews might not be willing to integrate such discussion into their own considerations fearing they would be engaging in a disrespectful and problematic form of cultural appropriation. Block however had different apprehensions. He recognized the dangers of cultural appropriation that would dilute Jewish specificity. Rather than a way for "newness to enter the world," he worried that the consumptive dynamics of Western thought might produce a loss of the historical and cultural specificity of *midrashic* interpretation. His counterpoint is a good one, and requires that our conversation continue.

Block's warning is closely related to another danger that must be faced by a pedagogy of Jewish particularity. Despite its divergence from the aims of multicultural pedagogy, to the extent that the project outlined here is read as a form of multicultural education it may fall prey to the theatrical marketplace of ideas and images this approach has introduced. Multicultural education has unfortunately created a form of voyeuristic entertainment fed by a curiosity for something different, a pedagogy of consuming the other. This market promotes a "tolerance for diversity" that, rather than leading to new forms of human solidarity, promotes fragmentation and the reinforcement of tribalization.[27] Read this way, a pedagogy of Jewish particularity can only be of fading *public* interest; servicing communal separation and complicit with a facile assumption of coexistence supported by expedient forms of territorial and functional segregation. Toronto's ethnic spatialization is a model of such ethnocultural dis-aggregation. To avoid this, a pedagogy of Jewish particularity must be presented in ways that prevent its objectification as a cultural exotic, something that can only be accomplished if as a pedagogy it is understood as engaging more than Jewish memory, more than Jewish politics.

This means that a pedagogy of Jewish particularity must attempt to avoid being rendered a form of academic *shtick*. The worst of the postmodern embrace of difference has been to encourage the performance of one's ethnocultural, gender, or sexual difference as a personal/communal style or manner that inflects one's argument or presentation with interesting color. In an academy that is all too often literally a marketplace of competing courses and texts, academics must, it seems, operate as petite bourgeoisie marketing our talents and skills in ways that differentiate our production from the increasing flood of material calling for attention. Here difference simply returns as modernist individualism. Even if one claims and enacts a communal voice that frames the substance and mode of one's expression, the academic marketplace functionally individualizes one's work, renders it *shtick* that might become chic. Only when particularity becomes part of a public discourse—without dilution into triviality—is it no longer depictable and dismissible as *shtick*.

A pedagogy of Jewish particularity cannot afford to be naive about the symbolic and material economy in which it is condemned to participate. While one might do one's best to show that what is at stake in the specifics of this pedagogy are vital questions of communal life within an interconnected biosphere, the institutions we have created for this discussion often undercut its force. But these institutions exist for good reasons. We treasure and support their further epistemological transformation because they secure opportunities to express our ideas and furnish the diverse and fertile ground for the joint discovery of self and Other. A pedagogy of Jewish particularity is unavoidably denominational and public; fundamentally ambivalent, it is not easily practiced. Such is the tenor of our times. If not now, when?

Notes

1. Wendy S. Hesford *Reframing Autobiography: Critical Pedagogy and the Politics of Identity* (Minneapolis: University of Minnesota Press, in press).

2. Emmanuel Levinas "Difficult Freedom" in *The Levinas Reader* [edited by Sean Hand], (Oxford:Basil Blackwell, 1989).

3. Zygmunt *Bauman Modernity and Ambivalence* (Ithaca: Cornell University Press 1991), p. 160

4. Bauman, op. cit, p. 97.

5. Jonathan Boyarin "Yiddish Science and the Postmodern" in *Thinking in Jewish* (Chicago: University of Chicago Press 1996), p.196.

6. Emmanuel Levinas *Otherwise Than Being or Beyond Essence* (translated by Alphonso Lingis), (Boston: Kluwer Academic Publishers 1991).

7. Richard Cohen *Elevations: The Height of the Good in Rosenzweig and Levinas* (Chicago: University of Chicago Press 1994).

8. Ze'ev Levy "Judaism and Chosenness: On Some Controversial Aspects from Spinoza to Contemporary Jewish Thought in Daniel H. Frank (ed.) *A People Apart: Chosenness and Ritual in Jewish Philosophical Thought* (Albany: State University of New York Press 1993), p. 91.

9. The biblical translation here is by Everett Fox *The Schocken Bible: Volume I The Five Books of Moses* (New York: Schocken Books 1995).

10. Henri Atlan "Chosen People" in Arthur A. Cohen and Paul Mendes-Flohr (Eds.) Contemporary Jewish Religious Thought: Original Essays on Critical Concepts, Movements, *and Beliefs* (New York: Free Press, 1987).

11. Levy, op. cit.

12. Ibid. p. 104.

13. Cohen, op. cit., p. 129.

14. Zygmunt Bauman *Life In Fragments: Essays in Postmodern Morality* (Oxford: Blackwell) p. 285.

15. Michael Wyschogrod *The Body of Faith: Judaism as Corporeal Election* (New York: Seabury Press, 1983).

16. David Novak, "The Election of Israel: Outline of a Philosophical Analysis" in Frank, op. cit., p. 36.

17. Nehama Leibowitz, *Studies in Shemot (Exodus) Part II* (Jerusalem: World Zionist Organization, 1976).

18. David Hartman, *A Living Covenant: The Innovative Spirit in Traditional Judaism* (New York: Free Press, 1985), p. 96.

19. Marla Brettschneider, *The Narrow Bridge: Jewish Views on Multiculturalism* (New Brunswick, NJ: Rutgers University Press 1996).

20. Jonathan Boyarin "The Tree of Knowledege and the Tree of Life" in Brettschneider, op. cit., p. 210.

21. Homi K.Bhabba, "How Newness Enters the World: Postmodern Space, Postcolonial Times and the Trials of Cultural Translation" in *The location of Culture* (New York: Routledge, 1994).

22. See in particular Roger I. Simon, "Pedagogy and the Call to Witness in Marc Chagall's *White Crucifixion*" in *Review of Education/Pedagogy/Cultural Studies* Volume 19, Nos. 2–3 (1997) pp. 169–192, and Roger I. Simon "The Pedagogy of Commemoration and the Formation of Collective Memories" *Educational Foundations* Volume 8 No. 1 Winter 1994 pp. 5–24.

23. Levinas, "Difficult Freedom" op. cit., p. 265.

24. Yosef Hayim Yerushalmi *Zakhor: Jewish History and Jewish Memory* (New York: Schocken Books, 1989), postscript.

25. Susan Handelman, *The Slayers of Moses: The Emergence of Rabbinic Interpretation in Modern Literary Theory* (Albany: State University of New York Press 1982).

26. Geoffrey H. Hartman and Sanford Budick (eds.) *Midrash and Literature* (New Haven: Yale University Press 1986).

27. Bauman, op. cit. 1995.

Chapter 12

Being Jewish, Teaching Social Foundations and Studying Race; Some Reflections

Alan Wieder

This essay has had many false starts. There have been more caveats than discussion. And although both might be viewed as reflective, neither speaks to the relationship of being Jewish to my work. The remainder of this essay will attempt to address that relationship by briefly discussing my upbringing and then more thoroughly exploring my work as a nonobservant Jewish professor of social foundations of education and as an oral historian/visual sociologist of race and education.

I was born in 1949 and raised in a Cleveland suburb where my neighborhood and friends were predominantly Jewish. My mother lit Shabbat candles when my two sisters and I were young but this ritual ended before I reached high school. We celebrated the Jewish holidays alternating between paternal and maternal families and I attended Hebrew school until I was bar mitzvahed. My friends throughout high school and college were other Jews and I spent a short time in a Jewish fraternity which I left because I preferred my own apartment. There was no question in my mind whether or not I was Jewish. I considered myself a Jew, but I did nothing to be a Jew. It was simply that the world I traveled in was Jewish. The all too famous Lenny Bruce line went something like this: If you're from New York you're Jewish even if you're not. If you're from **South Carolina** you're not Jewish even if you are. It was all too true.

This short autobiographical vignette could be the story of many of my suburban Jewish contemporaries. But how does it lead to social foundations and research on race and education? Might it be that my parents, who were far from leftists (I think my mother took elocution at the Workmen's Circle), continue to vote for Democratic presidential candidates in spite of their friend's protests? Of course, their friends are Jewish so what does it all mean? It might be the connection to my Aunt Eve, who spoke of the socialist circles she was involved with in Chicago. The truth of those memories, though, was that she usually ended up talking much less about ideology than she did about boys meeting girls and girls meeting boys. Is it her husband Alec, who studied the prophets and the philosophers and who I visited when I was already a doctoral student for spiritual discussions that always led to Heschel and Buber? This might be the right track, but it is important not to forget Uncle Al on the other side of the family, who did not hesitate to use racial ephitets and very well might have banned Buber from the seder table.

I went to study with Bernie Mehl at Ohio State University in 1973. He was originally from Brooklyn and had studied social foundations with B. O. Smith, Ken Benne, and Arch Anderson at the University of Illinois in the early fifties. He came to Ohio State after a short stay as a professor at Hampton Institute just before the *Brown* decision. I went to study with Bernie Mehl because he was radical, but he also represented the Jewish prophet-as-teacher that both Heschel and Buber described. He pushed students about social and political issues as well as personal and public morality in both large classes and individual encounters. I wrote about Bernie in an article entitled "Interaction and the Professor: A Visual Tribute to Bernie Mehl:"

> I cannot help but to think of Martin Buber when I think of Mehl. Late in Buber's life, he was asked by an interviewer how he felt about his many books, his many speeches, and his worldwide fame. He answered with a story about his teacher who was unknown but had a personal, everlasting, and significant effect on the world through his students.[1]

Bernie Mehl was my representation of the secular Rebbe in the hinterlands of the Midwest. He did not belong to a synagogue and he did not celebrate the holidays or traditions and his sons were not bar mitzvahed, yet his breadth, his metaphors, and his teachings all related to his Yiddishkeit as did his constant push for human interaction. He put it this way in the conclusion of his book *Classic Educational Ideas*:

> Impersonalism is not realized when people no longer talk to each other; it comes into being because people can't speak to each other. They can't speak

> to each other because real speech only takes place between real people. A real person stands up for his beliefs and actions. He blames himself for his mistakes and accepts credit for his accomplishments. He is unable to converse for effect or for promoting good manners. To be real is to be held accountable for successes, for failure, for racism, for birth, for love, for goodness, for evil and for death.[2]

Mehl cited Gunnar Myrdal and others as he spoke of white racism as America's most important issue. We read DuBois, Bowles and Gintis, Baldwin, Katz, Dr. King, Spring, Wright and Perkinson; but also Buber, Singer, Roth, and Heschel. Even as he was teaching the importance of understanding and dealing with racism, he was encouraging me to write my dissertation on Jewish immigration and education and he was urging me to understand my own Jewishness. So I wrote my dissertation; "Immigration, the Public School and the 20th Century American Ethos." I studied the educational and occupational aspirations of three generations of twentieth-century American Jews. I interviewed my grandmother's generation of immigrant Jews and I read Oscar Handlin, Irving Howe, and Mary Antin as well as the revisionist educational history that dealt with the "new immigration." I was courted by the Lubavitchers in Cleveland, whom I immediately rejected, but choosing to study with Bernie Mehl-the nonobservant Jew whose teachings centered on race-put me constantly in touch with being a Jew. The following quote is from the conclusion of the reworking of my dissertation:

> In a world where alienation and fragmentation seem to be rule rather than exception, the commitment and loyalty of the old Jewish family looks more and more inviting. But that is now a lost culture. If the public school is to become a vital force, it has to open up its doors to Blacks. And not just in numbers, but rather in an honest acceptance of the Black man into the American ethos. The aspirations the Jewish immigrant mother had for her children, the "American dream," college, and a good job, are the words of the Black mother today. The same energizing force the Jewish immigrant brought to the schools when they emigrated from Europe will be revitalized if we honestly open up the American school for the Black man as we did for the Jewish immigrant at the turn of the century.[3]

So there is no question that having a mentor who studied race and education and who I considered a twentieth-century Jewish prophet had an effect on my choosing to study race and education for the next twenty years. Although Bernie Mehl did not use interviews in his work, my being an oral historian at least has partial roots in his modeling of

Martin Buber both inside and outside of the classroom. I should also add that I learned photography at his side and although this is a bit of a leap from my considerations of being Jewish on my work, it is certainly related to our relationship as teacher and student and the interactive life that entailed.

There are also Jewish historical events that may or may not be relevant. The weaving of the academic and the spiritual has been a Jewish reality that includes the Talmudists, the Hasidim, and continues today in Michael Lerner's Jewish renewal work among other things. In terms of race much has been written on Jewish early involvement in the NAACP, the civil rights movement, and current discussions, exemplified by Cornel West and Michael Lerner's book *Jews and Blacks: Let the Healing Begin.*

So I am part of this all and it is certainly endemic to my work. While acknowledging the importance of all that I've said, it might be that a coincidental event brought together being Jewish and my work on race and education. While I was doing my research on Jewish immigration and writing the American dream stories of the people I interviewed, I had the occasion to visit the homes of African-American families in Columbus, Ohio. It was the winter of 1976–77 and the Midwest had been hit with extreme blizzards. The public schools in Columbus were closed because of the weather and the system initiated a program entitled "School Without Schools." The district did not want to keep the schools open during the summer to meet state-mandated attendance requirements, so classes met in family homes and children got credit for school attendance. I became involved in this program as a supervisor for Ohio State University student teachers. I visited homes of urban African American families who reminded me of the early twentieth-century Jews I had been interviewing. I was meeting African Americans who believed in the American dream and were living it for themselves and their children. I spoke with African-American parents who told me about the jobs they worked and their hopes and dreams for their elementary age children. My educated ignorance made for great irony.

Here I was studying the American dream through my Jewish ancestors while at the same time being raised on teacher education ideology that religiously believed in the culture of poverty and cultural deprivation that was exhibited in the United States through African-Americans. And here were African Americans who were living the American dream that I was writing about. It was more than ironic, it was surreal, but then in the end very real.

At the risk of redundancy it might be worthwhile to again mention three realities/events: (1) I studied for my doctorate with a nonobservant Jew who viewed white racism as America's most important issue. (2) Because of his urging I decided to write a dissertation on Jewish education. (3) While writing my dissertation I encountered urban African Americans who believed in the American dream and were working to live it. The next twenty years of my academic life were spent studying race and education. Initially I did work that was counterpoint to both the culture of poverty and cultural deprivation theory. I spent many years working on an oral history of school integration in New Orleans. In recent years I have done work on examples of white racism in South Carolina and its schools. And finally, I have done a great deal of documentary photographic work on African-American children.

This is the work that has been the heart and soul of my academic life. And although I could not possibly point to a definitive causal relationship between this work and being Jewish, the being Jewish aspect continues to appear. As I read for the work I do on race and education, I always find that I am also reading Jewish material and it relates to the work on race and education. I reread Buber yearly at the very least and it always touches the issues of race and education that I am studying. This was especially the case while analyzing some of the work on Afrocentric curriculum. The issues of the Black-Jewish debates and the relationship between the two groups are ever present even though they are not always prominent. So again, I cannot speak to a causal relationship, but Judaism and my work on race always seem to touch.

The final connection, though, is with some of the work that I am presently involved in and the work I plan to do in the future. Bernie Mehl was not alone when he would remind me that a person's best work is done when they reach back to their roots-when they reconsider their souls. I am not sure how this equates to some of the issues of ethnographic research regarding insiders and outsiders as researchers. And I am quite sure that Bernie was not suggesting that I abandon the work I was doing on race and education. He certainly could not have held up my dissertation as a model for work on Jews and education. Now though, after working on race and education for twenty years, I find it is personally important to again address being Jewish. This past year I have spent many hours doing participant observation and interviewing at the local Jewish day school. I have amassed over three hundred transcribed pages of interviews with the two Chabad rabbis who operate the school as well as some of their supporters and critics. I am not sure where the story leads. There is certainly irony in fundamentalist Jews settling in a Southern town. They are a great contrast to the general portrait of Southern Judaism as well as to the local Jewish population. They are not building a following and they don't appear to be concerned about such things, but I often wonder if they are the perfect Jewish missionaries because they seldom seem to be proselytizing. There are many other questions. Who locally supports the group and who are their critics? Why do some local Jews send their children to the school that they run? For me, the question that has the closest ties to social foundations is the question of authenticity. As I interviewed the rabbis and their wives, they were good-spirited and kind but I always left with the feeling that they felt they represented authentic Judaism. I felt that although it was not always overt, the lesson taught at the school was that they were showing the children how to be authentic Jews. It was not pounded in but it certainly was my reading of both their views and their school practices. Of course, why would I expect it to be otherwise? The point, of course, is that it is a belief that presumes that myself and all other Jews are inauthentic.

Authenticity is the issue that brings me to my Jewish education project of the future. What I would like to do is extend the work that anthropologist Barbara Myerhoff was doing at the time of her untimely and youthful death. Myerhoff's most famous work resulted in a book and film entitled *Number Our Days*. It was a study of a Jewish retirement center in Venice, California. The film is the only academic film that has ever won an Academy Award. At the time of her death Barbara Myerhoff was working on a study of Fairfax, a very diverse Jewish Los Angeles community. At the corner of Fairfax and Melrose sits Fairfax High School. The school has a long and storied history and the **"no"** and **"do not"** signs on the school fence are written in many languages. What is interesting is that many of the more religious Jews in Fairfax do not send their kids to the school. They attend private Jewish schools of various quality and character. So what I would like to do is a study of education in Fairfax, public and private. I see this project as the ultimate connection of Judaism and my work in social foundations. I also see it as a project that will force me to confront Judaism in America—my own included.

I began by mentioning that I left out many caveats. If there is a caveat, or an apology for that matter, it might be for the stream of consciousness of this essay. I have thought about this hard, however, and it could not have been written any other way. There are some interesting connections in my being Jewish and the work that I do. But the only thing that I can say about it with certainty is that I am Jewish and that has affected my work. I can also say that I think that I am now beginning a time period where this connection is becoming more concrete and that it offers an opportunity to explore both my field and my soul more deeply. In the end I am an educational storyteller who attempts to portray the "grassroots" stories of educational issues. For the past twenty years they have concerned racism and education. It might be that it is time to become more personal by pointing my "grassroots" work towards American Judaism and education.

Notes

1. Alan Wieder, "Interaction and the Professor: A Visual Tribute to Bernie Mehl" in *Teaching Education*, Winter/Spring 1995, pp. 2, 3, 4, 42, 72, and 94.
2. Bernard Mehl, *Classic Educational Ideas: From Sumeria to America* (Columbus, OH: Charles Merrill Publishing, 1972), p. 211.
3. Alan Wieder, *Immigration, the Public School, and the 20th Century American Ethos: The Jewish Immigrant as A Case Study* (Lanham, MD: University Press of America), pp. 106, 107.

Yizkor

Sherry Shapiro

She stamps,
  turns to look over her left shoulder
Dark eyes flirting
  moving the rythmns of memory
Carrying in her being, bound in her form, the sacred and the profane.

Your memory in my body rests uneasily
  as I experience the challenge of Deborah's tambourine
The emptiness of Sarah's womb
  the absolute commitment of Ruth's love.
You remind me of all possibilities.

Linking me to a history of struggle to survive with dignity
  I understand the straightness of your back
The stiffening of your neck
  the need to speak with all of your body
The word of life.

More difficult to understand is the laughter I see in your moves,
  yet hasn't escaped through your mouth.
Do you hold it with a sense of fear or fullness?
  Is the stranger still not welcome
In your circle carved out through shared touches.

What do you have to teach me in the memory of compassion
  in the memory of justice?
Where do I seek memories as blessings and loving testimonies?
  Is peace and dignity only for the dead?

Oseh shalom bi-m'romav, hu ya'aseh shalom aleinu v'al kol yisrael vimru-amen.

One who brings peace to the universe, will bring peace to all of us and to all the people of Israel and let us say

Amen.

Contributors

Svi Shapiro was born in London, England. During his youth he was an active member of a labor-Zionist youth movement, and lived and worked for two years in Israel. He is a Professor in the Social Foundations of Education and has been Chair of the Department of Educational Leadership and Cultural Foundations at the University of North Carolina, Greensboro. He is a contributor on educational issues to *Tikkun* magazine His most recent book, with David Purpel, is *Beyond Liberation and Excellence: Reconstructing the Public Discourse on Education* (1995). His work focuses on issues of social change and educational policy and practice. He lives in Greensboro with his wife Sherry and daughter Sarah.

Michael W. Apple is John Bascom Professor of Education at the University of Wisconsin, Madison. A former elementary and secondary school teacher and past-president of a teachers union, he has worked with unions, dissident groups, and educators throughout the world to democratize educational research, policy, and practice. Among his recent books are *Official Knowledge, Education and Power* (second edition), and *Cultural Politics and Education.*

Haim Dov Beliak is a graduate student in education at the Claremont Graduate School, where he is completing his Ph.D. in Higher Education Administration while serving as the Director of Mifgash: An On-Going Conversation Among Jewish Intellectuals. He was born in Munich, Germany and grew up in Mason City, Iowa and Phoenix, Arizona. He resides in Los Angles, with his spouse, Lynn and his children, Tamara, Ariel, and Hanan. Beliak is a graduate of Hebrew Union College and is an ordained rabbi. He has a A.B. degree from

Occidental College. In 1988–90 he embarked on a second formal career in education as a Jerusalem Fellow in Jerusalem, Israel.

David Bleich teaches in the English Department, in Jewish Studies, and in Women's Studies at the University of Rochester. He is the author of *Readings and Feelings* (1975), *Subjective Criticism* (1978)), *Utopia: The Psychology of a Cultural Fantasy* (1984), *The Double Perspective: Language, Literacy, and Social Relations* (1988). Forthcoming in 1997 is *Know and Tell: Genre and Discourse in the Teaching of Writing.*

Linda Bliss grew up in New York City and presently lives with her husband in Boone, North Carolina where she is an active member of the Boone Jewish community. They have two grown sons. She is an Adjunct Assistant Professor at Appalachian State University's Reich College of Education, where as a member of the Department of Leadership and Educational Studies, she teaches foundations of American Education. In 1995, she received her Ph.D. in the Social Foundations of Education from the University of North Carolina at Greensboro.

Alan A. Block is an Associate Professor in the Department of Education at the University of Wisconsin-Stout. He has published three books and numerous articles and book chapters concerning education and curriculum. He lives with his wife and two children in Menomonie, Wisconsin—very much a stranger to the land.

Miriyam Glazer is Associate Professor of Literature, Chair of the Literature Department, and Director of the Dortort Writers Institute at the University of Judaism in Los Angles. She is the editor of the forthcoming *Dreaming the Actual: Israeli Women Writers in the 1990's* (Suny Press). She has written frequently on Jewish-American women writers. Recent articles include "Daughters of Refugees of the Ongoing-Universal-Endless-Upheaval: The Quest for Narrative Power in Jewish-American Women's Fiction," in *Daughters of Valor* (Delaware); "'Crazy, of Course: Spiritual Romanticism and the Redeeming of Female Spirituality in Contemporary Jewish-American Women's Fiction," in *People of the Book: Thirty Scholars Reflect on Their Jewish Identity* (Wisconsin).

Barry Kanpol is Associate Professor of Educational Foundations at Penn State, Harrisburg. His main academic interests are in identity construction, multiculutral education and liberation theology as related to public school teachers' lives. He has published in numerous journals and is the author of a number of books, the most recent of which are *Teachers Talking Back and Breaking Bread* , and *Issues and Trends in Critical Pedagogy* both forthcoming in 1997.

Stephen Lerman was a high school teacher of mathematics for many years in England and in a Kibbutz school in Israel. Before teaching he was an active member of the zionist youth organization Habonim, including a period working full-time as a youth leader and for one year as general secretary. He is now Reader in Mathematics Education at South Bank University in London. He is President of the International Group for the Psychology of Mathematics Education and is also Chair of the British Society for Research into Learning Mathematics. His research interests include: philosophy of mathematics; equity issues; learning theories; and socio-cultural perspectives on mathematics teaching and learning.

David Purpel is a Professor in the Department of Educational Leadership at the University of North Carolina Greensboro. He is the author of *The Moral and Spiritual Crisis in Education* and (with Svi Shapiro) *Beyond Liberation and Excellence.*

Mara Sapon-Shevin is Professor of Education in the Teaching and Leadership Division of the School of Education at Syracuse University. A long-time peace and social justice activist, she teaches in the University's Inclusive Elementary and Special Education Teacher Education Program which prepares teachers for inclusive, heterogeneous classrooms. She is active in working with schools to promote the full inclusion of all students and the creation of cooperative school communities. She is Co-President for the International Association for the Study of Cooperation in Education, and gives workshops on cooperative learning and cooperative games for the classrooms. The author of many articles and book chapters on cooperative learning, full inclusion, diversity education and the politics of gifted education, she is the author of the book, *Playing Favorites: Gifted Education and the Disruption of Community* (SUNY), and of the forthcoming *Because We Can Change the World* (Allyn and Bacon).

Sherry Shapiro is an Associate Professor at Meredith College in Raleigh North Carolina. She is the Coordinator of the Dance Education Program teaching both undergraduate and graduate courses in dance education and educational studies. Her professional work focuses upon issues of feminist and critical pedagogy, and more specifically on ways in which knowledge is embodied, resisted and transformed. She is the author of the forthcoming *Pedagogy and the Politics of the Body: A Critical Praxis* (Garland), and editor of the volume, *Dance, Power and Difference: Critical and Feminist Perspectives on Dance Education* (Human Kinetics Press).

Roger I. Simon is a Professor at the Ontario Institute for Studies in Education at the University of Toronto. For over two decades, he has been engaged in his own struggles integrating Jewish experience and studies into his teaching and writing on education. Simon's current work is focused on the strengths and limits of testimony in the formation of historical memory. He is currently completing a book of essays entitled *Insurgent Commemorations.*

Shirley Steinberg is an Assistant Professor at Adelphi University. The author of many books and articles, her most recent book is, with Joe Kincheloe, *Kinderculture: The Corporate Construction of Childhood* (Westview). Her research interests in cultural studies and pedagogy include issues of Jewishness, identity, and popular culture. She is also the co-editor of the book (in press) *White Reign: Whiteness and Pedagogy in America* (St. Martins). She is the senior editor of the journal Taboo.

Arthur Waskow received his doctorate in US History from the University of Wisconsin (Madison) in 1963, and was ordained a Rabbi in 1995. He has served as a legislative assistant to a member of the US House of Representatives, as one of the original Fellows of the Institute for Policy Studies, as a member of the faculty of the Reconstructionist Rabbinical College, and as a visiting professor at Swarthmore College, Temple University, and Drew University. He has written books on US military strategy, racial conflict, Jewish history, and Jewish theology, including *Godwrestling; Down-to-Earth Judaism: Food, Money, Sex, and the Rest of Life*; and *Godwrestling–Round 2*.

Alan Weider is an oral historian/visual sociologist who teaches in the College of Education at the University of South Carolina. He has published widely on race and education and his books, *Race and Education: Narrative Essays, Oral Histories and Documentary Photographs*, was recently published by Lang.

Lynn Leon (cover artist) was born in Tynemouth, England. She studied Fine Art (photography) at the University of Northumbria at Newcastle where she attained her Master of Arts degree. She lives and works in North Yorkshire but travels frequently to Israel where she photographs, draws and exhibits her artwork.

Her work from the mid-80's consists of large composite black and white photographs which explore the nature of confinement and violence, whilst also dealing with the vulnerability of the female body. Some of her images contain references both to the Holocaust and to the latent tensions in Israel.

Her more recent work—small pen and ink drawings—are directly concerned with the political situation in Israel and are therefore more topical and provocative. She uses her Jewishness, her belief in the Middle-East peace process, and her interest in Surrealism as a basis for her work.

Lynn Leon has exhibited widely in England and Israel. her photographs and drawings were represented in the 'Rubies and Rebels' exhibition at the Barbican, London in 1996. Her image 'Censored' was used in all the publicity for this major exhibition. It was the first exhibition of its kind to deal with 'Jewish Female Identity in Contemporary British Art'.

Lynn Leon has work in a number of collections in USA, Canada, UK and Israel.

published widely on race and education and his books, *Race and Education: Narrative Essays, Oral Histories and Documentary Photographs* were recently published by Lang.

Lynn Leon (cover artist) was born in Tynemouth, England. She studied Fine Art/photography at the University of Northumbria at Newcastle where she attained the Master of Arts degree. She lives and works in North Yorkshire but travels frequently to Israel where she photographs, draws and exhibits her artworks.

Her work from the mid-80's consists of large-format black and white photographs which explore the nature of confinement and violence, whilst also dealing with the vulnerability of the female body. Some of her images contain references both to the Holocaust and to the Intifada in Israel.

Her more recent work—small pen and ink drawings—are directly concerned with the political situation in Israel and are therefore more topical and provocative. She uses her Jewishness, her belief in the Middle East peace process, and her interest in Surrealism as a basis for her work.

Lynn Leon has exhibited widely in England and Israel. Her photographs and drawings were represented in the 'Rubies and Rebels' exhibition at the Barbican, London in 1996. Her image 'Semtex' was used as the publicity for the major exhibition. It was the first exhibition of its kind to deal with Jewish Female Identity in Contemporary British Art.

Lynn Leon has work in a number of collections in USA, Canada, UK and Israel.

Index

COUNTERPOINTS

Studies in the Postmodern Theory of Education

General Editors
Joe L. Kincheloe & Shirley R. Steinberg

Counterpoints publishes the most compelling and imaginative books being written in education today. Grounded on the theoretical advances in criticalism, feminism and postmodernism in the last two decades of the twentieth century, Counterpoints engages the meaning of these innovations in various forms of educational expression. Committed to the proposition that theoretical literature should be accessible to a variety of audiences, the series insists that its authors avoid esoteric and jargonistic languages that transform educational scholarship into an elite discourse for the initiated. Scholarly work matters only to the degree it affects consciousness and practice at multiple sites. Counterpoints' editorial policy is based on these principles and the ability of scholars to break new ground, to open new conversations, to go where educators have never gone before.

For additional information about this series or for the submission of manuscripts, please contact:

Joe L. Kincheloe & Shirley R. Steinberg
637 West Foster Avenue
State College, PA 16801